Letters of a Nation

Letters of a Nation

A Collection of Extraordinary American Letters

Edited by Andrew Carroll

Kodansha International

New York • Tokyo • London

Kodansha America, Inc.
114 Fifth Avenue, New York, New York 10011, U.S.A.

Kodansha International Ltd.
17-14 Otowa 1-chome, Bunkyo-ku, Tokyo 112, Japan

Published in 1997 by Kodansha America, Inc.

Library of Congress Cataloging-in-Publication Data
Letters of a nation: a collection of extraordinary American letters/
edited by Andrew Carroll.
p. cm.
Includes index.
ISBN 1-56836-196-3
1. American letters. 2. United States—Civilization—Sources.
I. Carroll, Andrew.
PS672.L48 1997 97-25510
816.008—dc21 CIP

Book design by Linda Kosarin

Manufactured in the United States of America on acid-free paper

97 98 99 00 10 9 8 7 6 5 4 3 2 1

To my parents,

for their love, generosity, and support—and, of course, their letters.

Contents

LETTERS OF SLAVERY & THE CIVIL WAR

Letters of War

- *Part II* -

Letters of Humor & Personal Contempt

LETTERS OF LOVE & FRIENDSHP

LETTERS OF FAMILY

Letters on Death & Dying

Letters of Faith & Hope

Foreword

Finding one's way in the world today is a challenge for all of us. Increasingly we are seeing a breakdown of family and community values in our society, and many of our young people, rich and poor alike, are growing up morally confused. Our children need hope, a sense of purpose, and a steady internal compass to navigate the choppy seas they must face on the journey to adulthood.

But a culture that too often glamorizes materialism over faith, getting over giving, indifference over compassion, can leave us all—no matter our age—feeling spiritually impoverished. This is especially true for all those parents today who are working harder for less and struggling and sacrificing just to provide their children with basic needs. Adults, too, can get discouraged by the demands of life and yearn for direction and support.

During the times I feel most overwhelmed, I look inward to God for guidance and strength. But I also draw on the values and legacies of the great men and women of history who have lived before us—people such as W. E. B. Du Bois, Susan B. Anthony, Rabbi Stephen Wise, Dorothy Day, Phillis Wheatley, Dr. Martin Luther King Jr., Cesar Chavez, and Harriet Beecher Stowe, all of whom are featured in this wonderful anthology. Their words embolden me and remind me of what is important and meaningful in life.

In tough times I also look to the example of ordinary people of grace and courage, which is why I am heartened to find included here so many letters by lesser-known, though no less inspiring, heroes and heroines. From farmers and immigrants to slaves and pioneers, they have shown in their letters an ability to transform crisis into opportunity and to bring out the inherent goodness in others. We see men like Luis Rodriguez, a former gang member, who now teaches poetry to incarcerated young people, successfully motivating them to be "true warriors" for justice by renouncing violence and using their "creativity, heart (corazón), thoughts and words" instead.

And we see Urban League leader Lester Granger, who, along with seventy-six other African Americans, contributed to the United Jewish Appeal in 1943 after learning of Nazi atrocities against European Jews. Mr. Granger wrote: "[This donation] is a reaffirmation of our conviction that we are under one God, one people united in one cause. May this small gift stand as an additional testimonial to the bond of friendship that must grow between two peoples with a glorious history, and a still more glorious future." If only all of us could embrace in thought and deed Lester Granger's powerful words, we would not see the racial polarization so prevalent in our society today.

Too often we perceive the forces of history as a mighty wave we are powerless to change. But from the first Minutemen who confronted the British at Lexington, to freedom fighters like Frederick Douglass and Mother Jones who spoke out against inequality everywhere, the letters in this collection show us the brave souls who not only held fast against the currents of injustice but even helped turn the tide. Few had riches or fame or a formal education, but they had a spiritual wealth and character that proved far more valuable. And as they endured the most crushing social and historical pressures imaginable, they forged in their letters jewels of hope that gleam as brilliantly today as when they were first written.

Not all of the authors in this anthology, of course, are saints. And not all of the letters are meant to inspire—many will make us laugh, remind us of the costs of ambition and vanity, furnish us with eyewitness accounts of historic upheaval, and reveal to us the heartache of losing a loved one. But ultimately, the letters here affirm that regardless of our age, color, religion, gender, or ancestry, we—as individuals and as a nation—share universal aspirations and anxieties and a common resilience in times of personal and social crisis. Each of us, we discover, weaves a thread that contributes to the overall strength of our national fabric.

As you read through the letters in this book I hope that you, too, will be inspired. But I also hope you will be inspired *to write* letters for others to enjoy and find comfort in as well. After my parents passed away I remember rummaging through old personal belongings and coming upon their letters from when I was a child. I was astonished to see how much of what they wrote and taught me then influenced who I am now. I was fourteen years old the night my Daddy, a Baptist minister in a small southern town, passed away. He had holes in his shoes but two children out of college, one in college, another in divinity school, and a vision he had conveyed to me that I, a young Black girl, could be and do anything I wanted.

When my own three children approached adulthood I wrote a long, detailed letter to them offering the "lessons of life" I have learned along the way. Theirs is a far more complicated world than the one into which I was born, but I wanted them to know that the principles I hold dear—honesty, self-discipline, responsibility, faith, perseverance, and service to others—will *always* enable them to make the right choices in life.

Every one of us has experiences to share and wisdom to impart. Let us all then leave behind letters of love and friendship, family and devotion, hope and consolation, so that future generations will know what we valued and believed and achieved. They too will face enormous obstacles. They too will search for guidance in times of adversity and despair. And just as we have found strength and solace in the words of those who have come before us, so too will those who follow us look to our letters, find the encouragement they need, and make their own way.

Marian Wright Edelman
April 1997

ACKNOWLEDGMENTS

Looking back at the last four years, I find it extraordinary—and a bit terrifying—the degree to which serendipity and good fortune have helped bring this book to life. The most knowledgeable, gracious, and supportive people all seemed to appear at the precise time a nurturing hand was needed most.

First and foremost, I am indebted to my editor, Deborah Baker, for understanding my vision of the book from the start and, most importantly, for offering me the opportunity to see it realized. Deborah's assistance throughout has been invaluable, and it has been a joy to work with her—and the rest of the Kodansha staff—from day one. I am also grateful to my agent, Miriam Altshuler, for finding such a first-rate publisher as Kodansha for *Letters of a Nation*, and for her words of encouragement throughout the researching, writing, and editing of the book.

For the foreword, I am indebted to Marian Wright Edelman, who through her integrity, dedication, and compassion has influenced and inspired me more than anyone I know (except my own parents, of course). I am also extremely grateful to Jonah Edelman for his support during this project, particularly considering the enormous demands on his time directing Stand for Children. A large part of this book's soul would have been missing if it were not for Mrs. Edelman and Jonah, and I am forever grateful.

For providing valuable editorial assistance on the early drafts of this book I am grateful to Sunil Iyengar. Sunil has one of the most brilliant literary minds I have ever encountered, and his input was appreciated more than he will ever know. I am also grateful to Kelly Winograd, who generously helped type in countless letters as my deadline loomed. I couldn't have made it without her.

In locating obscure and unpublished letters, I was fortunate to speak with an extraordinary group of archivists, scholars, and professionals who gave of their time and expertise out of sheer kindness and a love of letters. They include: Nancy A. Pope of the Smithsonian's National Postal Museum; Aaron T. Kornblum, reference archivist at the United States Holocaust Memorial Museum; Elise Higdon; Megan Bartsch; Michelle Mallory; Eleanor Dore at the Martin Luther King Memorial Library; Andrew Turnage of the Association of Space Explorers; Katherine T. Collins, archivist of the Sons and Daughters of the 442nd Regimental Combat Team; Patricia Green at the Louisiana Division of the New Orleans Public Library; Stacey Swigart at the Valley Forge Historical Society; Karen Stevens of *Ms.* magazine and Mary Thom, editor of *Letters to Ms. 1972–1987*; Pat Lowe and Joe Carter at the Will Rogers Memorial Museum; Bernard Edelman, author of *Dear America: Letters Home from Vietnam*; the Honorable Ed Foreman; Debbie R. Henderson of the Japanese American National Museum; Joellen LeBashire of the Moorland Springarn Research Center at Howard University; Sally McClain, author of *Navajo Weapon;* Barbara Pathe of the American Red Cross; Gloria Roberts of the Planned Parenthood Federation of America; Merriam Saunders of the Ansel Adams Publishing Rights Trust; Margo Stipe of the Frank Lloyd Wright Foundation; Paul R. Wagner, coauthor of *Out of Ireland* and producer and director of the highly acclaimed documentary of the same name, and Kerby Miller, who served as an adviser on *Out of Ireland* and cowrote the book; Jill Westmoreland of the William Morris Agency; Frederic Woodbridge Wilson of the Harvard Theatre Collection; Donna Dillon of the Ronald Reagan Library; Lindsay Patterson, editor of *A Rock Against the Wind: African-American Poems and Letters of Love and Passion;* Lynn Sherr of ABC News and author of *Failure Is Impossible: Susan B. Anthony in Her Own Words;* Ze'ev Rosenkranz of the Jewish National & Hebrew University Library; Calman Levin of the Estate of Gertrude Stein; Elizabeth Barnett, literary executor of Edna St. Vincent Millay's works; Meg Merle-Smith at Harvard University; John A. Gable, executive director of the Theodore Roosevelt Association; Phyllis Theroux; the teachers who inspired my love for letters and literature—Neal Tonken, Karl Kroeber, Kenneth Koch, Andrew Delbanco, and John Elko; Michael E. Johnson, editor of *Space Autograph News* and *Autograph Research* in San Diego; Dr. Craig and Julie

Feied; W. Ronald Thompson and Heather Stanley in Belfast for assistance with the William Murphy letter; Professor Judy Yung of the University of California at Santa Cruz and author of *Unbound Feet: A Social History of Chinese Women in San Francisco* (Berkeley: University of California Press, 1995); Helen Bryan; Nancy Glynn at the Sharon Public Library in Sharon, Massachusetts; Rose Jefferson at the National Urban League; Virginia Smith and Louis L. Tucker at the Massachusetts Historical Society; Jimmy Gaines (the postman who brings my mail); Dr. Tom and Judy Bowles; Joe Rogers; George Bailey; Donna Nedderman; Michael Ketakis; Allison Bergmann at the American Foundation for the Blind; U.S. Coast Guard Historian Robert M. Browning Jr.; John Ferris, Alycia Vivona, and Raymond Teichman at the Franklin D. Roosevelt Library; Allen Mikaelian; the staff members of the Georgetown University Library, National Archives, the Harry S. Truman Library, and the Library of Congress, particularly Jeffrey Flannery, who patiently and courteously assisted me beyond the call of duty; Robbie and Brice Klein and my "pen" pals John Petrone, Dave "Dutch" Van Vlymen, and Jesse Friedman.

Finally, I wish to express my profound thanks to all those who generously shared their personal letters with me (or letters to which they owned the copyright), many of which are being published here for the first time. These kind souls include: Luis Rodriguez; Rose Price; Erwin Blonder (and his granddaughter Anne Tramer for telling me about her grandfather's letters); Scott Carpenter; the Honorable Ed Foreman; Chuck Jones; Melanie Behnke; Don Novella; David Rothenberg; Dr. Raya Czerner Schapiro; Helga Czerner Weinberg; John Campbell; William Lederer; Bertha Frothingham; Louise E. King; Margie Brauer; William Yaeger; Allison West; John Eisenhower; Michele Song; Pam Hirsch; William Ford and Jennifer Sullivan; Alfred Corn; William and Thomas Ewald; John Boettiger; and Chris B. and Norma Shumpert for sharing a part of their lives through their letters, and to the NAMES Project Foundation, particularly Scott Williams, for permitting me to reprint these letters from the book *A Promise to Remember: The NAMES Project Book of Letters*.

This book is dedicated to my parents, and I also wish to thank the rest of my family, and the many friends who emboldened and assisted me as this anthology was being researched and written. They were especially patient when I had to focus solely on the book, and no matter how many times I thank them, it will never be enough. No writer could have better, more loving support.

Introduction

At the end of a rather long and revealing letter to a dear friend, the poet Elizabeth Bishop implores: "Pray for me—and tear this up, too." The sentiment is an oft-repeated one. The famed environmentalist Rachel Carson contemplated having all her letters destroyed after her death; "I have shuddered every time I see announcement of the publication of some poor wretch's letters!" Carson wrote to her friend Dorothy Freeman. "It's just the principle of exposing something that is wholly private and personal and should be sacred."

Letters are sacred. From impassioned declarations of love to furious bursts of rage, they expose the most heartfelt emotions stirring within a person's soul. This power may seem a touch diminished, however, when the letters are neatly arranged, retyped, categorized, and introduced with a few formal remarks in a mass-produced anthology such as this one. But when we imagine letters as they first appeared to their recipients, noting the choice of the stationery; the distinctiveness of the penmanship—whether it flows elegantly from one line to the next or scrawls somewhat unevenly across the page; and any small sketches or other afterthoughts the sender may have added in the margins, the letters assume a greater resonance and value. We begin to understand why the possibility of something so personal and intimate being displayed publicly is, to some, an appalling one.

But there is another, almost competing sentiment that runs throughout many personal correspondences. It is a desire to chronicle for oneself and for posterity reflections and experiences that might otherwise be overlooked or forgotten. In the spring of 1945 a twenty-five-year-old American soldier, Joseph Fogg, found himself walking among the ruins of the most savage act of orchestrated genocide in the twentieth century—a Nazi concentration camp. "Am writing this from deep inside Germany," he reports to his parents. "In the following pages I shall attempt to record a sight that is well beyond the pale of verbal or written description—a sight that will sear my memory for all time to come. I cannot expect you to believe it—indeed I who have seen it cannot." Fogg's letter, published here for the first time, is as vivid today as it was when he penned it over fifty years ago.

Another young American soldier, writing from France in 1944, was more explicit about his desire to remember "the horrible details of war." Lt. Col. Erwin Blonder explains to his older brother and father back in the States: "I want these thoughts of mine recorded so in later years I can read them and use them in getting a better understanding of life instilled in my children." Five decades later he was able to do just that; he read the letter aloud at his fiftieth wedding anniversary in front of three generations of family members, many of whom had never known the particulars of his war experience. It, too, is published here for the first time.

Letters give us "a better understanding of life" because they provide us with immediate and often striking insight into human nature and the human experience. In this collection we hear the first impressions—some enthusiastic, others scathing—from English, Chinese, Irish, and Russian immigrants upon their arrival in this country. And from the native residents of this "new" world we hear *their* impressions of the incoming pilgrims and pioneers. The opening shots of the American Revolution echo as clearly today as they did over two hundred years ago in the letters of those who were there. We learn of the grinding and dehumanizing effects of slavery from those caught in its grasp. Through the eyes of a Confederate general we scan the fields of Gettysburg after one of the single bloodiest battles in American military history. We hear from Depression-era voices begging President Franklin D. Roosevelt for the smallest morsel of relief. Almost fifty years later we read the heartbreaking letter of an elderly woman facing the loss of her family farm after the government-imposed grain embargo. We also hear voices of social protest from civil rights workers, migrant farmers, suffragists, and antiwar activists. We may not all agree with their opinions, but they have influenced dramatically our nation's direction and, for that alone, merit attention.

The letters in this anthology explore not only the vast terrain of

America's history but the equally boundless, albeit internal, expanse of the human soul. We hear a profound reflection on immortality from a twenty-four-year-old soldier only weeks before he is killed in Vietnam. We learn of forgiveness by a father who asks the governor to spare the life of the man who murdered his son. We listen as a grown woman, adopted as a child, explains to her birth mother why she hopes to meet her and say, "Thank you for loving me enough to give me up so that I might have a better life." And from those facing their own death or the loss of a loved one, we read words of exemplary courage and tenderness. These letters reveal to us the spark of poetry within Americans from all walks of life, from slaves and soldiers to explorers and expatriates. And from the letters of more well-known Americans we discover the private fears and insecurities from which no amount of celebrity or social status can offer protection.

This book also strives to emphasize the varying styles, formats, and tones in which letters have been written. Some writers express themselves in lush, extravagant prose; others, in a few sharply worded sentences. Many dash off whimsical messages unencumbered by the dictates of grammar, syntax, or spelling. Edgar Allan Poe wrote rambling, almost emotionally delirious love letters to several women at the same time, while many of Benjamin Franklin's letters more closely resemble legal briefs—such as his letter to a young friend enumerating eight succinct reasons why he "should prefer old women to young ones" when choosing a wife. The eminent literary editor Maxwell Perkins wrote letters to his young daughters in verse and often embellished the stationery and envelopes with drawings. Through all these unique characteristics and nuances we gain a greater understanding not only of the personality of the sender but of the sheer versatility and variety of letters themselves—attributes that E-mail, for all its speed and convenience, ultimately lacks.

Letters, like people, defy easy categorization. This book has been arranged into essentially two parts—the first focusing on letters of a historical nature, the second on more personal themes such as friendship, family, humor, devotion, death, and hope. Within each chapter the letters are organized chronologically (with a few exceptions). The arrangement, however, is hardly a perfect one. The letter Scott Carpenter received on the eve of his May 1962 mission is a loving message from an awed and obviously proud father to his astronaut son, and it could have fit comfortably in "Letters of Family." But the letter also represents one of the most significant endeavors in our nation's history, Project Mercury, which successfully launched the first Americans into space. For narrative purposes, the Carpenter letter worked better as the concluding entry in the chapter on exploration and expansion.

Similarly, many of the letters in the more "personal" half of the book, such as Malcolm X's letter from the Holy Land, have historical significance as well. Malcolm X was one of America's most dynamic African American leaders and had professed throughout his life an intense hatred for whites. People of different colors, he often proclaimed, should not and could not coexist peacefully. But during his pilgrimage to Mecca, where he saw harmony between white and black Muslims, Malcolm X renounced his views and wrote optimistically to his followers back home of amity and reconciliation between the races. His message, featured in "Letters of Faith & Hope," mentions neither word by name—the letter, itself, is a symbol of hope.

The guiding criterion that determines the placement of each letter is primarily its content, not its author. In "Letters of Love & Friendship," for example, we find not only letters between lovers declaring their undying affection for one another (or their desire never to see one another again), but letters on the topic of love itself. Ayn Rand, the internationally known Objectivist philospher, explains to an inquiring fan her thoughts on love: "True love is profoundly selfish," Rand insists, "and a person who exists only for the sake of his loved one is not an independent entity, but a spiritual parasite." John Steinbeck offers a somewhat more sentimental definition in a letter to his teenaged son Thom: "[Love] is an outpouring of everything good in you—of kindness, and consideration and respect. Glory in it for one thing and be very glad and grateful for it." The circumstances under which the letters are written are also determining factors. After Union general David Hunter ordered his men to burn Henrietta Lee's house to the ground, Lee sent Hunter a furious message as riveting as any in the chapter on letters of "personal contempt." It was, instead, placed in "Letters of Slavery & the Civil War," due to the time it was written (1864) and because it counterbalanced an equally impassioned letter General Hunter himself wrote to his antagonist Jefferson Davis.

Whenever possible, private correspondences have been reprinted here in place of more public ones. When William Faulkner wrote his infamous "If I were a Negro" letter, addressed openly to black leaders in the United States, he also sent a more personal message to an acquaintance on race relations in America. The latter is featured in this collection. Ronald Reagan's poignant letter to the American people disclosing that he has Alzheimer's is not in this anthology. But the letter President Reagan sent to Soviet premier Leonid Brezhnev, just three weeks after Reagan was shot, is. Still recuperating from his wound, Reagan handwrote the letter as he sat in his pajamas in the White House solarium and shared with Brezhnev his desire "to find lasting peace" between the two superpowers. The letter, written in 1981, was not declassified until 1995.

While the letters themselves are undeniably the focus here, a handful are presented as a means to showcase an incredible story or an unusual relationship, such as the correspondence between the celibate priest Thomas Merton and the notoriously racy (some would say pornographic) novelist Henry Miller. Then there is the handwritten letter from Elvis Presley to President Richard M. Nixon that resulted in an Oval Office meeting and the famous photograph of the two men shaking hands. (Presley's letter has been included in the humor chapter, admittedly, for lack of a better category. "Letters of the Bizarre" would have been ideal, but a surprising dearth of other contenders prevented such a chapter from being added.)

On a more serious note, there is a letter in this collection—believed to be the first of its kind ever published—written by a Navajo "code talker" in 1944. Using a code based on their native language, the Navajo code talkers were stationed in the South Pacific by the American military in World War II to communicate top-secret military information. (The code was never broken.) Their participation in the war was one of the most prolonged, confidential military secrets in American history; even the code talkers's families did not know the extent of their involvement until over twenty years after the war. Another intriguing story is that of Mary Ewald's letter to Saddam Hussein demanding the release of her son Thomas. Tom Ewald, a twenty-four-year-old American living in Kuwait City, had been captured by Hussein's army and used as a "human shield" to prevent American forces from firing on Iraqi military installations. His mother's letter, printed here for the first time, and Ewald's fate are presented in full in "Letters of War."

Regardless of sender or circumstance, this anthology strives to ensure that the original spontaneity and emotive power of each letter is preserved. For the most part, the letters are printed in their entirety, errors and all. Typos, misspellings, and syntactically challenged sentences have been maintained. Expletives and curses have also survived the editor's red pen. (But they appear in only a few letters out of the more than two hundred here.) Every effort has been made to keep the body of the letters free of parenthetical comments, *sic*s, asterisks, and other notations. If, however, the sender left out a word that leaves a sentence unintelligible, or if there is a typo or two in an otherwise immaculate original, then the missing or misspelled material is inserted between brackets—[ ]—so as not to raise uncertainty on the reader's part. Consistent errors, such as the predilection among some to write contractions without an apostrophe (as in "dont" for "don't") or to misspell repeatedly certain words, are not acknowledged within the body of the letters. The notes preceding (and at times following) the letters will—along with putting the letters in context—alert readers to any other peculiarities and explain any important allusions. In some instances it was not possible either to locate or to account for every reference. But the most critical, assuming they could be found, are mentioned.

Unless otherwise noted, only ellipses in brackets—[. . .]—represent editorial deletions, and in almost all cases these have been made by third parties (families, estates, or other copyright owners) or by the writers themselves at a later date. Ellipses not in brackets represent a stylistic decision on the writer's part. A few letters, published previously, have had their salutations and closings removed due to space limitations. Others have been "tidied up" by those intending to make the letters more presentable. Although it was possible to track down the primary sources in most cases, some proved elusive.

The reasons behind featuring the letters in their complete and original form are manifold. There is something both captivating and fulfilling about a letter that beautifully expresses itself from top to bottom. And just as one would not cut from a painting sections considered less appealing than the rest or mar the canvas with explanatory notes, one similarly cannot tamper with a truly memorable letter without detracting from the overall import of the work. Great letters have a rhythm that is uniquely their own, and to snip and slice away chunks from the original or to break in repeatedly with commentary, this editor believes, disrupts a letter's natural flow and continuity. (Recognizing, however, that some rather exceptional sentiments have been expressed in otherwise unremarkable letters, these passages have been tucked into relevant headnotes or displayed as epigraphs throughout the book.) Further, while the omnipotent editor may know that the words or paragraphs deleted were supposedly of no consequence, the reader, coming upon "[. . .]," does not know if the offending material was deemed inappropriate because of length or substance or what. Better—for our purposes here—to let you, the reader, decide what to savor and what to discard.

This is not to deny that some wonderfully written letters are interrupted by seemingly tedious tangents. But even these occasional departures can, at times, prove subtly enlightening. Robert E. Lee, for instance, writes to his wife, Mary, over four years before the Civil War that he believes slavery to be a "moral and political evil." After some potentially controversial comments on the matter, Lee then describes how he is spending his Christmas (alone, mostly) and the gifts he has purchased for friends and family. Similarly, and before launching into what is considered to be one of the most brilliant and articulate letters on democratic governing, Thomas Jefferson discusses a variety of trivial matters with James Madison, particularly his concern over a lost package of rice. Though entirely unrelated to the weightier issues at hand, these minutiae offer us a more accurate portrait of Lee and Jefferson as husband and friend, respectively, preoccupied with the day-to-day details of life familiar to us all. Consequently they—as well as the other men and women of prominence included here—seem less the remote, one-dimensional historical giants we often perceive them to be. They become, instead, more accessible, more genuine, more human. And their triumphs (and defeats) become all the more extraordinary.

Years after she lamented the public release of private letters and considered destroying her own, Rachel Carson had a change of heart. Reading her eleven-year correspondence with her close friend Dorothy Freeman, one begins to understand why: the exchange represents friendship at its best—supportive, open, forgiving, thoughtful, and trusting. Reviewing the letters near the end of her life, Rachel Carson recognized this, too. She realized as well that no matter what should happen to her or to Freeman—and, tragically, Carson succumbed to cancer at the age of fifty-seven—there would always remain a tangible and permanent record of their friendship, a relationship that would be revived and relived every time another reader came upon their letters and the heartfelt messages therein. Writing to Freeman just a year before she died, Carson acknowledged: "It is giving me so much pleasure to go through these letters that I'm glad I've been a hoarder. They recall so many precious things that one forgets otherwise." So many indeed.

PART I

Letters of Arrival, Expansion, & Exploration

It seems almost an impossibility to me how anyone can look forward to living their life out in the same place and doing the same things that their fathers and grandfathers did before them. Today as I think of what the world is and that I have my life before me, nothing seems impossible. I wish that as in the story books, some fairy might place the mirror of life before me and tell me to look at whatever scene I wished. Yet if it could be so, I can hardly say but I should close my eyes and refuse to look. How many have wished and wondered about the mysterious future as I do, and yet if the curtain were permitted to be drawn aside, would shrink from doing it for fear of gazing upon rugged rocks and yawning graves, in place of the velvety paths they wished for.

Robert E. Peary, explorer, to his mother on his twentieth birthday; May 6, 1876

John Winthrop to His Wife Margaret

To John Winthrop and his fellow Puritans, England in the 1620s was an increasingly ominous place to live. Economic depression threatened even wealthy landowners like Winthrop, and the ascension of King Charles I, who was sympathetic to Roman Catholicism and impatient with Puritan reformers, did not bode well. In April 1630 Winthrop and one thousand other English men and women sailed to the New World, where they made their home in Massachusetts with Winthrop as governor. On September 9, 1630, eleven weeks after his arrival, Winthrop sent his wife Margaret, in England, the following letter describing the great challenges they faced and his hopes for their future well-being. (The Winthrops agreed, in their correspondence, to seek spiritual communion with one another on Mondays and Fridays.)

My dear wife,

The blessing of God all-sufficient be upon thee and all my dear ones with thee forever.

I praise the good Lord, though we see much morality, sickness, and trouble, yet (such is His mercy) myself and children with most of my family, are yet living, and in health, and enjoy prosperity enough, if the afflictions of our brethren did not hold under the comfort of it. The Lady Arbella is dead, and good Mr. Higginson, my servant, old Waters of Neyland, and many others. Thus the Lord is pleased still to humble us; yet he mixes so many mercies with His corrections, as we are persuaded He will not cast us off, but, in His due time, will do us good, according to the measure of our afflictions. He stays but till He hath purged our corruptions, and healed the hardness and error of our hearts, and stripped us of our vain confidence in this arm of flesh, that He may have us rely wholly upon Himself.

The French ship, so long expected, and given for lost, is now come safe to us, about a fortnight since, having been twelve weeks at sea; and yet her passengers (being but a few) all safe and well but one, and her goats but six living of eighteen. So as now we are somewhat refreshed with such goods and provisions as she brought, though much thereof hath received damage by wet. I praise God, we have many occasions of comfort here, and do hope, that our days of affliction will soon have an end, and that the Lord will do us more good in the end than we could have expected, that will abundantly recompense for all the troubles we have endured. Yet we may not look at great things here. It is enough that we shall have Heaven, though we should pass through Hell to it. We here enjoy God and Jesus Christ. Is not this enough? What would we have more? I thank God; I like so well to be here, as I do not repent my coming, and if I were to come again, I would not have altered my course, though I had foreseen all these afflictions. I never fared better in my life, never slept better, never had more content of mind, which comes merely of the Lord's good hand; for we have not the like means of these comforts here, which we had in England. But the Lord is all-sufficient, blessed be His holy name. If He please, He can still uphold us in this estate; but if He shall see good to make us partakers with others in more affliction, His will be done. He is our God, and may dispose of us as He sees good.

I am sorry to part with thee so soon, seeing we meet so seldom, and my much business hath made me too oft forget Mondays and Fridays. I long for the time, when I may see thy sweet face again, and the faces of my dear children. But I must break off, and desire to thee to commend me kindly to all my good friends, and excuse my not writing at this time. If God please once to settle me, I shall make amends. I will name now but such as are nearest to thee: my brother and sister Gostlin, Mr Leigh, etc., Castleins, my neighbor Cole and his good wife, with the rest of my good neighbors, tenants, and servants. The good Lord bless thee, and all our children and family. So I kiss my sweet wife and my dear children, and rest.

Thy faithful husband
Jo: Winthrop

Margaret Winthrop, pregnant at the time her husband wrote this, joined him in 1631. Tragically, the baby died en route.

Roger Williams to the Town of Providence, Rhode Island & Cotton Mather to His Uncle John Cotton

Although many of the first pilgrims were exceedingly intolerant of faiths different from their own, one of the earliest settlers, Roger Williams, actually subscribed to the idea of religious freedom. Williams was banished from the Massachusetts Bay by the revered minister John Cotton Sr. for suggesting that there be a separation of civil and religious authority and that they break from the Church of England. Moving to Rhode Island, Williams ultimately created a sanctuary for people of varying faiths, including Jews. In the early to mid-1650s, the citizens of Providence found themselves in a quarrel as to whether it was possible to respect religious differences and also to maintain shared laws and order. In the following letter to the town of Providence, Williams concedes it is an immense issue but nevertheless offers his views on reconciling religious freedom with the need for common laws.

1655

To the Town of Providence,

That ever I should speak or write a tittle, that tends to such an infinite liberty of conscience, is a mistake, and which I have ever disclaimed and abhorred. To prevent such mistakes, I shall at present only propose this case: There goes many a ship to sea, with many hundred souls in one ship, whose weal and woe is common, and is a true picture of a commonwealth, or a human combination or society. It hath fallen out sometimes, that both Papists and Protestants, Jews and Turks, may be embarked in one ship; upon which supposal I affirm, that all the liberty of conscience, that ever I pleaded for, turns upon these two hinges—that none of the Papists, Protestants, Jews, or Turks be forced to come to the ship's prayers or worship, nor compelled from their own particular prayers or worship, if they practice any. I further add, that I never denied, that notwithstanding this liberty, the commander of this ship ought to command the ship's course, yea, and also command that justice, peace, and sobriety be kept and practiced, both among the seamen and all the passengers. If any of the seamen refuse to perform their services, or passengers to pay their freight; if any refuse to help, in person or purse, towards the common charges or defence; if any refuse to obey the common laws and orders of the ship, concerning their common peace or preservation; if any shall mutiny and rise up against their commanders and officers; if any should preach or write that there ought to be no commanders or officers, because all are equal in Christ, therefore no masters nor officers, no laws or orders, nor corrections nor punishments; I say, I never denied, but in such cases, whatever is pretended, the commander or commanders may judge, resist, compel, and punish such transgressors, according to their deserts and merits. This if seriously and honestly minded, may, if it so please the Father of Lights, let in some light to such as willingly shut not their eyes.

I remain studious of your common peace and liberty.

Roger Williams

The passing of Roger Williams's antagonist, John Cotton Sr., in 1652 by no means stemmed the tide of religious persecution in the colonies. Cotton Mather, the grandson of John Cotton Sr. and Richard Mather, rose to eminence by publicly denouncing those he believed were undermining the old Puritan ways with inferior and "blasphemous" religions. In 1692 Mather struck his most notorious blow in defense of his own faith when he fanned the flames of suspicion against women he thought to be witches. In the following letter to his uncle, John Cotton Jr., Mather expresses enthusiasm for the demise of a small band of witches and reflects on a recent earthquake in Jamaica.

August 5, 1692

Reverend Sir,

Our good God is working of miracles. Five witches were lately executed, impudently demanding of God a miraculous vindication of their innocency. Immediately upon this, our God miraculously sent in five Andover witches, who made a most ample, surprising, amazing confession of all their villainies, and declared the five newly executed to have been of their company, discovering many more, but all agreeing in Burroughs being their ringleader, who, I suppose, this day receives his trial at Salem, whither a vast concourse of people is gone, my father this morning among the rest. Since those, there have come in other confessors; yea, they come in daily. About this prodigious matter my soul has been refreshed with some little short of miraculous answers of prayer, which are not to be written; but they comfort me with a prospect of a hopeful issue.

The whole town yesterday turned the lecture into a fast, kept in our meeting-house; God give a good return. But in the morning we were entertained with the horrible tidings of the late earthquake at Jamaica, on the 7th of June last. When, on a fair day, the sea suddenly swelled, and the earth shook and broke in many places; and in a minute's time, the rich town of Port-Royal, the Tyrus of the whole English America, but a very Sodom for wickedness, was immediately swallowed up, and the sea came rolling over the town. No less than seventeen-hundred souls of that one town are missing, besides other incredible devastations all over the island, where houses are demolished, mountains overturned, rocks rent, and all manner of destruction\ inflicted. The Non-conformist minister there escaped wonderfully with his life. Some of our poor New England people are lost in the ruins, and others have their bones broke. Forty vessels were sunk—namely all whose cables did not break; but no New England ones. Behold, an accident speaking to all our English America. I live in pains, and want your prayers. Bestow them, dear Sir, on Your,

Cotton Mather

William Cobbett to Miss Rachel Smither & John Downe to His Wife

As the small, vulnerable colonies grew into major cities and ports, emigration from England to America expanded dramatically. The poor sought employment, merchants came to establish new businesses, and the adventurous arrived simply to see the growing, industrious offspring of the motherland. "Ambitious to become the citizen of a free state," William Cobbett wrote to an acquaintance, "I have left my native country, England, for America." With high hopes and an "inclination to see the world," Cobbett arrived in Philadelphia in October 1792. After less than two years of living in America, however, he saw almost nothing positive about the new land and made the following unsparing appraisal to Miss Rachel Smither, a friend back in England.

Philadelphia, July 6, 1794

This country is good for getting money, that is to say, if a person is industrious and enterprising. In every other respect the country is miserable. Exactly the contrary of what I expected. The land is bad, rocky; houses wretched; roads impassable after the least rain. Fruit in quantity, but good for nothing. One apple or peach in England or France is worth a bushel of them here. The seasons are detestable. All is burning or freezing. There is no spring or autumn. The weather is so very inconstant that you are never sure for an hour, a single hour at a time. Last night we made a fire to sit by, and to-day it is scorching hot. The whole month of March was so hot that we could hardly bear our clothes, and three parts of the month of June there was a frost every night, and so cold in the day-time that we were obliged to wear great-coats. The people are worthy of the country—cheating, sly, roguish gang. Strangers make fortunes here in spite of all this, particularly the English. The natives are by nature idle, and seek to live by cheating, while foreigners, being industrious, seek no other means than those dictated by integrity, and are sure to meet with encouragement even from the idle and roguish themselves; for, however roguish a man may be, he always loves to deal with an honest man. You have perhaps heard of the plague being at Philadelphia last year. It was no plague; it was a fever of the country, and is by no means extraordinary among the Americans. In the fall of the year almost every person, in every place, has a spell of fever that is called fall-fever. It is often fatal, and the only way to avoid it is to quit the country. But this fever is not all. Every month has its particular malady. In July, for example, everybody almost, or at least one half of the people, are taken with vomitings for several days at a time; they often carry off the patient, and almost always children. In short, the country is altogether detestable.

The greatest part of my acquaintance in this country are French merchants from St. Domingo and Martinico. To one of those Islands I shall probably go in about eight or nine months; and in that case, if I live so long, I shall be in England in about three years. For I do not intend to stay much above a couple of years in the Islands. Take care of my trunk and box, if you please, till you see me or hear from me. My Nancy's kind love to you all, and accept of mine at the same time. Doctor Priestley is just arrived here from England. He has attacked our English laws and Constitution in print, and declared his sentiments in favour of those butchers in France. He has, however, been attacked in his turn by an Englishman here. I will send you one of these pieces by another ship. Accept my love, and God bless you.

Wm. Cobbett

Cobbett did, ultimately, return to England. Not everyone, however, found the New World to be such a "scourge." Another Englishman, John Downe, traveled to America to work as a weaver and earn enough to bring his wife and their children over as soon as possible. In the following letter, he offers his impressions of his new home.

New York, United States
August 12, 1830

My dear wife,

I have got a situation in a Factory, in a very pleasant vale about 7 miles from Hudson, and I am to have the whole management of the factory and the master is going to board me till you come in his house. A Farmer took me one day in his waggon into the country, from Hudson, to see a factory, and I dined with him, and he would not have a farthing, and told me I was welcome to come to his house at any time; they had on the table pudding, pyes, and fruit of all kind that was in season, and preserves, pickles, vegetables, meat, and everything that a person could wish, and the servants set down at the same table with their masters. They do not think of locking the doors in the country, and you can gather peaches, apples, and all kinds of fruit by the side of the roads. And I can have a barrel of cider holding 32 gallons, for 4*s*., and they will lend me the barrel till I have emptied it. And I can have 100 lbs. of Beef for 10*s*. English money. Lamb is about five farthings the pound, and the butcher brings it to your door. And as for the bullocks' heads, sheep and lambs', they are thrown away, no one will eat them. I went into the market yesterday at New York, and on the outside of the market there was bullocks' and sheep and lambs' heads laying underfoot like dogs' meat. They cut the tongue, and throw the rest away. And I can go into a store, and have as much brandy as I like to drink for three half-pence and all other spirits in proportion. If a man like work he need not want victuals. It is a foolish idea that some people have, that there is too many people come here, it is quite the reverse; there was more than 1000 emigrants came in the day after I landed, and there is four ships have arrived since with emigrants. But there is plenty of room yet, and will for a thousand years to come.

My dear Sukey, all that I want now is to see you, and the dear children here, and then I shall be happy, and not before. You know very well that I should not have left you behind me, if I had money to have took you with me. It was sore against me to do it. But I do not repent of coming, for you know that there was nothing but poverty before me, and to see you and the dear children want was what I could not bear. *I would rather cross the Atlantic ten times than hear my children cry for victuals once.* Now, my dear, if you can get the Parish to pay for your passage, come directly; for I have not a doubt in my mind I shall be able to keep you in credit. You will find a few inconveniences in crossing the Atlantic, but it will not be long, and when that is over, all is over, for I know that you will like America.

America is not like England, for here no man thinks himself your superior. There is no improper or disgusting equality, for Character has its weight and influence, and the man which is really your superior does not plume himself on being so. An American, however low his station, never feels himself abashed when entering the presence of the highest. This is a country where a man can stand as a man, and where he can enjoy the fruits of his own exertions, with rational liberty to its fullest extent.

There is much attention paid to dress as at any of the watering places in England. Out in the country where I have been you see the young women with their veils and parasols, at the lowest that I saw. Poverty is unknown here. You see no beggars.

Give all the little ones a kiss for me, etc.

Meriwether Lewis and William Clark to the Oto Indians

At the urging of President Thomas Jefferson, who had long wanted to see America expand into a great "Empire of Liberty," Congress appropriated funds in January 1803 for an exploration of the western lands leading to the Pacific. (The Louisiana Purchase from the French, which was being negotiated in early 1803, doubled the size of America by 1804.) Jefferson selected his private secretary, Captain Meriwether Lewis, to lead the voyage and instructed him in a lengthy letter of June 20, 1803, to find "the most direct & practicable water communication across this continent for the purpose of commerce." Jefferson also requested detailed information on the geography, minerals, climate, animals, flora, and native inhabitants and traders encountered along the way. Recognizing the enormity of the task, Lewis invited his trusted friend William Clark, under whom Lewis had served in the army, to share the "fatigues, dangers, and honors" of the expedition. While the journals of Lewis and Clark reflect heartfelt and even emotional reactions to the spectacular views they observed and the daring episodes they survived, the extant letters of their two-year journey are mostly straightforward reports of the data President Jefferson had requested. Lewis and Clark were not unaware of the historical import of their endeavor; apparently they simply felt no need to emphasize it in their letters. Lewis did, however, provide insight into the purpose of his travels—and his desire to continue them peacefully—in the following August 4, 1804, message to the Oto Indians and their chief, Petit Voleur, also known as Wear-ruge-nor. (The haphazard capitalizations, punctuation, and misspellings, including that of the name of the tribe, are in the original document.)

To the Petit Voleur, or Wear-ruge-nor, the great Chief of the Ottoes, to the Chiefs and Warriors of the Ottoes, and the Chiefs and Warriors of the Missouri nation residing with the Ottoes—

Children.—Convene from among you the old men of experience; the men, on the wisdom of whose judgement you are willing to risk the future happiness of your nations; and the warriors, to the strength of whose arms you have been taught to look for protection in the days of danger—When in Council tranquilly assembled, reflect on the time past, and that to come; do not deceive yourselves, nor suffer others to deceive you; but like men and warriors devoted to the real interests of their nation, Seek those truths; which can alone perpetuate happiness.

Children.—Commissioned and sent by the great Chief of the Seventeen great nations of America, we have come to inform you, as we go also to inform all the nations of red men who inhabit the borders of the Missouri, that a great council was lately held between this great chief of the Seventeen great nations of America, and your old fathers the french and Spaniards; and that in this great council it was agreed that all the white men of Louisiana, inhabiting the waters of the Missouri and Mississippi should obey the commands of this great chief; he has accordingly adopted them as his children and they now form one common family with us: your old traders are of this description; they are no longer the Subjects of France or Spain, but have become the Citizens of the Seventeen great nations of america, and are bound to obey the commands of their great Chief the President who is now your only great father.—

Children.—This council being concluded between your old fathers the french and Spaniards, and your great father the Chief of the Seventeen great nations of America, your old fathers the French and Spaniards in complyance with their engagements made in that council, have withdrawn all their troops from all their military posts on the waters of the Mississippi and missouri, and have Surrendered to our great chief all their fortifications and lands in this country, together with the mouths of all the rivers through which the traders bring goods to the red men on the troubled waters. These arrangements being made, your old fathers the french and Spaniards have gone beyond the great lake towards the rising Sun, from whence they never intend returning to visit their former red-children in this quarter; nor will they, or any other nation of white men, ever again display their flag on the troubled waters; because the mouths of all those rivers are in the possession of the great Chief of the Seventeen great nations of America, who will command his war chiefs to Suffer no vessel to pass—but those which Sail under the protection of his flag, and who acknowledge his Supreme authority.

Children.—From what has been said, you will readily perceive, that the great chief of the Seventeen great nations of America, has become your only father; he is the only friend to whom you can now look for protection, or from whom you can ask favours, or receive good councils, and he will take care that you shall have no just cause to regret this change; he will serve you, & not deceive you.

Children.—The great chief of the Seventeen great nations of America, impelled by his parental regard for his newly adopted children on the troubled waters, has sent us out to clear the road, remove every obstruction, and to make it the road of peace between himself and his red children residing there; to enquire into the Nature of their wants, and on our return to inform Him of them, in order that he may make the necessary arrangements for their relief, he has sent by us, one of his flags, a medal and Some cloathes, such as he dresses his war chiefs with, which he directed should be given to the great Chief of the Ottoe nation, to be kept by him, as a pledge of the Sincerity with which he now offers you the hand of friendship.

Children.—Know that the great chief who has thus offered you the hand of unalterable friendship, is the great Chief of the Seventeen great Nations of America, whose cities are as numerous as the stars of the heavens, and whose people like the grass of your plains, cover with their Cultivated fields and wigwams, the wide Extended country, reaching from the western borders of the Mississippi, to the great lakes of the East, where the land ends and the Sun rises from the face of the great waters.—

Children.—Know that this great chief, as powerfull as he is just, and as beneficent as he is wise, always entertaining a Sincere and friendly disposition towards the red people of America, has commanded us his war chiefs to undertake this long journey, which we have so far accomplished with great labour & much expence, in order to council with yourselves and his other red-children on the troubled waters, to give you his good advice; to point out to you the road in which you must walk to obtain happiness. He has further commanded us to tell you that when you accept his flag and medal, you accept therewith his hand of friendship, which will never be withdrawn from your nation as long as you continue to follow the councils which he may command his chiefs to give you, and shut your ears to the councils of Bad birds.

Children.—The road in which your great father and friend, has commanded us to tell you and your nation that you must walk in order to enjoy the benefit of his friendship, is, that you are to live in peace with all the *whitemen*, for they are his children; neither wage war against the *redmen* your neighbours, for they are equally his children and he is bound to protect them. injure not the persons of any traders who may come among you, neither destroy nor take their property from them by force; more particularly those traders who visit you under the protection of your great fathers flag. do not obstruct the passage of any boat, pirogue, or other vessel, which may be ascending or decending the Missouri River, more especially such as may be under cover of your great fathers flag neither injure any red or white man on board such vessels as may possess the flag, for by that Signal you may know them to be good men, and that they do not intend to injure you; they are therefore to be treated as friends, and as the common children of one great father, (the great chief of the Seventeen great nations of America.—

Children.—Do these things which your great father advises and be happy. Avoid the councils of bad birds; turn on your heel from them as you would from the precipice of an high rock, whose summit reached the Clouds, and whose base was washed by the gulph of human woes; lest by one false step you should bring upon your nation the displeasure of your great father, the great chief of the Seventeen great nations of America, who could consume you as the fire consumes the grass of the plains. The mouths of all the rivers through which the traders bring goods to you are in his possession, and if you displease him he could at pleasure shut them up and prevent his traders from coming among you; and this would of course bring all the Calamities of want upon you; but it is not the wish of your great father to injure you; on the contrary he is now pursuing the measures best Calculated to insure your happiness.—

Children.—If you open your ears to the councils of your great father, the great chief of the Seventeen great nations of America, & strictly pursue the advice which he has now given you through us, he will as soon as possible after our return, send a store of goods to the mouth of the river Platte to trade with you for your pelteries and furs; these goods will be furnished you annually in a regular manner, and in such quantities as will be equal to your necessities.

You will then obtain goods on much better terms than you have ever received them heretofore.

Children.—As it will necessarily take some time before we can return, and your great father send and establish this store of goods; he will permit your old traders who reside among you, or who annually visit you, to continue to trade with you, provided they give you good Council.

Children.—We are now on a long journey to the head of the Missouri; the length of this journey compelled us to load our boat and perogues with provisions, we have therefore brought but very few goods as presents for yourselves or any other nations which we may meet on our way. we are no traders, but we have come to consult you on the subject of your trade; to open the road and prepare the way, in order that your nation may hereafter receive a regular and plentifull supply of goods.

Children.—We are sorry that your absence from your town prevented our Seeing your great chief and yourselves; it would have given us much pleasure to have spoken to you personnally; but, as the cold season is fast advancing, and we have a long distance to travel, we could not wait your return.—

Children.—If your great Chief wishes to See your great father and speak with him, he can readily do so. Let your chief engage Some trader who may reside with you the ensuing winter, to take him and four of his principal chiefs or warriors with him to St. Louis when he returns thither on the ensuing spring; your great chief may take with him also an interpreter of his own choice, who shall be well paid for his services by your great father's Chiefs; the trader will also be well paid for his services by the Commandant at St. Louis. The commandant at St. Louis will furnish you with the necessary number of horses, and all other means to make your journey from thence to your great father's town Comfortable and Safe.

Children.—In order that the Commandant at St. Louis, as well as your great father, and all his chiefs may know you, you must take with you, the flag, the medal, and this parole which we now Send you. When your great father and his chiefs see those things, they will know that you have opened your ears to your great father's voice, and have come to hear his good Councils.

Our oldest son the Wear-ruge-nor. If the Situation of your nation is Such that you cannot with propriety leave them, you may Send Some of your principal men not exceeding five, to See your great father and hear his words. You must give them authority to act for you and your Nation. Your great father will receive them as his children, give them his good councils, and Send them back loaded with presents for their nation; your nation would then See that all we have told you is true, and that the great chief of the Seventeen great nations of America never Sends his red children from him to return with empty hands to their village.—

Our oldest son the Wear-ruge-nor.—Whomsoever you Send to your great father must carry the flag and this parole, in order that your great father and his chiefs may know that they have come to see them by our invitation. Send by them also all the flags and medals which you may have received from your old fathers the French and Spaniards, or from any other nation whatever, your father will give you new flags and new medals of his own in exchange for those which you send him. It is not proper since you have become the children of the great chief of the Seventeen great nations of America, that you should wear or keep those emblems of attachment to any other great father but himself, nor will it be pleasing to him if you continue to do so.

Children.—We hope that the great Spirit will open your ears to our councils, and dispose your mind to their observance. Follow these councils and you will have nothing to fear, because the great Spirit will Smile upon your nation, and in future ages will make you to outnumber the trees of the forest.

Signed and Sealed this 4th day of August 1804 at the council Bluff, by us, the friends of all red-men, and the war chiefs of the great chief of the Seventeen great nations of America.

Meriwether Lewis Captn.
1st U.S. Regt. Infantry.

William Clark
Capt. on the Missouri Expedition

Frithjof Meidell to His Mother & Father Pierre-Jean de Smet to George Thompson

"The whole country," the San Francisco Californian *exclaimed in May 1848, "resounds with the sordid cry of 'gold! GOLD!! GOLD!!!'" By May 1849, over a year after gold was first discovered in California, thousands of wagons were wheeling their way toward the West Coast as other prospectors went by sea, sailing around South America in crowded ships. By the end of 1849, over one hundred thousand people were digging, panning, and mining for gold in California. One of these individuals, Frithjof Meidell, was an immigrant from Scandinavia who traveled to northern California's Mill Valley but ultimately did not find his fortune. Meidell was nevertheless awed by America's frontier, and in a letter to his mother (and indirectly to his brother Ditmar), he writes of his excellent mental and physical well-being, due in part to the magnificence of the Sierra Nevadas.*

December 1, 1859

You may be sure that I am still well. As a matter of fact, I have never enjoyed better health, and as far as personal safety is concerned I now live in a country which is very different from what it was a few years ago. One is in no greater danger here than anywhere else. I am an almost full-fledged miner now, but I have not been so lucky as to find a good-sized nugget yet. And even if I should never strike it rich, I shall not be disappointed, for my ideas about California never caused me to entertain any very extravagant expectations.

I am now living in the Sierra Nevada Mountains, and you cannot imagine a more romantic country, rich as it is in the most magnificent scenery. I wish you could make a trip up here in the spring and see the flowers that cover every inch of ground. I had gathered quite a few seeds which I meant to send to you, but a mouse stole the package one night on a little "prospecting trip." I had always thought that our Norwegian field flowers, for color and scent, were inferior only to those of the tropics, but now it seems to me that their sisters here in the Sierra Nevada Mountains win the prize. Most of the time I have a bouquet of them in my cabin, and that is the only ornament it contains. On Sunday, which is here the busiest trading day in the week, you often see the hardy miners on their way to the grocery store with bouquets of these flowers in their hands. Arriving at the store, each miner compares his bouquet with those of the others, and if there is a lady present, which is rarely the case, she is immediately chosen as judge of the flowers. But the prize for the finest bouquet is, it grieves me to report, whisky.

I shall never be able to forget a walk I took last spring on a Sunday morning. For hours I wandered about without following any road or trail, until I was completely overwhelmed with admiration of all the splendor and glory that surrounded me. I sat down in order to enjoy the glorious view. Everything was as great as if God had just created it. Probably no human foot before mine had ever trodden on this splendid carpet of flowers. He had spread out here, and I was probably the first man to see the beautiful cedars and evergreen oak trees. He had planted here and there to provide shade for the flowers and a cool place for the birds to sing in. There was no trace of a human presence, and not even the smallest indication of an Indian trail could be found in this sacred spot. A strange feeling came over me. Never before had I felt God's greatness and omnipotence as strongly as I did here. None of His servants can describe in words His boundless goodness as well as He Himself had done it here with His flowers, birds, and natural beauty. One gorgeous range of mountains rose behind the other, and on to the horizon towered the still higher summits of the Sierras with their crowns of snow. I was alone with my Creator, and a feeling of awe and gratitude arose in my breast that I should have been given so much for nothing. I prayed to God without realizing that I did so.

Please do not believe now, dear Mother, after reading this, that I have grown melancholy in any way. I am in good spirits and full of courage, but my pen ran away with me, and I believe that the lonely life I lead here is to blame if I have shown any faintness of heart.

I had really planned to write a long letter to Ditmar, as I have several things to relate which I think would amuse him, but I do not have any more paper now. But I promise, my dear Ditmar, that you will hear from me soon. As far as your writing to me "at once" goes—that will do to tell the marines.

Whatever the motivation—the search for gold, religious independence, a more spacious plot of land—the reality of going west and growing up with the country, as the publisher Horace Greeley famously advised, was for many a brutal one. Death, starvation, attacks by American Indians and bandits, severe weather, and a host of other ills plagued those who attempted the journey. Father Pierre-Jean de Smet, a missionary-explorer, crisscrossed America numerous times and was familiar with these dangers. Known as "Black Robe" by the Indians, de Smet was born in Belgium and came to Missouri at the age of twenty to spread Christianity throughout America. De Smet maintained a prolific correspondence with friends, other priests, and those familiar with his work, and he was often asked for advice on traveling to the West. In the following letter, he candidly tells one inquirer what he thinks of such an attempt.

St. Louis University, Feb. 27, 1852.

Mr. George Thompson, *Chapel Hill, Perry Co., Ohio:*

Dear Sir.—

I acknowledge the receipt of your letter of the 15th instant, in which you ask me some information concerning Oregon. As it is asked by way of advice which may decide you and eight or ten more families, as you say, to emigrate to that country, I am indeed at a loss what to say, and I must acknowledge that till now I have never taken it upon me to encourage any one to undertake the journey. Oregon, no doubt, has great advantages, several of its valleys are beautiful and rich; the grazing, even in winter, is fine and abundant; and the great discoveries in California have opened up a large market for its products. In no country are cattle easier raised, and its wheat is most beautiful. The climate may be put down as fair, if you except the rainy season, which lasts between three and four months. I must say, at the same time, that it can bear no comparison with most of our Western States, all things well considered. The richness of the lands in general, with all the other advantages connected with it, are much greater here than there.

I left Oregon in the fall of 1846, and since that time extensive emigrations to that country have taken place; so that I think by this time the best and most suitable spots must have been taken up.

Besides, the great difficulty is to get there, for the road is long and dangerous. Last summer I paid a visit to different Indian nations as far as the Rocky Mountains, and returned to the States by the Oregon route, which I struck in the neighborhood of Independence Rock, about 200 miles above Fort Laramie. The scene we witnessed on this road presented indeed a melancholy proof of the uncertainty which attends our highest prospects in life. The bleached bones of animals everywhere strewed along the track, the hastily erected mound, beneath which lie the remains of some departed friend or relative, with an occasional tribute to his memory roughly inscribed on a board or headstone, and hundreds of graves left without this affectionate token of remembrance, furnished abundant evidence of the unsparing hand with which death has thinned their ranks. The numerous shattered fragments of the vehicles, provision, tools, etc., intended to be taken across these wild plains, tell us another tale of reckless boldness with which many entered upon this hazardous enterprise. It is rashness to undertake this long trip except with very good animals, with very strong vehicles and with a good supply of light provisions, such as tea, coffee, sugar, rice, dried apples, peaches, flour and peas or beans.

I remain, Dear Sir, etc.

Guri Endresen to Relatives in Norway & Washakie, a Shosone Indian, to Governor John W. Hoyt

Cultural misunderstandings and prejudices, incompatible notions of justice, competition for land, and many other differences, real and imagined, sparked bloody clashes between American Indians and pioneers from their first encounters with one another. Each accused the other of unspeakable cruelties, and each alleged that the aggression of the other was unprovoked. In the following letter to relatives back in Norway, Guri Endresen recounts the horrors she and her family endured at the hands of the Indians in Minnesota.

December 2, 1866

I have received your letter of April 14, this year, and I send you herewith my heartiest thanks for it, for it gives me great happiness to hear from you and to know that you are alive, well, and in general thriving. I must also report briefly to you how things have been going with me recently, though I must ask you to forgive me for not having told you earlier about my fate. I do not seem to have been able to do so much as to write to you, because during the time when the savages raged so fearfully here I was not able to think about anything except being murdered, with my whole family, by these terrible heathen. But God be praised, I escaped with my life, unharmed by them, and my four daughters also came through the danger unscathed.

Guri and Britha were carried off by the wild Indians, but they got a chance the next day to make their escape. When the savages gave them permission to go home to get some food, these young girls made use of the opportunity to flee and thus they got away alive, and on the third day after they had been taken, some Americans came along who found them on a large plain or prairie and brought them to people. I myself wandered aimlessly around on my land with my youngest daughter, and I had to look on while they shot my precious husband dead, and in my sight my dear son Ole was shot through the shoulder. But he got well again from this wound and lived a little more than a year and then was taken sick and died. We also found my oldest son Endre shot dead, but I did not see the firing of this death shot. For two days and nights I hovered about here with my little daughter, between fear and hope and almost crazy, before I found my wounded son and a couple of other persons, unhurt, who helped us to get away to a place of greater security. To be an eyewitness to these things and to see many others wounded and killed was almost too much for a poor woman; but, God be thanked, I kept my life and my sanity, though all my movable property was torn away and stolen. But this would have been nothing if only I could have had my loved husband and children—but what shall I say? God permitted it to happen thus, and I had to accept my heavy fate and thank Him for having spared my life and those of some of my dear children.

I must also let you know that my daughter Gjaertru has land, which they received from the government under a law that has been passed, called in our language "the Homestead law," and for a quarter-section of land they have to pay $16, and after they have lived there five years they receive a deed and complete possession of the property and can sell it if they want to or keep it if they want to. She lives about twenty-four American miles from here and is doing well. My daughter Guri is away in house service for an American about a hundred miles from here; she has been there working for the same man for four years; she is in good health and is doing well; I visited her recently, but for a long time I knew nothing about her, whether she was alive or not.

My other two daughters, Britha and Anna, are at home with me, are in health, and are thriving here. I must also remark that it was four years August 21 since I had to flee from my dear home, and since that time I have not been on my land, as it is only a sad sight because at the spot where I had a happy home, there are now only ruins left as reminders of the terrible Indians. Still I moved up here to the neighborhood again this summer. A number of families have moved back here again so that we hope after a while to make conditions pleasant once more. Yet the atrocities of the Indians are and will be fresh in memory. They have now been driven beyond the boundaries of the state, and we hope that they never will be allowed to come here again. I am now staying at the home of Sjur Anderson, two and half miles from my home.

I must also tell you how much I had before I was ruined in this way. I had 17 head of cattle, 8 sheep, 8 pigs, and a number of chickens; now I have 6 head of cattle, 4 sheep, 1 pig. Five of my cattle stayed on my land until February 1863, and lived on some hay and stacks of wheat on the land; and I received compensation from the government for my cattle and other movable property that I lost. Of the six cattle that I now have three are milk cows, and of these I have sold butter, the summer's product, a little over 230 pounds; I sold this last month and got $66 for it. In general I may say that one or another has advised me to sell my land, but I would rather keep it for a time yet, in the hope that some of my people might come and use it. It is difficult to get such good land again, and if you, my dear daughter, would come here, you could buy it and use it, and then it would not be necessary to let it fall into the hands of strangers.

And now in closing I must send my very warm greetings to my unforgettable dear mother, my dearest daughter and her husband and children, and in general to all my relatives, acquaintances, and friends. And may the Lord by his grace bend, direct, and govern our hearts so that we sometime with gladness may assemble with God in the eternal mansions where there will be no more partings, no sorrows, no more trials, but everlasting joy and gladness, and contentment in beholding God's face. If this be the goal for all our endeavors through the sorrows and cares of this life, then through his grace we may hope for a blessed life hereafter, for Jesus sake.

American Indians had their own perspective on the conflicts between their people and those settling in the lands they considered their own. A Shoshone Indian named Washakie explains, in the following 1878 message to Governor John W. Hoyt of the Wyoming territory, why he and his fellow Indians feel threatened.

Governor:

We are right glad, sir, that you have so bravely and kindly come among us. I shall, indeed, speak to you freely of the many wrongs we have suffered at the hands of the white man. They are things to be noted and remembered. But I cannot hope to express to you the half that is in our hearts. They are too full for words.

Disappointment; then a deep sadness; then a grief inexpressible; then, at times, a bitterness that makes us think of the rifle, the knife and the tomahawk, and kindles in our hearts the fires of desperation—that, sir, is the story of our experience, of our wretched lives.

The white man, who possesses this whole vast country from sea to sea, who roams over it at pleasure, and lives where he likes, cannot know the cramp we feel in this little spot, with the undying remembrance of the fact, which you know as well as we, that every foot of what you proudly call America, not very long ago belonged to the red man. The Great Spirit gave it to us. There was room enough for all his many tribes, and all were happy in their freedom. But the white man had, in ways we know not of, learned some things we had not learned; among them, how to make superior tools and terrible weapons, better for war than bows and arrows; and there seemed no end to the hordes of men that followed them from other lands beyond the sea.

And so, at last, our fathers were steadily driven out, or killed, and we, their sons, but sorry remnants of tribes once mighty, are cornered in little spots of the earth all ours of right—cornered like guilty prisoners, and watched by men with guns, who are more than anxious to kill us off.

Nor is that all. The white man's government promised that if we, the Shoshones, would be content with the little patch allowed us, it would keep us well supplied with everything necessary to comfortable living, and would see that no white man should cross our borders for our game, or for anything that is ours. *But it has not kept its word!* The white man kills our game, captures our furs, and sometimes feeds his herds upon our meadows. And your great and mighty government—Oh sir, I hesitate, for I cannot tell the half! It does not protect us in our rights. It leaves us without the promised seed, without tools for cultivating the land, without implements for harvesting our crops, without breeding animals better than ours, without the food we still lack, after all we can do, without the many comforts we cannot produce, without the schools we so much need for our children.

I say again, the government does not keep its word! And so,

after all we can get cultivating the land, and by hunting and fishing, we are sometimes nearly starved, and go half naked, as you see us!

Knowing all this, do you wonder, sir, that we have fits of desperation and think to be avenged?

Washakie

William Murphy to Family Members in Ireland

For five years, beginning in 1845, a plant disease ravaged the farms of Ireland and destroyed the country's basic food crop—the potato—causing widespread disease, malnutrition, and starvation. By 1850 over a million Irish men, women, and children were dead, and those who could afford to leave headed primarily for America. During and immediately following the famine over one and a half million Irish citizens came to the United States. One of them was a young man named William Murphy, who immigrated with his younger brother James and searched for work. Even when he found a steady job constructing railroad bridges, he was moved from Virginia to California and many states in between. In December 1880 Murphy wrote the following letter to his sister and her husband in Belfast to share his thoughts on his American experience.

Dear Sister and Brother,

I have to knock around so much at the work I follow that I am hardly ever more than a week or two in one place. And I make up my mind to write home every place I go. But when I get there, I think this way: "Well, I'm not going to be long here; perhaps the next place I go I can wait and get an answer." And so it goes.

No doubt you think, why don't I settle down like other people? I have asked myself that question a thousand times. I have gone further—I have tried to do so. But when I try, I soon get tired and the restless spirit gets the best of me all the time. The fact is, traveling is so natural to me that I might as well try to live without eating as without wandering around. But what difference does it make? Life is but a dream, and although I know that my last days will be spent in all probability amongst strangers, I almost wish sometimes the dream was over.

Don't think for a moment that I am despondent or downhearted. But just think for a second of the past that has gone, never to be recalled. It seems but yesterday since we were a happy and united family—mother, father, brothers, and sisters. Where are they now?

The grew together side by side,
They filled one hall with glee.
Their graves are scattered far and wide,
By mountain, stream and sea.

James, the latest of our loved and lost, laid him down to rest in the far away California. He like thousands more tried to find a fortune and instead he found a grave. But where could he find a more fitting resting place than in Lone Mountain? The last rays of the setting sun kiss his grave as it sinks behind the waters of the Great Pacific, and his spirit has crossed the Great Divide and joined the others in that better land beyond.

Dear sister and brother, may God bless and preserve you is the earnest prayer or your affectionate brother,

William

Walt Whitman to the Town of Santa Fé

In early 1883 the citizens of Santa Fé, New Mexico, asked the great American poet Walt Whitman to come to their town's anniversary celebration and read a poem honoring the city. Whitman, who was sixty-four at the time, declined the invitation. But he did send the following letter venerating the great influence the "Spanish character" has had on the United States and expressing his hopes for its continued presence.

Camden, New Jersey, July 20th, 1883

To Messrs Griffin, Martinez, Prince, and other Gentlemen
at Sante Fé:

Dear Sirs: —Your kind invitation to visit you and deliver a poem for the 333rd Anniversary of founding Santa Fé has reach'd me so late that I have to decline, with sincere regret. But I will say a few words off hand.

We Americans have yet to really learn our antecedants, and sort them, to unify them. They will be found ampler than has been supposed, and in widely different sources. Thus far, impress'd by New England writers and schoolmasters, we tacitly abandon ourselves to the notion that our United States have been fashion'd from the British Islands only, and essentially form a second England only—which is a very great mistake. Many leading traits for our future national personality, and some of the best ones, will certainly prove to have originated from other than British stock. As it is, the British and German, valuable as they are in the concrete, already threaten excess. Or rather, I should say, they have certainly reach'd that excess. To-day, something outside of them, and to counterbalance them, is seriously needed.

The seething materialistic and business vortices of the United States, in their present devouring relations, controlling and belittling everything else, are, in my opinion, but a vast and indispensable stage in the new world's development, and are certainly to be follow'd by something entirely different—at least by immense modifications. Character, literature, a society worthy of the name, are yet to be establish'd, through a nationality of noblest spiritual, heroic and democratic attributes—not one of which at present definitely exists—entirely different from the past, though unerringly founded on it, and to justify it.

To that composite American identity of the future, Spanish character will supply some of the most needed parts. No stock shows a grander historic retrospect—grander in religiousness and loyalty, or for patriotism, courage, decorum, gravity and honor. It is time to dismiss utterly the illusion-compound, half raw-head-and-bloody-bones and half Mysteries-of-Udolpho, inherited from the English writers of the past 200 years. It is time to realize—for it is certainly true—that there will not be found any more cruelty, tyranny, superstition, &c., in the *résumé* of past Spanish history than in the corresponding *résumé* of Anglo-Norman history. Nay, I think there will not be found so much.

Then another point, relating to American ethnology, past and to come, I will here touch upon at a venture. As to our aboriginal or Indian population—the Aztec in the South, and many a tribe in the North and West—I know it seems to be agreed that they must gradually dwindle as time rolls on, and in a few generations more leave only a reminiscence, a blank. But I am not at all clear about that. As America, from its many far-back sources and current supplies, develops, adapts, entwines, faithfully identifies its own—are we to see it cheerfully accepting and using all the contributions of foreign lands from the whole outside globe—and then rejecting the only ones distinctly its own—the autochthonic ones?

As to the Spanish stock of our Southwest, it is certain to me that we do not begin to appreciate the splendor and sterling value of its race element. Who knows but that element, like the course of some subterranean river, dipping invisibly for a hundred or two hundred years, is now to emerge in broadest flow and permanent action?

If I might assume to do so, I would like to send you the most cordial, heartfelt congratulations of your American fellow-countrymen here. You have more friends in the Northern and Atlantic regions than you suppose, and they are deeply interested in the development of the great Southwestern interior, and in what your festival would arouse to public attention.

Very respectfully, &c.,
Walt Whitman

Elinore Rupert Stewart to Her Former Employer Mrs. Coney

Elinore Rupert, a widow who lost her husband in a railroad accident, left Denver, Colorado, with her young daughter, Jerrine, to find employment in Burnt Fork, Wyoming. Her goal was to work for a rancher and eventually learn enough to be a homesteader herself. Four years after arriving in Wyoming, Elinore Rupert Stewart *was married and had realized her dream of running her own home and farm. After reflecting on all that she had accomplished (and thinking on all that was ahead), Stewart wrote the following to her former employer, Mrs. Coney, in Denver.*

January 23, 1913

Dear Mrs. Coney,—

I am afraid all my friends think I am very forgetful and that you think I am ungrateful as well, but I am going to plead not guilty. Right after Christmas Mr. Stewart came down with *la grippe* and was so miserable that it kept me busy trying to relieve him. Out here where we can get no physician we have to dope ourselves, so that I had to be housekeeper, nurse, doctor, and general overseer. That explains my long silence.

And now I want to thank you for your kind thought in prolonging our Christmas. The magazines were much appreciated. They relieved some weary night-watches, and the box did Jerrine more good than the medicine I was having to give her for *la grippe*. She was content to stay in bed and enjoy the contents of her box.

When I read of the hard times among the Denver poor, I feel like urging them every one to get out and file on land. I am very enthusiastic about women homesteading. It really requires less strength and labor to raise plenty to satisfy a large family than it does to go out to wash, with the added satisfaction of knowing that their job will not be lost to them if they care to keep it. Even if improving the place does go slowly, it is that much done to stay done. Whatever is raised is the homesteader's own, and there is no house-rent to pay. This year Jerrine cut and dropped enough potatoes to raise a ton of fine potatoes. She wanted to try, so we let her, and you will remember that she is but six years old. We had a man break the ground and cover the potatoes for her and the man irrigated them once. That was all that was done until digging time, when they were ploughed out and Jerrine picked them up. Any woman strong enough to go out by the day could have done every bit of the work and put in two or three times that much, and it would have been so much more pleasant than to work so hard in the city and then be on starvation rations in the winter.

To me, homesteading is the solution of all poverty's problems, but I realize that temperament has much to do with success in any undertaking, and persons afraid of coyotes and work and loneliness had better let ranching alone. At the same time, any woman who can stand her own company, can see the beauty of the sunset, loves growing things, and is willing to put in as much time at careful labor as she does over the washtub, will certainly succeed; will have independence, plenty to eat all the time, and a home of her own in the end.

Experimenting need cost the homesteader no more than the work, because by applying to the Department of Agriculture at Washington he can get enough seed and as many kinds as he wants to make a thorough trial, and it does n't even cost postage. Also one can always get bulletins from there and the Experiment Station of one's own State concerning any problem or as many problems as may come up. I would not, for anything, allow Mr. Stewart to do anything toward improving my place, for I want the fun and the experience myself. And I want to be able to speak from experience when I tell others what they can do. Theories are very beautiful, but facts are what must be had, and what I intend to give some time.

Here I am boring you to death with things that cannot interest you! You'd think I wanted you to homestead, would n't you? But I am only thinking of the troops of tired, worried women, sometimes even cold and hungry, scared to death of losing their places to work, who could have plenty to eat, who could have fires by gathering the wood, and comfortable homes of their own, if they but had the courage and determination to get them.

I must stop right now before you get so tired you will not answer. With much love to you from Jerrine and myself, I am

Yours affectionately,
Elinore Rupert Stewart

A Young Immigrant Woman to the *Jewish Daily Forward*
& Irma Czerner to First Lady Eleanor Roosevelt

Between 1881 and 1925 over two and a half million Jews came to America, fleeing pogroms in tsarist Russia and persecutions in neighboring Eastern Europe. The Jewish Daily Forward*—a Yiddish-language, working-class newspaper—inaugurated a column in January 1906 known as the "Bintel Brief," which invited readers to send in questions or concerns about life in America. The letters, mostly from recent Jewish immigrants struggling to survive on New York's Lower East Side, sought advice on matters ranging from employment to new social customs to interreligious marriage. Some used the opportunity to express their despair at not having attained the American dream. The following letter was written in 1907 by a young woman caught in a truly horrible situation.*

Dear Editor,

I am one of those unfortunate girls thrown by fate into a dark and dismal shop, and I need your counsel.

Along with my parents, sisters and brothers, I came from Russian Poland where I had been well educated. But because of the terrible things going on in Russia we were forced to emigrate to America. I am now seventeen years old, but I look younger and they say I am attractive.

A relative talked us into moving to Vineland, New Jersey, and here in this small town I went to work in a shop. In this shop there is a foreman who is an exploiter, and he sets prices on the work. He figures it out so that the wages are very low, he insults and reviles the workers, he fires them and then takes them back. And worse than all of this, in spite of the fact that he has a wife and several children, he often allows himself to "have fun" with some of the working girls. It was my bad luck to be one of the girls he tried to make advances to. And woe to any girl who doesn't willingly accept them.

Though my few hard-earned dollars mean a lot to my family of eight souls, I didn't want to accept the foreman's vulgar advances. He started to pick on me, said my work was no good, and when I proved to him he was wrong, he started to shout at me in the vilest language. He insulted me in Yiddish and then in English, so the American workers could understand too. Then, as if the Devil were after me, I ran home.

I am left without a job. Can you imagine my circumstances and that of my parents who depend on my earnings? The girls in the shop were very upset over the foreman's vulgarity but they don't want him to throw them out, so they are afraid to be witnesses against him. What can be done about this? I beg you to answer me.

Respectfully,
A Shopgirl

The editors advised the young woman to bring her story out into the open, where, in such a small town, the foreman would likely be dismissed and she would get her job back. (The eventual outcome of the shopgirl's plight is not known.) The second great wave of Jewish immigration came during the 1930s and 1940s when each year hundreds of thousands of Jews, desperate to leave Europe and the persecution of the Nazis, applied to become American citizens. One such man was a doctor named Erwin Froehlich, who lived with his mother, Paula, and watched as his sister, Irma, her husband, Max Czerner, and their family escaped safely to the United States. As Erwin's situation became more precarious, Irma Czerner tried everything she could to secure visas for him and their mother, all to no avail. As a last resort, Czerner wrote the following letter to Eleanor Roosevelt in the fall of 1941 imploring the First Lady to assist her brother and mother.

5335 Kimbark Avenue
Chicago, Illinois

Dear Lady:

The pictures of you and your family in the newspapers gave me the idea and the courage to do the unusual thing and approach you—although a stranger. I always liked and enjoyed the nice and happy expression of your face and always felt strongly attracted. I am sure you get many letters asking you for some favor. Therefore, I shall be brief.

Who am I? A refugee from Prague, Czechoslovakia, here with my husband and 3 children, two girls, seven and nine, and a boy two and a half years old.

What do I want? An affadavit for my mother and brother. We are earning enough to take care of them, but not so much that our affadavits alone would be sufficient. It is my anxious desire to give them quick and effective help that makes me turn to you. I am sure an affadavit from you as an outstanding personality would be one hundred per cent effective if only you would be willing to help me.

Who is my brother? Erwin Froehlich, Prague physician, 38 years old, single, lives with my mother. He is a specialist for gastroenterology and had made himself known already as an excellent young doctor by his medical ability, his good character and a number of works published in medical journals. Since the Occupation more than a year ago, he is no longer allowed to work in his profession. He and our mother were forced to move three times during one year and to share their four-room apartment with two other families. He is now working in a social institution without pay. Some of his publications are known in this country and I feel sure that some of the specialists in the USA would be glad to give references for him if required, including Professor Dr. Schindler at the University of Chicago, the inventor of the gastroscope.

Since I have no right to take much of your time with a long story, I will let these lines be enough, hoping that you will understand that behind the few facts and words given to you lies a world of anxiety and hope.

My husband and I can give you every possible assurance that my people would never be in any sense a burden to anybody should your kind help make my dreams come true and decide to sign the papers for them. They will of course live with us in our six-room apartment at the above address.

Should you decide to kindly help my dreams come true I would take the liberty of sending you the necessary forms for signature.

Very respectfully yours,
Irma Czerner

It is doubtful Eleanor Roosevelt ever saw the letter. On November 18, 1941, the head of the Visa Division for the Department of State, Mr. A. M. Warren, sent a form letter to Czerner, stating, "since there are no American consular offices operating in German-occupied territories, no action can be taken." In fact, America's strict immigration policy at the time prevented the great majority of Jews who applied for visas from entering the United States. Almost exactly one year after Irma Czerner's letter was written, her mother was sent to the Treblinka extermination camp. She was gassed on October 23, 1942. Erwin Froehlich was killed three months later at Auschwitz.

Two Letters to the *Chicago Defender*

Encouraged by black newspapers such as the Chicago Defender *and attracted by a rapidly expanding job market, African Americans from the South poured into northern cities at unprecedented levels in the early 1900s. The black population in Chicago, Illinois, alone went from 44,000 in 1910 to almost 110,000 in 1920. The* Chicago Defender *reported frequently on "The Great Migration," as it was called, and featured ads offering to pay the travel costs of workers willing to move to the city. The* Defender *received thousands of responses to the ads, as well as letters asking for advice, monetary support, and information on job openings. The following letter, dated May 20, 1917, is just one example.*

New Orleans, La.

Dear Sir: I am sure your time is precious, for being as you an editor of a newspaper such as the race has never owned and for which it must proudly bost of as being the peer in the pereoidical world. am confident that yours is a force of busy men. I also feel sure that you will spare a small amount of your time to give some needed information to one who wishes to relieve himselfe of the burden of the south. I indeed wish very much to come north anywhere in Ill. will do since I am away from the Lynchman's noose and torchman's fire. Myself and a friend wish to come but not without information regarding work and general suroundings. Now hon sir if for any reason you are not in position to furnish us with the information desired. please do the act of kindness of placing us in tuch with the organization who's business it is I am told to furnish said information. we are firemen machinist helpers practical painters and general laborers. And most of all, ministers of the gospel who are not afraid of labor for it put us where we are. Please let me hear from you.

The Defender *also provided its readers with a forum to discuss and debate openly both the advantages and the dangers of the migration. The following letter is a response to those who publicly discouraged African Americans from making the journey.*

August 26, 1916

I have read several articles recently from the pen of Race leaders advising the Negroes against going to the north for employment. I am thoroughly convinced that this advice is wrong, however honestly and well intended it is being given. These leaders give reasons why the Negro should stay in the south, but none of them give any good reason why our people should not go as the Chinaman, the Japanese, the Italian, the Pole, the Scandinavian and other foreigners who come to America for work have. So why should it be not profitable for the Negro to go to the same field for employment?

In the first place, there is but little work at the present for us in the south, except growing cotton, and cotton growing is so unprofitable under present conditions, that those who stick to it do so under starvation conditions. There is more cotton raised than the world has ready use for. The cotton grower is unable to hold his crop and make his own prices, therefore the speculator fixes the prices and the grower is the loser. Why then keep our people raising cotton for which there is no profitable market when he is needed in the mines and factories and farms of the north and west, producing the things which the world most needs?

Through this migration to the north and west, he has a golden opportunity to learn. We will get new ideas of life, new ideas of agriculture and manufacturing, new ideas of civilization, new ideas of a larger world. Many will return home when the weather gets cold but they will bring back with them these ideas and impart them to the folds at home. Others will come and go, and in this manner develop themselves as they could not otherwise do.

In the early days of our American civilization Horace Greeley said to the young man, "Go west!" The white man has gone westward until he has reached the east. I say to the young men of my race: "Go west!" Go east! Go north! Go south! Go everywhere the sun shines! Go everywhere there is found an opportunity to make a living and develop this wonderful world of ours.

W. J. Latham, Jackson, Mississippi

Wallace Stegner to David E. Pesonen

Calling it the "geography of promise," the author Wallace Stegner found a great source of inspiration and renewal in the American West. Stegner, who won the Pulitzer Prize in 1971, was an outspoken critic of the industrialization and overdevelopment of the West and warned of the conse-

quences of reckless expansion—not only to the environment but to Americans themselves. In the following long but heartfelt letter, Stegner writes to David Pesonen, a member of a commission assessing the potential uses of the nation's wilderness, and beseeches Pesonen to recognize the extraordinary value of these lands and what they represent to America and its people.

Los Altos, Calif.
Dec. 3, 1960

David E. Pesonen
Wildland Research Center
Agricultural Experiment Station
243 Mulford Hall
University of California
Berkeley 4, Calif.

Dear Mr. Pesonen:

I believe that you are working on the wilderness portion of the Outdoor Recreation Resources Review Commission's report. If I may, I should like to urge some arguments for wilderness preservation that involve recreation, as it is ordinarily conceived, hardly at all. Hunting, fishing, hiking, mountain-climbing, camping, photography, and the enjoyment of natural scenery will all, surely, figure in your report. So will the wilderness as a genetic reserve, a scientific yardstick by which we may measure the world in its natural balance against the world in its man-made imbalance. What I want to speak for is not so much the wilderness uses, valuable as those are, but the wilderness *idea,* which is a resource in itself. Being an intangible and spiritual resource, it will seem mystical to the practical-minded—but then anything that cannot be moved by a bulldozer is likely to seem mystical to them.

I want to speak for the wilderness idea as something that has helped form our character and that has certainly shaped our history as a people. It has no more to do with recreation than churches have to do with recreation, or than the strenuousness and optimism and expansiveness of what historians call the "American Dream" have to do with recreation. Nevertheless, since it is only in this recreation survey that the values of wilderness are being compiled, I hope you will permit me to insert this idea between the leaves, as it were, of the recreation report.

Something will have gone out of us as a people if we ever let the remaining wilderness be destroyed; if we permit the last virgin forests to be turned into comic books and plastic cigarette cases; if we drive the few remaining members of the wild species into zoos or to extinction; if we pollute the last clear air and dirty the last clean streams and push our paved roads through the last of the silence, so that never again will Americans be free in their own country from the noise, the exhausts, the stinks of human and automotive waste. And so that never again can we have the chance to see ourselves single, separate, vertical and individual in the world, part of our environment of trees and rocks and soil, brother to the other animals, part of the natural world and competent to belong in it. Without any remaining wilderness we are committed wholly, without chance for even momentary reflection and rest, to a headlong drive into our technological termite-life, the Brave New World of a completely man-controlled environment. We need wilderness preserved—as much of it as is still left, and as many kinds—because it was the challenge against which our character as a people was formed. The reminder and the reassurance that it is still there is good for our spiritual health even if we never once in ten years set foot in it. It is good for us when we are young, because of the incomparable sanity it can bring briefly, as vacation and rest, into our insane lives. It is important to us when we are old simply because it is there—important, that is, simply as idea.

We are a wild species, as Darwin pointed out. Nobody ever tamed or domesticated or scientifically bred us. But for at least three millennia we have been engaged in a cumulative and ambitious race to modify and gain control of our environment, and in the process we have come close to domesticating ourselves. Not many people are likely, any more, to look upon what we call "progress" as an unmixed blessing. Just as surely as it has brought us increased comfort and more material goods, it has brought us spiritual losses, and it threatens now to become the Frankenstein that will destroy us. One means of sanity is to retain a hold on the natural world, to remain, insofar as we can, good animals. Americans still have that chance, more than many peoples; for while we were demonstrating ourselves the most efficient and ruthless environment-busters in history, and slashing and burning and cutting our way through a wilderness continent, the wilderness was working on us. It remains in us as surely as Indian names remain on the land. If the abstract dream of human liberty and human dignity became, in America, something more than an abstract dream, mark it down at least partially to the fact that we were in subtle ways subdued by what we conquered.

The Connecticut Yankee, sending likely candidates from King Arthur's unjust kingdom to his Man Factory for rehabilitation, was over-optimistic, as he later admitted. These things cannot be forced, they have to grow. To make such a man, such a democrat, such a believer in human individual dignity, as Mark Twain himself, the frontier was necessary, Hannibal and the Mississippi and Virginia City, and reaching out from those the wilderness; the wilderness as opportunity and as idea, the thing that has helped to make an American different from and, until we forget it in the roar of our industrial cities, more fortunate than other men. For an American, insofar as he is new and different at all, is a civilized man who has renewed himself in the wild. The American experience has been the confrontation by old peoples and cultures of a world as new as if it had just risen from the sea. That gave us hope and our excitement, and the hope and excitement can be passed on to newer Americans, Americans who never saw any phase of the frontier. But only so long as we keep the remainder of our wild as a reserve and a promise—a sort of wilderness bank.

As a novelist, I may be perhaps forgiven for taking literature as a reflection, indirect but profoundly true, of our national consciousness. And our literature, as perhaps you are aware, is sick, embittered, losing its mind, losing its faith. Our novelists are the declared enemies of their society. There has hardly been a serious or important novel in this century that did not repudiate in part or in whole American technological culture for its commercialism, its vulgarity, and the way in which it has dirtied a clean continent and a clean dream. I do not expect that the preservation of our remaining wilderness is going to cure this condition. But the mere example that we can as a nation apply some other criteria than commercial and exploitative considerations would be heartening to many Americans, novelists or otherwise. We need to demonstrate our acceptance of the natural world, including ourselves; we need the spiritual refreshment that being natural can produce. And one of the best places for us to get that is in the wilderness where the fun houses, the bulldozers, and the pavements of our civilization are shut out.

Sherwood Anderson, in a letter to Waldo Frank in the 1920's, said it better than I can. "Is it not unlikely that when the country was new and men were often left alone in the fields and the forest they got a sense of bigness outside themselves that has now in some way been lost . . . Mystery whispered in the grass, played in the branches of trees overhead, was caught up and blown across the American line in clouds of dust as evening on the prairies . . . I am old enough to remember tales that strengthen my belief in a deep semi-religious influence that was formerly at work among our people. The flavor of it hangs over the best work of Mark Twain . . . I can remember old fellows in my home town speaking feelingly of an evening spent on the big empty plains. It had taken the shrillness out of them. They had learned the trick of quiet . . ."

We could learn it too, even yet; even our children and grandchildren could learn it. But only if we save, for just such absolutely non-recreational, impractical, and mystical uses as this, all the wild that still remains to us.

It seems to me significant that the distinct downturn in our literature from hope to bitterness took place almost at the precise time when the frontier officially came to an end, in 1890, and when the American way of life had begun to turn strongly urban and industrial. The more urban it has become, and the more frantic with technological change, the sicker and more embittered our literature, and I believe our people, have become. For myself, I grew up on the empty plains of Saskatchewan and Montana and in the mountains of Utah, and I put a very high valuation on what those places gave me. And if I had not been able periodically to renew myself in the mountains and deserts of western America I would be very nearly bughouse. Even when I can't get back to the country, the thought of the colored deserts of southern Utah, or the reassurance that there are still stretches of prairie where the world can be instantaneously perceived as disk and bowl, and where the little but intensely important human being is exposed to the five directions and the thirty-six winds, is a positive consolation. The idea alone can sustain me. But as the wilderess areas are progressively exploited or "improved," as the jeeps and bulldozers of uranium prospectors scar up the deserts and the roads are cut into the alpine timberlands, and as the remnants of the unspoiled and natural world are progressively eroded, every such loss is a little death in me. In us.

I am not moved by the argument that those wilderness areas which have already been exposed to grazing or mining are already deflowered, and so might as well be "harvested." For mining I cannot say much good except that its operations are generally short-lived. The extractable wealth is taken and the shafts, the tailings, and the ruins left, and in a dry country such as the American West the wounds men make in the earth do not quickly heal. Still, they are only wounds; they aren't absolutely mortal. Better a wounded wilderness than none at all. And as for grazing, if it is strictly controlled so that it does not destroy the ground cover, damage the ecology, or compete with the wildlife it is in itself nothing that need conflict with the wilderness feeling or the validity of the wilderness experience. I have known enough range cattle to recognize them as wild animals; and the people who herd them have, in the wilderness context, the dignity of rareness; they belong on the frontier, moreover, and have a look of rightness. The invasion they make on the virgin country is a sort of invasion that is as old as Neolithic man, and they can, in moderation, even emphasize a man's feeling of belonging to the natural world. Under surveillance, they can belong; under control, they need not deface or mar. I do not believe that in wilderness areas where grazing has never been permitted, it should be permitted; but I do not believe either that an otherwise untouched wilderness should be eliminated from the preservation plan because of limited existing uses such as grazing which are in consonance with the frontier condition and image.

Let me say something on the subject of the kinds of wilderness worth preserving. Most of those areas contemplated are in the national forests and in high mountain country. For all the usual recreational purposes, the alpine and forest wildernesses are obviously the most important, both as genetic banks and beauty spots. But for the spiritual renewal, the recognition of identity, the birth of awe, other kinds will serve every bit as well. Perhaps, because they are less friendly to life, more abstractly non-human, they will serve even better. On our Saskatchewan prairie, the nearest neighbor was four miles away, and at night we saw only two lights on all the dark rounding earth. The earth was full of animals—field mice, ground squirrels, weasels, ferrets, badgers, coyotes, burrowing owls, snakes. I knew them as my little brothers, as fellow creatures, and I have never been able to look upon animals in any other way since. The sky in that country came clear down to the ground on every side, and it was full of great weathers, and clouds, and winds, and hawks. I hope I learned something from knowing intimately the creatures of the earth; I hope I learned something from looking a long way, from looking up, from being much alone. A prairie like that, one big enough to carry the eye clear to the sinking, rounding horizon, can be as lonely and grand and simple in its forms as the sea. It is as good a place as any for the wilderness experience to happen; the vanishing prairie is as worth preserving for the wilderness idea as the alpine forests.

So are great reaches of our western deserts, scarred somewhat by prospectors but otherwise open, beautiful, waiting, close to whatever God you want to see in them. Just as a sample, let me suggest the Robbers' Roost country in Wayne County, Utah, near the Capitol Reef National Monument. In that desert climate the dozer and jeep tracks will not soon melt back into the earth, but the country has a way of making the scars insignificant. It is a lovely and terrible wilderness, such a wilderness as Christ and the prophets went out into; harshly and beautifully colored, broken and worn until its bones are exposed, its great sky without a smudge or taint from Technocracy, and in hidden corners and pockets under its cliffs the sudden poetry of springs. Save a piece of country like that intact, and it does not matter in the slightest that only a few people every year will go into it. That is precisely its value. Roads would be a desecration, crowds would ruin it. But those who haven't the strength or youth to go into it and live can simply sit and look. They can look two hundred miles, clear into Colorado; and looking down over the cliffs and canyons of the San Rafael Swell and the Robbers' Roost they can also look as deeply into themselves as anywhere I know. And if they can't even get to the places on the Aquarius Plateau where the present roads will carry them, they can simply contemplate the *idea*, take pleasure in the fact that such a timeless and uncontrolled part of the earth is still there.

These are some of the things wilderness can do for us. That is the reason we need to put into effect, for its preservation, some other principle than the principles of exploitation or "usefulness" or even recreation. We simply need that wild country available to us, even if we never do more than drive to its edge and look in. For it can be a means of reassuring ourselves of our sanity as creatures, a part of the geography of hope.

Very sincerely yours,
Wallace Stegner

Marion Carpenter to His Son, Astronaut Scott Carpenter

Committed to putting an astronaut into space, the National Aeronautics and Space Administration (NASA) sought out seven men in the fall of 1958 willing to participate in the most complicated and challenging expedition in America's history, Project Mercury. NASA needed men who met specific height and weight requirements, were experienced test pilots, had extensive knowledge of engineering and aircraft, and were in peak physical condition. Most importantly, though, they had to be daring, resourceful, and fearless in moments of crisis. NASA knew space was a hostile environment, and for an unprecedented venture the possibility of an astronaut's being killed during his mission was substantial. In April 1959 NASA introduced its team, and Malcolm Scott Carpenter, a thirty-four-year-old test pilot who had flown in Korea, was one of the chosen few. Carpenter's flight was scheduled for early May 1962 (it was postponed until—and completed successfully on—May 24), and the night before the momentous day, his father, a chemist, wrote him the following letter.

M. Scott Carpenter
PO Box 95 PALMER LAKE,
COLORADO

Dear Son,

Just a few words on the eve of your great adventure for which you have trained yourself and anticipated for so long—to let you know that we all share it with you, vicariously.

As I think I remarked to you at the outset of the space program, you are privileged to share in a pioneering project on a grand scale—in fact the grandest scale yet known to man. And I venture to predict that after all the huzzas have been uttered and the public acclaim is but a memory, you will derive the greatest satisfaction from the serene knowledge that you have discovered new truths. You can say to yourself: this I saw, this I experienced, this I know to be the truth. This experience is a precious thing; it is known to all researchers, in whatever field of endeavour, who have ventured into the unknown and have discovered new truths.

You are probably aware that I am not a particularly religious person, at least in the sense of embracing any of the numerous formal doctrines. Yet I cannot conceive of a man endowed with intellect, perceiving the ordered universe about him, the glory of the mountain top, the plumage of a tropical bird, the intricate complexity of a protein molecule, the utter and unchanging perfection of a salt crystal, who can deny the existence of some higher power. Whether he chooses to call it God or Mohammed or Buddha or Torquoise Woman or the Law of Probability matters little. I find myself in my writings frequently calling upon Mother Nature to explain things and citing Her as responsible for the order of the universe. She is a very satisfactory divinity for me. And so I shall call upon Her to watch over you and guard you and, if she so desires, share with you some of Her secrets which She is usually so ready to share with those who have high purpose.

With all my love,
Dad

Letters of a New Nation

*Y*ou will think me transported with Enthusiasm, but I am not. I am well aware of the Toil, and Blood, and Treasure, that it will cost Us to maintain this Declaration, and support and defend these States. Yet, through all the Gloom I can see the Rays of ravishing Light and Glory. I can see that the End is more than worth all the Means. And that Posterity will tryumph in that Day's Transaction, even altho We should rue it, which I trust in God We shall not.

John Adams to Abigail Adams; July 3, 1776

Israel Putnam, on Behalf of the Parish of Brooklyn, to the City of Boston

Not even the Boston Massacre in 1770 sparked the same degree of outrage in the colonies as the arrival of five hundred thousand pounds of East India Company tea into American ports. Turned away from New York and Philadelphia, merchant ships were allowed to dock in Boston after Massachusetts' Loyalist governor, Thomas Hutchinson, forced the city to accept the shipment. On December 16, 1773, a group of citizens boarded the ships and threw 340 chests of tea overboard. In retaliation, a furious British Parliament enacted the "Boston Port Act" (along with a slew of "Intolerable Acts," as they were called in the colonies), which shut down the Boston port, threatening the livelihood of thousands of colonial citizens. Word spread immediately of Boston's plight and letters of support, including the following, poured into the city.

August 11, 1774

Gentlemen,

With our hearts deeply impressed with the feelings of humanity towards our near and dear brethren of Boston, who are now suffering under a ministerial, revengeful hand, and at the same time full of gratitude to the patriotic inhabitants of the noble stand which they have made against all oppressive innovations, and with unfeigned love for all British America, who must, if Boston is subjugated, alternately fall a prey to ministerial ambition, we send you one hundred and twenty-five sheep, as a present from the inhabitants of the parish of Brooklyn, hoping thereby you may be enabled to stand more firm (if possible) in the glorious cause in which you are embarked, notwithstanding the repeated, unheard of daring attacks which the British Parliament are making upon the rights which you ought to enjoy as English-born subjects; and if so, we shall of consequence contribute our mite towards the salvation of British America, which is all our ambition.

In zeal in our country's cause, we are exceeded by none; but our abilities and opportunities do not admit of our being of that weight in the American scale as we would to God we were.

We mean, in the first place, to attempt to appease the fire (raised by your committing the India tea to the watery element as a merited oblation to Neptune) of an ambitious and vindictive minister, by the blood of rams and lambs; if that do not answer the end, we are ready to march in the van and to sprinkle the American altars with our hearts blood, if occasion should be.

The latent seeds of destruction which are implanted in the constitution of almost every state or empire have grown in England, in these last nine years, with amazing rapidity, and now are mature for harvest; and ere long we shall see reapers flocking from all parts of Europe, who will sweep their fields with the besom of destruction. This thought occasions a cloud of melancholy to arise in the breast of every descendant from Britain, which is only dissipated by the pleasing prospect every American has before him! Here we have an unbounded, fertile country, worth contending for with blood! Here bribery and corruption, which are certain forebodings of a speedy dissolution, are as yet only known by names. To us, ere long, Britain's glory will be transferred, where it will shine with accumulated brilliancy.

We cannot but rejoice with you on account of the union and firmness of the Continent. The public virtue now exhibited by the American exceeds all of its kind that can be produced in the annals of the Greeks and Romans. Behold them from North to South, from East to West, striving to comfort the Town of Boston, both by publishing their sentiments in regard to the present tyrannical administration, and by supporting their poor with provision, who, otherwise, in this present stagnation of business, would have reduced the opulent to a state of penury and despair in a short time.

You are held up as a spectacle to the whole world. All Christendom are longing to see the event of the America contest. And do, most noble citizens, play your part manfully, of which, we make no doubt, your names are either to be held in eternal veneration or execration. If you stand out, your names cannot be too much applauded by all Europe and all future generations, which is the hearty desire and wish of us, who are, with utmost respect, your most obedient and humble servants.

Israel Putnam
Committee of Correspondence for the Parish of Brooklyn

J. Palmer to "All Friends of Liberty" & The Committee of Safety to the "Several Towns in Massachusetts"

On September 5, 1774, fifty-five delegates of the first Continental Congress, including John Adams, George Washington, John Jay, and Patrick Henry, convened in Philadelphia to determine a unified course of action. The British Parliament initially scoffed at the meeting of "zealots of anarchy," as one member called them. But when the Continental Congress ruled, among other things, that all trade with Great Britain should cease, King George III ran out of patience. In a letter to one member of Parliament the king wrote: "I am not sorry that the line of conduct seems now chalked out. [. . . T]he New England governments are in a state of rebellion, blows must decide whether they are to be subject to this country or independent." In the spring of 1775, the first blows were struck at Lexington and Concord. The War of Independence had begun.

April 19, 1775
Wednesday Morning near 11 O'clock

To all friends of American liberty, be it known that this morning before break of day, a brigade, consisting of about 1000 or 1200 men, landed at Phipp's farm at Cambridge and marched to Lexington, where they found a company of our militia in arms, upon whom they fired without any provocation and killed 6 men and wounded 4 others. By an express from Boston we find another brigade are now upon their march from Boston supposed to be about 1000. The bearer Israel Bissel is charged to alarm the country quite to Connecticut, and all persons are desired to furnish him with fresh horses, as they may be needed. I have spoken with several men who have seen the dead and wounded.

J Palmer
one of the Committee of Safety

The news exploded throughout the colonies, and almost immediately afterward minutemen left for Massachusetts from Connecticut (led by then-patriot Benedict Arnold), New Hampshire, Rhode Island, and other nearby states. The Massachusetts Committee of Safety sent out another appeal for help, this time urging all citizens to be mindful of what was at stake.

Cambridge, April 28, 1775

Gentlemen:

The barbarous murders committed on our innocent brethren on Wednesday the 19th instant have made it absolutely necessary that we immediately raise an army to defend our wives and children from the butchering hands of an inhuman soldiery, who, incensed at the obstacles they met with in their bloody progress, and enraged at being repulsed from the field of slaughter, will, without doubt, take the first opportunity in their power to ravage this devoted country with fire and sword. We conjure, therefore, by all that is dear, by all that is sacred, that you give all assistance possible in forming the army. Our all is at stake. Death and devastation are the certain consequences of delay; every moment is infinitely precious; an hour lost may deluge your country in blood and entail perpetual slavery upon the few of your posterity who may survive the carnage. We beg and entreat, as you will answer it to your country, to your own conscience, and, above all, to God himself, that you will hasten and encourage, by all possible means, the enlistment of men to form the army, and send them forward to head quarters at Cambridge, with that expedition which the vast importance and instant urgency of the affair demands.

Committee of Safety

Anne Hulton, a "Loyalist Lady," to Mrs. Adam Lightbody

Not all of those living in the colonies were in favor of revolution, however; a host of personal, economic, and political reasons kept many loyal to the crown. One Loyalist, Anne Hulton, wrote frequently to her friend Mrs. Adam Lightbody in England to describe the fighting between the Rebels (the "banditti") and the Redcoats, led by the "honorable" Lord Percy. So fearful was Hulton of the "violent fury of the people" and the "shocking cruelty" against Loyalists that she eventually returned to England in late 1775. Although undated, the following letter to Mrs. Lightbody is presumed to have been written in the spring of 1775.

I acknowledged the receipt of My Dear Friends kind favor of the 20th Sept[r] the begin'ing of last Month, tho' did not fully Answer it, purposing as I intimated to write again soon, be assured as your favors are always very acceptable, so nothing you say, passes unnoticed, or appears unimportant to me. but at present my mind is too much agitated to attend to any subject but one, and it is that which you will be most desirous to hear particulars of, I doubt not in regard to your friends here, as to our Situation, as well as the Publick events. I will give you the best account I can, which you may rely on for truth.

On the 18th inst[t] at 11 at Night, about 800 Grenadiers & light Infantry were ferry'd across the Bay to Cambridge, from whence they march[d] to Concord, about 20 Miles. The Congress had been lately assembled at that place, & it was imagined that the General had intelligence of a Magazine being formed there & that they were going to destroy it.

The People in the Country (who are all furnished with Arms & have what they call Minute Companys in every Town ready to march on any alarm), had a signal it's supposed by a light from one of the Steeples in Town, Upon the Troops embark[g]. The alarm spread thro' the Country, so that before daybreak the people in general were in Arms & on their March to Concord. About Daybreak a number of the People appeared before the Troops near

Lexington. They were called to, to disperse. when they fired on the Troops & ran off, Upon which the Light Infantry pursued them & brought down about fifteen of them. The Troops went on to Concord & executed the business they were sent on, & on their return found two or three of their people Lying in the Agonies of Death, scalp'd & their Noses & ears cut off & Eyes bored out—Which exasperated the soldiers exceedingly—a prodigious number of People now occupying the Hills, woods, and Stone Walls along the road. The Light Troops drove some parties from the hills, but all along the road being inclosed with Stone Walls Served as a cover to the Rebels, from whence they fired on the Troops still running off whenever they had fired, but still supplied by fresh Numbers who came from many parts of the Country. In this manner were the Troops harrassed in their return for Seven or eight Miles, they were almost exhausted & had expended near the whole of their Ammunition when to their great joy they were relieved by a Brigade of Troops under the command of Lord Percy with two pieces of Artillery. The Troops now combatted with fresh Ardour, & marched in their return with undaunted countenances, receiving Sheets of fire all the way for many Miles, yet having no visible Enemy to combat with, for they never woud face 'em in an open field, but always skulked & fired from behind Walls, & trees, & out of Windows of Houses, but this cost them dear for the Soldiers enterd those dwellings, & put all the Men to death. Lord Percy has gained great honor by his conduct thro' this day of Severe Servise, he was exposed to the hottest of the fire & animated the Troops with great coolness & spirit. Several officers were wounded & about 100 Soldiers. The killed amount to near 50, as to the Enemy we can have no exact acc[t] but it said there was about ten times the Number of them engaged, & that near 1000 of 'em have fallen

The Troops returned to Charlestown about Sunset after having some of 'em marched near fifity miles, & being engaged from Daybreak in Action, without respite, or refreshment, & about ten in the Evening they were brought back to Boston. The next day the Country pourd down its Thousands, and at this time from the entrance of Boston Neck at Roxbury round by Cambridge to Charlestown is surrounded by at least 20,000 Men, who are raising batteries on three or four different Hills. We are now cut off from all communication with the Country & many people must soon perish with famine in this place. Some families have laid in store of Provissions against a Siege. We are threatned that whilst the Out Lines are attacked wth a rising of the Inhabitants within, & fire & sword, a dreadful prospect before us, and you know how many & how dear are the objects of our care. The Lord preserve us all & grant us an happy Issue out of these troubles.

For several nights past, I have expected to be roused by the firing of Cannon. Tomorrow is Sunday, & we may hope for one day of rest, at present a Solemn dead silence reigns in the Streets, numbers have packed up their effects, & quited the Town, but the General has put a Stop to any more removing, & here remains in Town about 9000 Souls (besides the Servants of the Crown) These are the greatest Security, the General declared that if a Gun is fired within the Town the inhabitants shall fall a Sacrifice. Amidst our distress & apprehension, I am rejoyced our British Hero was preserved, My Lord Percy had a great many & miraculous escapes in the late Action. This amiable Young Nobleman with the Graces which attracts Admiration, possesses the virtues of the heart, & all those qualities that form the great Soldier—Vigilent Active, temperate, humane, great Command of temper, fortitude in enduring hardships & fatigue, & Intrepedity in dangers. His Lordships behavior in the day of trial has done honor to the Percys. indeed all the Officers & Soldiers behaved with the greatest bravery it is said

I hope you and yours are all well & shall be happy to hear so. I would beg of you whenever you write to mention the dates of my Letters which you have rec'd since you wrote specialy my last of March 2[d]

I am not able at present to write to our Dear friends at Chester would desire the favor of you to write as soon as you receive this, & present my respects to your & my friends there, and likewise the same to those who are near you.

I wrote not long ago both to Miss Tylston & to my Aunt H:—have not heard yet from the Bahamas

Have never heard from Miss Gildart or Mr Earl yet

The Otter Man of War is just arrived Sunday Morn^g

What is marked with these Lines, you are at Liberty to make as publick as you please Let the merits of Lord Percy be known as far as you can.

George Washington to Martha Washington

Lacking discipline, ammunition, and experience, the American Rebels were in no position to take on the battle-ready Redcoats for an extended period of time. When the Second Continental Congress met in the summer of 1775 one of the most important orders of business was the nomination of a "Commander of All Continental Forces" who had the ability, energy, and willingness to train a ragged group of Rebels into a formidable army of soldiers. Only one man was nominated—George Washington—and the vote was unanimous. He accepted modestly (it was reported) and refused compensation for his position. Three days after his appointment, Washington reflected on the enormity of the task ahead and expressed his reservations about the position to his wife, Martha (nicknamed "Patsy").

Philadelphia, June 18, 1775

My Dearest:

I am now set down to write to you on a subject which fills me with inexpressible concern, and this concern is greatly aggravated and increased, when I reflect upon the uneasiness I know it will give you. It has been determined in Congress, that the whole army raised for the defence of the American cause shall be put under my care, and that it is necessary for me to proceed immediately to Boston to take upon me the command of it.

You may believe me, my dear Patsy, when I assure you, in the most solemn manner that, so far from seeking this appointment, I have used every endeavor in my power to avoid it, not only from my unwillingness to part with you and the family, but from consciousness of its being a trust too great for my capacity, and that I should enjoy more real happiness in one month with you at home, than I have the most distant prospect of finding abroad, if my stay were to be seven times seven years. But as it has been a kind of destiny, that has thrown me upon this service, I shall hope that my undertaking is designed to answer some good purpose. You might, and I suppose did perceive, from the tenor of my letters, that I was apprehensive I could not avoid this appointment, as I did not pretend to intimate when I should return. That was the case. It was utterly out of my power to refuse this appointment, without exposing my character to such censures, as would have reflected dishonor upon myself, and given pain to my friends. This, I am sure, could not, and ought not, to be pleasing to you, and must have lessened me considerably in my own esteem. I shall rely, therefore, confidently on that Providence, which has heretofore preserved and been bountiful to me, not doubting but that I shall return safe to you in the fall. I shall feel no pain from the toil or the danger of the campaign; my unhappiness will flow from the uneasiness I know you will feel from being left alone. I therefore beg, that you will summon your whole fortitude, and pass your time as agreeably as possible. Nothing will give me so much sincere satisfaction as to hear this, and to hear it from your own pen. My earnest and ardent desire is, that you would pursue any plan that is most likely to produce content, and a tolerable degree of tranquillity; as it must add greatly to my uneasy feelings to hear, that you are dissatisfied or complaining at what I really could not avoid.

As life is always uncertain, and common prudence dictates to every man the necessity of settling his temporal concerns, while it is in his power, and while the mind is calm and undisturbed, I have, since I came to this place (for I had not the time to do it before I left home) got Colonel Pendleton to draft a will for me, by the directions I gave him, which will I now enclose. The provision made for you in case of my death will, I hope, be agreeable.

I shall add nothing more, as I have several letters to write, but to desire that you will remember me to your friends, and to assure you that I am with the most unfeigned regard, my dear Patsy, your affectionate, &c.

G. Washington

Abigail Adams to John Adams

Abigail Adams, who was as dedicated to the cause of independence as her husband, John, wrote frequently to him in Philadelphia on the condition of wartime Boston, as well as to offer advice to the Continental Congress. In the following letter she castigates the Earl of Dunmore—the governor of Virginia, who ultimately took Britain's side in the war—and asks that John and his colleagues "remember the ladies" as they begin their deliberations on the Declaration of Independence.

Braintree, March 31, 1776

I wish you would ever write me a Letter half as long as I write you; and tell me if you may where your Fleet are gone? What sort of Defence Virginia can make against our common Enemy? Whether it is so situated as to make an able Defence? Are not the Gentery Lords and the common people vassals? Are they not like the uncivilized Natives Brittain represents us to be? I hope their Riffel Men, who have shewn themselves very savage and even Blood thirsty, are not a specimen of the Generality of the people.

I am willing to allow the Colony great merrit for having produced a Washington, but they have been shamefully duped by a Dunmore.

I have sometimes been ready to think that the passion for Liberty cannot be Eaquelly Strong in the Breasts of those who have been accustomed to deprive their fellow Creatures of theirs. Of this I am certain: that it is not founded upon the generous and christian principal of doing to others as we would that others should do unto us.

Do not you want to see Boston; I am fearful of the small pox, or I should have been in before this time. I got Mr. Crane to go to our House and see what state it was in. I find it has been occupied by one of the Doctors of a Regiment, very dirty, but no other damage has been done to it. The few things which were left in it are all gone. Crane has the key, which he never delivered up. I have wrote to him for it and am determined to get it cleaned as soon as possible and shut it up. I look upon it a new acquisition of property, a property which one month ago I did not value at a single Shilling, and could with pleasure have seen it in flames.

The Town in General is left in a better state than we expected, more oweing to a percipitate flight than any Regard to the inhabitants, tho some individuals discovered a sense of honour and justice and have left the rent of the Houses in which they were for the owners and the furniture unhurt, or if damaged sufficient to make it good.

Others have committed abominable Ravages. The Mansion House of your President is safe and the furniture unhurt, whilst both the House and the Furniture of the Solisiter General have fallen a prey to their own merciless party. Surely the very Fiends feel a Reverential awe for Virtue and patriotism, whilst they Detest the paricide and traitor.

I feel very differently at the approach of spring to which I did a month ago. We knew not then whether we could plant or sow with safety, whether when we had toiled we could reap the fruits of our own industry, whether we could rest in our own Cottages, or whether we should not be driven from the sea coasts to seek shelter in the wilderness, but now we feel as if we might sit under our own vine and eat the good of the land.

I feel a *gaieti de Coar* to which before I was a stranger. I think the Sun looks brighter, the Birds sing more melodiously, and

Nature puts on a more chearfull countanance. We feel a temporary peace, and the poor fugitives are returning to their deserted habitations.

Tho we felicitate ourselves, we sympathize with those who are trembling least the Lot of Boston should be theirs. But they cannot be in similar circumstances unless pusilanimity and cowardise should take possession of them. They have time and warning given them to see the Evil and shun it.—I long to hear that you have declared an independency—and by the way, in the new Code of Laws which I suppose it will be necessary for you to make, I desire you would Remember the Ladies, and be more generous and favourable to them than your ancestors. Do not put such unlimited power into the hands of the Husbands. Remember, all Men would be tyrants if they could. If perticular care and attention is not paid to the Ladies, we are determined to foment a Rebelion, and will not hold ourselves bound by any Laws in which we have no voice, or Representation.

That your Sex are Naturally Tyrannical is Truth so thoroughly established as to admit no dispute, but such of you as wish to be happy willingly give up the harsh title of Master for the more tender and endearing one of Friend. Why, then, not put it out of the power of the vicious and the Lawless to use us with cruelty and indignity with impunity. Men of Sense in all Ages abhor those customs which treat us only as the vassals of your Sex. Regard us then as Beings placed by providence under your protection, and in immitation of the Supreem Being, make use of that power only for our happiness.

Abigail

John Adams to Timothy Pickering & John Adams to Abigail Adams

The first draft of the Declaration of Independence was written by Thomas Jefferson, only thirty-three at the time, and submitted to the Continental Congress on June 28, 1776. After much debate, Congress ulti-

mately cut out substantial amounts of Jefferson's text before approving it on July 4. (Jefferson's greatest lament was the deletion, at the insistence of Southern delegates, of all references to the abolition of slavery.) Surprisingly, there are few contemporaneous accounts as to why Jefferson, one of the youngest and newest delegates, was selected to write the enormously influential document. Instead, there are mostly recollections—and many of them conflicting—by a handful of members written decades after the fateful event. In 1822 Timothy Pickering asked John Adams why Jefferson (whom Pickering despised) was chosen to write the Declaration. Adams responded:

6 August 1822

Sir:—

[. . .] You inquire why so young a man as Mr. Jefferson was placed at the head of the Committee for preparing a Declaration of Independence? I answer: It was the Frankfort advice, to place Virginia at the head of every thing. Mr. Richard Henry Lee might be gone to Virginia, to his sick family, for aught I know, but that was not the reason for Mr. Jefferson's appointment. There were three committees appointed at the same time. One for the Declaration of Independence, another for preparing articles of Confederation, and another for preparing a treaty to be proposed to France. Mr. Lee was chosen for the Committee of Confederation, and it was not thought convenient that the same person should be upon both. Mr. Jefferson came into Congress in June, 1775, and brought with him a reputation for literature, science, and a happy talent of composition. Writings of his were handed about, remarkable for the peculiar felicity of expression. Though a silent member in Congress, he was so prompt, frank, explicit and decisive upon committees and in conversation, not even Samuel Adams was more so, that he soon seized upon my heart; and upon this occasion I gave him my vote, and did all in my power to procure the votes of others. I think he had one more vote than any other, and that placed him at the head of the committee. I had the next highest number, and that placed me the second. The committee met, discussed the subject, and then appointed Mr. Jefferson and me to make the draught, I suppose because we were the first two on the list.

The sub-committee met. Jefferson proposed to me to make the draught. I said, "I will not."

"You should do it."

"Oh! no."

"Why will you not? You ought to do it."

"I will not."

"Why?"

"Reasons enough."

"What can be your reasons?"

"Reason first—You are a Virginian, and a Virginian ought to appear at the head of this business. Reason second—I am obnoxious, suspected, and unpopular. You are very much otherwise. Reason third—You can write ten times better than I can."

"Well," said Jefferson, "if you are decided, I will do as well as I can."

"Very well. When you have drawn it up, we will have a meeting."

A meeting we accordingly had, and conned the paper over. I was delighted with its high tone and flights of oratory with which it abounded, especially that concerning negro slavery, which, though I knew his Southern brethren would never suffer to pass in Congress, I certainly never would oppose. There were other expressions which I would not have inserted, if I had drawn it up, particularly that which called the King tyrant. I thought this too personal; for I never believed George to be a tyrant in disposition and in nature; I always believed him to be deceived by his courtiers on both sides of the Atlantic, and, in his official capacity only, cruel. I thought the expression too passionate, and too much like scolding, for so grave and solemn a document; but as Franklin and Sherman were to inspect it afterwards, I thought it would not become me to strike it out. I consented to report it, and do not now remember that I made or suggested a single alteration.

We reported it to the committee of five. It was read, and I do not remember that Franklin or Sherman criticized any thing. We were all in haste. Congress was impatient, and the instrument was reported, as I believe, in Jefferson's handwriting, as he first drew it. Congress cut off about a quarter of it, as I expected they would; but they obliterated some of the best of it, and left all that was exceptionable, if any thing in it was. I have long wondered that the original draught has not been published. I suppose the reason is, the vehement philippic against negro slavery.

As you justly observe, there is not an idea in it but what had been hackneyed in Congress for two years before. The substance of it is contained in the declaration of rights and the violation of those rights, in the Journals of Congress, 1774. Indeed, the essence of it is contained in a pamphlet, voted and printed by the town of Boston, before the first Congress met, composed by James Otis, as I suppose, in one of his lucid intervals, and pruned and polished by Samuel Adams.

Your friend and humble servant.

The momentousness of Congress's deliberations over the document that would seal, for better or for worse, the fate of the colonies was not lost on its participants, and particularly not on John Adams. In the following letter to his wife, and after addressing some personal matters (most notably, his friend James Warren's decision to refuse an appointment to become a judge), Adams expresses his concern for the fate of America.

Philadelphia 3 July, 1776

Abigail,

Your Favour of 17th June, dated at Plymouth, was handed me by Yesterdays Post. I was much pleased to find that you had taken a Journey to Plymouth, to see your Friends, in the long Absence of one whom you may wish to see. The Excursion will be an Amusement, and will serve your Health. How happy would it have made me to have taken this Journey with you?

I was informed, a day or two before the Receipt of your Letter, that you were gone to Plymouth, by Mrs. Polly Palmer, who was obliging enough in your Absence, to inform me of the Particulars of the Expedition to the lower Harbour against the Men of War. Her Narration is executed, with a Precision and Perspicuity, which would have become the Pen of an accomplished Historian.

I am very glad you had so good an opportunity of seeing one of our little American Men of War. Many Ideas, new to you must have presented themselves in such a Scene; and you will in future, better understand the Relations of Sea Engagements.

I rejoice extremely at Dr. Bulfinch's Petition to open an Hospital. But I do hope the Business will be done upon a larger Scale. I hope that one Hospital will be licensed in every county, if not in every Town. I am happy to find you resolved to be with the Children in the first Class. Mr. Whitney and Mrs. Katy Quincy are cleverly through Innoculation in this City.

I have one favour to ask, and that is, that in your future Letters, you would acknowledge the Receipt of all those you may receive from me, and mention their Dates. By this Means I shall know if any of mine miscarry.

The Information you give me, of our Friend's refusing his Appointment, has given me much Pain, Grief, and Anxiety. I believe I shall be obliged to follow his Example. I have not Fortune enough to support my Family, and, what is of more Importance, to support the Dignity of that exalted Station. It is too high and lifted up for me, who delight in nothing so much as Retreat, Solitude, Silence, and Obscurity. In private Life, no one has a Right to censure me for following my own Inclinations, in Retirement, Simplicity, and Frugality; in public Life, every Man has a Right to remark as he pleases, at least he thinks so.

Yesterday, the greatest Question was decided, which ever was debated in America, and a greater perhaps, never was nor will be decided among Men. A Resolution was passed without one dissenting Colony, "that these United Colonies are, and of right ought to be, free and independent States, and as such they have, and of Right ought to have, full power to make War, conclude Peace, establish Commerce, and to do all other Acts and Things which other States may rightfully do." You will see in a few days a Declaration setting forth the Causes which have impell'd Us to this mighty Revolution, and the Reasons which will justify it, in the sight of God and Man. A Plan of Confederation will be taken up in a few days.

When I look back to the year 1761, and recollect the argument concerning Writs of Assistance in the Superior Court, which I have hitherto considered as the Commencement of this Controversy between Great Britain and America, and run through the whole Period from that Time to this, and recollect the series of political Events, the Chain of Causes and Effects, I am surprised at the Suddenness as well as the Greatness of this Revolution. Britain has been fill'd with Folly, and America with Wisdom. At least, this is my Judgment. Time must determine. It is the Will of Heaven that the two Countries should be sundered forever. It may be the Will of Heaven that America shall suffer Calamities still more wasting, and Distresses yet more dreadfull. If this is to be the Case, it will have this good Effect, at least: It will inspire Us with many Virtues, which We have not, and correct many Errors, Follies, and Vices which threaten to disturb, dishonor and destroy Us. The Furnace of Affliction produces Refinement, in States as well as Individuals. And the new Governments we are assuming in every Part will require a Purification from our Vices, and an Augmentation of our Virtues, or they will be no Blessings. The people will have unbounded Power. And the people are extremely addicted to Corruption and Venality, as well as the Great.—I am not without Apprehensions from this Quarter. But I must submit all my Hopes and Fears to an overruling Providence, in which, unfashionable as the Faith may be, I firmly believe.

James Mitchell Varnum, at Valley Forge, to Nathanael Greene

Suffering rampant diseases and a shortage of food and supplies in the winter of 1778, George Washington's men at Valley Forge were in imminent danger of freezing and starving to death. An estimated twelve thousand men had marched into Valley Forge with General Washington in

December of 1777 to position themselves between the British in Philadelphia and the Continental Congress in York, Pennsylvania. But the severity of the weather, combined with bureaucratic incompetence, hampered relief efforts. Fearing for his men's lives, Brigadier General James Mitchell Varnum sent the following letter to Nathanael Greene, whom both Mitchell and Washington considered one of the most able commanders in the army.

Camp Valley Forge, February 12, 1778

Sir,

Inclosed you'll receive the Report of Yesterday. I must add to that the Situation of the Camp is such that in all human probability the Army must soon dissolve. Many of the Troops are destitute of Meat, and are several Days in arrear. The Horses are dying for want of Forage. The Country in the vicinity of the Camp is exhausted. There cannot be a moral Certainty of bettering our Circumstances while we continue here. What Consequences have we rationally to expect? Our Desertions are astonishingly great; the Love of Freedom, which once animated the Breasts of those born in the Country, is controlled by Hunger, the keenest of Necessities. If we consider the Relation in which we stand to the Troops, we cannot reconcile their Sufferings to the Sentiments of honest men. No political Considerations can justify the Measure. There is no local Object of so much moment as to conceal the Obligations which bind us to them. Should a blind Attachment to a preconcerted plan fatally disaffect, and in the End force the Army to Mutiny, then will the same Country, which now applauds our Hermitage, curse our Insensibility.

I have from the Beginning viewed the Situation with Horror! It is unparalleled in the History of Mankind to establish Winter Quarters in a Country wasted, and without a single Magazine. We now only feel some of the Effects which Reason from the beginning taught us to expect as inevitable. My Freedom upon this Occasion may be offensive; I should be unhappy, but Duty obliges me to speak without Reserve. My own Conscience will approve the Deed, when some may perhaps look back with Regret to the Time when the Evil in extreme might have been prevented. There is no

Alternative but immediately to remove the Army to places where they can be supplied, unless effectual Remedies can be applied upon the Spot, which I believe every Gentleman of the Army thinks impractical.

I am Sir with great Respect your very obedient Servant,
J. Varnum

Ultimately, thousands of men either perished or were sent in critical condition to area hospitals. But by spring, with Greene serving as the quartermaster general and with the arrival of fresh supplies, the army was once again prepared to fight.

Patrick Ferguson to His Fellow British Soldiers

The British soldiers and officers committed to maintaining America's allegiance to the crown were outraged by the "treasonous" acts of the Rebels. Patrick Ferguson, a major in the British army fighting in South Carolina, tried to rouse new recruits by reminding Loyalists of all that the Americans had done to deserve a swift and certain defeat. He sent out his appeal in the following letter.

Denard's Ford. Broad River,
Tryon County
October 1, 1780

Gentlemen,

Unless you wish to be eat up by an inundation of barbarians who have begun by murdering an unarmed son before the aged father, and afterwards lopped off his arms, and who, by their shocking cruelties and irregularities, give the best proof of their cowardice and want of discipline:—I say, if you wish to be pinioned, robbed, and murdered, and see your wives and daughters, in four days, abused by the dregs of mankind—in short, if you wish or deserve to live and bear the name of men, grasp your arms in a moment and run to camp.

The Backwater men have crossed the mountains: McDowell,

Hampton, Shelby, and Cleveland are at their head: so that you know what you have to depend on. If you choose to be degraded for ever and ever by a set of mongrels, say so at once, and let your women turn their backs upon you, and look out for real men to protect them.

Pat. Ferguson
(Major 71st Regiment).

Ferguson was killed six days later.

General George Washington to Colonel Nichola

Before the War of Independence was even over, George Washington received a letter from an officer in the Continental Army recommending "a kingdom with Washington as the head." The officer, Colonel Nichola (his first name has not been recorded), claimed the Colonies could "never become a nation under a [Democratic] form of government" and thought a monarchy, with Washington as king, would be ideal. Having personally just spent almost seven years in bloody conflict trying to sever the colonies from one monarchy, Washington was shocked by the suggestion and sent the following reply.

Newburgh May 22d '82

Sir,

With a mixture of great surprise & astonishment I have read with attention the Sentiments you have submitted to my perusal.—Be assured Sir, no occurrence in the course of the War, has given me more painful sensations than your information of there being such ideas existing in the Army as you have expressed, & I must view with abhorrence, and reprehend with severety—For the present, the communication of them will rest in my own bosom, unless some further agitation of the matter shall make a disclosure necessary.—

I am much at a loss to conceive what part of my conduct could have given encouragement to an address which to me seems big with the greatest mischiefs that can befall my Country.—If I am not deceived in the knowledge of myself, you could not have found a person to whom your schemes are more disagreeable—at the same time in justice to my own feeling I must add, that no man possesses a more sincere wish to see ample justice done to the Army than I do, and as far as my powers & influence, in a constitution, may extend, they shall be employed to the utmost of my abilities to effect it, should there be any occasion—Let me conjure you then, if you have any regard for your Country—concern for yourself or posterity—or respect for me, to banish these thoughts from your mind, & never communicate, as from yourself, or any one else, a sentiment of the like nature.—

With esteem I am Sir
Yr Most Obed Ser
G. Washington

Benjamin Franklin to Sir Joseph Banks

On October 19, 1781, the British suffered a fatal blow when Washington defeated General Charles Cornwallis's troops at Yorktown. Although small skirmishes continued, peace negotiations were initiated in 1782, and the final treaties were finally signed by both nations on September 3, 1783. The victory was met not unexpectedly with great joy throughout America, but many—particularly those most responsible for inciting the Revolution—were well aware of the great loss to the colonies in human lives and economic resources in the years of fighting. Benjamin Franklin, who had written stirring articles and proclamations on the necessity of independence from England, wrote the following letter to a British friend, Sir Joseph Banks, on the price that war exacts from all sides.

27 July 1783

Dear Sir,

I received your very kind letter by Dr. Blagden, and esteem myself much honour'd by your friendly Remembrance. I have been too much and too closely engag'd in public Affairs since his being here, to enjoy all the Benefit of his Conversation you were so good as to intend me. I hope soon to have more Leisure, and to spend a part of it in those Studies that are much more agreeable to me than political Operations.

I join with you most cordially in rejoicing at the return of Peace. I hope it will be lasting, and that Mankind will at length, as they call themselves reasonable Creatures, have Reason and Sense enough to settle their Differences without cutting Throats; for, in my opinion *there never was a good War, or a bad Peace*.

What vast additions to the Conveniences and Comforts of Living might Mankind have acquired, if the Money spent in Wars had been employ'd in Works of public utility! What an extension of Agriculture, even to the Tops of our Mountains; what Rivers rendered navigable, or joined by Canals; what Bridges, Aqueducts, new Roads, and other public Works, Edifices, and Improvements, rendering England a compleat Paradise, might have been obtain'd by spending those Millions in doing good, which in the last War have been spent in doing Mischief; in bringing Misery into thousands of Families, and destroying the Lives of so many thousands of working people who might have perform'd the useful labour!

I am pleas'd with the late astronomical Discoveries made by our Society. Furnish'd as all Europe now is with Academies of Science, with nice Instruments and the Spirit of Experiment, the progress of human knowledge will be rapid, and discoveries made of which we have at present no Conception. I begin to be almost sorry I was born so soon, since I cannot have the happiness of knowing what will be known 100 years hence.

I wish continued success to the Labours of the Royal Society, and that you may long adorn their chair; being with the highest esteem,

Dear Sir, I your most obedient and most humble servant,
B. Franklin

P.S. Dr. Blagden will acquaint you with the experiment of a vast Globe sent up into the Air, much talked of here, and which, if prosecuted, may furnish means of new knowledge.

Paul Revere to William Eustis

Despite serving faithfully in the Continental Army for several years, a young soldier named Robert Shurtliff did not receive the pension guaranteed to all veterans. The situation, however, was unique: Robert Shurtliff was, in fact, Deborah Sampson, believed to be the first American woman to fight as a soldier for her country. Dressed in men's clothing, Sampson enlisted in the army and was assigned to the Fourth Massachusetts Regiment. In June of 1782, during a battle in New York, Sampson was shot in the leg but returned to her regiment after a brief recuperation. Soon after, her regiment was ordered to march several hundred miles through driving blizzards, and Sampson was eventually hospitalized for pneumonia. Again, she recovered and went back to fight. After the war Sampson was honorably discharged and eventually married Benjamin Gannett, had children, and worked on a farm. But as the years went on working became difficult, owing in part to her past injury and hospitalizations, and her family slipped into poverty. Paul Revere, a neighbor who sympathized with Gannett's plight, assisted her in her efforts to receive a pension. In 1804 he wrote the following letter to William Eustis, a Massachusetts representative in Congress.

Sir,

Mrs. Deborah Gannett of Sharon informed me, that she has inclosed to your care a petition to Congress in favour of Her. My works for manufacturing Copper, being at Canton, but a short distance from the neighbourhood where she lives; I have been induced to enquire her situation, and character, since she quitted the Male habit, and Soldier's uniform, for the more decent apparel of her own sex; and since she has been married and become a Mother:—Humanity, and Justice obliges me to say, that every person with whom I have conversed about Her, and it is not a few, speak of Her as a woman of handsom talents, good morals, a dutifull Wife, and an affectionate parent. She is now much out of health. She has several Children, her Husband is a good sort of man, 'tho of small force in business; they have a few acres of poor land which they cultivate, but they are really poor.

She told me, she had no doubt that her ill health is in consequence of her being exposed when she did a Soldier's duty; and that while in the army, she was wounded.

We commonly form our idea of the person whom we hear spoken of, whom we have never seen, according as their actions are described. When I heard her spoken of as a Soldier, I formed the idea of a tall, masculine female, who had a small share of understanding, without education, and one of the meanest of her sex.—When I saw and discoursed with her I was agreeably supprised to find a small, effeminate, and conversable Woman, whose education entitled her to a better situation in life.

I have no doubt your humanity will prompt you to do all in your power to get her some relief. I think her cause much more deserving than the hundreds to whom Congress has been generous.

I am sir with esteem and respect your humble servant.

Paul Revere

A short time later Congress added to the Massachusetts Pension Rolls the name "Deborah Sampson Gannett, who served as a soldier in the Army of the United States during the late Revolutionary War, and who was seriously wounded therein."

Alexander Hamilton to George Washington & Thomas Jefferson to James Madison

Deliberations on the new Constitution began in late May 1787 and lasted four months. Fifty-five delegates met in Philadelphia to create a Constitution for what was increasingly becoming one nation of "united" states. Although the delegates quarreled over innumerable issues, one of the most intense concerned the amount of power the federal government should be granted. Men such as Patrick Henry wanted a smaller, less centralized federal government and claimed that the public sentiment was in their favor, while others, like Alexander Hamilton, argued for a strong federal government that could quickly and effectively address national problems. Disagreement grew so fierce that Hamilton feared the Constitution would never be written. Hamilton believed public opinion was gradually shifting in his favor, and he expressed his views in the following letter, written on July 3, 1787, from New York, to George Washington, whose opinion Hamilton knew would carry tremendous weight in any discussion.

Dr. Sir,

In my passage through the Jerseys and since my arrival here I have taken particular pains to discover the public sentiment and I am more and more convinced that this is the critical opportunity for establishing the prosperity of this country on a solid foundation. I have conversed with men of information not only of this City but from different parts of the state; and they agree that there has been an astonishing revolution for the better in the minds of the people. The prevailing apprehension among thinking men is that the Convention, from a fear of shocking the popular opinion, will not go far enough. They seem to be convinced that a strong, well mounted government will better suit the popular palate than one of a different complexion. Men in office are indeed taking all possible pains to give an unfavourable impression of the Convention; but the current seems to be running strongly the other way.

A plain but sensible man, in a conversation I had with him yesterday, expressed himself nearly in this manner. The people begin to be convinced that their "excellent form of government" as they have been used to call it, will not answer their purpose; and that they must substitute something not very remote from that which they have lately quitted.

These appearances though they will not warrant a conclusion that the people are yet ripe for such a plan as I advocate, yet serve to prove that there is no reason to despair of their adopting one equally energetic, if the Convention should think proper to propose it. They serve to prove that we ought not to allow too much weight to objections drawn from supposed repugnancy of the people to an efficient constitution. I confess I am more and more inclined to believe that former habits of thinking are regaining their influence with more rapidity than is generally imagined.

Not having compared ideas with you, Sir, I cannot judge how far our sentiments agree; but as I persuade myself the genuineness of my representations will receive credit with you, my anxiety for the event of the deliberations of the Convention induces me to make this communication of what appears to be the tendency of the public mind. I own to you Sir that I am seriously and deeply distressed at the aspect of the Councils which prevailed when I left Philadelphia. I fear that we shall let slip the golden opportunity of rescuing the American empire from disunion anarchy and misery. No motley or feeble measure can answer the end or will finally receive the public support. Decision is true wisdom and will be not less reputable to the Convention than salutary to the community.

I shall of necessity remain here ten or twelve days; if I have reason to believe that my attendance at Philadelphia will not be mere waste of time, I shall after that period rejoin the Convention.

I shall remain with sincere esteem Dr Sir Yr. Obed ser A Hamilton

Washington replied with a short letter that reflected his displeasure with the direction the Convention was heading and agreed, in essence, with

Hamilton: "The Men who oppose a strong & energetic government," Washington wrote on July 10, "are, in my opinion, narrow minded politicians." Thomas Jefferson was serving as the minister to France at the time and could not be present at the Constitutional Convention to express his own fears of a powerful, centralized federal government. But he was sent a draft copy of the Constitution by his friend James Madison, who reported the main arguments being made at the time. After a few paragraphs of personal business, Jefferson tells Madison—in what has become one of the most famous letters ever written on democratic government—precisely what he does and does not like about the new Constitution.

Paris, December 20, 1787

Dear Sir,—

My last to you was of October the 8th, by the Count de Moustier. Yours of July the 18th, September the 6th and October the 24th, were successfully received, yesterday, the day before, and three or four days before that. I have only had time to read the letters; the printed papers communicated with them, however interesting, being obliged to lie over till I finish my despatches for the packet, which despatches must go from hence the day after to-morrow. I have much to thank you for; first and most for the cyphered paragraph respecting myself. These little informations are very material towards forming my own decisions. I would be glad even to know, when any individual member thinks I have gone wrong in any instance. If I know myself, it would not excite ill blood in me, while it would assist to guide my conduct, perhaps to justify it, and to keep me to my duty, alert. I must thank you too, for the information in Thomas Burke's case; though you will have found by a subsequent letter, that I have asked of you a further investigation of that matter. It is to gratify the lady who is at the head of the convent wherein my daughters are, and who, by her attachment and attention to them, lays me under great obligations. I shall hope, therefore, still to receive from you the result of all the further inquiries my second letter had asked. The parcel of rice which you informed had miscarried, accompanied my letter to the

Delegates of South Carolina. Mr. Mourgoin was to be the bearer of both, and both were delivered together into the hands of his relation here, who introduced him to me, and who, at a subsequent moment, undertook to convey them to Mr. Bourgoin. This person was an engraver, particularly recommended to Dr. Franklin and Mr. Hopkinson. Perhaps he may have mislaid the little parcel of rice among his baggage. I am much pleased that the sale of western lands is so successful. I hope they will absorb all the certificates of our domestic debt speedily, in the first place, and that then, offered for cash, they will do the same by our foreign ones.

The season admitting only of operations in the cabinet, and these being in a great measure secret, I have little to fill a letter. I will therefore make up the deficiency, by adding a few words on the constitution proposed by our convention.

I like much the general idea of framing a government, which should go on of itself, peaceably, without needing continual recurrence to the State legislatures. I like the organization of the government into legislative, judiciary and executive. I like the power given the legislature to levy taxes, and for that reason solely, I approve of the greater House being chosen by the people directly. For though I think a House so chosen, will be very far inferior to the present Congress, will be very illy qualified to legislate for the Union, for foreign nations, &c., yet this evil does not weigh against the good, of preserving inviolate the fundamental principle, that the people are not to be taxed but by representatives chosen immediately by themselves. I am captivated by the compromise of the opposite claims of the great and little States, of the latter to equal, and the former to proportional influence. I am much pleased too, with the substitution of the method of voting by person, instead of that of voting by States; and I like the negative given to the Executive, conjointly with a third of either House; though I should have liked it better had the judiciary been associated for that purpose, or invested separately with a similar power. There are other good things of less moment.

I will now tell you what I do not like. First, the omission of a bill of rights, providing clearly, and without the aid of sophism, for freedom of religion, freedom of the press, protection against standing armies, restriction of monopolies, the eternal and unremitting force of the habeas corpus laws, and trials by jury in all matters of fact triable by the laws of the land, and not by the laws of nations. To say, as Mr. Wilson does, that a bill of rights was not necessary, because all is reserved in the case of the general government which is not given, while in the particular ones, all is given which is not reserved, might do for the audience to which it was addressed; but it is surely a *gratis dictum*, the reverse of which might just as well be said; and it is opposed by strong influences from the body of the instrument, as well as from the omission of the cause of our present Confederation, which had made the reservation in express terms. It was hard to conclude, because there has been a want of uniformity among the States as to the cases triable by jury, because some have been so incautious as to dispense with this mode of trial in certain cases, therefore, the more prudent States shall be reduced to the same level of calamity. It would have been much more just and wise to have concluded the other way, that as most of the States had preserved with jealousy this sacred palladium of liberty, those who wandered, should be brought back to it; and to have established general right rather than general wrong. For I consider all the ill as established, which may be established. I have a right to nothing, which another has a right to take away; and Congress will have a right to take away trials by jury in all civil cases. Let me add, that a bill of rights is what the people are entitled to against every government on earth, general or particular, and what no just government should refuse, or rest on inference.

The second feature I dislike, and strongly dislike, is the abandonment, in every instance, of the principle of rotation in office, and most particularly in the case of the President. Reason and experience tell us, that the first magistrate will always be re-elected if he may be re-elected. He is then an officer for life. This once observed, it becomes of so much consequence to certain nations, to have a friend or a foe at the head of our affairs, that they will interfere with money and with arms. A Galloman, or an

Angloman, will be supported by the nation he befriends. If once elected, and at a second or third election out-voted by one or two votes, he will pretend false votes, foul play, hold possession of the reigns of government, be supported by the States voting for him, especially if they be the central ones, lying in a compact body themselves, and separating their opponents; and they will be aided by one nation in Europe, while the majority are aided by another. The election of a President of America, some years hence, will be much more interesting to certain nations of Europe, than ever the election of a King of Poland was. Reflect on all the instances in history, ancient and modern, of elective monarchies, and say if they do not give foundation for my fears; the Roman Emperors, the Popes while they were of any importance, the German Emperors till they became hereditary in practice, the Kings of Poland, the Deys of the Ottoman dependencies. It may be said, that if elections are to be attended with these disorders, the less frequently they are repeated the better. But experience says, that to free them from disorder, they must be rendered less interesting by a necessity of change. No foreign power, nor domestic party, will waste their blood and money to elect a person, who must go out at the end of a short period. The power of removing every fourth year by the vote of the people, is a power which they will not exercise, and if they were disposed to exercise it, they would not be permitted. The King of Poland is removable every day by the diet. But they never remove him. Nor would Russia, the Emperor, &c., permit them to do it.

Smaller objections are, the appeals on matters of fact as well as laws; and the binding all persons, legislative, executive and judiciary by oath, to maintain that constitution. I do not pretend to decide, what would be the best method of procuring the establishment of the manifold good things in this constitution, and of getting rid of the bad. Whether by adopting it, in hopes of future amendment; or after it shall have been duly weighed and canvassed by the people, after seeing the parts they generally dislike, and those they generally approve, to say to them, "We see now what you wish. You are willing to give to your federal government such and such powers; but you wish, at the same time, to have such and such fundamental rights secured to you, and certain sources of convulsion taken away. Be it so. Send together deputies again. Let them establish your fundamental rights by a sacrosanct declaration, and let them pass the parts of the constitution you have approved. These will give powers to your federal government sufficient for your happiness."

This is what might be said, and would probably produce a speedy, more perfect and more permanent form of government. At all events, I hope you will not be discouraged from making other trials, if the present one should fail. We are never permitted to despair of the commonwealth. I have thus told you freely what I like, and what I dislike, merely as a matter of curiosity; for I know it is not in my power to offer matter of information to your judgment, which has been formed after hearing and weighing everything which the wisdom of man could offer on these subjects. I own, I am not a friend to a very energetic government. It is always oppressive. It places the governors indeed more at their ease, at the expense of the people. The late rebellion in Massachusetts has given more alarm, than I think it should have done. Calculate that one rebellion in thirteen States in the course of eleven years, is but one for each State in a century and a half. No country should be so long without one. Nor will any degree of power in the hands of government, prevent insurrections. In England, where the hand of power is heavier than with us, there are seldom half a dozen years without an insurrection. In France, where it is still heavier, but less despotic, as Montesquieu supposes, than in some other countries, and where there are always two or three hundred thousand men ready to crush insurrections, there have been three in the course of the three years I have been here, in every one of which greater numbers were engaged than in Massachusetts, and a great deal more blood was spilt. In Turkey, where the sole nod of the despot is death, insurrections are the events of every day. Compare again with the ferocious depredations of their insurgents, with the order, the moderation and the almost self-extinguishment of ours. And say, finally, whether peace is best preserved by giving energy to the government, or information to the people. This last is the most certain, and the most legitimate engine of government. Educate and inform the whole mass of people. Enable them to see that it is their interest to preserve peace and order, and they will preserve them. And it requires no very high degree of education to convince them of this. They are the only sure reliance for the preservation of our liberty. After all, it is my principle that the will of the majority should prevail. If they approve the proposed constitution in all its parts, I shall concur in it cheerfully, in hopes they will amend it, whenever they shall find it works wrong. This reliance cannot deceive us, as long as we remain virtuous; and I think we shall be so, as long as agriculture is our principal object, which will be the case, while there remains vacant lands in any part of America. When we get piled upon one another in large cities, as in Europe, we shall become corrupt as in Europe, and go to eating one another as they do there. I have tired you by this time with disquisitions which you have already heard repeated by others, a thousand and a thousand times; and therefore, shall only add assurances of the esteem and attachment with which I have the honor to be, dear Sir, your affectionate friend and servant.

Th: Jefferson

P.S. The instability of our laws is really an immense evil. I think it would be well to provide in our constitutions, that there shall always be a twelvemonth between the engrossing a bill and passing it; that it should then be offered to its passages without changing a word; and that if circumstances should be thought to require a speedier passage, it should take two-thirds of both Houses, instead of a bare majority.

Jefferson's arguments proved persuasive. Despite being initially (and adamantly) opposed to the amendments Jefferson described, James Madison himself would become one of their most vocal proponents. Almost three years after the Constitution was ratified and the first national elections had been held in 1789, Madison wrote the first ten amendments to the Constitution, enumerating the Bill of Rights Jefferson believed to be so necessary.

The Hebrew Congregation of Newport, Rhode Island, to George Washington & Washington's Response

In as early as the mid-1600s Jews traveled to America and contributed significantly to the creation of the United States as an independent and sovereign nation. Despite their contributions, however, many colonial Jews were persecuted solely because of their faith. When members of the Hebrew Congregation of Touro Synagogue in Newport, Rhode Island, one of the oldest synagogues in America, learned that George Washington was visiting their city, they sent the president the following letter emphasizing the freedoms upon which the nation was founded and anticipating his agreement.

August 17, 1790

Sir,

Permit the Children of the Stock of Abraham to approach you with the most cordial affection and esteem for your person and merits—and to join with our fellow-citizens in welcoming you to New Port.

With pleasure we reflect on those days—those days of difficulty and danger, when the God of Israel, who delivered David from the peril of the sword—shielded your head in the day of battle:—and we rejoice to think that the same Spirit, who rested in the bosom of the greatly beloved Daniel, enabling him to preside over the Provinces of the Babylonish Empire, rests, and ever will rest upon you, enabling you to discharge the arduous duties of Chief Magistrate in these States.

Deprived as we have hitherto been of the invaluable rights of free citizens, we now, (with a deep sense of gratitude to the Almighty Disposer of all events) behold a Government, (erected by the Majesty of the People) a Government which to bigotry gives no sanction, to persecution no assistance—but generously affording to All liberty of conscience, and immunities of citizenship—deeming every one, of whatever nation, tongue, or language equal parts of the great governmental machine. This so ample and extensive federal union whose basis is Philanthropy, mutual confidence, and public virtue, we cannot but acknowledge to be the work of the Great God, who ruleth in the armies of Heaven, and among the inhabitants of the Earth, doing whatsoever seemeth him good.

For all the blessings of civil and religious liberty which we enjoy under an equal and benign administration we desire to send up our thanks to the Ancient of days, the great Preserver of Men—beseeching him that the Angel who conducted our forefathers through the wilderness into the promised land, may graciously conduct you through all the dangers and difficulties of this mortal life—and when like Joshua full of days, and full of honor, you are gathered to your Fathers, may you be admitted into the heavenly Paradise to partake of the water and the tree of immortality.

Done and signed by the order of the Hebrew Congregation in New Port Rhode Island August 17th, 1790.

Moses Sexias Warden

Washington replied:

Gentlemen,

While I receive with much satisfaction your address replete with expressions of affection and esteem; I rejoice in the opportunity of assuring you that I shall always retain a grateful remembrance of the cordial welcome I experienced in my visit to New Port from all classes of Citizens.

The reflection on the days of difficulty and danger which are past is rendered the more sweet from a consciousness that they are succeeded by days of uncommon prosperity and security. If we have wisdom to make the best of the advantages with which we are now favored, we cannot fail, under the just administration of a good government to become a great and a happy people.

The Citizens of the United States of America have a right to applaud themselves for having given to mankind examples of an enlarged and liberal policy, a policy worthy of imitation.

All possess alike liberty of conscience and immunities of citizenship. It is now no more that toleration is spoken of, as if it was by the indulgence of one class of people, that another enjoyed the exercise of their inherent natural rights. For happily the government of the United States, which gives to bigotry no sanction, to persecution no assistance, requires only that they who live under its protection should demean themselves as good citizens, in giving it on all occasions their effectual support.

It would be inconsistent with the frankness of my character not to avow that I am pleased with your favorable opinion of my administration, and fervent wishes for my felicity.

May the children of the Stock of Abraham, who dwell in this land, continue to merit and enjoy the good will of the other inhabitants, while every one shall sit in safety under his own vine and fig-tree, and there shall be none to make him afraid.

May the Father of all mercies scatter light and not darkness in our paths, and make us all in our several vocations useful here, and in his own due time and way everlastingly happy.

G Washington

Benjamin Banneker to Thomas Jefferson & Jefferson's Response

Thomas Jefferson's bold declaration in 1776 that "all men are created equal" resonated, whether intentionally or not, in the hearts and minds of blacks throughout the colonies. Jefferson was profoundly ambivalent on the issue of race. Though he sharply condemned slavery in his first draft of the Declaration of Independence, he himself owned slaves. Several passages in his Notes on the State of Virginia *lament the prejudice toward blacks in America, yet in the same book he writes: "In reason [blacks are] much inferior, as I think one could scarcely be found capable of tracing and comprehending the investigations of Euclid; and that in imagination they are dull, tasteless, and anomalous." Benjamin Banneker, a black mathematician, inventor, writer, and social critic, was familiar with these sentiments and sent the following letter to Jefferson, who was serving as secretary of state at the time.*

Maryland Baltimore County
Near Ellicotts' Lower Mills, August 19th, 1791

Thomas Jefferson, Secretary of State.

Sir: I am fully sensible of the greatness of that freedom, which I take with you on the present occasion, a liberty which seemed to me scarcely allowable, when I reflected on that distinguished and dignified station in which you stand, and the almost general prejudice and prepossession which is so prevalent in the world against those of my complexion.

I suppose it is a truth too well attested to you, to need a proof here, that we are a race of beings who have long laboured under the abuse and censure of the world, that we have long been considered rather as brutish than human, and scarcely capable of mental endowments.

Sir, I hope I may safely admit, in consequence of that report which hath reached me, that you are a man far less inflexible in sentiments of this nature than many others, that you are measurably friendly and well disposed towards us, and that you are willing and ready to lend your aid and assistance to our relief, from those many distresses and numerous calamities, to which we are reduced.

Now, sir, if this is founded in truth, I apprehend you will readily embrace every opportunity to eradicate that train of absurd and false ideas and opinions, which so generally prevails with respect to us, and that your sentiments are concurrent with mine, which are that one universal Father hath given Being to us all, and that he hath not only made us all of one flesh, but that he hath also without partiality afforded us all the same sensations, and endued us all with the same faculties, and that however variable we may be in society or religion, however diversified in situation or colour, we are all of the same family, and stand in the same relation to him.

Sir, if these are sentiments of which you are fully persuaded, I hope you cannot but acknowledge, that it is the indispensable duty of those who maintain for themselves the rights of human nature, and who profess the obligations of christianity, to extend their power and influence to the relief of every part of the human race, from whatever burden or oppression they may unjustly labour under, and this I apprehend a full conviction of the truth and obligation of these principles should lead all to.

Sir, I have long been convinced that if your love for yourselves and for those inesteemable laws, which preserve to you the rights of human nature, was found on sincerity, you could not but be solicitous that every individual of whatever rank or distinction, might with you equally enjoy the blessings thereof, neither could you rest satisfied, short of the most active diffusion of your exertions in order to their promotions from any state of degradation to which the unjustifiable cruelty and barbarism of men have reduced them.

Sir, I freely and cheerfully acknowledge that I am of the African race, and in that colour which is natural to them of the deepest dye, and it is under a sense of the most profound gratitude to the Supreme Ruler of the universe that I now confess to you that I am not under that state of tyrannical thraldom and inhuman captivity to which too many of my brethren are doomed; but that I have abundantly tasted of the fruition of those blessings which proceed from that free and unequalled liberty with which you are favoured and which, I hope you will willingly allow you have received from the immediate hand of that Being, from which proceedeth every good and perfect gift.

Sir, suffer me to recall to your mind that time in which the arms and tyranny of the British Crown were exerted with every powerful effort in order to reduce you to a State of Servitude, look back I entreat you on the variety of dangers to which you were exposed; reflect on that time in which every human aid appeared unavailable, and in which even hope and fortitude wore the aspect of inability to the conflict and you cannot but be led to a serious and grateful sense of of your miraculous and providential preservation; you cannot but acknowledge that the present freedom and tranquility which you enjoy you have mercifully received and that it is the peculiar blessing of Heaven.

This sir, was a time which you clearly saw into the injustice of a state of slavery and in which you had just apprehensions of the horrors of its condition, it was now, sir, that your abhorrence thereof was so excited, that you publickly held forth this true and valuable doctrine, which is worthy to be recorded and remembered in all succeeding ages. "We hold these truths to be self-evident, that all men are created equal, and that they are endowed by their creator with certain unalienable rights, that among these are life, liberty and the pursuit of happiness."

Here, sir, was a time in which your tender feelings for yourselves had engaged you thus to declare, you were then impressed with proper ideas of the great valuation of liberty and the free possession of those blessings to which you were entitled by nature; but, sir, how pitiable is it to reflect that although you were so fully convinced of the benevolence of the Father of mankind and of his equal and impartial distribution of those rights and privileges which he had conferred upon them, that you should at the same time counteract his mercies in detaining by fraud and violence so numerous a part of my brethren under groaning captivity and cruel oppression, that you should at the same time be found guilty of that most criminal act which you most professedly detested in others with respect to yourselves.

Sir, I suppose that your knowledge of the situation of my brethren is too extensive to need a recital here; neither shall I presume to prescribe methods by which they may be relieved, otherwise than by recommending to you and all others to wean yourselves from those narrow prejudices which you have imbibed with respect to them and as Job proposed to his friends, "put your souls in their souls stead," thus shall your hearts be enlarged with kindness and benevolence towards them, and thus shall you need neither the direction of myself or others, in what manner to proceed herein.

And now, sir, although my sympathy and affection for my

brethren hath caused my enlargement thus far, I ardently hope that your candour and generosity will plead with you in my behalf when I make known to you that it was not originally my design; but that having taken up my pen in order to direct to you as a present, a copy of an almanac, which I have calculated for the succeeding year, I was unexpectedly and unavoidably led thereto.

This calculation, sir, is the production of my arduous study in this my advanced stage of life; for having long had unbounded desires to become acquainted with the secrets of nature, I have had to gratify my curiosity herein through my own assiduous application to astronomical study, in which I need not to recount to you the many difficulties and disadvantages which I have had to encounter.

And although I had almost declined to make my calculation for the ensuing year, in consequence of that time which I had allotted therefore being taken up at the Federal Territory by the request of Mr. Andrew Ellicott, yet finding myself under several engagements to printers of this state, to whom I had communicated my design, on my return to my place of residence I industriously applied myself thereto which I hope I have accomplished with correctness and accuracy, a copy of which I have taken the liberty to direct to you and which I humbly request you will favourably receive. Although you may have the opportunity of perusing it after its publication yet I chose to send it to you in manuscript previous thereto that you might not only have an earlier inspection but that you might also view it in my own handwriting.

And now, sire, I shall conclude and subscribe myself, with the most profound respect, your most obedient humble servant,

B. Banneker

Jefferson replied:

Philadelphia, Aug. 30, 1791

Sir,—I thank you sincerely for your letter of the 19th instant, and for the Almanac it contained. Nobody wishes more than I do to see such proofs as you exhibit, that nature has given to our black brethren talents equal to those of other colours of men, and that the appearance of a want of them is owing only to the degraded condition of their existence, both in Africa and America. I can add with truth that no one wishes more ardently to see a good system commenced for raising the condition both of their body and mind to what it ought to be, as fast as the imbecility of their present existence, and other circumstances which cannot be neglected, will admit. I have taken the liberty of sending your Almanac to Monsieur de Condorcet, Secretary of the Sciences at Paris, and member of the Philanthropic Society; because I considered it a document to which your whole colour had a right for their justification against the doubts which have been entertained of them.

I am, with great esteem, Sir, your most obedient humble servant,

Th: Jefferson

Benjamin Rush to John Adams

For the British, the signing of the Declaration of Independence was an act of unpardonable treason. And at the time the document was announced, a military victory over Great Britain was anything but assured. Dr. Benjamin Rush, one of the delegates to the Continental Congress and a signer of the Declaration, was a close friend of John Adams and other founding fathers. In the following letter to Adams, Rush laments that twenty-five years after all their sacrifices in the summer of 1776, they are already being forgotten. And, worst of all, Rush is appalled that the only men being honored during the recent Fourth of July festivities are military men such as George Washington, who Rush claimed acted like a slave "master" over the American people and whom he loathed so much he could barely (if at all) mention him by name in his letters.

Philadelphia, July 20th, 1811

Dear Old Friend,

The 4th of July has been celebrated in Philadelphia in the manner I expected. The military men, and particularly one of them, ran away with all the glory of the day. Scarcely a word was said of the solicitude and labors and fears and sorrows and sleepless nights of the men who projected, proposed, defended and subscribed the Declaration of Independence. Do you recollect your memorable speech upon the day on which the vote was taken? Do you recollect the pensive and awful silence which pervaded the house when we were called up, one after another, to the table of the President of Congress to subscribe what was believed by many at that time to be our own death warrants? The silence and the gloom of the morning were interrupted, I well recollect, only for a moment by Colonel Harrison of Virginia, who said to Mr. Gerry at the table: "I shall have a great advantage over you, Mr. Gerry, when we are all hung for what we are now doing. From the size and weight of my body I shall die in a few minutes, but from the lightness of your body you will dance in the air an hour or two before you are dead." This speech procured a transient smile, but it was soon succeeded by the solemnity with which the whole business was conducted.

Of the farewell addresses you mention in your letter it is hardly safe to speak, they are so popular in our country; but I cannot help mentioning a remark I heard made by one of our Democrats a day or two after the last of them was published. "He has treated us as a master would do his slaves, were he about to transfer them to a new master. As a *servant* of the public, he should have been more modest."

How is it that the old tories love him exclusively of all the whigs of the Revolution? The names of the Adamses, Hancock, the Lees, and Franklin are all more or less disliked or hated by them. One of them a few years ago, in viewing the statue of Dr. Franklin in a niche over our City Library door, said with a malignant sneer, "But for that fellow, we should never have had independence."

There was a time when these things irritated and distressed me, but I now hear and see them with the same indifference or pity that I hear the ravings and witness the antic gestures of my deranged patients in our Hospital. We often hear of "prisoners at large." The majority of mankind are *madmen at large*. They differ in their degrees of sanity, but I have sometimes thought the most prominent in this general mental disease are those men who by writing and reasoning attempt to cure them.

I visited the late Reverend Mr. Marshall of this city in his last illness. A few days before his death he thanked me affectionately for my services to him and his family, and afterwards said some kind of flattering things to me upon the pursuits and labors of my life. I replied to the latter by saying that I had aimed to do all the good I could to my fellow citizens, but that I had been so much thwarted and opposed that I did not know that any of my labors had ever been attended with success. "Well, well," said this dying saint, "remember your Saviour at the day of judgment will not say, 'Well done, thou *successful*, but well done thou *faithful* servant.' You have been 'faithful,' Doctor, and that is enough."

Let us, my dear friend, console ourselves for the unsuccessful efforts of our lives to serve our fellow creatures by recollecting that we have aimed well, that we have faithfully strove to tear from their hands the instruments of death with which they were about to destroy themselves, that we have attempted to take off their fancied crowns and royal robes and to clothe them with their own proper dresses, and that we have endeavored to snatch the poisoned bowl from their lips and to replace it with pleasant and wholesome food. We shall not I hope lose our reward for these well-intended labors of love. "She did all that she could," was once both the acquittal and the praise of a pious woman in the New Testament, and pronounced too by those lips which must finally decide the merit and demerit of all human actions. They are full of consolation to those who have aimed well.

Adieu! my dear old friend, and believe me to be, with unabated respect and affection, yours truly,

Benjn: Rush

Letters of Slavery & the Civil War

In every human Breast, God has implanted a Principle, which we call Love of Freedom; it is impatient of Oppression, and pants for Deliverance; and by the Leave of our modern Egyptians I will assert, that the same Principle lives in us. God grant Deliverance in his own Way and Time, and get him honour upon all those whose Avarice impels them to help forward the Calamities of their fellow Creatures. This I desire not for their Hurt, but to convince them of the strange Absurdity of their Conduct whose Words and Actions are so diametrically opposite. How well the Cry for Liberty, and the reverse Disposition for the exercise of oppressive Power over others agree—I humbly think it does not require the Penetration of a Philosopher to determine.

Phillis Wheatley, former slave and acclaimed poet,
to Rev. Samson Occom; February 11, 1774

President Andrew Jackson to Secretary of War Lewis Cass

Angered by tariffs in 1828 and 1832 that Southern states felt benefited the North at their expense, South Carolina threatened to secede from the Union. By an overwhelming majority members of a South Carolina state convention adopted an ordinance that pronounced the federally imposed tariffs "unauthorized by the Constitution" and therefore "null [and] void." President Andrew Jackson, a Southerner who had supported states's rights in the past, was nevertheless furious with South Carolina's declaration and vowed publicly that if the federal government clashed with the South he would take to the field himself and "die with the Union." Jackson even threatened to hang his former vice president, John C. Calhoun, who had lent his support to South Carolina. On December 17, 1832, President Jackson sent the following letter to his secretary of war, Lewis Cass.

My D. Sir,

I can judge from the signs of the times Nullification, & secession, or in the language of truth, *disunion* is gaining strength, and we must be prepared to act with promptness, and crush the monster in its cradle, before it matures to manhood. We must be prepared for the crisis.

The moment that we are informed that the Legislature of So Carolina has passed laws to carry her rebellious ordinance into effect which I expect tomorrow we must be prepared to act. Tenders of service is coming to me daily and from New York we can send to the bay of Charleston with steamers, such number of troops as we may please to order in five days.

We will want three Divisions of artillery, each composed of nines, twelves, & Eighteen pounders—one for the East, one for the West, and one for the center divisions. How many of these calibers, are ready for field service.

How many musketts with their compleat equipments are ready for service. How many swords & pistols & what quantity of hand ammunition for Dragoons—Brass pieces for the field, how many, & what caliber.

At as early a day as possible, I wish a report from the ordnance Department, on this subject, stating with precision, how many pieces of artillery of the caliber, are ready for the field—how many good musketts, et, etc, and at what place in depart—

yrs respectfully

Andrew Jackson

Despite claims that it would "repel force with force," the legislature of South Carolina was, at the time, alone in its willingness to fight for secession. Congress authorized the president to use the full army and navy to enforce his decision, which finally convinced secessionists to negotiate. A compromise was reached, and, for the time being, no blood was shed.

Frederick Douglass to His Former Master, Capt. Thomas Auld & Douglass to Harriet Tubman

Unquestionably the most eminent African American figure of his time, Frederick Douglass was born a slave and escaped bondage at the age of twenty-one, fleeing from Maryland to Massachusetts in 1838. Douglass secretly taught himself to read and write and, while technically a fugitive, went on to become a renowned orator and writer. (It was illegal in most Southern states, and even punishable by death in some, to teach a slave to read or write.) His Narrative of the Life of Frederick Douglass, an American Slave *was a profoundly influential autobiography that exposed many Americans to the physical and mental torment of being a slave. Douglass, who was beginning to gain national acclaim for his abolitionist efforts, wrote the following letter—which was published openly in the* North Star *on September 8, 1848—to his former master, Capt. Thomas Auld.*

SIR—The long and intimate, though by no means friendly, relation which unhappily subsisted between you and myself, leads me to hope that you will easily account for the great liberty which I now take in addressing you in this open and public manner. The same fact may possibly remove any disagreeable surprise which you may experience on again finding your name coupled with mine, in any other way than in an advertisement, accurately describing my person, and offering a large sum for my arrest. In thus dragging you again before the public, I am aware that I shall subject myself to no inconsiderable amount of censure. I shall probably be charged with an unwarrantable, if not a wanton and reckless disregard of the rights and properties of private life. There are those north as well as south who entertain a much higher respect for rights which are merely conventional, than they do for rights which are personal and essential. Not a few there are in our country, who, while they have no scruples against robbing the laborer of the hard earned results of his patient industry, will be shocked by the extremely indelicate manner of bringing your name before the public. Believing this to be the case, and wishing to meet every reasonable or plausible objection to my conduct, I will frankly state the ground upon which I justify myself in this instance, as well as on former occasions when I have thought proper to mention your name in public. All will agree that a man guilty of theft, robbery, or murder, has forfeited the right to concealment and private life; that the community have a right to subject such persons to the most complete exposure. However much they may desire retirement, and aim to conceal themselves and their movements from the popular gaze, the public have a right to ferret them out, and bring their conduct before the proper tribunals of the country for investigation. Sir, you will undoubtedly make the proper application of these generally admitted principles, and will easily see the light in which you are regarded by me; I will not therefore manifest ill temper, by calling you hard names. I know you to be a man of some intelligence, and can readily determine the precise estimate which I entertain of your character. I may therefore indulge in language which may seem to others indirect and ambiguous, and yet be quite well understood by yourself.

I have selected this day on which to address you, because it is the anniversary of my emancipation; and knowing no better way, I am led to this as the best mode of celebrating that truly important event. Just ten years ago this beautiful September morning, yon bright sun beheld me a slave—a poor degraded chattel—trembling at the sound of your voice, lamenting that I was a man, and wishing myself a brute. The hopes which I had treasured up for weeks of a safe and successful escape from your grasp, were powerfully confronted at this last hour by dark clouds of doubt and fear, making my person shake and my bosom to heave with the heavy contest between hope and fear. I have no words to describe to you the deep agony of soul which I experienced on that never-to-be-forgotten morning—for I left by daylight. I was making a leap in the dark. The probabilities, so far as I could by reason determine them, were stoutly against the undertaking. The preliminaries and precautions I had adopted previously, all worked badly. I was like one going to war without weapons—ten chances of defeat to one of victory. One in whom I had confided, and one who had promised me assistance, appalled by fear at the trial hour, deserted me, thus leaving the responsibility of success or failure solely with myself. You, sir, can never know my feelings. As I look back to them, I can scarcely realize that I have passed through a scene so trying. Trying, however, as they were, and gloomy as was the prospect, thanks be to the Most High, who is ever the God of the oppressed, at the moment which was to determine my whole earthly career, His grace was sufficient; my mind was made up. I embraced the golden opportunity, took the morning tide at the flood, and a free man, young, active, and strong is the result.

I have often thought I should like to explain to you the grounds upon which I have justified myself in running away from you. I am almost ashamed to do so now, for by this time you may have discovered them yourself. I will, however, glance at them. When yet but a child about six years old, I imbibed the determination to run away. The very first mental effort that I now remember on my part, was an attempt to solve the mystery—why am I a slave? and with this question my youthful mind was troubled for many days, pressing upon me more heavily at times than others. When I saw the slave-driver whip a slave-woman, cut the blood out of her neck, and heard her piteous cries, I went away into the corner of the fence, wept and pondered over the mystery. I had, through some medium, I know not what, got some idea of God, the Creator of all mankind, the black and the white, and that he had made the blacks to serve the whites as slaves. How he could do this and be *good*, I could not tell. I was not satisfied with this theory, which made God responsible for slavery, for it pained me greatly, and I have wept over it long and often. At one time, your first wife, Mrs. Lucretia, heard me singing and saw me shedding tears, and asked of me the matter, but I was afraid to tell her. I was puzzled with this question, till one night while sitting in the kitchen, I heard some of the old slaves talking of their parents having been stolen from Africa by white men, and were sold here as slaves. The whole mystery was solved at once. Very soon after this, my Aunt Jinny and Uncle Noah ran away, and the great noise made about it by your father-in-law, made me for the first time acquainted with the fact, that there were free states as well as slave states. From that time, I resolved that I would some day run away. The morality of the act I dispose of as follows: I am myself; you are yourself; we are two distinct persons, equal persons. What you are, I am. You are a man, and so am I. God created both, and made us separate beings. I am not by nature bond to you, or you to me. Nature does not make your existence depend upon me, or mine to depend upon yours. I cannot walk upon your legs, or you upon mine. I cannot breathe for you, or you for me; I must breathe for myself, and you for yourself. We are distinct persons, and are each equally provided with faculties necessary to our individual existence. In leaving you, I took nothing but what belonged to me, and in no way lessened your means for obtaining an *honest* living. Your faculties remained yours, and mine became useful to their rightful owner. I therefore see no wrong in any part of the transaction. It is true, I went off secretly; but that was more your fault than mine. Had I let you into the secret, you would have defeated the enterprise entirely; but for this, I should have been really glad to have made you acquainted with my intentions to leave.

You may perhaps want to know how I like my present condition. I am free to say, I greatly prefer it to that which I occupied in Maryland. I am, however, by no means prejudiced against the state as such. Its geography, climate, fertility, and products, are such as to make it a very desirable abode for any man; and but for the existence of slavery there, it is not impossible that I might again take up my abode in that state. It is not that I love Maryland less, but freedom more. You will be surprised to learn that people at the north labor under the strange delusion that if the slaves were emancipated at the south, they would flock to the north. So far from this being the case, in that event, you would see many old and familiar faces back again to the south. The fact is, there are few here who would not return to the south in the event of emancipation. We want to live in the land of our birth, and to lay our bones by the side of our fathers; and nothing short of an intense love of personal freedom keeps us from the south. For the sake of this most of us would live on a crust of bread and a cup of cold water.

Since I left you, I have had a rich experience. I have occupied stations which I never dreamed of when a slave. Three out of the ten years since I left you, I spent as a common laborer on the wharves of New Bedford, Massachusetts. It was there I earned my first free dollar. It was mine. I could spend it as I pleased. I could buy hams or herring with it, without asking any odds of anybody. That was a precious dollar to me. You remember when I used to make seven or eight, or even nine dollars a week in Baltimore, you would take every cent of it from me every Saturday night, saying that I belonged to you, and my earnings also. I never liked this conduct on your part—to say the best, I thought it a little mean. I would not have served you so. But let that pass. I was a little awkward about counting money in New England fashion when I first landed in New Bedford. I came near betraying myself several times. I caught myself saying phip, for fourpence; and at one time a man actually charged me with being a runaway, whereupon I was silly enough to become one by running away from him, for I was greatly afraid he might adopt measures to get me again into slavery, a condition I then dreaded more than death.

I soon learned, however, to count money, as well as to make it, and got on swimmingly. I married soon after leaving you; in fact, I was engaged to be married before I left you; and instead of finding my companion a burden, she was truly a helpmate. She went to live at service, and I to work on the wharf, and though we toiled hard the first winter, we never lived more happily. After remaining in New Bedford for three years, I met with William Lloyd Garrison, a person of whom you have *possibly* heard, as he is pretty generally known among slaveholders. He put it into my head that I might make myself serviceable to the cause of the slave, by devoting a portion of my time to telling my own sorrows, and those of other slaves, which had come under my observation. This was the commencement of a higher state of existence than any to which I had ever aspired. I was thrown into society the most pure, enlightened, and benevolent, that the country affords. Among these I have never forgotten you, but have invariably made you the topic of conversation—thus giving you all the notoriety I could do. I need not tell you that the opinion formed of you in these circles is far from being favorable. They have little respect for your honesty, and less for your religion.

But I was going on to relate to you something of my interesting experience. I had not long enjoyed the excellent society to which I have referred, before the light of its excellence exerted a beneficial influence on my mind and heart. Much of my early dislike of white persons was removed, and their manners, habits, and customs, so entirely unlike what I had been used to in the kitchen-quarters on the plantations of the south, fairly charmed me, and gave me a strong disrelish for the coarse and degrading customs of my former condition. I therefore made an effort so to improve my mind and deportment, as to be somewhat fitted to the station to which I seemed almost providentially called. The transition from degradation to respectability was indeed great, and to get from one to the other without carrying some marks of one's former condition, is truly a difficult matter. I would not have you think that I am now entirely clear of all plantation peculiarities, but my friends here, while they entertained the strongest dislike of them, regard me with that charity to which my past life somewhat entitles me, so that my condition in this respect is exceedingly pleasant. So far as my domestic affairs are concerned, I can boast of as comfortable a dwelling as your own. I have an industrious and neat companion, and four dear children—the oldest a girl of nine years, and three fine boys, the oldest eight, the next six, and the youngest four years old. The three oldest are now going regularly to school—two can read and write, and the other can spell, with tolerable correctness, words of two syllables. Dear fellows! they are all in comfortable beds, and are sound asleep, perfectly secure under my own roof. There are no slaveholders here to rend my heart by snatching them from my arms, or blast a mother's dearest hopes by tearing them from her bosom. These dear children are ours—not to work up into rice, sugar, and tobacco, but to watch over, regard, and protect, and to rear them to the paths of wisdom and virtue, and, as far as we can, to make them useful to the world and to themselves. Oh! sir, a slaveholder never appears to me so completely an agent of hell, as when I think of and look upon my dear children. It is then that my feelings rise above my control. I meant to have said more with respect to my own prosperity and happiness, but thoughts and feelings which this recital has quickened, unfits me to proceed further in that direction. The grim horrors of slavery rise in all their ghastly terror before me; the wails of millions pierce my heart and chill my blood. I remember the chain, the gag, the bloody whip; the death-like gloom overshadowing the broken spirit of the fettered bondman; the appalling liability of his being torn away from wife and children, and sold like a beast in the market. Say not that this is a picture of fancy. You well know that I wear stripes on my back, inflicted by your direction; and that you, while we were brothers in the same church, caused this right hand, with which I am now penning this letter, to be closely tied to my left, and my person dragged at the pistol's mouth, fifteen miles, from the Bay side to Easton, to be sold like a beast in the market, for the alleged crime of intending to escape from your possession. All this, and more, you remember, and know to be perfectly true, not only of yourself, but of nearly all of the slaveholders around you.

At this moment, you are probably the guilty holder of at least three of my own dear sisters, and my only brother, in bondage. These you regard as your property. They are recorded on your ledger, or perhaps have been sold to human flesh-mongers, with a view to filling your own ever-hungry purse. Sir, I desire to know how and where these dear sisters are. Have you sold them? or are they still in your possession? What has become of them? are they living or dead? And my dear old grandmother, whom you turned out like an old horse to die in the woods—is she still alive? Write and let me know all about them. If my grandmother be still alive, she is of no service to you, for by this time she must be nearly eighty years old—too old to be cared for by one to whom she has ceased to be of service; send her to me at Rochester, or bring her to Philadelphia, and it shall be the crowning happiness of my life to take care of her in her old age. Oh! she was to me a mother and a father, so far as hard toil for my comfort could make her such. Send me my grandmother! that I may watch over and take care of her in her old age. And my sisters—let me know all about them. I would write to them, and learn all I want to know of them, without disturbing you in any way, but that, through your unrighteous conduct, they have been entirely deprived of the power to read and write. You have kept them in utter ignorance, and have therefore robbed them of the sweet enjoyments of writing or receiving letters from absent friends and relatives. Your wickedness and cruelty, committed in this respect on your fellow-creatures, are greater than all the stripes you have laid upon my back or theirs. It is an outrage upon the soul, a war upon the immortal spirit, and one for which you must give account at the bar of our common Father and Creator.

The responsibility which you have assumed in this regard is truly awful, and how you could stagger under it these many years is marvelous. Your mind must have become darkened, your heart hardened, your conscience seared and petrified, or you would have long since thrown off the accursed load, and sought relief at the hands of a sin-forgiving God. How, let me ask, would you look upon me, were I, some dark night, in company with a band of hardened villains, to enter the precincts of your elegant dwelling, and seize the person of your own lovely daughter, Amanda, and carry her off from your family, friends, and all the loved ones of her youth—make her my slave—compel her to work, and I take her wages—place her name on my ledger as property—disregard her personal rights—fetter the powers of her immortal soul by denying her the right and privilege of learning to read and write—feed her coarsely—clothe her scantily, and whip her on the naked back occasionally; more, and still more horrible, leave her unprotected—a degraded victim to the brutal lust of fiendish overseers, who would pollute, blight, and blast her fair soul—rob her of all dignity—destroy her virtue, and annihilate in her person all the graces that adorn the character of virtuous womanhood? I ask, how would you regard me, if such were my conduct? Oh! the vocabulary of the damned would not afford a word sufficiently infernal to express your idea of my God-provoking wickedness. Yet, sir, your treatment of my beloved sisters is in all essential points precisely like the case I have now supposed. Damning as would be such a deed on my part, it would be no more so than that which you have committed against me and my sisters.

I will now bring this letter to a close; you shall hear from me again unless you let me hear from you. I intend to make use of you as a weapon with which to assail the system of slavery—as a means of concentrating public attention on the system, and deepening the horror of trafficking in the souls and bodies of men. I shall make use of you as a means of exposing the character of the American church and clergy—and as a means of bringing this guilty nation, with yourself, to repentance. In doing this, I entertain no malice toward you personally. There is no roof under which you would be more safe than mine, and there is nothing in my house which you might need for your comfort, which I would not readily grant. Indeed, I should esteem it a privilege to set you an example as to how mankind ought to treat each other.

I am your fellow-man, but not your slave.
Frederick Douglass

Remarkably, Douglass and his former master reconciled. Thirty years after this letter was written, Douglass and Auld met face-to-face at Auld's deathbed, and Douglass later described the meeting as "deeply emotional" and cordial. Douglass was especially heartened to learn that Auld had taken Douglass's grandmother into his home, where his family had cared for her. Concerning his fellow abolitionists, Douglass was well aware of the sacrifices made by others and expressed his praise for them in both public forums and private messages. Douglass was especially impressed with Harriet Tubman, a fugitive slave who could neither read nor write but who went on to assist—at tremendous personal risk—hundreds of slaves escape to freedom through the Underground Railroad. When a biography of Tubman, referred to as the "Moses of Her People," was written in 1868, Tubman asked Douglass for an endorsement. He responded with the following letter.

Rochester, August 29, 1868

Dear Harriet:

I am glad to know that the story of your eventful life has been written by a kind lady, and that the same is soon to be published. You ask for what you do not need when you call upon me for a word of commendation. I need such words from you far more than you can need them from me, especially where your superior labors and devotion to the cause of the lately enslaved of our land are known as I know them. The difference between us is very marked. Most that I have done and suffered in the service of our cause has been in public, and I have received much encouragement at every step of the way. You, on the other hand, have labored in a private way. I have wrought in the day—you in the night. I have had the applause of the crowd and the satisfaction that comes of being approved by the multitude, while the most that you have done has been witnessed by a few trembling, scarred, and foot-sore bondmen and women, whom you have led out of the house of bondage, and whose heartfelt *"God bless you"* has been your only reward. The midnight sky and the silent stars have been the witnesses of your devotion to freedom and of your heroism. Excepting John Brown—of sacred memory—I know of no one who has willingly encountered more perils and hardships to serve our enslaved people than you have. Much that you have done would seem improbable to those who do not know you as I know you. It is to me a great pleasure and a great privilege to bear testimony to your character and your works, and to say to those to whom you may come, that I regard you in every way truthful and trustworthy.

Your friend,

Frederick Douglass

A "Dear Friend" to Harriet Beecher Stowe

A wrenching account of the relentless cruelties endured by slaves, Harriet Beecher Stowe's Uncle Tom's Cabin *had a powerful effect on the minds of those unfamiliar with the horrors of slavery. The book was published in 1852 and sold three hundred thousand copies in the United States within the year. The following letter, known only as a "note from a lady, an intimate friend [of Stowe]" and reprinted in its entirety from* The Life and Letters of Harriet Beecher Stowe, *is just one example of the searing impression the book made on its readers.*

My Dear Mrs. Stowe,—

I sat up last night until long after one o'clock, reading and finishing "Uncle Tom's Cabin." I could *not leave* it any more than I could have left a dying child; nor could I restrain an almost hysterical sobbing for an hour after I laid my head upon my pillow. I thought I was a thoroughgoing abolitionist before, but your book has awakened so strong a feeling of indignation and of compassion, that I seem never to have had *any* feeling on this subject till now. But what can we do? Alas! Alas! what *can* we do? This storm of feeling has been raging, burning like a very fire in my bones all the livelong night, and through all my duties this morning it haunts me,—I *cannot* away with it. Gladly would I have gone out in the midnight storm last night, and, like the blessed martyr of old, been stoned to death, if that could have rescued these oppressed and afflicted ones. But that would avail nothing. And now what am I doing? Just the most foolish thing in the world. Writing to you, who need no incitement; to you, who have spun from your very vitals this tissue of agony and truths; for I know, I feel, that there are burning drops of your heart's best blood here concentrated. To *you*, who need no encouragement or sympathy of mine, and whom I would not insult by praise,—oh, no, you stand on too high an eminence for praise; but methinks I see the prayers of the poor, the blessings of those who are ready to perish, gathering in clouds about you, and forming a halo round your beloved head. And surely the tears of gentle, sympathizing childhood, that are dropping about many a Christian hearthstone over the wrongs and cruelties depicted by you so touchingly, will water the sod and spring up in bright flowers at your feet. And better still, I *know*,—I see, in the flushing cheek, the clenched hand and indignant eye of the young man, as he dashes down the book and paces the room to hide the tears that he is too proud to show, too powerless to restrain, that you are sowing seed which shall yet spring up to the glory of God, to the good of the poor slave, to the enfranchisement of our beloved though guilty country.

Robert E. Lee to His Wife Mary

Though by no means an abolitionist, Robert E. Lee—who was ultimately to be appointed head of the Confederate Army of Northern Virginia in April 1861—considered slavery to be an appalling stain on American society. In the following letter to his wife, Mary Custis Lee, written over four years before the Civil War, Lee articulates his views on slavery and its inevitable demise.

Fort Brown, Texas, December 27, 1856

The steamer has arrived from New Orleans, bringing in full files of papers and general intelligence from the "States." I have enjoyed the former very much, and, in the absence of particular intelligence, have perused with much interest the series of the *Alexandria Gazette* from the 20th of November to the 8th of December inclusive. Besides the usual reading matter, I was interested in the relation of local affairs, and inferred, from the quiet and ordinary course of events, that all in the neighborhood was going on well. I trust it may be so, and that you and particularly all at Arlington and our friends elsewhere are well.

The steamer brought the President's message to Congress, and the reports of the various heads of the departments, so that we are now assured that the Government is in operation and the Union in existence. Not that I had any fears to the contrary, but it is satisfactory always to have facts to go on; they restrain supposition and conjecture, confirm faith, and bring contentment. I was much pleased with the President's message and the report of the Secretary of War. The views of the President on the domestic institutions of the South are truthfully and faithfully expressed.

In this enlightened age there are few, I believe, but will acknowledge that slavery as an institution is a moral and political evil in any country. It is useless to expatiate on its disadvantages. I think it, however, a greater evil to the white than to the black race, and while my feelings are strongly interested in behalf of the latter, my sympathies are stronger for the former. The blacks are immeasurably better off here than in Africa, morally, socially, and physically. The painful discipline they are undergoing is necessary for their instruction as a race, and, I hope, will prepare and lead them to better things.

How long their subjection may be necessary is known and ordered by a wise and merciful Providence. Their emancipation will sooner result from a mild and melting influence than the storms and contests of fiery controversy. This influence, though slow, is sure. The doctrines and miracles of our Saviour have required nearly two thousand years to convert but a small part of the human race, and even among Christian nations what gross errors still exist!

While we see the course of the final abolition of slavery onward, and we give it the aid of our prayers and all justifiable means in our power, we must leave the progress as well as the result in his hands, who sees the end and who chooses to work by slow things, and with whom a thousand years are but as a single day; although the abolitionist must know this, and must see that he has neither the right nor the power of operating except by moral means and suasion; and if he means well to the slave, he must not create angry feelings in the master. That although he may not approve the mode by which it pleases Providence to accomplish its purposes, the result will never be the same; that the reasons he gives for interferences in what he has no concern holds good for every kind of interference with our neighbors when we disapprove their conduct. Is it not strange that the descendants of those Pilgrim Fathers who crossed the Atlantic to preserve the freedom of their opinion have always proved themselves intolerant of the spiritual liberty of others?

I hope you had a joyous Christmas at Arlington, and that it may be long and often repeated. I thought of you all and wished to be with you. Mine was gratefully but silently passed. I endeavored to find some little presents for the children in the garrison to add to their amusement, and succeeded better than I had anticipated. The stores are very barren of such things here, but by taking the week beforehand in my daily walks I picked up little by little something for all. Tell Mildred I got a beautiful Dutch doll for little Emma Jones—one of those crying babies that can open and shut their eyes, turn their head, etc. For the two other girls, Puss Shirley and Mary Sewell, I found French teapots to match cups given to them by Mrs. Waite; then by means of knives and books I satisfied the boys. After dispensing my presents I went to church; the discourse was on the birth of our Saviour. It was not as simply or touchingly told as it is in the Bible. By previous invitation I dined with Major Thomas at 2 p.m. on roast turkey and plum pudding. He and his wife were there alone. I had provided a pretty singing bird for the little girl, and passed the afternoon in my room. God bless you all.

Abolitionist John Brown to His Pastor

On October 16, 1859, a fiercely outspoken white abolitionist named John Brown led a group of eighteen men—five black and thirteen white—on a raid at Harpers Ferry, Virginia, to steal munitions from the town's armory and to rally the slaves. The effort was a disaster. Pursued by a young lieutenant colonel named Robert E. Lee, Brown and his remaining men (ten were killed, including two of Brown's sons) were rounded up and put on trial for treason against the state. The outcome was not unexpected; Brown and the rest of his men were given a sentence of death. Writing from his cell in the Charles Town Prison four days before his execution, Brown sent the following letter to his pastor, D. R. Tilden.

Charlestown, 28 November, 1859

TO THE HON. D. R. TILDEN
My Dear Sir,—

Your most kind and comforting letter of the 23rd inst. is received. I have no language to express the feelings of gratitude and obligation I am under for your kind interest in my behalf ever since my disaster. The great bulk of mankind estimate each other's actions and motives by the measure of success or otherwise that attends them through life. By that rule, I have been one of the worst and one of the best of men. I do not claim to have been one of the latter, and I leave it to an impartial tribunal to decide whether the world has been the worse or the better for my living or dying in it. My present great anxiety is to get as near in readiness for a different field of action as I well can, since being in a good measure relieved from the fear of my poor broken-hearted wife and children would come to immediate want. May God reward a thousandfold all the kind efforts made in their behalf! I have enjoyed remarkable cheerfulness and composure of mind ever since my confinement; and it is a great comfort to feel assured that I am permitted to die for a cause—not merely to pay the debt of nature, as all must. I feel myself to be most unworthy of so great distinction. The particular manner of dying assigned to me gives me but very little uneasiness. I wish I had the time and the ability to give you, my dear friend, some little idea of what is daily, and I might almost say hourly, passing within my prison walls; and could my friends but witness only a few of these scenes, just as they occur, I think they would feel very well reconciled to my being here, just what I am, and just as I am. My whole life before had not afforded me one half the opportunity to plead for the right. In this, also, I find much to reconcile me to both my present condition and my immediate prospect. I may be very insane; and I am so, if insane at all. But if that be so, insanity is like a very pleasant dream to me. I am not in the least degree conscious of my ravings, of my fears, or of any terrible visions whatever; but fancy myself entirely composed, and that my sleep, in particular, is as sweet as that of a healthy, joyous little infant. I pray God that He will grant me a continuance of the same calm but delightful dream, until I come to know of those realities which eyes have not seen and which ears have not heard. I have scarce realized that I am in prison or in irons at all. I certainly think I was never more cheerful in my life.

I intend to take the liberty of sending by express to your care some trifling articles for those of my family who may be in Ohio, which you can hand to my brother Jeremiah when you may see him, together with fifteen dollars I have asked him to advance to them. Please excuse me so often in troubling you with my letters or any of my matters. Please also remember me most kindly to Mr. Griswold, and to all others who love their neighbors. I write Jeremiah to your care.

Your friend in truth,
John Brown

Jefferson Davis to Franklin Pierce

Six weeks after Abraham Lincoln was elected president, South Carolina seceded from the Union. Three weeks later Mississippi broke, followed by Florida, Alabama, Georgia, and Louisiana. Recognizing it would need a "president" of its own, the Southern states chose as their leader Jefferson Davis, who had served as secretary of war under President Franklin Pierce and, as a senator from Mississippi, was an outspoken advocate for the rights of slaveholders. Davis was concerned by the likelihood of a civil war but believed unconditionally in the South's right to secede. One month before he would be sworn in as the provisional president of the Confederacy, Davis wrote the following letter to Pierce. (Caleb Cushing, whom Davis refers to, was a Northerner who had served with him in Pierce's Cabinet.)

Washington
Jan. 20, 1861

Dear Friend,

I have often and sadly turned my thoughts to you during the troublous times through which we have been passing and now I come to the hard task of announcing to you that the hour is at hand which closes my connection with the United States, for the independence and Union of which my Father bled and in the service of which I have sought to emulate the example he set for my guidance. Mississippi, not as a matter of choice but of necessity, has resolved to enter on the trial of secession. Those who have driven her to this alternative threaten to deprive her of the right to require that her government shall rest on the consent of the governed, to substitute foreign force for domestic support, to reduce a state to the condition from which the colony rose.

When Lincoln comes in he will have but to continue in the path of his predecessor to inaugurate a civil war, and, leave a *soi-disant* democratic administration responsible for the rest.

Genl. Cushing was here last week and when we parted it seemed like taking leave of a Brother.

I leave immediately for Missi. and know not what may devolve upon me after my return. Civil war has only horror for me, but whatever circumstances demand shall be met as a duty and I trust be so discharged that you will not be ashamed of our former connection or cease to be my friend.

Do me the favor to write to me often, address Hurricane P.O. Warren County, Missi.

May God bless you is ever the prayer of your friend
Jefferson Davis

At 4:30 A.M. on April 12, 1861, South Carolina militiamen opened fire on Fort Sumter in Charleston Harbor. The Civil War had officially begun.

Sullivan Ballou to His Wife Sarah

The Battle of Bull Run, which took place just twenty-five miles from the White House, was the first major clash of the war. Civilians from neighboring areas rode out to the perimeter of the battlefield—some with binoculars and picnic baskets—to watch the fighting unfold. Well aware that the battle might be their first and last, soldiers made preparations accordingly, including writing letters home to loved ones. Major Sullivan Ballou, of the Second Rhode Island Volunteers, addressed the following letter to his wife, Sarah, in Smithfield.

July 14, 1861
Camp Clark, Washington

My very dear Sarah,

The indications are very strong that we shall move in a few days—perhaps tomorrow. Lest I should not be able to write again, I feel impelled to write a few lines that may fall under your eye when I shall be no more. Our movements may be of a few days' duration and full of pleasure—and it may be one of some conflict and death to me. "Not my will, but thine, O God be done." If it is necessary that I should fall on the battlefield for my Country, I am ready.

I have no misgivings about, or lack of confidence in, the cause in which I am engaged, and my courage does not halt or falter. I know how strongly American Civilization now leans on the triumph of the Government, and how great a debt we owe to those who went before us through the blood and sufferings of the Revolution. And I am willing—perfectly willing—to lay down all my joys in this life, to help maintain this Government, and to pay that debt . . .

Sarah my love for you is deathless. It seems to bind me with mighty cables that nothing but Omnipotence could break; and yet my love of Country comes over me like a strong wind and bears me unresistibly on with all these chains to the battlefield.

The memories of the blissful moments I have spent with you come creeping over me, and I feel most gratified to God and to you that I have enjoyed them so long. And hard it is for me to give them up and burn to ashes the hopes of future years, when, God willing, we might still have lived and loved together, and seen our sons grown up to honorable manhood around us. I have, I know, but few and small claims upon Divine Providence, but something whispers to me—perhaps it is the wafted prayer of my little Edgar—that I shall return to my loved ones unharmed. If I do not my dear Sarah, never forget how much I love you, and when my last breath escapes me on the battlefield, it will whisper your name. Forgive my many faults, and the many pains I have caused you. How thoughtless and foolish I have often times been! How gladly would I wash out with my tears every little spot upon your happiness, and struggle with all the misfortunes of this world to shield you and your children from harm. But I cannot. I must watch you from the Spirit-land and hover near you, while you buffet the storm, with your precious little freight, and wait with sad patience till we meet to part no more.

But, O Sarah! if the dead can come back to this earth and flit unseen around those they loved, I shall always be near you; in the gladdest days and darkest nights, advised to your happiest scenes and gloomiest hours, *always*, *always*, and if there be a soft breeze upon your cheek, it shall be my breath; as the cool air fans your throbbing temple, it shall be my spirit passing by. Sarah do not mourn me dead; think I am gone and wait for thee, for we shall meet again.

As for my little boys—they will grow up as I have done, and never know a father's love and care. Little Willie is too young to remember me long, and my blue-eyed Edgar will keep my frolics with him among the dim memories of childhood. Sarah, I have unlimited confidence in your maternal care and your development of their character, and feel that God will bless you in your holy work.

Tell my two Mothers I call God's blessing upon them. O! Sarah. I wait for you there; come to me and lead thither my children.

Sullivan

The Union Army was ultimately defeated at Bull Run, and of the more than 70,000 Southern and Northern soldiers who went into battle, some 4,500 were killed, wounded, or captured. Major Sullivan Ballou was among the dead.

President Abraham Lincoln to Horace Greeley

Throughout the war President Lincoln endured a relentless barrage of criticism and outright contempt for his policies on slavery—including from people who felt he was not doing enough to end it. Horace Greeley, the influential newspaper editor and publisher, excoriated Lincoln in a lengthy public letter (printed in Greeley's own New York Tribune*) for lack of fortitude in abolishing slavery and punishing slaveholders. Greeley was particularly displeased that Lincoln was not enforcing the Confiscation Act, which freed the slaves of Rebel masters (even though the U.S. Government had no jurisdiction over slaveholders). Although Lincoln had privately denounced slavery, he had, in fact, lessened his public condemnation of it for fear of angering Unionist slaveholders in the border states. Three days after Greeley's letter was published, Lincoln wrote the following reply.*

Executive Mansion
Washington, August 22, 1862

Hon. Horace Greeley:
Dear Sir

I have just read yours of the 19th. addressed to myself through the New-York Tribune. If there be in it any statements, or assumptions of fact, which I may know to be erroneous, I do not, now and here, controvert them. If there be in it any inferences which I may believe to be falsely drawn, I do not now and here, argue against them. If there be perceptable in it an impatient and dictatorial tone, I waive it in deference to an old friend, whose heart I have always supposed to be right.

As to the policy I "seem to be pursuing" as you say, I have not meant to leave any one in doubt.

I would save the Union. I would save it in the shortest way under the Constitution. The sooner the national authority can be restored, the nearer the Union will be "the Union as it was." If there be those who would not save the Union, unless they could at the same time *save* slavery, I do not agree with them. If there be those who would not save the Union unless they could at the same time *destroy* slavery, I do not agree with them. My paramount object in this struggle *is* to save the Union, and is *not* either to save or to destroy slavery. If I could save the Union without freeing *any* slave I would do it, if I could save it by freeing *all* the slaves I would do it; and if I could save it by freeing some and leaving others alone I would also do that. What I do about slavery, and the colored race, I do because I believe it helps to save the Union; and what I forbear, I forbear because I do *not* believe it would help to save the Union. I shall do *less* whenever I shall believe what I am doing hurts the cause, and I shall do *more* whenever I shall believe doing more will help the cause. I shall try to correct errors when shown to be errors; and I shall adopt new views so fast as they shall appear to be true views.

I have here stated my purpose according to my view of *official* duty; and I intend no modification of my oft-expressed *personal* wish that all men everywhere could be free.

Yours,
A. Lincoln

Unknown to Greeley, Lincoln had already drafted a preliminary copy of the Emancipation Proclamation declaring that "all persons held as slaves within any State, or designated part of a State, the people whereof shall then be in rebellion against the United States, shall be then, thenceforward, and forever free."

Louisa Alexander to Her Husband Archer

On September 22, 1862, Abraham Lincoln issued his Emancipation Proclamation, which would take effect on January 1, 1863. "If my name ever goes into history," Lincoln remarked, "it was for this act." Confederate President Jefferson Davis called the document the "most execrable measure recorded in the history of guilty man." Rebel slaveholders simply ignored it—the Union Army would have to defeat them first before it could be enforced—but slaves who escaped bondage now had a better chance of maintaining their freedom. Taking advantage of this opportunity, a slave named Archer Alexander fled his master in February 1863 and gained employment from a sympathetic minister, William Greenleaf Eliot, in a free state. Nine months later Archer wrote to his wife, still a slave, reporting that he had finally earned enough money to purchase her freedom legally from her master, Mr. Jim. The following letter is her reply.

Naylor's Store, Nov. 16, 1863.

My Dear Husband,—I received your letter yesterday, and lost no time in asking Mr. Jim if he would sell me, and what he would take for me. He flew at me, and said I would never get free only at the point of the Baynot, and there was no use in my ever speaking to him any more about it. I don't see how I can ever get away except you get soldiers to take me from the house, as he is watching me night and day. If I can get away I will, but the people here are all afraid to take me away. He is always abusing Lincoln, and calls him an old Rascoll. He is the greatest rebel under heaven. It is a sin to have him loose. He says if he had hold of Lincoln he would chop him up into mincemeat. I had good courage all along until now, but now I am almost heart-broken. Answer this letter as soon as possible.

I am your affectionate wife,
Louisa Alexander.

Two weeks after he received this letter, Archer Alexander convinced a German farmer to help his wife and their daughter, Nellie, escape. The attempt was successful.

Lewis Douglass to His Fiancée Amelia Loguen

Although Abraham Lincoln wanted to see slavery abolished, he was not unaware of the political necessity of the Emancipation Proclamation; the Union Army was suffering and desperately needed new recruits. Who better, Lincoln knew, than free and fugitive blacks who passionately wanted to see the South defeated? Blacks constituted less than 1 percent of the North's population, but by the end of the war they would represent nearly 10 percent of the Northern army. One of the most famous regiments in the war was the all-black Fifty-fourth Massachusetts Volunteer Infantry. As part of a larger effort to capture Charleston, the Fifty-fourth spearheaded the assault on Fort Wagner, which protected the entrance to Charleston Harbor. The Fifty-fourth was ordered to take the fort, considered virtually impregnable, on July 18, 1863. Before the attack, Lewis Douglass—one of Frederick Douglass's two sons serving in the Fifty-fourth—sent the following letter to his finacée, Amelia Loguen.

Morris Island. S.C. July 20

My Dear Amelia:

I have been in two fights, and am unhurt. I am about to go in another I believe to-night. Our men fought well on both occasions. The last was desperate—we charged that terrible battery on Morris

Island known as Fort Wagner, and were repulsed with a loss of 3 killed and wounded. I escaped unhurt from amidst that perfect hail of shot and shell. It was terrible. I need not particularize—the papers will give a better account than I have time to give. My thoughts are with you often, you are as dear as ever, be good enough to remember it as I no doubt you will. As I said before we are on the eve of another fight and I am very busy and have just snatched a moment to write you. I must necessarily be brief. Should I fall in the next fight killed or wounded I hope to fall with my face to the foe.

If I survive I shall write you a long letter. DeForrest of your city is wounded, George Washington is missing, Jacob Carter is missing, Chas Reason is wounded, Chas Whiting, Chas Creamer all wounded. The above are in hospital.

This regiment has established its reputation as a fighting regiment, not a man flinched, though it was a trying time. Men fell all around me. A shell would explode and clear a space of twenty feet. Our men would close up again, but it was no use—we had to retreat, which was a very hazardous undertaking. How I got out of that fight alive I cannot tell, but I am here. My Dear girl I hope again to see you. I must bid you farewell should I be killed. Remember if I die I die in a good cause. I wish we had a hundred thousand colored troops—we would put an end to this war. Good Bye to all.

Your own loving Lewis
Write soon

The Fifty-fourth was repelled, losing almost half of its men. (Both of Douglass's sons survived.) Nevertheless, whites who had doubted that blacks would have the courage to fight were astounded by the bravery of the Fifty-fourth. "It is not too much to say that if this Massachusetts 54th had faltered when its trial came, two hundred thousand troops for whom it was a pioneer would never have put into the field," the New York Tribune *later wrote. "But it did not falter. It made Fort Wagner such a name for the colored race as Bunker Hill has been for ninety years to the white Yankees."*

Hannah Johnson to President Lincoln

Of the estimated 180,000 blacks who fought in the Civil War, approximately 36,000 gave their lives for the Union. But despite their sacrifices and public recognition for their bravery, they still suffered indignities and humiliations at the hands of whites unfamiliar with seeing blacks in positions of equality. Black soldiers were often denied the same clothing given to whites, white doctors were less willing to treat them (the death rate from disease among blacks was double that of the rest of the army), and they were paid less for the same service. Writing from Buffalo, New York, the mother of a soldier in the Fifty-fourth sent the following letter (through a friend, Carrie Coburn) to the president in hopes that he would ensure equal pay and treatment for black soldiers.

Buffalo July 31 1863

Excellent Sir

My good friend says I must write to you and she will send it My son went in the 54th regiment. I am a colored woman and my son was strong and able as any to fight for his country and the colored people have as much to fight for as any. My father was a Slave and escaped from Louisiana before I was born morn forty years agone I have but poor edication but I never went to schol, but I know just as well as any what is right between man and man. Now I know it is right that a colored man should go and fight for his country, and so ought to a white man. I know that a colored man ought to run no greater risques than a white, his pay is no greater his obligation to fight is the same. So why should not our enemies be compelled to treat him the same, Made to do it.

My son fought at Fort Wagoner but thank God he was not taken prisoner, as many were I thought of this thing before I let my boy go but then they said M^r. Lincoln will never let them sell our colored soldiers for slaves, if they do he will get them back quck he will rettallyate and stop it. Now Mr Lincoln dont you think you oght to stop this thing and make them do the same by the colored man they have lived in idleness all their lives on stolen labor and made savages of the colored people, but they now are so furious because they are proving themselves to be men, such as have come away and got some edication. It must not be so. You must put the rebels to work in State prisons to making shoes and things, if they sell our colored soldiers, till they let them all go. And give their wounded the same treatment. it would seem cruel, but their no other way, and a just man must do hard things sometimes, that shew him to be a great man. They tell me some do you will take back the Proclamation, don't do it. When you are dead and in Heaven, in a thousand years that action of yours will make the Angels sing your praises I know it. Ought one man to own another, law for or not, who made the law, surely the poor slave did not. so it is wicked, and a horrible Outrage, there is no sense in it, because a man has lived by robbing all his life and his father before him, should he complain because the stolen things found on him are taken. Robbing the colored people of their labor is but a small part of the robbery their souls are almost taken, they are made bruits of often. You know all about this

Will you see that the colored men fighting now, are fairly treated. You ought to do this, and do it at once, Not let the thing run along meet it quickly and manfully, and stop this, mean cowardly cruelty. We poor oppressed ones, appeal to you, and ask fair play.

Yours for Christs sake
Hannah Johnson.

Hon. Mr. Lincoln The above speaks for itself Carrie Coburn

Lincoln is not believed to have responded to this letter, and according to Frederick Douglass, who met with the president over the grievances of black soldiers, Lincoln reportedly stated: "The employment of colored troops at all was a great gain to the colored people [and] their enlistment was a serious offence to popular prejudice. [. . .] That they were not to receive the same pay as white soldiers seemed a necessary concession to smooth the way to their employment as soldiers." Black soldiers continued to protest, and Congress finally equalized their pay with that of whites in June 1864.

President Abraham Lincoln to General "Fighting Joe" Hooker

Throughout the war President Lincoln wrote hundreds of messages to his generals giving them orders or requesting updates, and many reflected Lincoln's frustrations with their losses, delays, and inactivity. To General George B. McClellan he wrote in October 1862: "I have just read your despatch about sore-tongued and fatigued horses. Will you pardon me for asking what the horses of your army have done since the battle of Antietam that fatigues anything?" McClellan is the same general Lincoln famously told, "If [you are] not using the Army I should like to borrow it for awhile." In January 1863 Lincoln sent the following stern letter to the notoriously outspoken Joseph "Fighting Joe" Hooker, whom Lincoln had recently appointed to lead the Potomac Army (replacing Ambrose Burnside, who had only recently replaced George McClellan).

Executive Mansion
Washington, January 26, 1863

Major-General Hooker:
General:

I have placed you at the head of the Army of the Potomac. Of course I have done this upon what appear to me to be sufficient reasons. And yet I think it best for you to know that there are some things in regard to which, I am not quite satisfied with you. I believe you to be a brave and skilful soldier, which, of course, I like. I also believe you do not mix politics with your profession, in which you are right. You have confidence in yourself, which is a valuable, if not an indispensable quality. You are ambitious, which, within reasonable bounds, does good rather than harm. But I think that during Gen. Burnside's command of the Army you have taken counsel of your ambition, and thwarted him as much as you could, in which you did a great wrong to the country, and to a most meritorious and honorable brother officer. I have heard, in such way as to believe it, of your recently saying that both the Army and the Government needed a Dictator. Of course it was not *for* this, but in spite of it, that I have given you the command. Only those generals who gain successes, can set up dictators. What I now ask of you is military success, and I will risk the dictatorship. The government will support you to the utmost of its ability, which is neither more nor less than it has done and will do for all commanders. I much fear that the spirit which you have aided to infuse into the Army, of criticising their Commander and withholding confidence from him, will now turn upon you. I shall assist you as far as I can, to put it down. Neither you, nor Napoleon, if he were alive again, could get any good out of an army, while such a spirit prevails in it. And now, beware of rashness. Beware of rashness, but with energy, and sleepless vigilance, go forward and give us victories.

Yours very truly,
A. Lincoln

General Hooker's leadership also proved disastrous, and in June 1863 he was replaced with yet another commander, George Gordon Meade.

Union General David Hunter to Confederate President Jefferson Davis & Henrietta Lee to General Hunter

Enraged by reports that black soldiers were being executed or forced back into slavery by Southern troops instead of being taken prisoner as white soldiers were, Union general David Hunter declared he would retaliate with equal brutality. In the following letter to Jefferson Davis, with whom Hunter had been friends as a young man, General Hunter states his intentions to the Confederate president in no uncertain terms.

HILTON HEAD, Port Royal, S.C., April 23rd 1863.

The United States flag must protect all its defenders, white, black or yellow. Several negroes in the employ of the Government, in the Western Department, have been cruelly murdered by your authorities, and others sold into slavery. Every outrage of this kind against the laws of war and humanity, which may take place in this Department, shall be followed by the immediate execution of the

Rebel of highest rank in my possession; man for man, these executions will certainly take place, for every one murdered, or sold into a slavery worse than death. On your authorities will rest the responsibility of having inaugurated this barbarous policy, and you will be held responsible, in this world and in the world to come, for all blood thus shed.

In the month of August last you declared all those engaged in arming the negroes to fight for their country, to be felons, and directed the immediate executions of all such, as should be captured. I have given you long enough to reflect on your folly. I now give you notice, that unless this order is immediately revoked, I will at once cause the execution of every rebel officer, and every rebel slaveholder in my possession. This sad state of things may be kindly ordered by an all wise Providence, to induce the good people of the North to act earnestly, and to realize that they are at war. Thousands of lives may thus be saved.

The poor negro is fighting for liberty in its truest sense; and Mr Jefferson has beautifully said,—"in such a war, there is no attribute of the Almighty, which will induce him to fight on the side of the oppressor."

You say you are fighting for liberty. Yes you are fighting for liberty: liberty to keep four millions of your fellow-beings in ignorance and degradation;—liberty to separate parents and children, husband and wife, brother and sister;—liberty to steal the products of their labor, exacted with many a cruel lash and bitter tear,—liberty to seduce their wives and daughters, and to sell your own children into bondage;—liberty to kill these children with impunity, when the murder cannot be proven by one of pure white blood. This is the kind of liberty—the liberty to do wrong—which Satan, Chief of fallen Angels, was contending for when he was cast into Hell. I have the honor to be, very respectfully, Your mo. ob. serv.

D. Hunter

There is no record of a reply from Davis, and it could not be determined if Hunter ever carried through with his threat. Over a year later, Hunter himself was on the receiving end of a furious letter accusing barbarity.

Hunter had ordered the destruction of a house owned by Mrs. Henrietta Lee, who then sent the Union general the following letter.

Jefferson County, Virginia
July 20, 1864

General Hunter:

Yesterday your underling, Captain Martindale, of the First New York Cavalry, executed your infamous order and burned my house. You have had the satisfaction ere this of receiving from him the information that your orders were fulfilled to the letter; the dwelling and every out-building, seven in number, with their contents, being burned. I, therefore, a helpless woman whom you have cruelly wronged, address you, a Major-General of the United States army, and demand why this was done? What was my offence? My husband was absent, in exile. He had never been a politician or in any way engaged in the struggle now going on, his age preventing. This fact your chief of staff, David Strother, could have told you. The house was built by my father, a Revolutionary soldier, who served the whole seven years for your independence. There was I born; there the sacred dead repose. It was my house and my home, and there has your niece (Miss Griffith), who has tarried among us all this horrid war up to the present time, met with all kindness and hospitality at my hands. Was it for this that you turned me, my young daughter, and little son out upon the world without a shelter? Or was it because my husband is the grandson of the Revolutionary patriot and "rebel," Richard Henry Lee, and the near kinsman of the noblest of Christian warriors, the greatest of generals, Robert E. Lee? Heaven's blessing be upon his head forever. You and your Government have failed to conquer, subdue, or match him; and disappointment, rage, and malice find vent on the hopeless and inoffensive.

Hyena-like, you have torn my heart to pieces! for all hallowed memories clustered around that homestead, and demon-like, you have done it without even the pretext of revenge, for I never saw or harmed you. Your office is not to lead, like a brave man and soldier, your men to fight in the ranks of war, but your work has been to separate yourself from all danger, and with your incendiary band steal unaware upon helpless women and children, to insult and destroy. Two fair homes did you ruthlessly lay in ashes, giving not a moment's warning to the startled inmates of your wicked purpose; turning mothers and children out of doors, you are execrated by your own men for the cruel work you give them to do.

In the case of Colonel A. R. Boteler, both father and mother were far away. Any heart but that of Captain Martindale (and yours) would have been touched by that little circle, compromising a widowed daughter just risen from her bed of illness, her three fatherless babies—the oldest not five years old—and her heroic sister. I repeat, any man would have been touched at that sight but captain Martindale. One might as well hope to find mercy and feeling in the heart of a wolf bent on his prey of young lambs, as to search for such qualities in his bosom. You have chosen well your agent for such deeds, and doubtless will promote him.

A colonel of the Federal army has stated that you deprived forty of your officers of their commands because they refused to carry on your malignant mischief. All honor to their names for this, at least! They are men; they have human hearts and blush for such a commander!

I ask who that does not wish infamy and disgrace attached to him forever would serve you? Your name will stand on history's page as the Hunter of weak women, and innocent children the Hunter to destroy defenceless villages and refined and beautiful homes—to torture afresh the agonized hearts of widows; the Hunter of Africa's poor sons and daughters, to lure them on to ruin and death of soul and body; the Hunter with the relentless heart of a wild beast, the face of a fiend and the form of a man. Oh, Earth, behold the monster! Can I say, "God forgive you?" No prayer can be offered for you. Were it possible for human lips to raise your name heavenward, angels would thrust the foul thing back again, and demons claim their own. The curses of thousands, the scorns of manly and upright, and the hatred of the true and honorable, will follow you and yours through all time, and brand your name infamy! infamy!

Again, I demand why you have burned my home? Answer as you must answer before the Searcher of all hearts, why have you added this cruel, wicked deed to your many crimes?

Hunter is not believed to have replied.

Confederate General George E. Pickett to La Salle Corbell

In three days of fighting at Gettysburg—from July 1st to the 3rd, 1863—51,000 American men were killed and tens of thousands more wounded. (In the almost ten years of American military presence in Vietnam, 58,000 Americans were killed.) Considered one of the greatest and most pivotal battles of the Civil War, Gettysburg halted Robert E. Lee's steady march up the Shenandoah Valley and into Pennsylvania and all but broke the spirit of the Confederate Army. General George E. Pickett had been chosen by Lee to command the final assault on the Union Army at Gettysburg. Horrified by what he had seen and racked with guilt, Pickett sent the following letter to his beloved, La Salle Corbell, three days after the combat was over.

Headquarters, July 6, 1863

On the Fourth—far from a glorious Fourth to us or to any with love for his fellow-men—I wrote you just a line of heart-break. The sacrifice of life on that blood-soaked field on the fatal third was too awful for the heralding of victory, even for our victorious foe, who, I think, believe as we do, that it decided the fate of our cause. No words can picture the anguish of that roll-call—the breathless waits between the responses. The "Here" of those who, by God's mercy, had miraculously escaped the awful rain of shots and shell was a sob—a gasp—a knell—for the unanswered name of his comrade called before his. There was no tone of thankfulness for having been spared to answer to their names, but rather a toll, and an unvoiced wish that they, too, had been among the missing.

But for the blight to your sweet young life, but for you, only you, my darling, your soldier would rather by far be out there, too, with his brave Virginians—dead—

Even now I can hear them cheering as I gave the order, "Forward"! I can feel their faith and trust in me and their love for our cause. I can feel the thrill of their joyous voices as they called out all along the line, "We'll follow you, Marse George. We'll follow you—we'll follow you." Oh, how faithfully they kept their word—following me on—on—to their death, and I, believing in the promised support, led them on—on—on—Oh, God!

I can't write you a love letter to-day, my Sallie, for with my great love for you and my gratitude to God for sparing my life to devote to you, comes the over-powering thought of those whose lives were sacrificed—of the broken-hearted widows and mothers and orphans. The moans of my wounded boys, the sight of the dead, upturned faces, flood my soul with grief—and here am I whom they trusted, whom they followed, leaving them on that field of carnage—leaving them to the mercy of—and guarding four thousand prisoners across the river back to Winchester. Such a duty for men who a few hours ago covered themselves with glory eternal.

Well, my darling, I put the prisoners all on their honor and gave them equal liberties with my own soldier boys. My first command to them was to go and enjoy themselves the best they could, and they have obeyed my order. To-day a Dutchman and two of his comrades came up and told me they were lost and besought me to help them find their commands. They had been with my men and had gotten separated from their own comrades. So I sent old Floyd off on St. Paul to find out where they belonged and deliver them.

This is too gloomy and too poor a letter for so beautiful a sweetheart, but it seems sacrilegious, almost, to say I love you, with the hearts that are stilled to love on the field of battle.

Your
Soldier

Fugitive Slave Spotswood Rice to His Former Master's Wife Kittey Diggs

By the fall of 1864 the Civil War, at long last, seemed to be nearing its conclusion. Union spirits were lifted by the conquests at Gettysburg and Vicksburg. One soldier, Spotswood Rice, was especially heartened by the prospect of victory; Rice was a slave-turned-soldier whose children were still being held by his former master, Mr. Diggs, and his wife, Kittey. From a hospital in St. Louis, Missouri, Rice sent the following letter to Mrs. Diggs.

I received a leteter from Cariline telling me that you say I tried to steal to plunder my child away from you now I want you to understand that mary is my Child and she is a God given rite of my own and you may hold on to hear as long as you can but I want you to remembor this one thing that the longor you keep my Child from me the longor you will have to burn in hell and the qwicer youll get their for we are now makeing up a bout one thoughsand blacke troops to Come up tharough and want to come through Glasgow and when we come wo be to Copperhood rabbels and to the Slaveholding rebbels for we dont expect to leave them there root neor branch but we thinke how ever that we that have Children in the hands of you devels we will trie your [vertues?] the day that we enter Glasgow I want you to understand kittey diggs that where ever you and I meets we are enmays to each orthere I offered once to pay you forty dollers for my own Child but I am glad now that you did not accept it Just hold on now as long as you can and the worse it will be for you you never in your life befor I came down hear did you give Children any thing not eny thing whatever not even a dollers worth of expencs now you call my children your pro[per]ty not so with me my Children is my own and I expect to get them and when I get ready to come after mary I will have bout a powrer and autherity to bring hear away and to exacute vengencens on them that holds my Child you will then know how to talke to me I will assure that and you will know how to talk rite too I want you now to just hold on to hear if you want to iff your conchosence tells thats the road go that road and what it will brig you to kittey diggs I have no fears about getting mary out of your hands this whole Government gives chear to me and you cannot help your self

Spotswood Rice

The fate of Rice and his children could not be determined.

Mollie E. to President Lincoln

Just as they had done during the War of Independence, women throughout the United States contributed to the war effort in numerous ways. They organized food drives, knitted desperately needed clothing and blankets, raised funds for relief efforts, served as army nurses, comforted soldiers in hospitals, and even worked as spies. The following letter to President Lincoln is just one example of the desire among women to involve themselves directly in the war.

Gallia Furnace, Ohio
Sept 9 1864

Mr Abram Lincen

Dear Sir I write you these few lines hoping you will consider it I appeal to you for aid there is fifteen young Ladies of the most worthy families that is in this part of the country we wish to do something for our Country we have been wanting to do something Ever since this Cruel war broke out but Circumstances will not permit it. but we cannot wait eny longer we must do something We have sent all that is Near and dear to us and we must help them in some way We are willing to be sworn in for one year or more eny lenght of time it makes No difference to us. But we must do something to help, save that Beautifful Flag that has Waved so long, oer the Land of the Free and the home of the brave I could get up a Regt. in one day of young Ladies of high Rank but I hope you will give us pen something that is helping to save that old Flag We have but one young man in this Part of the Country most Evry man is gone out to help serve that Stary Banner and we must go to we live back in the Country so fur that we Cannot do much here has Evry thing is so quiet. I will Close now hoping you will do something for us I will not send you my full Name Now but if you will do anything for us you May have all

your most Humble Servant
Miss Mollie E.

There is no known reply to this letter, and, since women were not allowed to enlist, it is unlikely Miss Mollie E. and the other ladies would have been encouraged to do so. It is believed, however, that hundreds of women dressed up in men's clothing—just as Deborah Sampson had done in the American Revolution—and fought in disguise.

General William T. Sherman to the Mayor and Councilmen of Atlanta

In the mind of General William Tecumseh Sherman, who made famous the phrase "War is hell," there was no doubt as to the integrity of the North's cause. Sherman was renowned as a fierce—some would say tyrannical—military leader, and in September 1864 he gave orders for the city of Atlanta to be evacuated and burned. Despite appeals from the citizens of Atlanta, including reminders that there were elderly and pregnant women whom it would be difficult and even perilous to move, Sherman's decision was final. He explained himself to the mayor and council members of the city.

Headquarters Military Division of the
Mississippi in the Field, Atlanta, Georgia,

James M. Calhoun, Mayor, E. E. Rawson and S. C. Wells,
representing City Council of Atlanta.

Gentleman: I have your letter of the 11th, in the nature of a petition to revoke my orders removing all the inhabitants from

Atlanta. I have read it carefully, and give full credit to your statements of distress that will be occasioned, and yet shall not revoke my orders, because they were not designed to meet the humanities of the case, but to prepare for the future struggles in which millions of good people outside of Atlanta have a deep interest. We must have *peace*, not only at Atlanta, but in all America. To secure this, we must stop the war that now desolates our once happy and favored country. To stop war, we must defeat the rebel armies which are arrayed against the laws and Constitution that all must respect and obey. To defeat those armies, we must prepare the way to reach them in their recesses, provided with the arms and instruments which enable us to accomplish our purpose. Now, I know the vindictive nature of our enemy, that we may have many years of military operations from this quarter; and, therefore, deem it wise and prudent to prepare in time. The use of Atlanta for warlike purposes is inconsistent with its character as a home for families. There will be no manfacturers, commerce, or agriculture here, for the maintenance of families, and sooner or later want will compel the inhabitants to go. Why not *go now*, when all the arrangements are completed for the transfer, instead of waiting till the plunging shot of contending armies will renew the scenes of the past month? Of course, I do not apprehend any such thing at this moment, but you do not suppose this army will be here until the war is over. I cannot discuss this subject with you fairly, because I cannot impart to you what we propose to do, but I assert that our military plans make it necessary for the inhabitants to go away, and I can only renew my offer of services to make their exodus in any direction as easy and comfortable as possible.

You cannot qualify war in harsher terms than I will. War is cruelty, and you cannot refine it; and those who brought war into our country deserve all the curses and maledictions a people can pour out. I know I had no hand in making this war, and I know I will make more sacrifices to-day than any of you to secure peace. But you cannot have peace and a division of our country. If the United States submits to a division now, it will not stop, but will go on until we reap the fate of Mexico, which is eternal war. The

United States does and must assert its authority, wherever it once had power; for, if it relaxes one bit to pressure, it is gone, and I believe that such is the national feeling. This feeling assumes various shapes, but always comes back to that of Union. Once admit the Union, once more acknowledge the authority of the national Government, and, instead of devoting your houses and streets and roads to the dread uses of war, I and this army become at once your protectors and supporters, shielding you from danger, let it come from what quarter it may. I know that a few individuals cannot resist a torrent of error and passion, such as swept the South into rebellion, but you can point out, so that we may know those who desire a government, and those who insist on war and its desolation.

You might as well appeal against the thunder-storm as against these terrible hardships of war. They are inevitable, and the only way the people of Atlanta can hope once more to live in peace and quiet at home, is to stop the war, which can only be done by admitting that it began in error and is perpetuated in pride.

We don't want your Negroes, or your horses, or your lands, or any thing you have, but we do want and will have a just obedience to the laws of the United States. That we will have, and if it involves the destruction of your improvements, we cannot help it.

You have heretofore read public sentiment in your newspapers, that live by falsehood and excitement; and the quicker you seek for truth in other quarters, the better. I repeat then that, by the original compact of government, the United States had certain rights in Georgia, which have never been relinquished and never will be; that the South began the war by seizing forts, arsenals, mints, custom-houses, etc., etc., long before Mr. Lincoln was installed, and before the South had one jot or tittle of provocation. I myself have seen in Missouri, Kentucky, Tennessee, and Mississippi, hundreds and thousands of women and children fleeing from your armies and desperadoes, hungry and with bleeding feet. In Memphis, Vicksburg, and Mississippi, we fed thousands upon thousands of the families of rebel soldiers left on our hands, and whom we could not see starve. Now that war comes to you, you feel very different. You deprecate its horrors, but did not feel them when you sent car-loads of soldiers and ammunition, and moulded shells and shot, to carry war into Kentucky and Tennessee, to desolate the homes of hundreds and thousands of good people who only asked to live in peace at their old homes, and under the Government of their inheritance. But these comparisons are idle. I want peace, and believe it can only be reached through union and war, and I will ever conduct war with a view to perfect an early success.

But, my dear sirs, when peace does come, you may call on me for any thing. Then will I share with you the last cracker, and watch with you to shield your homes and families against danger from every quarter.

Now you must go, and take with you the old and feeble, feed and nurse them, and build for them, in more quiet places, proper habitations to shield them against the weather until the mad passions of men cool down, and allow the Union and peace once more to settle over your old homes in Atlanta. Yours in haste,

W. T. Sherman, *Major-General commanding*

General Robert E. Lee to His Army

On April 7, 1865, Ulysses S. Grant wrote to Robert E. Lee recommending that he consider surrendering to spare any further "effusion of blood." Later that evening Lee wrote back asking what the terms of surrender would be. Grant responded: "I would say that, peace being my greatest desire, there is but one condition I would insist upon, namely: that the men and officers surrendered shall be disqualified for taking up arms against the Government of the United States." Lee asked that they meet in person. On April 9, Grant met Lee, with whom he had served in the Mexican War, and officially accepted his surrender. At Lee's request he then ordered that rations of food be sent to Lee's starving soldiers. The next day, Lee addressed the following message to his troops.

Headquarters, Army of Northern Virginia
April 10, 1865

After four years of arduous service, marked by unsurpassed courage and fortitude, the Army of Northern Virginia has been compelled to yield to overwhelming numbers and resources. I need not tell the survivors of so many hard-fought battles, who have remained steadfast to the last, that I have consented to this result from no distrust of them; but, feeling that valor and devotion could accomplish nothing that could compensate for the loss that would have attended the continuation of the contest, I have determined to avoid the useless sacrifice of those whose past services have endeared them to their countrymen. By the terms of the agreement, officers and men can return to their homes and remain there until exchanged. You will take with you the satisfaction that proceeds from the consciousness of duty faithfully performed; and I earnestly pray that a merciful God will extend to you His blessing and protection. With an increasing admiration of your constancy and devotion to your country, and a grateful remembrance of your kind and generous consideration of myself, I bid you an affectionate farewell.

R. E. Lee, General

General Ulysses S. Grant to His Wife Julia

"Whatever may have been my political opinions before," wrote Ulysses S. Grant to his father on April 21, 1861, "I have but one sentiment now. That is we have a Government, and laws and a flag and they must all be sustained. There are but two parties now, Traitors & Patriots and I want hereafter to be ranked with the latter." Four years later, and on the verge of winning the nation's most consequential war since the American Revolution, Grant neither boasted about his victory nor condemned the South. The tone of his correspondence, in fact, was one of sympathy. In a short letter to his wife, Julia Dent Grant, he wrote the following.

In the Field Raleigh Apl. 25th 1865

Dear Julia,

We arrived here yesterday and as I expected to return to-day did not intend to write until I returned. Now however matters have taken such a turn I suppose Sherman will finish up matters by tomorrow night and I shall wait to see the result.

Raleigh is a very beautiful place. The grounds are large and filled with the most beautiful spreading oaks I ever saw. Nothing has been destroyed and the people are anxious to see peace restored so that further devastation need not take place in the country. The suffering that must exist in the South the next year, even with the war ending now, will be beyond conception. People who talk now of further retalliation and punishment, except of the political leaders, either do not conceive of the suffering endured already or they are heartless and unfeeling and wish to stay at home, out of danger, whilst the punishment is being inflicted.

Love and Kisses for you and the children,

ULYS.

Frances Watkins Harper to William Still

While the end of the Civil War brought an overwhelming sense of relief and joy to most Americans, the celebratory mood was tempered by the news that Abraham Lincoln had been shot on April 14. Many blacks, in particular, saw Lincoln as the "Great Emancipator" and were shocked and devastated when he died on April 15. A prominent African American poet and lecturer, Frances Ellen Watkins Harper used her renowned literary and oratorical skills to spread the antislavery message throughout the United States. In a letter to fellow abolitionist William Still, Harper reflects on slavery and the assassination of the man who hastened its demise.

Boston

Sorrow treads on the footsteps of the nation's joy. A few days since the telegraph thrilled and throbbed with a nation's joy. To-day a nation sits down beneath the shadow of its mournful grief. Oh, what a terrible lesson does this event read to us! A few years since slavery tortured, burned, hung and outraged us, and the nation passed by and said, they had nothing to do with slavery where it was, slavery would have something to do with them where they were. Oh, how fearfully the judgments of Ichabod have pressed upon the nation's life! Well, it may be in the providence of God this blow was needed to intensify the nation's hatred of slavery, to show the utter fallacy of basing national reconstruction upon the votes of returned rebels, and rejecting loyal black men; making (after all the blood poured out like water, and wealth scattered like chaff) a return to the old idea that a white rebel is better or of more account in the body politic than a loyal black man.

Moses, the meekest man on earth, led the children of Israel over the Red Sea, but was not permitted to see them settled in Canaan. Mr. Lincoln has led us through another Red Sea to the table land of triumphant victory, and God has seen fit to summon for the new era another man. It is ours then to bow to the Chastener and let our honored and loved chieftain go. Surely the everlasting arms that have hushed him so strangely to sleep are able to guide the nation through its untrod future; but in vain should be this fearful baptism of blood if from the dark bosom of slavery springs such terrible crimes. Let the whole nation resolve that the whole virus shall be eliminated from its body; that in the future slavery shall only be remembered as a thing of the past that shall never have the faintest hope of a resurrection.

Letters of War

*H*ow I wish this cruel business of war could be completed quickly. Entirely aside from longing to return to you (and stay there) it is a terribly sad business to total up the casualties each day—even in an air war—and to realize how many youngsters are gone forever. A man must develop a veneer of callousness that lets him consider such things dispassionately; but he can never escape a recognition of the fact that back home the news brings anguish and suffering to families all over the country. Mothers, fathers, brothers, sisters, wives and friends must have a difficult time preserving any comforting philosophy and retaining any belief in the eternal rightness of things. War demands real toughness of fiber—not only in the soldiers that must endure, but in the homes that must sacrifice their best.

General Dwight D. Eisenhower to his wife Mamie;
April 16, 1944

Clara Barton to Jessie Gladden

Known as the "Angel of the Battlefield," Clara Barton tended to sick and wounded soldiers during the Civil War and worked afterward to locate missing prisoners of war. A small woman (she stood barely five feet tall) who suffered from poor health most of her life, Barton was forty when she began her work behind the lines in hospitals and at training camps nursing soldiers, cooking food, helping with letters home, and providing solace to those who were dying. Believing her efforts to be inadequate, Barton traveled to the front lines and assisted injured soldiers on the battlefield, often at grave personal risk. After the war she was determined to assist victims of natural disasters in peacetime, and in 1881 she founded the American Red Cross, which is now the nation's foremost volunteer emergency services organization. At the age of seventy-six Barton was asked to affirm her support for the American soldier, and she responded with the following.

Washington, D.C., Nov. 7, 1898

Jessie L. Gladden,
P. O. Box 528,
Pueblo, Col.

Dear Madame,

I am in receipt of your request for a brief expression "relative to the noble work of our soldiers and sailors." I was with our boys constantly during the four years of our Civil War, and during the entire time of the late Spanish-American War; and being thoroughly American myself, it is needless for me to say I love and admire the American soldier, and think him equal, if not the superior, of any warrior of any time. He is not only brave but he is generous; and when he has fought for a principle and won, he has no desire to crush his foe, but is eager to abide by the old Latin maxim of "live and let live;" and he forgets and forgives, and lends a helping hand when a disposition to do the right thing is shown. The soldiers of this country know me and my feelings for them too well to need any extended assurance of my faithfulness to them; and they know that as long as I live there will be no truer friend to them than,

Yours sincerely,
Clara Barton

Theodore Roosevelt to Mrs. William Brown Meloney

The embodiment of rugged masculinity and adventure, Theodore Roosevelt did not take kindly to pacifists. When, in 1914, hostilities between Germany and America's European Allies exploded, the former president demanded that the United States involve itself militarily. President Woodrow Wilson argued that America should remain neutral, proclaiming in one speech: "There is such a thing as being too proud to fight. There is such a thing as a nation being so right that it does not need to convince others by force." Roosevelt scoffed at this and publicly called President Wilson "yellow." Eight months before the United States finally declared war on Germany, Roosevelt wrote the following letter to a friend, Mrs. William Brown Meloney.

August 5, 1916

Dear Mrs. Meloney:

There are a good many things that America needs, if Santa Claus could only give them!

Here are a few of them.

1. That every molly-coddle, professional pacifist, and man who is "too proud to fight" when the nation's quarrel is just, should be exiled to those out of the way parts . . . where the spirit of manliness has not yet penetrated.

2. That every decent young man should have a family, a job, and the military training which will enable him to keep this country out of war by making it dangerous for any ruthless military people to attack us.

3. That every youngster should have a good and wise mother; and every good woman a child for her arms.

4. That we may all of us become an efficient, patriotic, and nobly proud people—too proud either to inflict wrong or to endure it.

Good luck, Always yours

Theodore Roosevelt

Adrian Edwards to His Mother

At the age of thirty-four, Adrian Edwards, a lawyer from Carrollton, Illinois, became one of the two million American men who volunteered to serve in World War I. In early May 1918, writing from "somewhere in France," Edwards penned the following letter to his mother to be delivered to her in the event of his death.

My dear Mother:

I am about to go into battle and have instructed the company clerk to send you this letter in case I become a casualty, hence the receipt of this letter by you will indicate that I am either with God or a prisoner in the hands of the enemy.

Since I will never become a prisoner of the foe if I remain conscious and able to fight, it is doubtful if I will ever be an inmate of a German prison camp.

Do not grieve that I am among the missing, but rather rejoice that you have given a son in sacrifice to make the greatest military caste of all time lay down the sword—to save civilization, to prevent future wars, to punish the Germans, who have disregarded every law of God and mankind, whose only god is the god of war and military force—and to make the world safe for democracy.

I desire that you view the matter in the light and spirit of the

Spartan mothers of old, who, when their sons went forth to battle for freedom and their native land, said to their sons: "Either come home proudly bearing your shield before you, or upon it."

War was absolutely necessary on the part of my country, and although I was thirty-four years old and nobody expected me to go, yet some one had to go; some one must make the sacrifice, some mother must lose her son.

In the light of these facts, and knowing our country's great need, I volunteered, and have never for one moment regretted my decision, and I will not, although my life and a useful career must end. Life is not the highest boon of existence. There are ideals that are superhuman, interests greater than life itself, for which it is worth while fighting, suffering, and dying.

If possible after the war, I would like for my remains to be brought to America and interred at White Hall. I have provided well for your support, as I have a $10,000 insurance policy with the Government and several thousand with the old-line companies. My friends, Thompson and Jess, have these policies and other valuable papers.

Good-bye, Mother; I will see you in the next world. You may know I died fighting for you, my country, and all that life holds dear.

Your son
Adrian

Only days after writing this letter, Adrian Edwards was killed in battle.

Helen Keller to Eugene V. Debs

In the early to mid-1900s, Helen Keller grew increasingly famous for her ability—despite being both blind and deaf—to articulate her views on a range of social issues. Born into an extremely conservative southern family, Keller was a staunch feminist and pacifist who joined the Socialist Party of America in 1909. There she became friends with the party's leader, Eugene V. Debs. In the following letter to Debs, who had just learned he would be going to prison for publicly expressing his antiwar views, Keller expresses her own unwavering opposition to war as well as her deep admiration for Debs and his cause.

March 11, 1919
Forest Hills, New York

Dear Comrade,—

Of course the Supreme Court has sustained the decision of the lower court in your case. To my mind, the decision has added another laurel to your wreath of victories. Once more you are going to prison for upholding the liberties of the people.

I write because my heart cries out, it will not be still. I write because I want you to know that I should be proud if the Supreme Court convicted me of abhorring war, and doing all in my power to oppose it. When I think of the millions who have suffered in all the wicked wars of the past, I am shaken with the anguish of a great impatience. I want to fling myself against all brute powers that destroy the life, and break the spirit of man.

In the persecution of our comrades there is one satisfaction. Every trial of men like you, every sentence against them, tears away the veil that hides the face of the enemy. The discussion and agitation that follow the trials define more sharply the positions that must be taken before all men can live together in peace, happiness and security.

We were driven into the war for liberty, democracy and humanity. Behold what is happening all over the world today! Oh where is the swift vengence of Jehovah that it does not fall upon the hosts of those who are marshalling machine-guns against hungry-stricken peoples? It is the complacency of madness to call such acts "preserving law and order." What oceans of blood and tears are shed in their name! I have come to loathe traditions and institutions that take away the rights of the poor and protect the wicked against judgment.

The wise fools who sit in the high places of justice fail to see that in revolutionary times like the present vital issues are settled, not by statutes, decrees and authorities, but in spite of them. Like the Girondines of France they imagine that force can check the onrush of revolution. Thus they sow the wind, and unto them shall be the harvest of the whirlwind.

You dear comrade! I have long loved you because you are an apostle of brotherhood and freedom. For years I have thought of you as a dauntless explorer going toward the dawn, and, like a humble adventurer, I have followed in the trail of your footsteps. From time to time the greetings that have come back to me from you have made me very happy, and now I reach out my hand and clasp yours through prison bars.

With heartfelt greetings and with a firm faith that the cause for which you are now martyred shall be all the stronger because of your sacrifice and devotion, I am,

Yours for the Revolution,—May it come swiftly, like a shaft sundering the dark.

Helen Keller

Stand up! ye wretched ones who labor.
Stand up! ye galley-slaves of want.
Man's reason thunders from its crater
'Tis the eruption none can daunt
Of the past let us cleanse the tables
Mass enslaved, fling back the call;
Old earth is changing her foundations
We have been nothing, now be all
'Tis the last cause to battle!
Close the ranks, each in place,
The staunch old International
Shall be the Human race.

Frank Lloyd Wright to Lewis Mumford

In the years leading up to World War II many Americans were ambivalent about, if not adamantly opposed to, their country's entry into another major conflict. The great American architect Frank Lloyd Wright, a lifelong pacifist, was against U.S. involvement and voiced his sentiments frequently and openly. In May 1941, Wright's close friend Lewis Mumford, who was considered to be, among many other things, one of the greatest critics of urban architecture, publicly denounced Wright's antiwar views and accused Wright of condemning the British Empire without saying a word about the "Slave Empire" of Germany. "You are not man enough," Mumford argued, "to state openly the only terms on which Americans could purchase peace or security in such a world—namely by active cooperation [in the war]." Ironically, Mumford had recently submitted a glowing profile of Wright and his architectural work to The New Yorker *magazine. Wright knew of the profile but was nevertheless enraged by Mumford's attack and could not contain his enmity. On June 3, 1941, he sent Mumford the following letter.*

My dear Lewis:

When, because of a difference of feeling and judgement, you can shamelessly insult one who has trusted your sincerity, admired your ability, and praised you as a manly man, well, Lewis, I can understand your anguish and desire for revenge—but I say such reactions as yours are certainly not trustworthy when and wherever the welfare of our nation is at stake—I believe it to be, and you say you believe it to be, in danger.

Be ashamed Lewis, some day—but take your time. I am human grass roots in the service of the culture of a beloved country. I can give you time.

For the same reason that I despise eclecticism and reaction I despise your attitude toward war and Empire. There is no good Empire; there never was a just war. I despise your attitude now as I despised the setting sun all Europe mistook for dawn. It was called the "Renaissance."

If going to war is now your way, you have never really settled anything for yourself nor ever will settle anything for anyone else. Yours is the mind that would throw the dead cat back and forth across the backyard fence.

And I don't mean what you mean when I say "I love English." I love my England. You love yours. I hate master-empire or slave-empire. So my England is not your England and I am thankful.

You prate of culture, Lewis. Organic character is the basis of true greatness in that or in any individual concern or in any nation. War is the negation of this potentiality now as ever and forever. You knew that and yet sometime ago you wrote to me that you "had been busy getting the United States ready to fight and having accomplished that to your satisfaction you were ready to go back and write another book."

Christ, Lewis, is it possible that you are unable to see your own hypocrisy? Why do you try to hide behind what you call mine?

No honest believer in truth or beauty in his right mind could do what you say you have done. Time will discover you a deserter. A traitor on a battle-field that did you honor only to discover in you a vengeful, conceited writer, another writer out of ideas. The Chinese say it well: "He who runs out of ideas first strikes the first blow."

You standing for the time-cursed expedient with the frightened crowds! What a disappointment! And yet I could take it all from you because you are young and still be your friend if I believed you sincere in your anguish and desire for revenge. But you are not.

You prate of "downtrodden democracies" and of "defending slaves," only to justify your own impotence and rage. Why not honestly examine your own heart? What you would see there is what you accuse me of . . . hypocrisy.

Listen my young friend! I liked to call and talk to you occasionally when I got to the great city but I see now that you, too, are yellow with this strange but ancient sickness of the soul: the malady that has thrown down civilization after civilization by meeting force with force. Is meeting force with force the only way you see? Then I am sorry for you—you amateur essayist on culture. It is not the only way I see. I—a builder—see that there is still a chance for democracy on this continent just because the leaders of our culture are not all like Lewis Mumford, as he snarls and shows his teeth now.

Goodbye, Lewis, I shall read your "brief" in The New Yorker with shame. I shall read it knowing your real opinion is worthless whatever you may write.

Lewis Mumford ultimately lost a son in the war, and years later he and Wright reconciled.

President Franklin D. Roosevelt to Prime Minister Winston Churchill

When Winston Churchill became England's prime minister in May 1940, after the Nazi invasion of Denmark and Norway, he implored the United States for weapons and material aid. But the United States, still unwilling to become directly or significantly involved, responded with a relatively small supply of arms and ammunition. Then, on December 7, 1941, Pearl Harbor was attacked, and the American public was galvanized. One day later America announced its entry into the war. In a secret two-sentence cable, probably the shortest in the six-year history of the Churchill/Roosevelt correspondence, the American president informed his ally and friend of his nation's momentous decision.

December 8, 1941.

To the Former Naval Person
London

The Senate passed the all-out declaration of war eighty-two to nothing, and the House has passed it three hundred eighty-eight to one. Today all of us are in the same boat with you and the people of the Empire and it is a ship which will not and cannot be sunk.

F.D.R.

First Lady Eleanor Roosevelt to the President & An African American Soldier, "George," to His Sister

Over one million African American men would go on to serve their country in World War II, but they had to eat, live, train, and fight in segregated units. One of the earliest proponents of desegregating the armed services was First Lady Eleanor Roosevelt. In the following letter, addressed directly to the president, she recommends a meeting between black leaders such as Walter White (executive secretary of the National Association for the Advancement of Colored People [NAACP]), T. Arnold Hill (former industrial secretary of the Urban League), and A. Philip Randolph (president of the Brotherhood of Sleeping Car Porters) with Secretary of War Henry L. Stimson.

I have just heard that no meeting was ever held between colored leaders like Walter White, Mr. Hill and Mr. Randolph, with the secretary of War and Navy on the subject of how the colored people can participate in the services.

There is growing feeling amongst the colored people, and they are creating a feeling among many white people. They feel they should be allowed to participate in any training that is going on, in the aviation, army, navy, and have opportunities for service.

I would suggest that a conference be held with the attitude of the gentlemen: these are our difficulties, how do you suggest that we make a beginning to change the situation?

There is no use of going into a conference unless they have the intention of doing something. This is going to be very bad politically, besides being intrinsically wrong, and I think you should ask that a meeting be held and if you can not be present yourself, you should ask them to give you a report and it might be well to have General Watson present.

E. R.

A meeting did take place after Eleanor Roosevelt's letter, and Mssrs. White, Hill, and Randolph met with the president himself at the White House. Two days later, the White House issued a statement that "the services of the Negroes would be utilized on a fair and equitable basis." In fact, no changes were made and African American soldiers continued to suffer institutional discrimination and even physical abuse at the hands of white soldiers and officers. Although the background of the soldier who wrote the following letter is not known, the letter reflects the honor he felt serving his country and his dismay at how he and other African Americans were being treated.

Somewhere in France
March 19, 1945

Dear Sis:

Don't be surprised when you receive this letter and find that I am giving serious thought to our race, its problems and its contributions to the welfare of mankind. I shall hope to be able to write a series of letters of this nature.

As you know, Sis, I'm not in a combat unit so I can only write of general conditions behind the "Lines." My story will be the same way that many will have to tell someday.

I am in the Service Force. It is a very important branch of service. It's all work. Yes, the hours are sometimes very long. However, I can work with that certain satisfaction that my work behind the "Lines" is the only direct support that the men "Up Front" have. If that convoy with supplies is late because it was not started promptly as ordered the men "Up Front" may meet with capture, unnecessary hardship or even death, because the ammunition or rations were not at the proper place at the proper time. If that Liberty ship isn't unloaded as soon as possible it may miss the convoy and sometimes cost our government the ship and the lives of the men aboard. So you can see why the cry behind the "Lines" is, "Work so that your Combat Buddy may live."

All of us have many reasons for wanting to stay in the States. Yet we know that the war can't be won by our attending dances and enjoying weekend passes. Yes, we too are "Red Blooded Americans" and have as much at stake as anybody. Yes, we have a share in the American Way of Life. We came from all parts of America but we are still Americans. We hope that the American People won't forget that if we can work and fight for the Democratic Way, that we are entitled to enjoy every privilege it affords when this mess is over.

The going is tough over here. Daily you are thinking of that darling wife, dear mother or sweetheart. You know that feeling that one gets when the mailman passes and doesn't have any mail. It's funny, Sis, but true. When all around me was covered with snow, we lived in tents. Now that the snow is gone, we are living in houses. Well, what do you think of that? I would call all of this mental torture.

To add to this mental torture we read of those darn strikes and riots over there. We are here to help make the world a decent place for all men to live.

Even though we are in the war we have instances of inter-American conflicts. Yes, Sis, I've met many of the Apostles of Jim Crowisms on foreign soil. Over in England they would try to spread their Doctrine at the Dances, Cafés and Public Houses (Beer Gardens). The way they acted whenever we were around you wouldn't think that we were Americans, too.

Yes, there have been times when the colored and white boys would just fight it out. At this time it seemed like the Negro soldier would have to fight two wars over here. You get pretty low in spirit and just say, "Away with it all." My language would be familiar with the marines. You know me, Sis. I have named the times of such happenings "The Down Beat."

Victory is in sight. We are all confident in the ability of our men "Up Front." I thank God for giving the soldier of color the intestinal fortitude to go on and do a good job in spite of the odds that have been against him. We still have men fighting and dying in the Theatres of War. The colored men stuck to their assigned jobs; if they didn't the men "Up Front" would have known better than anyone else. In closing, Sis, I will write a few words penned by the great Negro poet Dunbar, "Out of the hell and dawn of it all, cometh good."

Best wishes,
Your Brother
George

It would not be until 1948, when President Harry Truman issued Executive Order 9981, that the official policy of the military would be enforced as: "equality of treatment and opportunity for all persons in the armed forces without regard to race, color, religion, or national origin."

Shirley Band to the *U. S. Coast Guard Magazine*

Tens of millions of American women contributed to the war effort at home and abroad, serving as air raid wardens, fund-raisers, radio operators, gunner's mates, and nurses. Hundreds of thousands of women joined the Women's Army Corps, the Navy's Women Accepted for Volunteer Emergency Service (WAVES), and the Coast Guard's SPARs (derived from the Coast Guard motto: Semper Paratus, *"Always Ready"). The following letter to the* U. S. Coast Guard Magazine *demonstrates the hope of one young woman, Shirley Band, to participate in winning the war.*

[Dear Editor]:

Why aren't girls of seventeen and eighteen permitted to join the SPARS, while boys of seventeen are allowed in the Coast Guard? Is it fair to make girls between seventeen and twenty sit at home and pray for their twenty-first birthday to hurry, while the boys of the same age, (and mentally, if not less) are fighting the enemy in rough and dangerous waters? No! It is absolutely wrong. There is a saying, "All is fair in love and war," but honestly, is it fair for us to twiddle our thumbs, while boys are getting their arms and legs shot off?

I am a girl nearing my seventeenth birthday. I expect to finish high school in a few months. What am I going to do after I graduate? Buy war bonds and stamps? We all know that is not enough. I am a normal, healthy, American girl, willing to do more than buy stamps and bonds. Of course, I can join the Red Cross, or the American Women's Voluntary Services, but why not leave that for the older women. I want to join the SPARS, knowing I am taking the place of a Coast Guardsman, and relieving him for actual fighting duty. I want to be an aid to my country, directly, not indirectly.

If my brothers and friends are old enough to join the Coast Guard and Navy at seventeen and up, I certainly should be permitted to join very soon, on my seventeenth birthday. So, please, who ever is in charge of the Spars, please lower the enlistment age to seventeen and make my seventeenth birthday the happiest.

I know I am speaking for millions of girls who feel the same way about this subject.

The policy was not changed.

Iwao Matsushita to Attorney General Francis Biddle

"It was not in keeping with our American concept of freedom and the rights of citizens," wrote Chief Justice Earl Warren in 1977 on the internment of Japanese Americans during World War II. "It demonstrates the cruelty of war when fear, get-tough military psychology, propaganda, and racial antagonism combine with one's responsibility for public security to produce such acts." Warren, who had been attorney general of California in 1942, played a prominent role in encouraging the U.S. Government to force 120,000 Japanese Americans out of their homes and into internment and War Relocation Authority camps. In some cases husbands and wives, and even entire families, were split apart. Iwao Matsushita, detained in Montana, was separated from his wife, Hanaye, detained in Idaho. In the following letter Matsushita pleads to the attorney general of the United States, Francis Biddle, to let him join his wife so that they could at least be incarcerated together.

Fort Missoula, Montana
Jan. 2, 1943

The Honorable Francis Biddle,
Attorney General,
Washington, D.C.
Dear Mr. Biddle,

I, Iwao Matsushita, an alien Japanese, have been detained in Fort Missoula, since Dec. 28, 1941, and I was recently notified about my internment order, despite the fact the Hearing Board made a recommendation for my release.

Since I read your article in a magazine last spring, regarding your policy of treating "alien enemies"—the words, you mentioned, you even didn't like to use—you have been occupying the innermost shrine of my heart as my only refuge and savior. So when I received your internment order, I was naturally greatly disappointed, because according to your intrepretation in the magazine, you intern only those aliens whom you consider to be potentially dangerous to the public safety.

Now, my conscience urges me to make a personal heart-to-heart appeal to you. Kindly allow me to make a brief statement about myself.

I was born a Christian in a Methodist minister's family, educated in an American Mission School, came to this country in 1919 from sheer admiration of the American way of life. I have always been living, almost half and best part of my life, in Seattle, Wash., and never went to Japan for the last twenty-four years, despite the fact there were many such opportunities, simply because I liked this country, and the principles on which it stands.

I have never broken any Federal, State, Municipal, or even traffic laws, and paid taxes regularly. I believe myself one of the most upright persons. I have never been, am not, and will never be potentially dangerous to the safety of the United States. There isn't an iota of dangerous elements in me, nor should there be any such evidence against me.

On the contrary I have done much good to the American

public. For instance, several years ago, I taught Japanese Language in the University of Washington, Seattle, without any compensation to help out the institution, which couldn't get appropriation for that purpose from the State. I might prove to be of some service in this capacity.

I am quite sure that my life history and my statement regarding loyalty in the hearing record will certainly convince you that I am a bona fide loyal resident.

My wife, with whom I have never been separated even for a short time during the last twenty-five years, and who has the same loyalty and admiration for this country, is living helplessly and sorrowfully in Idaho Relocation Center. You are the only person who can make us join in happiness and let us continue to enjoy the American life.

Therefore, please give my case your special reconsideration and let me anticipate your favorable answer.

Yours respectfully,
Iwao Matsushita

One year after this letter was written, Matsushita and his wife were re-united in Hunt, Iowa. In August 1988, forty-three years after the end of World War II, a law was enacted to recompense the victims of the internments; every living Japanese American who had been detained received a payment of twenty thousand dollars, along with an official apology from the United States of America.

George Saito to His Father

Ironically, a regiment composed entirely of Japanese American soldiers—most of whom were the sons of parents detained in the camps—went on to become one of the most highly decorated units in World War II. Military leaders were originally reluctant to let Japanese Americans fight, but they finally relented and created the 442nd Regimental Combat Team. The 442nd gained acclaim for saving members of the 141st Regiment's First Battalion, known as "The Lost Battalion," who were trapped by the

Germans in Italy and went without food or supplies for eight days. Although the cause was deemed hopeless, the 442nd was sent in and, after a ferocious battle, successfully carried out the rescue. (Approximately 800 members of the 442nd were killed trying to save 211 members of the 141st.) One of the members of the unit, George Saito, was serving overseas with his brother, Calvin, while the rest of the Saito family was being held in an internment camp in the States. The following letter was written by George on July 11, 1944—over three and a half months before the famed Lost Battalion rescue—to his father, Kiichi Saito, four days after his brother was killed in action.

Dear "dad"—

I believe the War Dept. has notified you of our loss of "Calvin"—Dad I am writing you now because I've just learned of his passing—July 7th was the immemorable day—

I can imagine what a shock it was to you, as it was to me, because it happened so soon—on the 12th day of combat—

A few events and action leading up to the time of his loss as related by a member of his company, are—On the 6th of July his unit was attacking a hill held by the enemy—After a hard fight with even a little hand to hand combat, they took the hill—The Jerries, after being shoved off were reforming for a counter-attack—In the confusion and disorder of battle, "Cal" being the radio-man, somehow, got a call thru to the artillery to open fire on the enemy—He personally directed and guided the firing on the enemy positions which routed the enemy—His action and doing his job well at this one instance, explained the fellows, saved many of his buddies—Their unit held that hill that night but the next morning the enemy barraged the hill with mortars and he happened to be one of the unlucky ones—His passing was instantaneous—All of the fellows were telling me what a good soldier and radio-man he was and that his loss was keenly felt—

Well dad—now that the inevitable has happened I guess you're wondering about his remains—Right now I can't do much for we're still in battle and I am writing you while at our gun position, but as I understand things now—they will bury him here in Italy and after the war you can ask the Government to transfer them to an American cemetary in the States. His personal belongings will be shipped to you in time—

Dad—this is not time to be preaching to you but I have something on my chest which I want you to hear—In spite of "Cal" 's supreme sacrifice don't let anyone tell you that he was foolish or made a mistake to "volunteer" Of what I've seen in my travels on our mission I am more than convinced that we've done the right thing in spite of what has happened in the past—America is a damn good country and don't let anyone tell you otherwise—

Well dad, the Germans are beginning to throw a few shells our way now so maybe I'd better get down in my hole If there is anything also that you'd like to know except the place I shall only be too glad to let you know In time tho' when we're allowed I'll give you the exact location—

Cheer up "dad" and do take care of yourself—Regards to all—

Your loving son
"George"

Tragically, three months after sending his father this letter, George Saito was also killed in battle.

Erwin Blonder to His Father and Brother

Twenty-three years old at the time, Second Lt. Erwin Blonder was a forward artillery observer—one of the most dangerous positions in battle—fighting near Bruyères, France, in September 1944. Newly married, Blonder did not want his wife or sister-in-law, Dorothy, to know of his situation, but he wanted his family, back in Ohio, to know he was alive and well. He sent the following letter to his father and his older brother, Jerome, who were managing a family business that distributed wall coverings throughout the Midwest.

September 30, 1944

Dear Dad and Jerry,

I am writing this letter to you to get certain things off my mind. I am telling this to you because I want to spare Shirlee the horrible details of war and I don't want this letter shown to either her, Mother, or even Dorothy. Another reason I am writing this to you is that I want these thoughts of mine recorded so in later years I can read them and use them in getting a better understanding of life instilled in my children.

I am well and in the best spirits possible for times like these. As I now write the guns are booming out sending their missiles of death to the enemy. I am not writing this to be dramatic but to show what thoughts are passing through my mind.

As you know, I have been transferred to another Battalion. The reason was one that had nothing to do with me personally but one that was a matter of necessity. As far as Mother and Shirlee are concerned, I am with the Service Battery of the Battalion. They worry enough without knowing what my real job is. I hope I am doing the right thing.

I am a Forward Observer for the Battalion. My job is to go along with the Infantry and conduct the firing of Field Artillery as the situation demands. I have seen and experienced things that I never dreamed of seeing and will never forget. The most honest words ever spoken were when Sherman said "War is Hell." Never were truer words spoken. It is a living hell that men endure because of things we are willing to give our lives for.

Now to relate a few of my own personal experiences. As you all know by now our campaign here has considerably slowed down because the enemy is trying to prevent us from reaching the borders of Germany.

You all read about our crossing a river and establishing ourselves permanently on the other side. We walked all night through a fog to reach the point we were going to cross. We arrived at dawn and I was the second artilleryman to cross. We had to wade across. The river was waist deep and the current was strong.

A rope was tied across so we could use it to steady ourselves. When I plunged in my thoughts were not upon the cold water and getting wet but getting to the other side and getting a place of cover in case the enemy fired on us. The river was 50 feet wide and I got across and up the bank to the protection of a farm house. The next thing I knew I saw two Germans coming down a road on bicycles. An Infantry man waited until they came near the house and then stepped out and stuck a gun in front of them. They stopped and shouted Comrade and easily gave up. Nothing happened and I pushed out with the Infantry. We came to a wreck and I couldn't get observation to shoot and I started back to a better point for observation. As I started across an open field a German sniper started to fire at me. I fell and layed on the ground. I started to run again and a bullet whizzed over my head and again I fell flat on my stomach. I was never so scared in my life. I had to get back and couldn't stay there forever. Then I thought of the words of a friend. "A rifle bullet has to hit you before it does any damage." I debated with myself, the pros and cons of this argument. Then I came to the conclusion that this sniper couldn't watch forever. So with a fervent prayer to God I started to run again and safely made my destination. Here we call this type of thing "Sweat it out." We moved over hill and forest and encountered a few Germans. I have never seen men get hit standing near me and I saw an artillery shell chew up one of my men. At least he never knew what hit him. I have seen many dead Germans. I used to be afraid of dead people but they don't bother me anymore. I have been in artillery barrages where you sit and wait for each shell to burst. Waiting for the uncertain future to come. You don't have time to think of the future but only what you are going to do next. You figure and figure but never seem to get anywhere. You see Germans moving a thousand yards away from you and you bring artillery fire on them. They scatter like a barrel of chickens do when an auto comes down the road. You kill a few and wound some. You don't stop to think whether it is right or wrong but know that the more Germans you kill the quicker the war will be won. That seems to be the only thing they understand.

I have seen the suffering and experienced the suffering of the Infantryman. They are magnificent and have the dirtiest job to do. I have lived with them and eaten with them. They bitch and complain and cuss and swear. But they get their job done and do it well. They have protected me and have kept me out of tight spots.

My only thought is to get home safely to my wife, so she and I can live our lives the way we have always dreamed. I would gladly accept the hard work and worries of a thousand Blonder Company's. What I wouldn't give to file the bills again or talk to the painters and uncultured paperhangers. I hope that when peace descends upon the world again, we will prove capable of having peace. I don't want my children to endure the things I have.

These are a few thoughts that run through my mind. I fervently pray that it will all end very soon. The news sounds optimistic but here in a foxhole with shells bursting around you have to be a braver man than I am to be an optimist. There seems to be no end.

I know that everything is OK at home. I dream of all of you. Please don't show this letter to Shirlee, Dorothy, or Mom but save it for me for after the war. Give my regards to everyone. Take good care of yourselves until I return.

Erwin

This letter was written three weeks before Blonder and his unit, the First Battalion of the 141st Regiment, were fighting in Italy and suddenly found themselves surrounded by Germans. Attempts to drop them supplies failed repeatedly, and by the fourth day they had nothing to eat and had to drink from a nearby swamp. Blonder's feet froze and he was unable to walk. Finally, after eight days of insufferable conditions, the First Battalion was saved by the 442nd Regiment. Blonder was carried off the field on a stretcher and taken to a military hospital in France to recuperate. He returned to the United States on Christmas Eve 1944 and was awarded the Silver Star. Erwin Blonder is still happily married to Shirlee Blonder.

Willson Price to Rosalie "Rose" James

Their mission was one of the great secrets of World War II. They were the Navajo "code talkers," American Indians recruited by the United States Marine Corps to communicate extremely sensitive military messages in the South Pacific. The Navajos used a code based on their native language to relay and receive information on troop movements, planned invasions, supply and ammunition demands, and other highly confidential matters. Although the Allied forces ultimately broke the Japanese code, the Japanese military could not penetrate the Navajo-based code—an advantage for the United States that proved invaluable in such battles as those at Iwo Jima and Okinawa. While all soldiers had to be cautious about divulging information on their location and responsibilities, the code talkers were censored more than any other troops. Their role was so confidential, in fact, that it was not disclosed until twenty-four years after the war. Even family members were not allowed to know. The strain of this secrecy proved trying, as demonstrated in the following letter (which has been edited slightly for clarity) by Willson Price, a Navajo writing to his beloved, Rosalie "Rose" James.

UNITED STATES MARINE CORPS
CAMP JOSEPH H. PENDLETON
OCEANSIDE, CALIFORNIA

July 22nd, 1944

Dearest Rose!

Your letter was received here yesterday afternoon. Glad to hear from you. I really don't have anything to tell you like I always do, because things are so different to me nowadays. That's why. I don't even care to write to any body not even my own folks.

I don't know when was the last time I wrote to them.

I hope they know where I am at this point in time.

I think that I mentioned to you that I was at sea for pretty near two months, and finally came back here at camp and am still going to school.

I really don't have any idea how long this school will be.

Remember some time ago, I had told you I was going on an other leave. But that has been changed.

I am not going. I don't think I will see you again, before I leave here for overseas again. I think we are about due, the way the training has been going the last three months.

I know it is pretty hard to say this. I really don't know what I mean to you. Why don't you just forget me and find some one else. That way you'll be happy and nothing to worry about. It's no use, for you, worrying yourself out. Just for your own good and health. I am not saying this because I dislike you. No that's not it. It's for you, I sure hate to see you worrying. Even though you promised me you will wait until I returned, but it's pretty hard to say. You might never see me again, the way this war has been going and the way the Marine Corps has been operating. I mean to face landing on the beach head, which I would hate to see again. But I think I have to face it. It does not matter, death. So what. I have not been out of this place for the week end, because I don't have time for it.

Everything is just fine around here, nothing much doing.

I think that will be all for this time. Good-by and so long.

God will care for you.

Love,
Price

When Willson Price returned to the States after the war, Rosalie James was waiting for him. They married and had four children, and Mrs. Price did not learn of her husband's role as a code talker until 1969, when their mission was finally declassified. Willson Price went on to fight in Korea and Vietnam, and, by the time he retired in 1972, he had served thirty years' active duty in the Marines—the longest of any code talker. He died in March 1993 at the age of seventy-two.

Joseph Fogg to His Parents

Disqualified for military service because of poor eyesight, Joseph G. Fogg volunteered as an ambulance driver with an American field service unit attached to the British Eighth Army. In April 1945, Fogg, 25, helped evacuate the Bergen-Belsen concentration camp in Germany. Sickened and outraged by what the Nazis had done, Fogg wrote the following account to his parents back in the States.

April 30

Dear Folks:

Am writing this from deep inside Germany. You are probably familiar with the story behind that. At any rate censorship apparently still denies an explanation.

In the following pages I shall attempt to record a sight that is well beyond the pale of verbal or written description—a sight that will sear my memory for all time to come. I cannot expect you to believe it—indeed I who have seen it cannot.

The Story.

We were called a long distance on emergency duty to transport a hospital to work in a newly liberated concentration camp. It was a camp for "political" prisoners of all nationalities—Russians, Czechs, Hungarians, Poles, French, Germans, etc. (many of them Jews)—located well away from any civilization. It is heavily barbwired and well screened from outside view by pine trees. Control towers are located at intervals on the perimeter such as you have seen in any prison at home—also dugouts and machine gun emplacements are displaced within the camp itself. The guards consisted of upwards of three hundred fifty élite SS troops and I don't know how many SS women. Near the camp in palatial barracks lived many more SS soldiers. The prisoners lived in rows of one story, green wooden barracks—the men being segregated from the women. Before launching into a description of the poor wretches themselves and conditions within, you must realize that I am only narrating what we saw today which is *after* the British had worked night and day for more than a week to ameliorate the situation. Also, any figures are only approximate. I doubt if exact ones will ever be known. The total number of men, women and children in the camp has been estimated at 53,000. The *daily* death rate is now about 350—an enormous decrease since work has begun.

The daily diet of *les miserables* consisted of one loaf of filthy bread to each 8 persons and a disgusting turnip and beetroot soup. For the last seven days prior to liberation they were given nothing. The result has been malnutrition on an unimaginable scale. Moreover, the barracks were (and many still are) so jammed with the poor devils that many had not even room to lie down. In one hut which I estimated to be 50 ft by 150 ft were 1250 women! In the entire camp there was not one latrine! The prisoners urinated etc outside on the ground. Those too weak to move simply evacuated where they lay—the stench inside was unbearable and the filth both inside and out indescribable. Each morning those strong enough dragged the ones who had died overnight outside the hut. Many dropped in their tracks during the day. The Germans cremated the bodies in a large crematorium in the center of camp, but towards the end they were unable to keep pace with the death rate and when the camp was liberated a pile of corpses table high stretching for hundreds of yards was left. I saw about 1,000 that had not yet been buried. The physical aspect and condition of those still alive can only be characterized as grotesque. They are living skeletons. I had never realized that people so thin could still be capable of motion. Children of seven or eight are scarcely the size of 2 yr. olds. All of them have a dazed look—the look of people who are long past caring about anything. Simply waiting for an end they know is inevitable. Although latrines have been brought in, many still stick to their old habits—incapable of helping themselves. Actually they are lower than animals, having wasted away without, their brains have atrophied within. They would be far better off with a merciful death.

About 50 of the SS guards were taken in the camp. Many were beaten to death by infuriated British soldiers. The rest were placed on the prisoners' diet and forced to bury the thousands of corpses lying about. Every move they made was on the double. When an order from General Dempsey came through the other day that the SS men were to be treated as prisoners of war, there were only a handful left who will ever be capable of much physical activity again. Same is true of the SS women.

You can easily imagine that the medical problems presented by this ghastly scene are enormous. Medical supplies, personnel, facilities are totally inadequate. Typhus is rampant and the most elaborate precautions must be taken. There is about one nurse and one medical officer to each 600 persons. Many of the prisoners are helping out and are being trained as nurses, orderlies etc. SS barracks have been made into hospital wards. Patients evacuated (by ambulances and lorries) from the camp are taken first to the "human laundry" where German men and women scrub and delouse them (some are too weak to survive this process). Their clothes are burned. About 650 are brought out daily. Thousands have not yet been touched and must live in the same filth until facilities are adequate to cope with them. Latrines have been placed everywhere as well as washing facilities. Food has been brought in, but diet is a very delicate problem for starving persons.

In startling contrast to this appalling misery and squalor and scarcely a mile away are the barracks of the SS soldiers, the very acme of luxury. The SS officers club is a large, modern structure furnished in the most lavish manner with loot from all over the continent. In the wine cellars are thousands of bottles (empty) of the choicest wines and liqueurs. A huge spotless kitchen with every modern convenience. We have had a field day looting the place.

I do not believe that people reared as we have been are capable of comprehending the type of mentality that can revel in such abysmal degradation of helpless human beings. It does not so much inspire hate (except at first) as stark disbelief. The only possible conclusion to reach is that the race should be exterminated—wiped from the face of the earth. If there are some who would argue a soft peace for these monstrous criminals, I would go to the end of the world to bring them back to this camp. I do not wish to sound dramatic, but I can assure you that I have been profoundly moved today. I have seen scores of medical men used to every type of suffering, absolutely bereft of speech.

Our own work has been mainly concerned with transporting medical personnel and supplies to this place. We presume and dread that shortly we will take some part in the evacuation of these wretches. It is certainly not our type of work, but has taught me more about the enemy than a thousand campaigns ever could. Personally, I am well and comfortable, though it is quite chilly here. British orders about fraternization with Germans are very strict (2 yrs in prison). Americans more lenient. You will note the A.P.O. number. For a long period we were unable to write at all and when finally permitted could say nothing—hence my silence. I am homesick again. Will request more vitamins, our diet being rather meager at the moment. The whirlwind conclusion of the Italian campaign has surprised no one more than myself. The walls are rapidly crumbling. Again I must apologize for my scanty correspondence. Hope you will convey my fondest regards to Uncle John, Aunt Lolette, and Kate Cushings etc and will send more observations along shortly.

best love

Joe

Harry S. Truman to Irv Kupcinet

Finally, in August 1945, after more than six years of fighting and with tens of millions of people killed worldwide, World War II was over. Although the world celebrated the end of the war, there was also intense debate about the use of the atomic bomb to bring it to a conclusion. "I realize the tragic significance of the atomic bomb," President Harry Truman said in a radio address before the Japanese finally surrendered, "[but we] have used it in order to shorten the agony of war, in order to save the lives of thousands and thousands of young Americans." Eighteen years later Truman felt just as strongly. He was still being criticized for his judgment, and he was grateful to those who supported him. In July of 1963, Irv Kupcinet of the Chicago Sun Times *wrote a favorable column on Truman and his decision, and Truman wrote the following letter in response.*

August 5, 1963

Dear Kup:

I appreciated most highly your column of July 30th, a copy of which you sent me.

I have been rather careful not to comment on the articles that have been written on the dropping of the bomb for the simple reason that the dropping of the bomb was completely and thoroughly explained in my Memoirs, and it was done to save 125,000 youngsters on the American side and 125,000 on the Japanese side from getting killed and that is what it did. It probably also saved a half million youngsters on both sides from being maimed for life.

You must always remember that people forget, as you said in your column, that the bombing of Pearl Harbor was done while we were at peace with Japan and trying our best to negotiate a treaty with them.

All you have to do is to go out and stand on the keel of the Battleship in Pearl Harbor with the 3,000 youngsters underneath it who had no chance whatever of saving their lives. That is true of two or three other battleships that were sunk in Pearl Harbor. Altogether, there were between 3,000 and 6,000 youngsters killed at that time without any declaration of war. It was plain murder.

I knew what I was doing when I stopped the war that would have killed a half million youngsters on both sides if those bombs had not been dropped. I have no regrets and, under the same circumstances, I would do it again—and this letter is not confidential.

Sincerely yours,
Harry S. Truman

Despite writing that the letter was not confidential, Truman told his secretary to hold it. The letter was never sent.

President John F. Kennedy to Soviet Leader Nikita Khrushchev

Four years after the end of World War II the Soviet Union developed its own atomic bomb, precipitating an arms race with the United States that led to the buildup of enough nuclear weapons to destroy both countries—if not the world. This possibility seemed a likelihood in October 1962, when an American U-2 spy plane photographed the installation of Soviet nuclear missiles in Cuba. President Kennedy called the act "a deliberately provocative and unjustified change in the status quo," ordered a naval quarantine around Cuba, and demanded that the Soviet Union dismantle and remove all missiles. As Soviet ships, presumably carrying more missiles, approached the American warships surrounding Cuba, the world held its breath. The Soviet ships ultimately turned back, but the conflict was not over—the more serious matter of the existing missiles had to be resolved. On October 26 Kennedy received a long, emotional letter from Soviet Premier Nikita Khrushchev on the horrors of nuclear war and with an offer to remove the missiles if the United States would end the quarantine and agree not to invade Cuba. Before Kennedy could answer, a second letter from Khrushchev was received the next morning. Its tone was stern and Khrushchev insisted on more concessions, including the removal of American missiles in Turkey. Robert Kennedy, serving as the U.S. Attorney General, advised his brother to ignore the second letter and respond to the first. Kennedy agreed and, in an attempt to end the most potentially catastrophic military crisis ever, sent Khrushchev the following reply on October 27.

Dear Mr. Chairman,

I have read your letter of October 26th with great care and welcomed the statement of your desire to seek a prompt solution to the problem. The first thing that needs to be done, however, is for work to cease on offensive missile bases in Cuba and for all weapons systems in Cuba capable of offensive use to be rendered inoperable, under effective United Nations arrangements.

Assuming this is done promptly, I have given my representatives in New York instructions that will permit them to work out this weekend—in cooperation with the Acting Secretary-General and your representatives—an arrangement for a permanent solution to the Cuban problem along the lines suggested in your letter of October 26th. As I read your letter, the key elements of your proposal—which seems generally acceptable as I understand them—are as follows:

1. You would agree to remove these weapons systems from Cuba under appropriate United Nations observation and supervision; and undertake, with suitable safeguards, to halt the further introduction of such weapons systems into Cuba.

2. We, on our part, would agree—upon the establishment of adequate arrangements through the United Nations to ensure the carrying out and continuation of these commitments—(a) to remove promptly the quarantine measures now in effect and (b) to give reassurances against an invasion of Cuba. I am confident that other nations of the Western Hemisphere would be prepared to do likewise.

If you will give your representative similar instructions, there is no reason why we should not be able to complete these arrangements and announce them to the world within a couple of days. The effect of such a settlement on easing world tensions would enable us to work toward a more general arrangement regarding "other armaments," as proposed in your second letter which you made public. I would like to say again that the United States is very interested in reducing tensions and halting the arms race; and if your letter signifies that you are prepared to discuss a détente affecting NATO and the Warsaw Pact, we are quite prepared to consider with our allies any useful proposals.

But the first ingredient, let me emphasize, is the cessation of work on missile sites in Cuba and measures to render such weapons inoperable, under effective international guarantees. The continuation of this threat, or a prolonging of this discussion concerning Cuba by linking these problems to the broader questions of European and world securities, would surely lead to an intensification of the Cuban crisis and a grave risk to the peace of the world. For this reason I hope we can quickly agree along the lines outlined in this letter and in your letter of October 26th.

Sincerely,
John F. Kennedy

Kennedy also verbally agreed, in a message forwarded to the Soviet ambassador, that he would remove America's missiles in Turkey. On October 28, Khrushchev accepted the conditions in Kennedy's letter, and the Cuban Missile Crisis was resolved.

Columbia Student Mark Rudd to Columbia University President Grayson Kirk & Bill Clinton to Col. Eugene Holmes

No other foreign war in America's history sparked the same degree of protest and outrage as the Vietnam War, with countless young men burning draft cards, declaring themselves conscientious objectors, and fleeing the United States to live abroad. Peace marches and rallies often exploded into violent confrontations, the worst being the deaths of four Kent State University students after National Guardsmen fired into a crowd of antiwar demonstrators. In spring 1968 Columbia University students raided the main administration building in response to the administration's support of the war and the university's affiliation with the Institute for Defense Analyses (IDA), which conducted weapons evaluation for the Defense Department. Columbia's president, Grayson Kirk, was infuriated by the students' actions: "Our young people, in disturbing numbers, appear to reject all forms of authority, from whatever source derived, and they have taken refuge in a turbulent and inchoate nihilism whose sole objectives are destruction. I know of no time in our history when the gap between the generations has been wider or more potentially dangerous." Student leader Mark Rudd responded with the following letter, dated April 22, attacking President Kirk and Columbia's vice president, David Truman. ("CC," which Rudd refers to, is the abbreviation for Contemporary Civilization, a mandatory class for all Columbia undergraduates that focuses on the "foundational" texts of Western philosophy.)

Dear Grayson,

Your charge of nihilism is indeed ominous; for if it were true, our nihilism would bring the whole civilized world, from Columbia to Rockefeller Center, crashing down upon all our heads. Though it is not true, your charge does represent something: you call it the generation gap. I see it as a real conflict between those who run things now—you, Grayson Kirk—and those who feel oppressed by, and disgusted with, the society you rule—we, the young people.

You might want to know what is wrong with this society, since, after all, you live in a very tight, self-created dream world. We can point to the war in Vietnam as an example of the unimaginable wars of aggression you are prepared to fight to maintain your control over your empire (now you've been beaten by the Vietnamese, so you call for a tactical retreat). We can point to your using us as cannon fodder to fight your war. We can point out your mansion window to the ghetto below you've helped to create through your racist University expansion policies, through your unfair labor practices, through your city government and your police. We can point to this University, your University, which trains us to be lawyers and engineers, and managers for your IBM, your Socony Mobil, your IDA, your Con Edison (or else to be scholars and teachers in more universities like this one). We can point, in short, to our own meaningless studies, our identity crises, and our revulsion with being cogs in your corporate machines as a product of and reaction to a basically sick society.

Your cry of "nihilism" represents your inability to understand our positive values. If you were ever to go into a freshman CC class you would see that we are seeking a rational basis for society. We do have a vision of the way things could be: how the tremendous resources of our economy could be used to eliminate want, how people in other countries could be free from your domination, how a university could produce knowledge for progress, not waste, consumption, and destruction (IDA), how men could be free to keep what they produce, to enjoy peaceful lives, to create. These are positive values, but since they mean the destruction of your order, you call them "nihilism." In the movement we are beginning to call this vision "socialism." It is a fine and honorable name, one which implies absolute opposition to your corporate capitalism and your government; it will soon be caught up by other young people who want to exert control over their own lives and their society.

You are quite right in feeling that the situation is "potentially dangerous." For if we win, we will take control of your world, your corporation, your University and attempt to mold a world in which we and other people can live as human beings. Your power is directly threatened, since we will have to destroy that power before we take over. We begin by fighting you about your support of the war in Vietnam and American imperialism—IDA and the School of International Affairs. We will fight you about your control of black people in Morningside Heights, Harlem, and the campus itself. And we will fight you about the type of mis-education you are trying to channel us through. We will have to destroy at times, even violently, in order to end your power and your system—but that is a far cry from nihilism.

Grayson, I doubt if you will understand any of this, since your fantasies have shut out the world as it really is from your thinking. Vice President Truman says the society is basically sound; you say the war in Vietnam was a well-intentioned accident. We, the young people, whom you so rightly fear, say that society is sick and you and your capitalism are the sickness.

You call for order and respect for authority; we call for justice, freedom, and socialism. There is only one thing left to say. It may sound nihilistic to you, since it is the opening shot in a war of liberation. I'll use the words of LeRoi Jones, whom I'm sure you don't like a whole lot: "Up against the wall, motherfucker, this is a stick-up."

Yours for freedom,
Mark

Other students, however, expressed their opposition to the war more diplomatically. One young man tried to reach a compromise position by not entirely serving and not entirely resisting. His name is William Jefferson Clinton, and he worked to get himself into his local Reserve Officers'

Training Corps (R.O.T.C.) so he would not have to fight overseas. In the following letter to the director of his local R.O.T.C. program, Clinton, 23, explains his feelings about the war and why he wishes to play no part in it.

December 3, 1969

Dear Colonel Holmes:

I am sorry to be so long in writing. I know I promised to let you hear from me at least once a month, and from now on you will, but I have had to have some time to think about this first letter. Almost daily since my return to England I have thought about writing, about what I want to and ought to say.

First, I want to thank you, not just for saving me from the draft, but for being so kind and decent to me last summer, when I was as low as I've ever been. One thing which made the bond we struck in good faith somewhat palatable to me was my high regard for you personally. In retrospect, it seems that the admiration might not have been mutual had you known a little more about me, about my political beliefs and activities. At least you might have thought me more fit for the draft than for R.O.T.C.

Let me try to explain. As you know, I worked for two years in a very minor position on the Senate Foreign Relations Committee. I did it for the experience and the salary but also for the opportunity, however small, of working every day against a war I opposed and despised with a depth of feeling I had reserved solely for racism in America before Vietnam. I did not take the matter lightly but studied it carefully, and there was a time when not many people had more information about Vietnam at hand than I did.

I have written and spoken and marched against the war. One of the national organizers of the Vietnam Moratorium is a close friend of mine. After I left Arkansas last summer, I went to work in the national headquarters of the Moratorium, then to England to organize the Americans here for demonstrations Oct. 15 and Nov. 16.

Interlocked with the war is the draft issue, which I did not begin to consider separately until early 1968. For a law seminar at

Georgetown I wrote a paper on the legal arguments for and against allowing, within the Selective Service System, the classification of selective conscientious objection, for those opposed to participation in a particular war, not simply to "participation in war in any form."

From my work I came to believe that the draft system itself is illegitimate. No government really rooted in limited, parliamentary democracy should have the power to make its citizens fight and kill and die in a war they may oppose, a war which even possibly may be wrong, a war which, in any case, does not involve immediately the peace and freedom of the nation.

The draft was justified in World War II because the life of the people collectively was at stake. Individuals had to fight, if the nation was to survive, for the lives of their countrymen and their way of life. Vietnam is no such case. Nor was Korea an example, where in my opinion, certain military action was justified but the draft was not, for the reasons stated above.

Because of my opposition to the draft and the war, I am in great sympathy with those who are not willing to fight, kill, and maybe die for their country (i.e., the particular policy of a particular government) right or wrong. Two of my friends at Oxford are conscientious objectors. I wrote a letter of recommendation for one of them to his Mississippi draft board, a letter which I am more proud of than anything else I wrote at Oxford last year. One of my roommates is a draft resister who is possibly under indictment and may never be able to go home again. He is one of the bravest, best men I know. His country needs men like him more than they know. That he is considered a criminal is an obscenity.

The decision not to be a resister and the related susbsequent decisions were the most difficult of my life. I decided to accept the draft in spite of my beliefs for one reason: to maintain my political viability within the system. For years I have worked to prepare myself for a political life characterized by both practical political ability and concern for rapid social progress. It is a life I still feel compelled to try to lead. I do not think our system of government is by definition corrupt, however dangerous and inadequate it has been in recent years. (The society may be corrupt, but that is not the same thing, and if that is true we are all finished anyway.)

When the draft came, despite political convictions, I was having a hard time facing the prospect of fighting a war I had been fighting against, and that is why I contacted you. R.O.T.C. was the one way left in which I could possibly, but not positively, avoid both Vietnam and resistance. Going on with my education, even coming back to England, played no part in my decision to join R.O.T.C. I am back here, and would have been at Arkansas Law School because there is nothing else I can do. In fact, I would like to have been able to take a year out perhaps to teach in a small college or work on some community action project and in the process to decide whether to attend law school or graduate school and how to begin putting what I have learned to use.

But the particulars of my personal life are not nearly as important to me as the principles involved. After I signed the R.O.T.C. letter of intent I began to wonder whether the compromise I had made with myself was not more objectionable than the draft would have been, because I had no interest in the R.O.T.C. program in itself and all I seemed to have done was to protect myself from physical harm. Also, I began to think I had deceived you, not by lies—there were none—but by failing to tell you all the things I'm writing now. I doubt that I had the mental coherence to articulate them then.

At that time, after we had made our agreement and you had sent my 1-D deferment to my draft board, the anguish and loss of my self-regard and self-confidence really set in. I hardly slept for weeks and kept going by eating compulsively and reading until exhaustion brought sleep. Finally, on Sept. 12 I stayed up all night writing a letter to the chairman of my draft board, saying basically what is in the preceding paragraph, thanking him for trying to help in a case where he really couldn't, and stating that I couldn't do the R.O.T.C. after all and would he please draft me as soon as possible.

I never mailed the letter, but I did carry it on me every day until I got on the plane to return to England. I didn't mail the letter because I didn't see, in the end, how my going in the army would achieve anything except a feeling that I had punished myself and gotten what I deserved. So I came back to England to try to make something of this second year of my Rhodes scholarship.

And that is where I am now, writing to you because you have been good to me and have a right to know what I think and feel. I am writing too in the hope that my telling this one story will help you to understand more clearly how so many fine people have come to find themselves still loving their country but loathing the military, to which you and other good men have devoted years, lifetimes, of the best service you could give. To many of us, it is no longer clear what is service and what is disservice, or if it is clear, the conclusion is likely to be illegal.

Forgive the length of this letter. There was much to say. There is still a lot to be said, but it can wait. Please say hello to Col. Jones for me.

Merry Christmas.
Sincerely,
Bill Clinton

While Clinton was campaigning for the presidency twenty-two years later, this letter was released to the media and—coming on the heels of another scandal—almost destroyed his election prospects. Clinton argued that he did, ultimately, put himself into the draft. Critics countered he did so only after receiving a low lottery number that virtually assured he would not be drafted. Candidate Clinton, of course, survived the ordeal and became President Clinton in January 1993 and was reelected in November 1996.

John "Soup" Campbell to Edward Van Every Jr.

The last American troops left Vietnam in March 1973, after approximately ten years of military involvement. Over 58,000 Americans were killed in all, and many more were permanently wounded. Some who returned were confronted with hostility—even spat upon and called "baby killers"—by those who opposed the war. But after a time the mood of the country changed and Vietnam veterans were increasingly given the honor and respect accorded to veterans of other wars. In 1982 the nation formally recognized their sacrifices with the creation of the Vietnam Veterans Memorial (known as "The Wall") in Washington, D.C. Since its dedication it has become the most visited memorial in Washington, and each year tens of thousands of people leave letters, poems, flowers, and other personal items in memory of those who died. The following letter was left in June 1985 by John Campbell and addressed to Eddie Van Every, a twenty-two-year-old who had served in Campbell's company.

June 8, 1985

Dear Eddie,

Although it's been fifteen years since you've been gone, it feels like it could have been fifteen days. Many times I have regretted not getting to know you better than I did. There was a quiet, sensitive goodness about you. You were one of the guys that had been with the unit awhile and was getting "short." I knew about your girl, your Mom & Dad and that you wanted to put your time in and get home. If anyone knew you at all, they liked you a lot.

I'll never forget being awakened at 3 that morning by the hysterical crying of Denny Newbill and Jerry Hall. "One of our guys is dead!" was all I could get out of Newbill. When Jerry told me it was you, I can remember demanding an answer—"Oh God, Why? Why any of us? Why Eddie?" I never did get any concrete answers. Our whole company felt a tremendous loss. When I left in August, there was still a sense of grief around. Things never did get back to "normal."

I hope you don't mind, but recently I made contact with your parents. They've moved twice and are now retired in Missouri, trusting in the Lord that you are at peace. They can't afford to travel much, so I've sent them pictures of the Memorial and your name. They're good people, too. I hope to meet them some day.

For years, I felt your life, as well as the other 58,000 lives, was wasted and anyone who wasn't there, could not or would not understand what we went through. That's changing now. People are beginning to realize that we were doing our jobs and doing them well. We had to pay the price and until recently, we were the ones tagged as losers, not our government. So if your names on this wall make it harder to send guys half way around the world to die, then maybe it wasn't a total waste.

I love you, brother. I pray some day we can welcome each other home. Peace.

John "Soup" Campbell
335th Radio Research Co.
Can Tho, Vietnam
Aug. 1969 to Aug. 1970

President Ronald Reagan to Soviet Leader Leonid Brezhnev

Just over three weeks after John Hinckley Jr. shot President Ronald Reagan outside the Hilton Hotel in Washington, D.C., Reagan attempted to improve relations between the United States and the Soviet Union. "As I sat in the sun-filled White House solarium in robe and pajamas that spring," Reagan later reflected, "I wondered how to get the process started. Perhaps having come so close to death made me feel I should do whatever I could in the years God had given me to reduce the threat of nuclear war." Reagan ordered an end to the grain embargo against the USSR and decided to write a personal message to the Soviet leader, Leonid Brezhnev. On April 24, 1981, still recuperating from his gunshot wound, Reagan sent Brezhnev the following letter, which was not declassified until 1995. (The handwritten message is reprinted here verbatim, including Reagan's propensity to use "it's" for "its.")

THE WHITE HOUSE
WASHINGTON

My Dear Mr. President

In writing the attached letter I am reminded of our meeting in San Clemente a decade or so ago. I was Governor of California at the time and you were concluding a series of meetings with

President Nixon. Those meetings had captured the imagination of all the world. Never had peace and good will among men seemed closer at hand.

When we met I asked if you were aware that the hopes and aspirations of millions and millions of people throughout the world were dependent on the decisions that would be reached in your meetings.

You took my hand in both of yours and assured me that you were aware of that and that you were dedicated with all your heart and mind to fulfilling those hopes and dreams.

The people of the world still share that hope. Indeed the peoples of the world, despite differences in racial and ethnic origin, have very much in common. They want the dignity of having some control over their individual destiny. They want to work at the craft or trade of their own choosing and to be fairly rewarded. They want to raise their families in peace without harming anyone or suffering harm themselves. Government exists for their convenience, not the other way around.

If they are incapable, as some would have us believe, of self government, then where among them do we find any who are capable of governing others?

Is it possible that we have permitted ideology, political and economic philosophies, and governmental policies to keep us from considering the very real, everyday problems of our peoples? Will the average Soviet family be better off or even aware that the Soviet Union has imposed a government of it's own choice on the people of Afghanistan? Is life better for the people of Cuba because the Cuban military dictate who shall govern the people of Angola?

It is often implied that such things have been made necessary because of territorial ambitions of the United States; that we have imperialistic designs and thus constitute a threat to your own security and that of the newly emerging nations. There not only is no evidence to support such a charge, there is solid evidence that the United States, when it could have dominated the world with no risk to itself, made no effort whatsoever to do so.

When World War II ended, the United Sates had the only undamaged industrial power in the world. Our military might was at it's peak—and we alone had the ultimate weapon, the nuclear weapon, with the unquestioned ability to deliver it anywhere in the world. If we had sought world domination then, who could have opposed us?

But the United States followed a different course—one unique in all the history of mankind. We used our power and wealth to rebuild the war-ravaged economies of the world, including those nations who had been our enemies. May I say there is absolutely no substance to charges that the United States is guilty of imperialism or attempts to impose it's will on other countries by use of force.

Mr. President, should we not be concerned with eliminating the obstacles which prevent our people—those we represent—from achieving their most cherished goals? And isn't it possible some of those obstacles are born of govt. objectives which have little to do with the real needs and desires of our people?

It is in this spirit, in the spirit of helping the people of both our nations, that I have lifted the grain embargo. Perhaps this decision will contribute to creating the circumstances which will lead to the meaningful and constructive dialogue which will assist us in fulfilling our joint obligation to find lasting peace.

Sincerely
Ronald Reagan

Brezhnev's lengthy reply respectfully disagreed with many of President Reagan's assertions. Regarding the claim that America "made no effort" to dominate the world after World War II, Brezhnev countered, "Actually, the USA did the maximum it could using a wide array of military, political, and economic means to achieve what American leaders themselves called 'Pax Americana.'" The Soviet premier went on to list other policies and actions, from the formation of NATO in 1949 to the expansion of America's military presence in the 1980s, as evidence that the Soviet Union had reason to feel threatened by the United States. He concluded, "We will never set up the fire of war. You know very well, as we do, what such a fire would lead to." Brezhnev died before the two men had an opportunity to meet face-to-face, and Reagan, who later described Brezhnev's letter as "an icy reply," lamented: "So much for my first attempt at personal diplomacy."

Mary Ewald to Iraqi President Saddam Hussein

Interested in pursuing a career in international finance, twenty-four-year-old Thomas Ewald accepted a senior position at a Kuwaiti bank and moved to Kuwait City on July 30, 1990. Before leaving the United States, Ewald and his parents contacted the Department of State in Washington, D.C., and the American embassy in Kuwait to verify the safety of traveling to and living in the Middle Eastern city. The Ewalds were told unconditionally that there was nothing to worry about. But only three days after Ewald's arrival the Iraqi army commenced a massive, full-scale invasion of Kuwait, overrunning Kuwait City in a matter of hours. Ewald hid in a safe house for eleven days until he was captured and taken to Baghdad with other American and British hostages to be used as "human shields." Unable to get any help from the State Department, Tom's mother, Mary—a scholar and poet who had traveled to the Middle East many times and had studied Arabic cultures extensively—decided to appeal to Saddam Hussein directly. During the Labor Day weekend of 1990 Mrs. Ewald and her husband, William, traveled from their home in Connecticut to the Iraqi embassy in Washington, where they hand-delivered the following letter.

President Saddam Hussein
c/o Ambassador al-Machat

Dear Mr. President:

I am writing to request you to send my student son, Thomas Hart Benton Ewald, home to his family. He was taken, I think, from the SAS Hotel in Kuwait City.

I feel I have the obligation to appeal to you for two reasons. First, my family has been a staunch friend to the Arabs. My husband, Tom's father, was on the White House Staff when

President Eisenhower caused the French, British, and Israelis to pull out of Suez. One of the first non-Arab meetings at the Washington Mosque was the one which I, as president of the Radcliffe (Harvard) Club of Washington, arranged to explain Muslim culture. I am also a poet who has written about Arabia. I have sent my youngest, well-loved son to work in an Arab country, hoping he would help bring peace between our cultures. Instead, after two days, he was caught up in war. It seems unjust that I, who have given to you so generously, should have my son taken away from me in return. You have the power to right this wrong.

Second, my son is asthmatic, so severely crippled as a child that we thought we could never raise him. He needs medication and a doctor's care. I beg you, in the name of Allah, let my son go.

Yours truly,
Mary Ewald

Incredibly, Hussein received the letter and ordered that Ewald be released. Thomas Ewald returned to the United States alive and well on September 14, 1990. The remaining hostages were not released until December 6, one week after the United Nations Security Council authorized the United States and its allies "to use all necessary means" to remove Iraqi forces from Kuwait.

Letters of Social Concern, Struggle, & Contempt

You might be wondering just what kind of people become engaged in an endeavor of this nature. My impression is that the volunteers are both realistic and idealistic: realistic in the sense that they are aware of the inherent danger in the world situation today and have a deep conviction that Americans must live the ideals which they have preached for so long—peace, freedom, equality, individual worth, and human brotherhood; idealistic in their belief and hope that through contributing two years of their life they can assist in some small way in the ultimate realization of these ideals for all mankind.

Peace Corps volunteer, in Ghana, writing home; 1961

Massa Hadjo, a Sioux Indian, to the *Chicago Tribune*

Wovoka, a messianic figure of the Paiute Indian tribe who initiated the Ghost Dance religion, prophesied that whites would be driven out of America and that Native Indians would recover their country. Whites who heard about Wovoka and the Ghost Dance religion were terrified, and after army officers and Indian Bureau agents witnessed the dance itself and reported back to the U.S. Government, the official word was blunt: Stop the Ghost Dancing. The army's attempts to do so led to several violent encounters with the Indians and, ultimately, the massacre of three hundred Indians at Wounded Knee. After an editorial appeared in the Chicago Tribune *condemning the Indians and their dance, Massa Hadjo, a Sioux, responded with the following letter, published on December 5, 1890.*

[Editor]:

You say, "If the United States army would kill a thousand or so of the dancing Indians there would be no more trouble." I judge by the above language you are a "Christian," and are disposed to do all in your power to advance the cause of Christ. You are doubtless a worshipper of the white man's Saviour, but are unwilling that the Indians should have a "Messiah" of their own.

The Indians have never taken kindly to the Christian religion as preached and practiced by the whites. Do you know why this is the case? Because the Good Father of all has given us a better religion—a religion that is all good and no bad, a religion that is adapted to our wants. You say if we are good, obey the Ten Commandments and never sin any more, we may be permitted eventually to sit upon a rock and sing praises to God forevermore, and look down upon our heathen fathers, mothers, brothers and sisters who are howling in hell.

It won't do. The code of morals as practiced by the white race will not compare with the morals of the Indians. We pay no lawyers or preachers, but we have not one-tenth part of the crime that you do. If our Messiah does come we shall not try to force you into our belief. We will never burn innocent women at the stake or pull men to pieces with horses because they refuse to join in our ghost dances. You white people had a Messiah, and if history is to be believed nearly every nation has had one. You had twelve Apostles; we have only eleven, and some of those are already in the military guard-house. We also had a Virgin Mary and she is in the guard-house. You are anxious to get hold of our Messiah, so you can put him in irons. This you may do—in fact, you may crucify him as you did that other one, but you cannot convert the Indians to the Christian religion until you contaminate them with the blood of the white man. The white man's heaven is repulsive to the Indian nature, and if the white man's hell suits you, keep it. I think there will be white rogues enough to fill it.

Elizabeth Cady Stanton to Susan B. Anthony & Anthony to Stanton

"When I think of all the wrongs that have been heaped upon womankind," Elizabeth Cady Stanton wrote to a friend in 1871, "I am ashamed that I am not forever in a condition of chronic wrath." Stanton, one of the leading suffragists of her time, worked closely with Susan B. Anthony, Lucretia Mott, Lucy Stone, and other prominent advocates to secure voting rights for women and to enact laws giving women control over their property and equal custody over their children. Stanton and Anthony toured the country together giving speeches, organizing conventions, circulating petitions, and editing their feminist newspaper, The Revolution. *The two did not agree on everything and even criticized one another publicly, but they maintained a strong friendship for over fifty years. The following letter by Stanton is a response to Anthony's suggestion that they consider changing the name of their newspaper—which was considered too bold by some—and a request that Stanton travel to Washington, D.C., for a conference.*

St. Louis, December 28, 1869

My Dear Susan,—

As to changing the name of the *Revolution*, I should consider it a great mistake. If all these people who for twenty years have been afraid to call their souls their own begin to prune us and the *Revolution*, we shall become the same galvanized mummies they are. There could not be a better name than *Revolution*. The establishing of woman on her rightful throne is the greatest revolution the world has ever known or ever will know. To bring it about is no child's play. You and I have not forgotten the conflict of the last twenty-years—the ridicule, persecution, denunciation, detraction, the unmixed bitterness of our cup for the past two years, when even friends crucified us. A journal called the *Rosebud* might answer for those who come with kid gloves and perfumes to lay immortal wreaths on the monuments which in sweat and tears others have hewn and built; but for us and for that great blacksmith of ours who forges such red-hot thunderbolts for Pharisees, hypocrites, and sinners, there is no name like the *Revolution*.

It does not seem to me worth while for me to take that long trip to Washington when I have all I can do all winter out here in the West. This field is ripe for the harvest. I am doing more good in stirring up these Western women than in talking to those old Washington politicians. I do not want to manage other people, neither do I want other people to manage me. I stand ready to pay anybody you can get to go to Washington in my stead. But of course I stand by you to the end. I would not see you crushed by rivals even if to prevent it required my being cut into inch bits. If you will promise solemnly to let me free in May, I will wear the yoke a few months longer, bravely and patiently. But I do hate conventions, for I dislike to be in a position where any set of people have the right to say, "For the sake of the cause don't do this or that." In fact I had rather give you five hundred dollars than go to Washington. But if your life depends on me, I will be your stay and staff to the end. No power in heaven, hell or earth can separate us, for our hearts are eternally wedded together. Ever yours, and here I mean *ever*.

Ultimately they did not change the name of The Revolution, *and Stanton did go to the convention. Despite decades of tireless work, however, she and Anthony did not see their ultimate dream—the right of women to vote—realized in their lifetime. (The Nineteenth Amendment to the U.S. Constitution was not ratified until August 1920—fourteen years after Anthony died, and almost eighteen years after Stanton.) In the last letter she wrote to Stanton, in October 1902, Anthony looked back on all they had done together and on all that was yet to be.*

My Dear Mrs. Stanton:—

I shall indeed by happy to spend with you November 12, the day on which you round out your four-score and seven, over four years ahead of me, but in age as in all else I follow you closely. It is fifty-one years since first we met and we have been busy through every one of them, stirring up the world to recognize the rights of women. The older we grow the more keenly we feel the humiliation of disenfranchisement and the more vividly we realize its disadvantages in every department of life and most of all in the labor market.

We little dreamed when we began this contest, optimistic with the hope and buoyancy of youth, that half a century later we would be compelled to leave the finish of the battle to another generation of women. But our hearts are filled with joy to know that they enter upon this task equipped with a college education, with business experience, with the fully admitted right to speak in public—all of which were denied to women fifty years ago. They have practically but one point to gain—the suffrage; we had all. These strong, courageous, capable young women will take our place and complete our work. There is an army of them where we were but a handful. Ancient prejudice has become so softened, public sentiment so liberalized and women have so thoroughly demonstrated their ability as to leave no doubt that they will carry our cause to victory.

And we, dear, old friend, shall move on to the next sphere of existence—higher and larger, we cannot fail to believe, and one where women will not be placed in an inferior position but will be welcomed on a plane of perfect intellectual and spiritual equality.

Ever lovingly yours,
Susan B. Anthony

Several days after this letter was written Elizabeth Cady Stanton passed away. Anthony was devastated and wrote to a friend soon after: "Well, it is an awful hush—it seems impossible—that the voice is hushed—that I have loved to hear for fifty years—longed to get her opinion of things—before I knew exactly where I stood—It is all at sea—but the Laws of Nature are still going on—with no shadow or turning—What a world it is—it goes right on & on—no matter who lives or who dies."

Mary Tape to the San Francisco Board of Education

Like many immigrant parents, Mary Tape wanted her children to learn the customs and language of her new land and to receive a good education. But the Board of Education in San Francisco, the city to which Tape emigrated from China, believed differently. Despite the fact that Tape's daughter, Mamie, was born in America and therefore was a U.S. citizen, the board did not want any child of Chinese immigrant parents in their public schools. Mary Tape and her husband, Joseph, petitioned the schools repeatedly but were rejected each time. The board even ruled that any principal who admitted a "Mongolian" child, as the Chinese children were called, would be fired. Angered by the injustice of the situation, Mary Tape sent the following letter to the Board of Education and the school superintendent, Andrew Moulder.

1769 Green Street,
San Francisco, April 8, 1885

To the Board of Education—

DEAR SIRS: I see that you are going to make all sorts of excuses to keep my child out of the Public schools. Dear sirs, Will you please to tell me! Is it a disgrace to be Born a Chinese? Didn't God make us all!!! What right have you to bar my children out of the school because she is a chinese Decend. They is no other worldy reason that you could keep her out, except that. I suppose, you all goes to churches on Sundays! Do you call that a Christian act to compell my little children to go so far to a school that is made in purpose for them. My children don't dress like the other chinese. They look just as phunny amongst them as the Chinese dress in Chinese look amongst you Caucasians. Besides, if I had any wish to send them to a chinese school I could have sent them two years ago without going to all this trouble. You have expended a lot of Public money foolishly, all because of one poor little Child. Her playmates is all Caucasians ever since she could toddle around. If she is good enough to play with them! Then is she not good enough to be in the same room and studie with them? You had better come and see for yourselves. See if the Tape's is not the same as other Caucasians, except in features. It seems no matter how a Chinese may live and dress so long as you know they Chinese. Then they are hated as one. There is not any right or justice for them.

You have seen my husband and child. You told him it wasn't Mamie Tape you object to. If it were not Mamie Tape you object to, then why didn't you let her attend the school nearest her home! Instead of first making one pretense of some kind to keep her out? It seems to me Mr. Moulder has a grudge against this Eight-year-old Mamie Tape. I know they is no other child I mean Chinese child! Care to go to your public Chinese school. May you Mr. Moulder, never be persecuted like the way you have persecuted little Mamie Tape. Mamie Tape will never attend any of the Chinese schools of your making! Never!!! I will let the world see sir What justice there is When it is govern by the Race prejudice men! Just because she is of the Chinese decend, not because she don't dress like you because she does. Just because she is decended of Chinese parents I guess she is more of a American than a good many of you that is going to prevent her being Educated.

Mrs. M. Tape

The case went to the Superior Court of San Francisco, which ruled in Tape's favor and called the board's actions unconstitutional. The board appealed, but the Supreme Court of California upheld the Superior Court's decision. Nevertheless, Mamie Tape never attended her local public school; despite the rulings, the Board of Education established a separate school above a grocery store in Chinatown for Mamie and other Chinese American children.

Mother Jones to President Theodore Roosevelt & Jones to Governor James H. Peabody

A passionate spokesperson for the rights of workers and anti–child labor laws, Mary Harris "Mother" Jones fought doggedly to bring attention to these issues through letters, speeches, marches, and other forms of social protest throughout the country—"[I have] no abiding place," she once said, "but wherever a fight is going on against wrong, I am always there." In the following letter, Jones implores President Theodore Roosevelt, who was visiting Oyster Bay, New York, at the time, to sponsor federal laws that would end child labor practices in America.

NEW YORK, July 30th, 1903.

The Hon. Theodore Roosevelt, President U.S.A.
Your Excellency:

Twice before I have written to you requesting an audience that I might lay my mission before you and have your advice on a matter which bears upon the welfare of the whole nation. I speak for the emancipation from mills and factories of the hundreds of thousands of young children who are yielding up their lives for the commercial supremacy of the nation. Failing to receive a reply to either of the letters, I yesterday went to Oyster Bay, taking with me three of these children that they might plead to you personally.

Secretary Barnes informed us that before we might hope for an interview, we must first lay the whole matter before you in a letter. He assured me of its delivery to you personally, and also that it would receive your attention.

I have espoused the cause of the laboring class in general and of suffering children in particular. For what affects the child must ultimately affect the adult. It was for them that our march of principle was begun. We sought to bring the attention of the public upon these little ones, so that ultimately sentiment would be aroused and the children freed from the workshops and sent to school. I know of no question of to-day that demands greater attention from those who have at heart the perpetuation of the Republic.

The child of to-day is the man or woman of to-morrow, the citizen and the mother of still future citizens. I ask Mr. President, what kind of citizen will be the child who toils twelve hours a day, in an unsanitary atmosphere, stunted mentally and physically, and surrounded with immoral influences? Denied education, he cannot assume the true duties of citizenship, and enfeebled physically and mentally, he falls a ready victim to the perverting influences which the present economic conditions have created.

I grant you, Mr. President, that there are State laws which should regulate these matters, but results have proven that they are inadequate. In my little band are three boys, the oldest 11 years old, who have worked in mills a year or more without interferences from the authorities. All efforts to bring about reform have failed.

I have been moved to this crusade, Mr. President, because of actual experiences in the mills. I have seen little children without the first rudiments of education and no prospect of acquiring any. I have seen other children with hands, fingers and other parts of their tiny bodies mutilated because of their childish ignorance of machinery. I feel that no nation can be truly great while such conditions exist without attempted remedy.

It is to be hoped that our crusade will stir up a general sentiment in behalf of enslaved childhood, and secure enforcement of present laws.

But that is not sufficient.

As this is not alone the question of the separate States, but of the whole Republic, we come to you as the chief representative of the nation.

I believe that Federal laws should be passed governing this evil and including a penalty for violation. Surely, Mr. President, if this is practicable—and I believe that you will agree that it is—you can advise me of the necessary steps to pursue.

I have with me three boys who have walked a hundred miles serving as living proof of what I say. You can see and talk with them, Mr. President, if you are interested. If you decide to see these children, I will bring them before you at any time you may set. Secretary Barnes has assured me of an early reply, and this should be sent care of the Ashland Hotel, New York City.

Very respectfully yours,
MOTHER JONES

The president's secretary, B. F. Barnes, responded by saying that the president was not unsympathetic to her cause, and that an anti–child labor law was passed under his administration when he was governor of New York, but there was nothing the president could do on a federal level. (Jones vehemently disagreed and went on to campaign against Roosevelt in 1904.) Eight months later, Jones proved to be even more defiant in the face of authority after the governor of Colorado tried to expel her from the state. Jones had been aiding workers striking against the Colorado Fuel and Iron Company when the governor ordered that she be "deported" and had her placed on a train heading out of Denver. She returned immediately, got a hotel room down the street from the governor's office, and fired off the following letter.

Denver, Colorado, March 26, 1904

Governor James H. Peabody

Mr. Governor, you notified your dogs of war to put me out of the state. They complied with your instructions. I hold in my hand a letter that was handed to me by one of them, which says "under no circumstances return to this state." I wish to notify you, governor, that you don't own the state. When it was admitted to the sisterhood of states, my fathers gave me a share of stock in it; and that is all they gave to you. The civil courts are open. If I break a law of state or nation it is the duty of the civil courts to deal with me. That is why my forefathers established those courts to keep dictators and tyrants such as you from interfering with civilians. I am right here in the capital, after being out nine or ten hours, four or five blocks from your office. I want to ask you, governor, what in the Hell are you going to do about it?

The governor did nothing.

W. E. B. Du Bois to Vernealia Fareira

Scholar, author, professor, and one of the founders of the National Association for the Advancement of Colored People, William Edward Burghardt (W. E. B.) Du Bois was one of the most influential black leaders of the first half of the twentieth century. After graduating from Fisk University and then from Harvard's doctorate program, Du Bois went on to write The Souls of Black Folk *and many other acclaimed works. A teacher in Berwyn, Pennsylvania, familiar with Du Bois's appreciation for hard work and scholastic accomplishment, wrote to Du Bois about a bright young student, Vernealia Fareira, who would not apply herself to her studies. On January 7, 1905, Du Bois sent Fareira the following letter.*

Dear Miss Fareira:

I wonder if you will let a stranger say a word to you about yourself? I have heard that you are a young woman of some ability but that you are neglecting your school work because you have become hopeless of trying to do anything in the world. I am very sorry for this. How any human being whose wonderful fortune it is to live in the 20th century should under ordinarily fair advantages despair of life is almost unbelievable. And if in addition to this that person is, as I am, of Negro lineage with all the hopes and yearnings of hundreds of millions of human souls dependent in some degree on her striving, then her bitterness amounts to crime.

There are in the U.S. today tens of thousands of colored girls who would be happy beyond measure to have the chance of educating themselves that you are neglecting. If you train yourself as you easily can, there are wonderful chances of usefulness before you: you can join the ranks of 15,000 Negro women teachers, of hundreds of nurses and physicians, of the growing number of clerks and stenographers, and above all of the host of homemakers. Ignorance is a cure for nothing. Get the very best training possible & the doors of opportunity will fly open before you as they are flying before thousands of your fellows. On the other hand every time a colored person neglects an opportunity, it makes it more difficult for others of the race to get such an opportunity. Do you want to cut off the chances of the boys and girls of tomorrow?

Margaret Sanger to the Readers of *The Woman Rebel*

An outspoken advocate for women's reproductive rights, Margaret Sanger opened the first birth control clinic in America in Brooklyn, New York, and went on to become the founder of Planned Parenthood Federation of America. The police raided and closed Sanger's clinic in 1916 under New York State's Comstock Law, which forbade the discussion and dissemination of birth control information, and Sanger was imprisoned for thirty days. It was not, however, her first encounter with the law. In March

1914 she began publishing The Woman Rebel, *a monthly newspaper that featured such articles as "The Prevention of Contraception," "Abortion in the United States," and "Can You Afford to Have a Large Family?" The post office refused to mail the newspaper and informed Sanger that if she continued to send it through the mails she could be arrested. Sanger did not relent, and she soon found herself in a courtroom facing the possibility of a jail term. In October she decided it would be safer to flee the country for Europe, which was more tolerant of birth control issues, and let passions cool. (She returned a year later, and the case against her was thrown out in February 1916.) Before leaving, Sanger wrote the following letter, which she published in* The Woman Rebel.

En Route to Exile
October, 1914

Comrades and Friends,—

Every paper published should have a message for its readers. It should deliver it and be done. *The Woman Rebel* had for its aim the imparting of information for the prevention of conception. (None of the suppressed issues contained such information.) It was not the intention to labor for years advocating the idea, but to give the information directly to those who desired it. The March, May, July, August, September and October issues have been suppressed and confiscated by the Post Office. They have been mailed regularly to all subscribers. If you have not received your copies, it has been because the U.S. Post Office has refused to carry them on to you.

My work in the nursing field for the past fourteen years has convinced me that the workers desire the knowledge of prevention of conception. My work among women of the working class proved to me sufficiently that it is they who are suffering because of the law which forbids the imparting of information. To wait for this law to be repealed would be years and years hence. Thousands of unwanted children may be brought into the world in the meantime, thousands of women made miserable and unhappy.

Why should we wait?

Shall we who have heard the cries and seen the agony of dying women respect the law which has caused their deaths?

Shall we watch in patience the murdering of 25,000 women each year in the United States from criminal abortions?

Shall we fold our hands and wait until a body of sleek and well fed politicians get ready to abolish the cause of such slaughter?

Shall we look upon a piece of parchment as greater than human happiness, greater than human life?

Shall we let it destroy our womanhood, or hold millions of workers in bondage and slavery? Shall we who respond to the throbbing pulse of human needs concern ourselves with indictments, courts, and judges, or shall we do our work first and settle with these evils after?

This law has caused the perpetuation of quackery. It has created the fake and quack who benefit by its existence.

Jail has not been my goal. There is special work to be done and I shall do it first. If jail comes after, I shall call upon all to assist me. In the meantime, I shall attempt to nullify the law by direct action and attend to the consequences afterward.

Over 100,000 working men and women in the United States shall hear from me.

The Boston Tea Party was a defiant and revolutionary act in the eyes of the British Government, but to the American Revolutionist it was but an act of courage and justice.

Yours fraternally,
Margaret Sanger

Nicola Sacco to His Daughter Ines

Despite evidence to the contrary, eyewitness accounts that the two men were not at the scene of the crime, and a written confession by a known criminal, Nicola Sacco and Bartolomeo Vanzetti were convicted of murder in 1920 and sentenced to die in the electric chair. What convicted Sacco and Vanzetti, it is believed, is the fact that they were immigrants and radicals; the judge who conducted the trial privately referred to the two men as "those anarchist bastards," and the prosecuting attorney repeatedly ques-

tioned them on their political beliefs, though these beliefs had nothing to do with the crime (a payroll holdup). During their more than seven years of confinement, both men spent time writing to friends, supporters, and family members. The following letter was written by Sacco to his daughter, Ines.

July 19, 1927. Charlestown State Prison

My Dear Ines:

I would like that you should understand what I am going to say to you, and I wish I could write you so plain, for I long so much to have you hear all the heart-beat eagerness of your father, for I love you so much as you are the dearest little beloved one.

It is quite hard indeed to make you understand in your young age, but I am going to try from the bottom of my heart to make you understand how dear you are to your father's soul. If I cannot succeed in doing that, I know that you will save this letter and read it over in future years to come and you will see and feel the same heart-beat affection as your father feels in writing it to you.

I will bring with me your little and so dearest letter and carry it right under my heart to the last day of my life. When I die, it will be buried with your father who loves you so much, as I do also your brother Dante and holy dear mother.

You don't know Ines, how dear and great your letter was to your father. It is the most golden present that you could have given to me or that I could have wished for in these sad days.

It was the greatest treasure and sweetness in my struggling life that I could have lived with you and your brother Dante and your mother in a neat little farm, and learn all your sincere words and tender affection. Then in the summer-time to be sitting with you in the home nest under the oak tree shade—beginning to teach you of life and how to read and write, to see you running, laughing, crying and singing through the verdent fields picking the wild flowers here and there from one tree to another, and from the clear, vivid stream to your mother's embrace.

The same I wished to see for other poor girls, and their

brothers, happy with their mother and father as I dreamed for us—but it was not so and the nightmare of the lower classes saddened very badly after your father's soul.

For the things of beauty and of good in this life, mother nature gave to us all, for the conquest and the joy of liberty. The men of this dying old society, they brutally have pulled me away from the embrace of your brother and your poor mother. But, in spite of all, the free spirit of your father's faith still survives, and I have lived for it and for the dream that some day I would have come back to life, to the embrace of your dear mother, among our friends and comrades again, but woe is me!

I know that you are good and surely you love your mother, Dante and all the beloved ones—and I am sure that you love me also a little, for I love you much and then so much. You do not know Ines, how often I think of you every day. You are in my heart, in my vision, in every angle of this sad walled cell, in the sky and everywhere my gaze rests.

Meantime, give my best paternal greetings to all the friends and comrades, and doubly so to our beloved ones. Love and kisses to your brother and mother.

With the most affectionate kiss and ineffable caress from him who loves you so much that he constantly thinks of you. Best warm greetings from Bartolo to you all.

Your Father

Despite post-trial discoveries of new evidence that cast further doubt on their guilt, Sacco and Vanzetti were not allowed a retrial. The two men were executed on August 23, 1927.

Two Letters to President Franklin D. Roosevelt & Minnie A. Hardin to First Lady Eleanor Roosevelt

Four years after Wall Street crashed in October 1929, approximately fourteen million Americans were unemployed—almost one quarter of the workforce. Taking families into account, a full forty million Americans were without a dependable source of income. During Franklin D. Roo-

sevelt's twelve years as president, he and Eleanor Roosevelt received millions of letters, many of which were desperate pleas for assistance from those caught up in the Great Depression. The following are just two examples.

Phila., Pa.
November, 26, 1934

Honorable Franklin D. Roosevelt.
Washington, D.C.
Dear Mr. President:

I am forced to write to you because we find ourselves in *a very serious condition*. For the last three or four years we have had depression and *suffered* with my *family* and little children *severely*. Now Since the Home Owners Loan Corporation opened up, I have been going there in order to save my home, because there has been unemployment in my house for more than three years. You can imagine that I and my family have suffered from lack of water supply in my house for more than two years. Last winter I did not have coal and the pipes burst in my house and therefore could not make heat in the house. Now winter is here again and we are suffering of cold, no water in the house, and we are facing to be forced out of the house, because I have no money to move or pay so much money as they want when after making settlement I am mother of little children, am sick and losing my health, and we are eight people in the family, and where can I go when I don't have money because no one is working in my house. The Home Loan Corporation wants $42. a month rent or else we will have to be on the street. I am living in this house for about ten years and when times were good we would put our last cent in the house and now I have *no money, no home and no wheres to go*. I beg of you to please help me and my family and little children for the sake of a sick mother and suffering family to give this your immediate attention so we will not be forced to move or put out in the street.

Waiting and Hoping that you will act quickly.

Thanking you very much I remain

Mrs. E. L.

The plight of Mrs. E. L. and her family is not known; nor is the fate of the writer of the following anonymous letter, dated September 3, 1935, from Picayune, Mississippi.

Dear Sir I am ritening you a few Lines to Let you no how they are treating we colored people on this releaf I went up to our home Vister and re [ap]plied for some Thing to do an Some Thing to eat and She told me that she has nothing for me at all and to they give all the worke to White people and give us nothing an Sir I wont you to no how we are treated here

So please help us if you can

Not everyone, however, was in favor of relief efforts to alleviate the suffering of the poor. The following letter, dated December 14, 1937, was sent to the First Lady by a furious "taxpaying" woman in Columbus, Indiana.

Mrs. F. D. Roosevelt
Washington, D. C.

Mrs. Roosevelt:

I suppose from your point of view the work relief, old age pensions, slum clearance and all the rest seems like a perfect remedy for all the ills of this country, but I would like for you to see the results, as the other half see them.

We have always had a shiftless, never-do-well class of people whose one and only aim in life is to live without work. I have been rubbing elbows with this class for nearly sixty years and have tried to help some of the most promising and have seen others try to help them, but it can't be done. We cannot help those who will not try to help themselves and if they do try, a square deal is all they need, and by the way that is all this country needs or ever has needed: a square deal for all and then, let each paddle their own canoe, or sink.

There has never been any necessity for any one who is able to work, being on relief in this locality, but there have been many eating the bread of charity and they have lived better than ever before. I have had taxpayers tell me that their children came from school and asked why they couldn't have nice lunches like the children on relief.

The women and children around here have had to work at the fields to help save the crops and several women fainted while at work and at the same time we couldn't go up or down the road without stumbling over some of the reliefers, moping around carrying dirt from one side of the road to the other and back again, or else asleep. I live alone on a farm and have not raised any crops for the last two years as there was no help to be had. I am feeding the stock and have been cutting the wood to keep my home fires burning. There are several reliefers around here now who have been kicked off relief, but they refuse to work unless they can get relief hours and wages, but they are so worthless no one can afford to hire them.

As for the clearance of the real slums, it can't be done as long as their inhabitants are allowed to reproduce their kind. I would like for you to see what a family of that class can do to a decent house in a short time. Such a family moved into an almost new, neat, four-room house near here last winter. They even cut down some of the shade trees for fuel, after they had burned everything they could pry loose. There were two big idle boys in the family and they could get all the fuel they wanted, just for the cutting, but the shade trees were closer and it was taking a great amount of fuel, for they had broken out several windows and they had but very little bedding. There were two women there all the time and three part of the time and there was enough good clothing tramped in the mud around the yard to have made all the bedclothes they needed. It was clothing that had been given them and they had worn it until it was too filthy to wear any longer without washing, so they threw it out and begged more. I will not try to describe their filth for you would not believe me. They paid no rent while there and left between two suns owing everyone from whom they could get a nickels worth of anything. They are just a fair sample of the class of people on whom so much of our hard earned tax money is being squandered and on whom so much sympathy is being wasted.

As for the old people on beggars' allowances: the taxpayers have provided homes for all the old people who never liked to work, where they will be neither cold nor hungry: much better homes than most of them have ever tried to provide for themselves. They have lived many years through the most prosperous times of our country and had an opportunity to prepare for old age, but they spent their lives in idleness or worse and now they expect those who have worked like slaves, to provide a living for them and all their worthless descendants. Some of them are asking for from thirty to sixty dollars a month when I have known them to live on a dollar a week rather than go to work. There is many a little child doing without butter on its bread, so that some old sot can have his booze and tobacco: some old sot who spent his working years loafing around pool rooms and saloons, boasting that the world owed him a living.

Even the child welfare has become a racket. The parents of large families are getting divorces, so that the mothers and children can qualify for aid. The children have to join the ranks of the "unemployed" as they grow up, for no child that has been raised on charity in this community has ever amounted to anything.

You people who have plenty of this worlds goods and whose money comes easy, have no idea of the heart-breaking toil and self-denial which is the lot of the working people who are trying to make an honest living, and then to have to shoulder all these unjust burdens seems like the last straw. During the worst of the depression many of the farmers had to deny their families butter, eggs, meat, etc. and sell it to pay their taxes and then had to stand by and see the dead-beats carry it home to their families by the arm load, and they knew their tax money was helping pay for it. One woman saw a man carry out eight pounds of butter at one time. The crookedness, selfishness, greed and graft of the crooked politicians is making one gigantic racket out of the new deal, and it is making this a nation of dead-beats and beggars and if it continues the people who will work will soon be nothing but slaves for the pampered poverty rats and I am afraid these human parasites are going to become a menace to the country unless they are disfranchised. No one should have the right to vote theirself a living at the expense of the taxpayers. They learned their strength at the last election and also learned that they can get just about what they want by "voting right." They have had a taste of their coveted life of idleness, and at the rate they are increasing, they will soon control the country. The twentieth child arrived in the home of one chronic reliefer near here some time ago.

Is it any wonder the taxpayers are discouraged by all this penalizing of thrift and industry to reward shiftlessness, or that the whole country is on the brink of chaos?

Minnie A. Hardin
Columbus, Ind.

Richard Wright to the *American Mercury*

Before leaving the United States for good in 1947 to live in France, Richard Wright encountered almost every conceivable form of oppression. Raised in the South in the early 1900s, he endured the worst of Jim Crow laws and institutionally sanctioned racism. His formal education consisted of a few years in dilapidated, segregated schools. Wright educated himself by reading the works of H. L. Mencken, Sinclair Lewis, Sherwood Anderson, and other prominent writers of the time. A passion for words and literature was ignited, and Wright, who empathized with the poor and working class, began contributing to leftist publications and literary magazines. His first published work, Uncle Tom's Children, *was relatively well received, but* Native Son, *published in 1940, transformed Wright into an internationally known novelist and social critic. Drawing from his own experiences, Wright created in Bigger Thomas,* Native Son*'s protagonist, a rebellious young African American formed—some would say deformed—by systematic racism in the United States. The book's relentless attack on America earned its author considerable scorn, particularly from* *white reviewers and critics. Burton Rascoe, writing for the monthly literary magazine* American Mercury, *deplored the novel's unapologetic rage. Wright read Rascoe's review and replied with the following.*

SIR:

Mr. Burton Rascoe's review of my book, *Native Son*, under the heading *Negro Novel and White Reviewers*, certainly introduces some brand new and unheard of principles into American literary criticism. What in God's name has "He is a handsome young man; his face is fine and intelligent . . ." got to do with the merits or shortcomings of a novel? I had hoped that the *Mercury*'s review of *Native Son* would be as objective as my treatment of Bigger, but I suppose that's hoping for too much from the *Mercury* these days.

Mr. Rascoe hopes that now, with *Native Son* out of my system, I'll give some sweetness and light. No, not yet. I'll be dishing out this for quite some time to come. Understated in Mr. Rascoe's review is this attitude: "Why in the world does a Negro writer want to bother with such stuff when he can write differently and be liked for it and paid for it?" The answer is simply this: I don't choose to. I prefer to write out of the background of my experience in an imaginative fashion. I don't prefer to streamline my stuff to what the public will like. It is no fault of mine that *Native Son* is selling; it was not written to sell, but to convey in terms of words an American-Negro experience of life. Too often when a Negro writes something which wins a prize, or sells, and which carries in it a note of protest, a white reviewer rises to ask: "What is he yelling about? He's making money, isn't he?" Has the *Mercury* fallen that low?

Following his personal line, Mr. Rascoe implied that I tried to insult the members of the Dutch Treat Club. What rot! I don't think a single person in that audience misunderstood my remarks (not a speech!) to the extent that Mr. Rascoe did. When I attended that luncheon my book had been off the press for about two weeks; I knew that very few of those present had read it. I took the occasion to remark that I hoped that they would meet Bigger Thomas if they had the time; that is, I expressed my hope that they would read the book. Only a "Negro-baiter" could twist such a statement and make it mean something else.

As an artist I reserve the right to depict the actions of people I do not agree with, Aristotle to the contrary! After reading Mr. Rascoe's review, I wondered why he did not reprint Buckley's speech and let it stand as his view; it would have been more clean-cut and honest. Yes; while writing the book I realized that Max's speech would be "utterly loathsome" to many people. That is why Max said:

> Of all things, men do not like to feel that they are guilty of wrong, and if you make them feel guilty, they will try desperately to justify it on any grounds; but failing that, and seeing no immediate solution that will set things right without too much cost to their lives and property, they will kill that which evoked in them the condemning sense of guilt. . . .

Does not this fall in line with Mr. Rascoe's statement that "We Americans are constitutionally for the underdog, so long as it does not seriously interfere with the business at hand of getting along"? I know that and that is why I wrote as I did. Max's speech anticipated every point raised by Mr. Rascoe. Read the book again, Mr. Rascoe, and pay close attention to Max's speech, which was directed toward men of your attitude. And remember that the author wrote that book, in the words of Max, as a "test symbol" to determine if 100 per cent Americans would feel "utterly loathsome" when confronted with one of their own historical mistakes! *Mr. Rascoe ran true to form!*

Richard Wright

Katherine Anne Porter to Dr. William Ross

Katherine Anne Porter was no fan of Communism, but she, like many writers and artists, was appalled by the "witch hunts" of the 1940s and 1950s led by Senator Joe McCarthy and others determined to root out Communist sympathizers. When Porter, a Pulitzer Prize–winning writer of poems, novels, biographies, screenplays, and librettos, was invited to teach at Colorado State College, she was asked to sign an "oath of allegiance" to the United States government (and against Communism). Porter found the request offensive and sent the school's president, Dr. William Ross, the following letter.

March 4, 1951

Dear Dr. Ross,

I cannot possibly sign the oath of allegiance you sent me, and I'm sorry I was not told in your first letter that this would be required of me, for a good deal of time and trouble would have been spared both of us.

This is the first time I've encountered this dangerous nonsense, but I have known from the beginning what my answer must be. My memory goes back easily thirty years to the time this law was passed in Colorado, in a time of war, fright and public hysteria being whipped up by the same kind of people who are doing this work now. Only now we're worse for thirty years of world disaster.

I believed then, and still do believe, that this requirement of an oath of allegiance was more of a device for embarrassing and humiliating honest persons than an effective trap for traitors and subversive people. We, all of us, do quite a lot of ceremonial oath-taking on many important occasions of life as an act of faith, a public testimony of honorable intention, and it is the mere truth that an oath binds only those persons who meant to keep their promises anyway, with or without an oath. The others cannot be touched or controlled in any such way. We all know this so why assist at such a cynical fraud.

I'm entirely hostile to the principle of Communism and to every form of totalitarian society, whether it calls itself

Communism, Fascism, or whatever. I feel indeed that Communism and Fascism are two names for the same thing, that the present struggle is really a civil war between two factions of totalitarianism. But Fascism is older, more insidious, harder to identify, easier to disguise. No one can be a Communist without knowing what he is doing. A man may be a most poisonous Fascist without even in the least recognizing his malady.

It is not the oath itself that troubles me. There is nothing in it I do not naturally and instinctively observe as I have and will. My people are the old stock. They helped to found colonies, to break new trails, and to survey wildernesses. They set up little log cabin academies, all the way from Virginia and Pennsylvania to Kentucky and clear into Texas. They have fought in all the wars, they have been governors of states, and military attachés, and at least one ambassador among us. We're not suspect, nor liable to the questionings of the kind of people we would never have invited to our tables.

You can see what the root of my resentment is. My many family branches helped to make this country. My feeling about my country and its history is as tender and intimate as about my own parents, and I really suffer to have them violated by the irresponsible acts of cheap politicians who prey on public fears in times of trouble and force their betters into undignified positions.

Our duty, Dr. Ross, is to circumvent them. To see through them and stop them in their tracks in time and not to be hoodwinked or terrorized by them, not to rationalize and excuse that weakness in us which leads us to criminal collusion with them for the sake of our jobs or the hope of being left in peace. That is not the road to any kind of safety. Nothing really effective is being done here against either Communism or Fascism, at least not by the politicians because they do not want anything settled. Their occupation and careers would be gone. We're going to be made sorry very soon for our refusal to reject unconditionally the kind of evil that disguises itself as patriotism, as love of virtue, as religious faith, as the crusador against the internal enemy. These people are themselves the enemy.

I do not propose to sit down quietly and be told by them what my duty is to my country and my government. My feelings and beliefs are nothing they could understand. I do not like being told that I must take an oath of allegiance to my government and flag under the threat of losing my employment if I do not. This is blackmail, and I have never been blackmailed successfully yet and do not intend to begin now.

So please destroy the contract we have made, as it is no longer valid. I know I run some little risk of nasty publicity in this matter. I hope not. I am not in the least a martyr. I have no time for heroics and indeed distrust them deeply. I am an artist who wishes to be left in peace to do my work. I hope that work will speak in the long run very clearly for me and all my kind, will be in some sort my testimony and my share of the battle against the elements of corruption and dissolution that come upon us so insidiously from all sides we hardly know where to begin to oppose them.

You may say this is a great how-do-you-do about a small matter. I can only say it is not a small matter when added to all other small matters of the kind that finally make an army of locusts.

Dr. Ross, I thank you for your courteous letter and hope you will take my word that this letter has nothing personal in it. That towards you I intend nothing but human respect in the assurance that I believe I understand your situation which must be extremely difficult.

What has this kind of meanness and cheapness to do with education? What is wrong that undesirable applicants for the faculty are not quietly discovered and refused before they are appointed? Why must a person like me be asked to do a stupid, meaningless thing because one person with a bad political record got into your college once? No, I can't have it, and neither can you. The amusing side of all this brou-ha-ha is I really did not expect to have any occasion to mention the flag or the laws of Colorado or the Communist Alger Hiss or even the Fascist Senator McCarthy. I meant to talk about literature, life understood and loved in terms of the human heart in the personal experience. The life of the imagination and the search for the true meanings of our fate in this world, of the soul as a pilgrim on a stony path and of faithfulness to an ideal good and tenacity in the love of truth. Whether or not we ever find it, we still must look for it to the very end.

Any real study of great literature must take in human life at every possible level and search out every dark corner. And its natural territory is the whole human experience, no less. It does not astonish me that young people love to hear about these things, love to talk about them, and think about them. It is sometimes surprising to me how gay my classes can be, as if we had found some spring of joy in the tragic state to which all of us are born. This is the service the arts do, and the totalitarian's first idea is to destroy exactly this. They can do great harm but not for long. I am not in the least afraid of them.

With my sincere good wishes, and apologies for this overlong letter,

Yours,
Katherine Anne Porter

William Faulkner to David Kirk

"If I were a Negro," the Nobel Prize–winning southern writer William Faulkner wrote in an open letter to the "Leaders of the Negro Race," "I would say [. . .]: 'We must learn to deserve equality so that we can hold and keep it after we get it. We must learn responsibility, the responsibility of equality. We must learn that there is no such thing as a 'right' without any ties to it." The letter, which was published in the prominent black magazine Ebony *and reiterated Faulkner's earlier public admonition to "Go slow" on desegregation, incensed civil rights activists both black and white. Faulkner's opinions were criticized for being patronizing, and his advice to blacks to "be more flexible" was considered, by many, to be misplaced. About six months before the* Ebony *letter appeared Faulkner wrote a somewhat more personal letter to David Kirk, who was organizing an interracial dialogue among students in Alabama, articulating in greater detail his views on segregation in America.*

8 March 1956 Oxford, Miss.

Dear Mr. Kirk:

Your letter of March 1st. is at hand several days. I wanted to think first before I tried to answer.

I wont try to tell you what to do in order to meet the problems you will face. The reason is, these problems will be individual ones, peculiar to the time and the place they will occur in. I mean, rise into sight, when they will have to be coped with.

I have found that the greatest help in meeting any problem with decency and self-respect and whatever courage is demanded, is to know where you yourself stand. That is, to have in words what you believe and are acting from.

I have tried to simplify my own standards by and from which I act, as follows, which I pass on to you.

1. Segregation is going, whether we like it or not. We no longer have any choice between segregation or un-segregation. The only choice we now have is, how, by what means. That is, shall segregation be abolished by force, from outside our country, despite everything we can do; or shall it be abolished by choice, by us in the South who will have to bear the burden of it, before it is forced on us.

I vote that we ourselves choose to abolish it, if for no other reason than, by voluntarily giving the Negro the chance for whatever equality he is capable of, we will stay on top; he will owe us gratitude; where, if his equality is forced on us by law, compulsion from outside, he will be on top from being the victor, the winner against opposition. And no tyrant is more ruthless than he who was only yesterday the oppressed, the slave.

That is the simple expediency of this matter, apart from the morality of it. Apart from the world situation in which we are steadily losing ground against the powers which decree that individual freedom must perish. We must have as many people as possible on the side of us who believe in individual freedom. There are seventeen million Negroes. Let us have them on our side, rather than on that of Russia.

That is the problem, as I see it. Why dont you get in touch with the Student Council or the TAR HEEL editorial board at North Carolina, Chapel Hill? They have handled the question splendidly. I can think of nothing which would do more to hold intact integrity and decency and sanity in this matter, than a sort of inter-State University organization for simple decency and rationality among Southern college men and women, young men and women. A confederation of older men like me would not carry half this weight. I can imagine nothing which would carry more weight than a sane, sober union of student representatives from all the Southern schools, standing for the simple things which democracy means and which we have got to show the world that we do mean if we are to survive: the simple principles of due process of the majority will and desire based on decency and fairness to all as ratified by law.

This may be difficult at first. It is a sad commentary on human nature that it is much easier, simpler, much more fun and excitement, to be *against* something you can see, like a black skin, than to be *for* something you can only believe in as a principle, like justice and fairness and (in the long view) the continuation of individual freedom and liberty.

And remember this too, when you have to meet these individual problems: you will be dealing with cowards. Most segregationalists are afraid of something, possibly Negroes; I dont know. But they seem to function only as mobs, and mobs are always afraid of something, of something they doubt their ability to cope with singly and in daylight.

Consult your friends, if you like, send me a copy of your letter to me, with a copy of this, under a covering letter, to the editor of the N. C. TARHEEL, and see what comes of it. And let me know.

Yours sincerely,
William Faulkner

Dr. Martin Luther King Jr. to Eight Fellow Clergymen

Confined in a small jail for "civil disobedience" in Birmingham, Alabama, Dr. Martin Luther King Jr. learned that eight prominent clergymen, all white, had issued an "Appeal for Law and Order and Common Sense" essentially condemning King. They believed his marches, sit-ins, and demonstrations—although nonviolent—were nevertheless igniting the flames of fear and racial strife in the towns and cities in which they occurred. The clergymen recommended that King try to solve racial problems through the local and federal courts. Results would come more slowly, they conceded, but at least there would be no possibility of confrontation or social discord. Despite his imprisonment King felt it necessary to respond immediately to their criticisms, as well as to their praise for the Birmingham Police Department, led by Eugene "Bull" Connor, who assaulted demonstrators with fire hoses and police dogs. Initially written in the margins of a newspaper and on scraps of paper in his cell (he was then provided a notepad by his attorneys), King's "Letter from a Birmingham Jail" has since become one of the most famous letters in American history.

April 16, 1963

My dear Fellow Clergymen,

While confined here in the Birmingham city jail, I came across your recent statement calling our present activities "unwise and untimely." Seldom, if ever, do I pause to answer criticism of my work and ideas. If I sought to answer all of the criticisms that cross my desk, my secretaries would be engaged in little else in the course of the day, and I would have no time for constructive work. But since I feel that you are men of genuine good will and your criticisms are sincerely set forth, I would like to answer your statement in what I hope will be patient and reasonable terms.

I think I should give the reason for my being in Birmingham, since you have been influenced by the argument of "outsiders coming in." I have the honor of serving as president of the Southern Christian Leadership Conference, an organization operating in every southern state, with headquarters in Atlanta,

Georgia. We have some eighty-five affiliate organizations all across the South—one being the Alabama Christian Movement for Human Rights. Whenever necessary and possible we share staff, educational and financial resources with our affiliates. Several months ago our local affiliate here in Birmingham invited us to be on call to engage in a nonviolent direct-action program if such were deemed necessary. We readily consented and when the hour came we lived up to our promises. So I am here, along with several members of my staff, because we were invited here. I am here because I have basic organizational ties here.

Beyond this, I am in Birmingham because injustice is here. Just as the eighth century prophets left their little villages and carried their "thus saith the Lord" far beyond the boundaries of their hometowns; and just as the Apostle Paul left his little village of Tarsus and carried the gospel of Jesus Christ to practically every hamlet and city of the Graeco-Roman world, I too am compelled to carry the gospel of freedom beyond my particular hometown. Like Paul, I must constantly respond to the Macedonian call for aid.

Moreover, I am cognizant of the interrelatedness of all communities and states. I cannot sit idly by in Atlanta and not be concerned about what happens in Birmingham. Injustice anywhere is a threat to justice everywhere. We are caught in an inescapable network of mutuality, tied in a single garment of destiny. Whatever affects one directly affects all indirectly. Never again can we afford to live with the narrow, provincial "outside agitator" idea. Anyone who lives in the United States can never be considered an outsider anywhere in this country.

You deplore the demonstrations that are presently taking place in Birmingham. But I am sorry that your statement did not express a similar concern for the conditions that brought the demonstrations into being. I am sure that each of you would want to go beyond the superficial social analyst who looks merely at effects, and does not grapple with underlying causes. I would not hesitate to say that it is unfortunate that so-called demonstrations are taking place in Birmingham at this time, but I would say in more emphatic terms that it is even more unfortunate that the white power structure of this city left the Negro community with no other alternative.

In any nonviolent campaign there are four basic steps: (1) collection of the facts to determine whether injustices are alive, (2) negotiation, (3) self-purification, and (4) direct action. We have gone through all of these steps in Birmingham. There can be no gainsaying of the fact that racial injustice engulfs this community.

Birmingham is probably the most thoroughly segregated city in the United States. Its ugly record of police brutality is known in every section of this country. Its unjust treatment of Negroes in the courts is a notorious reality. There have been more unsolved bombings of Negro homes and churches in Birmingham than any city in this nation. These are the hard, brutal and unbelievable facts. On the basis of these conditions Negro leaders sought to negotiate with the city fathers. But the political leaders consistently refused to engage in good faith negotiation.

Then came the opportunity last September to talk with some of the leaders of the economic community. In these negotiating sessions certain promises were made by the merchants—such as the promise to remove the humiliating racial signs from the stores. On the basis of these promises Rev. Shuttlesworth and the leaders of the Alabama Christian Movement for Human Rights agreed to call a moratorium on any type of demonstrations. As the weeks and months unfolded we realized that we were the victims of a broken promise. The signs remained. Like so many experiences of the past we were confronted with blasted hopes, and the dark shadow of a deep disappointment settled upon us. So we had no alternative except that of preparing for direct action, whereby we would present our very bodies as means of laying our case before the conscience of the local and national community. We were not unmindful of the difficulties involved. So we decided to go through a process of self-purification. We started having workshops on nonviolence and repeatedly asked ourselves the questions, "Are you able to accept blows without retaliating?" "Are you able to endure the ordeals of jail?" We decided to set our direct-action program around the Easter season, realizing that with the exception of

Christmas, this was the largest shopping period of the year. Knowing that a strong economic withdrawal program would be the by-product of direct action, we felt that this was the best time to bring pressure on the merchants for the needed changes. Then it occurred to us that the March election was ahead and so we speedily decided to postpone action until after election day. When we discovered that Mr. Connor was in the run-off, we decided again to postpone action so that the demonstrations could not be used to cloud the issues. At this time we agreed to begin our nonviolent witness the day after the run-off.

This reveals that we did not move irresponsibly into direct action. We too wanted to see Mr. Connor defeated; so we went through postponement after postponement to aid in this community need. After this we felt that direct action could be delayed no longer.

You may well ask, "Why direct action? Why sit-ins, marches, etc.? Isn't negotiation a better path?" You are exactly right in your call for negotiation. Indeed, this is the purpose of direct action. Nonviolent direct action seeks to create such a crisis and establish such creative tension that a community that has constantly refused to negotiate is forced to confront the issue. It seeks so to dramatize the issue that it can no longer be ignored. I just referred to the creation of tension as a part of the work of the nonviolent resister. This may sound rather shocking. But I must confess that I am not afraid of the word tension. I have earnestly worked and preached against violent tension, but there is a type of constructive nonviolent tension that is necessary for growth. Just as Socrates felt that it was necessary to create a tension in the mind so that individuals could rise from the bondage of myths and half-truths to the unfettered realm of creative analysis and objective appraisal, we must see the need of having nonviolent gadflies to create the kind of tension in society that will help men to rise from the dark depths of prejudice and racism to the majestic heights of understanding and brotherhood. So the purpose of the direct action is to create a situation so crisis-packed that it will inevitably open the door to negotiation. We, therefore, concur with you in your call for negotiation. Too long has our beloved Southland been bogged down in the tragic attempt to live in monologue rather than dialogue.

One of the basic points in your statement is that our acts are untimely. Some have asked, "Why didn't you give this new administration time to act?" The only answer that I can give to this inquiry is that the new administration must be prodded about as much as the outgoing one before it acts. We will be sadly mistaken if we feel that the election of Mr. Boutwell will bring the millenium to Birmingham. While Mr. Boutwell is much more articulate and gentle than Mr. O'Connor, they are both segregationists, dedicated to the task of maintaining the status quo. The hope I see in Mr. Boutwell is that he will be reasonable enough to see the futility of massive resistance to desegregation. But he will not see this without pressure from the devotees of civil rights. My friends, I must say to you that we have not made a single gain in civil rights without determined legal and nonviolent pressure. History is the long and tragic story of the fact that privileged groups seldom give up their privileges voluntarily. Individuals may see the moral light and voluntarily give up their unjust posture; but as Reinhold Neibuhr has reminded us, groups are more immoral than individuals.

We know through painful experience that freedom is never voluntarily given by the oppressor; it must be demanded by the oppressed. Frankly, I have never yet engaged in a direct action movement that was "well-timed," according to the timetable of those who have not suffered unduly from the disease of segregation. For years now I have heard the words "Wait!" It rings in the ear of every Negro with a piercing familiarity. This "Wait" has almost always meant "Never." It has been a tranquilizing thalidomide, relieving the emotional stress for a moment, only to give birth to an ill-formed infant of frustration. We must come to see with the distinguished jurist of yesterday that "justice too long delayed is justice denied." We have waited for more than 340 years for our constitutional and God-given rights. The nations of Asia and Africa are moving with jetlike speed toward the goal of political independence, and we still creep at horse and buggy pace toward the gaining of a cup of coffee at a lunch counter. I guess it is easy for those who have never felt the stinging darts of segregation to say, "Wait." But when you have seen vicious mobs lynch your mothers and fathers at will and drown your sisters and brothers at whim; when you have seen hate-filled policemen curse, kick, brutalize and even kill your black brothers and sisters with impunity; when you see the vast majority of your twenty million Negro brothers smothering in an airtight cage of poverty in the midst of an affluent society; when you suddenly find your tongue twisted and your speech stammering as you seek to explain to your six-year-old daughter why she can't go to the public amusement park that has just been advertised on television, and see tears welling up in her little eyes when she is told that Funtown is closed to colored children, and see the depressing clouds of inferiority begin to form in her little mental sky, and see her begin to distort her little personality by unconsciously developing a bitterness toward white people; when you have to concoct an answer for a five-year-old son asking in agonizing pathos: "Daddy, why do white people treat colored people so mean?"; when you take a cross-country drive and find it necessary to sleep night after night in the uncomfortable corners of your automobile because no motel will accept you; when you are humiliated day in and day out by nagging signs reading "white" and "colored"; when your first name becomes "nigger" and your middle name becomes "boy" (however old you are) and your last name becomes "John," and when your wife and mother are never given the respected title "Mrs."; when you are harried by day and haunted by night by the fact that you are a Negro living constantly at tiptoe stance never quite knowing what to expect next, and plagued with inner fears and outer resentments; when you are forever fighting a degenerating sense of "nobodiness"; then you will understand why we find it difficult to wait. There comes a time when the cup of endurance runs over, and men are no longer willing to be plunged into an abyss of injustice where they experience the blackness of corroding despair. I hope, sirs, you can understand our legitimate and unavoidable impatience.

You express a great deal of anxiety over our willingness to

break laws. This is certainly a legitimate concern. Since we so diligently urge people to obey the Supreme Court's decision of 1954 outlawing segregation in the public schools, it is rather strange and paradoxical to find us consciously breaking laws. One may well ask, "How can you advocate breaking some laws and obeying others?" The answer is found in the fact that there are two types of laws: there are *just* and there are *unjust* laws. I would agree with St. Augustine that "An unjust law is no law at all."

Now what is the difference between the two? How does one determine when a law is just or unjust? A just law is a man-made code that squares with the moral law or the law of God. An unjust law is a code that is out of harmony with the moral law. To put it in the terms of Saint Thomas Aquinas, an unjust law is a human law that is not rooted in eternal and natural law. Any law that uplifts human personality is just. Any law that degrades human personality is unjust. All segregation statutes are unjust because segregation distorts the soul and damages the personality. It gives the segregator a false sense of superiority, and the segregated a false sense of inferiority. To use the words of Martin Buber, the great Jewish philosopher, segregation substitutes an "I-it" relationship for the "I-thou" relationship, and ends up relegating persons to the status of things. So segregation is not only politically, economically and sociologically unsound, but it is morally wrong and sinful. Paul Tillich has said that sin is separation. Isn't segregation an existential expression of man's tragic separation, an expression of his awful estrangement, his terrible sinfulness? So I can urge men to disobey segregation ordinances because they are morally wrong.

Let us turn to a more concrete example of just and unjust laws. An unjust law is a code that a majority inflicts on a minority that is not binding on itself. This is difference made legal. On the other hand a just law is a code that a majority compels a minority to follow that it is willing to follow itself. This is sameness made legal.

Let me give another explanation. An unjust law is a code inflicted upon a minority which that minority had no part in enacting or creating because they did not have the unhampered right to vote. Who can say that the legislature of Alabama which set up the segregation laws was democratically elected? Throughout the state of Alabama all types of conniving methods are used to prevent Negroes from becoming registered voters and there are some counties without a single Negro registered to vote despite the fact that the Negro constitutes a majority of the population. Can any law set up in such a state be considered democratically structured?

These are just a few examples of unjust and just laws. There are some instances when a law is just on its face and unjust in its application. For instance, I was arrested Friday on a charge of parading without a permit. Now there is nothing wrong with an ordinance which requires a permit for a parade, but when the ordinance is used to preserve segregation and to deny citizens the First Amendment privilege of peaceful assembly and peaceful protest, then it becomes unjust.

I hope you can see the distinction I am trying to point out. In no sense do I advocate evading or defying the law as the rabid segregationist would do. This would lead to anarchy. One who breaks an unjust law must do it *openly*, *lovingly* (not hatefully as the white mothers did in New Orleans when they were seen on television screaming, "nigger, nigger, nigger"), and with a willingness to accept the penalty. I submit that an individual who breaks a law that conscience tells him is unjust, and willingly accepts the penalty by staying in jail to arouse the conscience of the community over its injustice, is in reality expressing the very highest respect for the law.

Of course, there is nothing new about this kind of civil disobedience. It was seen sublimely in the refusal of Shadrach, Meshach and Abednego to obey the laws of Nebuchadnezzar because a higher moral law was involved. It was practiced superbly by the early Christians who were willing to face hungry lions and the excruciating pain of chopping blocks, before submitting to certain unjust laws of the Roman Empire. To a degree academic freedom is a reality today because Socrates practiced civil disobedience.

We can never forget that everything Hitler did in Germany was "legal" and everything the Hungarian freedom fighters did in Hungary was "illegal." It was "illegal" to aid and comfort a Jew in Hitler's Germany. But I am sure that if I had lived in Germany during that time I would have aided and comforted my Jewish brothers even though it was illegal. If I lived in a Communist country today where certain principles dear to the Christian faith are suppressed, I believe I would openly advocate disobeying these anti-religious laws. I must make two honest confessions to you, my Christian and Jewish brothers. First, I must confess that over the last few years I have been gravely disappointed with the white moderate. I have almost reached the regrettable conclusion that the Negro's great stumbling block in the stride toward freedom is not the White Citizen's Counciler or the Ku Klux Klanner, but the white moderate who is more devoted to "order" than to justice; who prefers a negative peace which is the absence of tension to a positive peace which is the presence of justice; who constantly says, "I agree with you in the goal you seek, but I can't agree with your methods of direct action"; who paternalistically feels that he can set the timetable for another man's freedom; who lives by the myth of time and who constantly advised the Negro to wait until a "more convenient season." Shallow understanding from people of good will is more frustrating than absolute misunderstanding from people of ill will. Lukewarm acceptance is much more bewildering than outright rejection.

I had hoped that the white moderate would understand that law and order exist for the purpose of establishing justice, and that when they fail to do so they become dangerously structured dams that block the flow of social progress. I had hoped that the white moderate would understand that the present tension of the South is merely a necessary phase of the transition from an obnoxious negative peace, where the Negro passively accepted his unjust plight, to a substance-filled positive peace, where all men will respect the dignity and worth of human personality. Actually, we who engage in nonviolent direct action are not the creators of tension. We merely bring to the surface the hidden tension that is already alive. We bring it out in the open where it can be seen and dealt with. Like a boil that can never be cured as long as it is covered up but must be opened with all its pus-flowing ugliness to the natural medicines of air and light, injustice must likewise be exposed, with all of the tension its exposing creates, to the light of human conscience and the air of national opinion before it can be cured.

In your statement you asserted that our actions, even though peaceful, must be condemned because they precipitate violence. But can this assertion be logically made? Isn't this like condemning the robbed man because his possession of money precipitated the evil act of robbery? Isn't this like condemning Socrates because his unswerving commitment to truth and his philosophical delvings precipitated the misguided popular mind to make him drink the hemlock? Isn't this like condemning Jesus because His unique God-consciousness and never-ceasing devotion to His will precipitated the evil act of crucifixion? We must come to see, as federal courts have consistently affirmed, that it is immoral to urge an individual to withdraw his efforts to gain his basic constitutional rights because the quest precipitates violence. Society must protect the robbed and punish the robber.

I had also hoped that the white moderate would reject the myth of time. I received a letter this morning from a white brother in Texas which said: "All Christians know that colored people will receive equal rights eventually, but it is possible that you are in too great of a religious hurry. It has taken Christianity almost two thousand years to accomplish what it has. The teachings of Christ take time to come to earth." All that is said here grows out of a tragic misconception of time. It is the strangely irrational notion that there is something in the very flow of time that will inevitably cure all ills. Actually time is neutral. It can be used either destructively or constructively. I am coming to feel that the people of ill will have used time much more effectively than the people of good will. We will have to repent in this generation not merely for the vitriolic words and actions of the bad people, but for the appalling silence of the good people. We must come to see that human progress never rolls in on the wheels of inevitability. It comes through the tireless efforts and persistent work of men willing to be co-workers with God, and without this hard work time itself becomes an ally of the forces of social stagnation. We must use time creatively, and forever realize that the time is always right to do right. Now is the time to make real the promise of democracy, and transform our pending national elegy into a creative psalm of brotherhood. Now is the time to lift our national policy from the quicksand of racial injustice to the solid rock of human dignity.

You spoke of our activity in Birmingham as extreme. At first I was rather disappointed that fellow clergymen would see my nonviolent efforts as those of the extremist. I started thinking about the fact that I stand in the middle of two opposing forces in the Negro community. One is a force of complacency made up of Negroes who, as a result of long years of oppression, have been so completely drained of self-respect and a sense of "somebodiness" that they have adjusted to segregation, and, of a few Negroes in the middle class who, because of a degree of academic and economic security, and because at points they profit by segregation, have unconsciously become insensitive to the problems of the masses. The other force is one of bitterness and hatred, and comes perilously close to advocating violence. It is expressed in the various black nationalistic groups that are springing up over the nation, the largest and best known being Elijah Muhammad's Muslim movement. This movement is nourished by the contemporary frustration over the continued existence of racial discrimination. It is made up of people who have lost faith in America, who have absolutely repudiated Christianity, and who have concluded that the white man is an incurable "devil." I have tried to stand between these two forces, saying that we need not follow the "do-nothingism" of the complacent or the hatred and despair of the black nationalist. There is the more excellent way of love and nonviolent protest. I'm grateful to God that, through the Negro church, the dimension of nonviolence entered our struggle. If this philosophy had not emerged, I am convinced that by now many streets of the South would be flowing with floods of blood. And I am further convinced that if our white brothers dismiss us as "rabble-rousers" and "outside agitators" those of us who are working through the channels of nonviolent direct action and refuse to support our nonviolent efforts, millions of Negroes, out of frustration and despair, will seek solace and security in black nationalist ideologies, a development that will lead inevitably to a frightening racial nightmare.

Oppressed people cannot remain oppressed forever. The urge for freedom will eventually come. This is what happened to the American Negro. Something within has reminded him of his birthright of freedom; something without has reminded him that he can gain it. Consciously and unconsciously, he has been swept in by what the Germans call the *Zeitgeist*, and with his black brothers of Africa, and his brown and yellow brothers of Asia, South America and the Caribbean, he is moving with a sense of cosmic urgency toward the promised land of racial justice. Recognizing this vital urge that has engulfed the Negro community, one should readily understand public demonstrations. The Negro has many pent-up resentments and latent frustrations. He has to get them out. So let him march sometime; let him have his prayer pilgrimages to the city hall; understand why he must have sit-ins and freedom rides. If his repressed emotions do not come out in these nonviolent ways, they will come out in ominous expressions of violence. This is not a threat; it is a fact of history. So I have not said to my people "get rid of your discontent." But I have tried to say that this normal and healthy discontent can be channeled through the creative outlet of nonviolent direct action. Now this approach is being dismissed as extremist. I must admit that I was initially disappointed in being so categorized.

But as I continued to think about the matter I gradually gained a bit of satisfaction from being considered an extremist. Was not Jesus an extremist in love—"Love your enemies, bless them that curse you, pray for them that despitefully use you." Was not Amos an extremist for justice—"Let justice roll down like waters and righteousness like a mighty stream." Was not Paul an extremist for the gospel of Jesus Christ—"I bear in my body the marks of the Lord Jesus." Was not Martin Luther an extremist—"Here I stand; I can do none other so help me God." Was not John Bunyan an extremist—"I will stay in jail to the end of my days before I make a butchery of my conscience." Was not Abraham Lincoln an extremist—"This nation cannot survive half slave and half free." Was not Thomas Jefferson an extremist—"We hold these truths to be self-evident, that all men are created equal." So the question is not whether we will be extremist but what kind of extremist we will be. Will we be extremists for hate or will we be extremists for love? Will we be extremists for the preservation of injustice—or will we be extremists for the cause of justice? In that dramatic scene of Calvary's hill, three men were crucified. We must not forget that all three were crucified for the same crime—the crime of extremism. Two were extremists for immorality, and thusly fell below their environment. The other, Jesus Christ, was an extremist for love, truth and goodness, and thereby rose above his environment. So, after all, maybe the South, the nation and the world are in dire need of creative extremists.

I had hoped that the white moderate would see this. Maybe I was too optimistic. Maybe I expected too much. I guess I should have realized that few members of a race that has oppressed another race can understand or appreciate the deep groans and the passionate yearnings of those that have been oppressed and still fewer have the vision to see that injustice must be rooted out by strong, persistent and determined action. I am thankful, however, that some of our white brothers have grasped the meaning of this social revolution and committed themselves to it. They are still all too small in quantity, but they are big in quality. Some like Ralph McGill, Lillian Smith, Harry Golden, and James Dabbs have written about our struggle in eloquent, prophetic and understanding terms. Others have marched with us down nameless streets of the South. They have languished in filthy roach-infested jails, suffering the abuse and brutality of angry policemen who see them as "dirty nigger-lovers." They, unlike so many of their moderate brothers and sisters, have recognized the urgency of the moment and sensed the need for powerful "action" antidotes to combat the disease of segregation.

Let me rush on to mention my other disappointment. I have been so greatly disappointed with the white church and its leadership. Of course, there are some notable exceptions. I am not unmindful of the fact that each of you has taken some significant stands on this issue. I commend you, Rev. Stallings, for your Christian stance on this past Sunday, in welcoming Negroes to your worship service on a non-segregated basis. I commend the Catholic leaders of this state for integrating Springhill College several years ago.

But despite these notable exceptions I must honestly reiterate that I have been disappointed with the church. I do not say that as one of the negative critics who can always find something wrong with the church. I say it as a minister of the gospel, who loves the church; who was nurtured in its bosom; who has been sustained by its spiritual blessings and who will remain true to it as long as the cord of life shall lengthen.

I had the strange feeling when I was suddenly catapulted into the leadership of the bus protest in Montgomery several years ago that we would have the support of the white church. I felt that the white ministers, priests and rabbis of the South would be some of our strongest allies. Instead, some have been outright opponents, refusing to understand the freedom movement and misrepresenting its leaders; all too many others have been more cautious than courageous and have remained silent behind the anesthetizing security of the stained-glass windows.

In spite of my shattered dreams of the past, I came to Birmingham with the hope that the white religious leadership of this community would see the justice of our cause, and with deep moral concern, serve as the channel through which our just grievances would get to the power structure. I had hoped that each of you would understand. But again I have been disappointed. I have heard numerous religious leaders of the South call upon their worshippers to comply with a desegregation decision because it is the *law*, but I have longed to hear white ministers say, "Follow this decree because integregation is morally *right* and the Negro is your brother." In the midst of blatant injustices inflicted upon the Negro, I have watched white churches stand on the sideline and merely mouth pious irrelevancies and sanctimonious trivialities. In the midst of a mighty struggle to rid our nation of racial and economic injustice, I have heard so many ministers say, "Those are social issues with which the gospel has no real concern," and I have watched so many churches commit themselves to a completely otherwordly religion which made a strange distinction between body and soul, the sacred and the secular.

So here we are moving toward the exit of the twentieth century with a religious community largely adjusted to the status quo, standing as a tail-light behind other community agencies rather than a headlight leading men to higher levels of justice.

I have traveled the length and breadth of Alabama, Mississippi and all the other southern states. On sweltering summer days and crisp autumn mornings I have looked at her beautiful churches with their lofty spires pointing heavenward. I have beheld the impressive outlay of her massive religious education buildings. Over and over again I have found myself asking, "What kind of people worship here? Who is their God? Where were their voices when the lips of Governor Barnett dripped with words of interposition and nullification? Where were they when Governor Wallace gave the clarion call for defiance and hatred? Where were their voices of support when tired, bruised and weary Negro men and women decided to rise from the dark dungeons of complacency to the bright hills of creative protest?"

Yes, these questions are still in my mind. In deep disappointment, I have wept over the laxity of the church. But be assured that my tears have been tears of love. There can be no deep disppointment where there is not deep love. Yes, I love the church; I love her sacred walls. How could I do otherwise? I am in the rather unique position of being the son, the grandson and the great-grandson of preachers. Yes, I see the church as the body of Christ. But, oh! How we have blemished and scarred that body through social neglect and fear of being noncomformists.

There was a time when the church was very powerful. It was during that period when the early Christians rejoiced when they were deemed worthy to suffer for what they believed. In those days the church was not merely a thermometer that recorded the ideas and principles of popular opinion; it was a thermostat that transformed the mores of society. Wherever the early Christians entered a town the power structure got disturbed and immediately sought to convict them for being "disturbers of the peace" and "outside agitators." But they went on with the conviction that they were a "colony of heaven," and had to obey God rather than man. They were small in number but big in commitment. They were too God-intoxicated to be "astronomically intimidated." They brought an end to such ancient evils as infanticide and gladiatorial conquest.

Things are different now. The contemporary church is often a weak, ineffectual voice with an uncertain sound. It is so often the arch-supporter of the status quo. Far from being disturbed by the presence of the church, the power structure of the average community is consoled by the church's silent and often vocal sanction of things as they are.

But the judgment of God is upon the church as never before. If the church of today does not recapture the sacrificial spirit of the early church, it will lose its authentic ring, forfeit the loyalty of millions, and be dismissed as an irrelevant social club with no meaning for the twentieth century. I am meeting young people every day whose disappointment with the church has risen to outright disgust.

Maybe again, I have been too optimistic. Is organized religion too inextricably bound to the status quo to save our nation and the world? Maybe I must turn my faith to the inner spiritual church, the church within the church, as the true *ecclesia* and the hope of the world. But again I am thankful to God that some noble souls from the ranks of organized religion have broken loose from the paralyzing chains of conformity and joined us as active partners in the struggle for freedom. They have left their secure congregations and walked the streets of Albany, Georgia, with us. They have gone through the highways of the South on torturous rides for freedom. Yes, they have gone to jail with us. Some have been kicked out of their churches, and lost support of their bishops and fellow ministers. But they have gone with the faith that right defeated is stronger than evil triumphant. These men have been the leaven in the lump of the race. Their witness has been the spiritual salt that has preserved the true meaning of the gospel in these troubled times. They have carved a tunnel of hope through the dark mountain of disappointment.

I hope the church as a whole will meet the challenge of this decisive hour. But even if the church does not come to the aid of justice, I have no despair about the future. I have no fear about the outcome of our struggle in Birmingham, even if our motives are presently misunderstood. We will reach the goal of freedom in Birmingham and all over the nation, because the goal of America is freedom. Abused and scorned though we may be, our destiny is tied with the destiny of America. Before the Pilgrims landed at Plymouth we were here. Before the pen of Jefferson etched across the pages of history the majestic words of the Declaration of Independence, we were here. For more than two centuries our foreparents labored in this country without wages; they made cotton king; and they built the homes of their masters in the midst of brutal injustice and shameful humiliation—and yet out of a bottomless vitality they continued to thrive and develop. If the inexpressible cruelties of slavery could not stop us, the opposition we now face will surely fail. We will win our freedom because the sacred heritage of our nation and the eternal will of God are embodied in our echoing demands.

I must close now. But before closing I am impelled to mention one other point in your statement that troubled me profoundly. You warmly commended the Birmingham police force for keeping "order" and "preventing violence." I don't believe you would have so warmly commended the police force if you had seen its angry violent dogs literally biting six unarmed, nonviolent Negroes. I don't believe you would so quickly commend the policemen if you would observe their ugly and inhuman treatment of Negroes here in the city jail; if you would watch them push and curse old Negro women and young Negro girls; if you would see them slap and kick old Negro men and young boys; if you will observe them, as they did on two occasions, refuse to give us food because we wanted to sing our grace together. I'm sorry that I can't join you in your praise for the police department.

It is true that they have been rather disciplined in their public handling of the demonstrators. In this sense they have been rather publicly "nonviolent." But for what purpose? To preserve the evil system of segregation. Over the last few years I have consistently preached that nonviolence demands that the means we use must be as pure as the ends we seek. So I have tried to make it clear that it is wrong to use immoral means to attain moral ends. But now I must affirm that it is just as wrong, or even more so, to use moral means to preserve immoral ends. Maybe Mr. Connor and his policemen have been rather publicly nonviolent, as chief Pritchett was in Albany, Georgia, but they have used the moral means of nonviolence to maintain the immoral end of flagrant racial injustice. T. S. Eliot has said that there is no greater treason than to do the right deed for the wrong reason.

I wish you had commended the Negro sit-inners and demonstrators of Birmingham for their sublime courage, their willingness to suffer and their amazing discipline in the midst of the most inhuman provocation. One day the South will recognize its real heroes. They will be the James Merediths, courageously and with a majestic sense of purpose facing jeering and hostile mobs and the agonizing loneliness that characterizes the life of the pioneer. They will be the old, oppressed, battered Negro women, symbolized in a seventy-two-year-old woman of Montgomery, Alabama, who rose up with a sense of dignity and with her people decided not to ride the segregated buses, and responded to one who inquired about her tiredness with ungrammatical profundity: "My feet is tired, but my soul is rested." They will be the young high school and college students, young ministers of the gospel and a host of their elders courageously and nonviolently sitting-in at lunch counters and willingly going to jail for conscience's sake.

One day the South will know that when these disinherited children of God sat down at lunch counters they were in reality standing up for the best in the American dream and the most sacred values in our Judeo-Christian heritage, and thusly, carrying our whole nation back to those great wells of democracy which were dug deep by the Founding Fathers in the formulation of the Constitution and the Declaration of Independence.

Never before have I written a letter this long (or should I say a book?). I'm afraid that it is much too long to take your precious time. I can assure you that it would have been much shorter if I had been writing from a comfortable desk, but what else is there to do when you are alone for days in the dull monotony of a narrow jail cell than write long letters, think strange thoughts, and pray long prayers?

If I have said anything in this letter that is an overstatement of the truth and indicative of an unreasonable impatience, I beg you to forgive me. If I have said anything in this letter that is an understatement of the truth and is indicative of my having a patience that makes me patient with anything less than brotherhood, I beg God to forgive me.

I hope this letter finds you strong in the faith. I also hope that circumstances will soon make it possible for me to meet each of you, not as an integrationist or a civil rights leader, but as a fellow clergyman and a Christian brother. Let us all hope that the dark clouds of racial prejudice will soon pass away and the deep fog of misunderstanding will be lifted from our fear-drenched communities and in some not too distant tomorrow the radiant stars of love and brotherhood will shine over our great nation with all of their scintillating beauty.

Yours for the cause of Peace and Brotherhood,
Martin Luther King, Jr.

"Jim," a Student Civil Rights Worker, to His Parents

They were mostly college students, white, and from the North, and in the summer of 1964, 650 of these young men and women traveled to Mississippi to organize civil rights efforts and voter registration drives throughout the state. The challenges they faced were daunting; the mayor of Jackson met them with tanks and riot gear, and a public opinion poll taken in June indicated that 65 percent of all Americans opposed the Mississippi Summer Project, as it was known. The students were undeterred, and they arrived for orientation in the middle of June, when they were taught how to dress and speak "southern" and how to act in the face of a threatening crowd or full-scale riot. The students were even teargassed, briefly, to give them a sense of what it might be like. One participant described the intensity of the training in a letter home to his parents. ("Lee," alluded to in the song "We'll Never Turn Back," is Herbert Lee, a black voter-registration worker killed in Mississippi several years earlier.)

Dear Folks,

A great deal of tension and a great deal of camaraderie here at Oxford. Workshops and role-playing are constant. We staged one situation, a screaming mob lining the steps to the courthouse while a small band of registrants tried to get through. The inevitable happened—what will actually happen in Mississippi happened. The chanting mob (instructed to be as brutal as possible, and to pull no punches) turned into a clawing, pounding mob, and we volunteer registrants were down in our crunched-up ball. Casualties? A couple of scratches, a sprained ankle, and one camerman who got swept up was a little bit shaken. It seems like brutal play, and it is. We've got to be ready for anything, and we must prepare for it ourselves. Once we get south we are nonviolent; we must get whatever there is in our systems out now, and we must also learn to take the worst. Some of the staff members walk around carrying sections of hose. This strangely terrible training in brutality may well save lives. (I must confess, I have not been able to take part in even the screaming of a mob scene, much less the pummeling. Wherever possible, I am among the victims.)

We have registration workshops, too. And lecturers came from all over the country to speak to us. And we sing. What "We Shall Overcome" is to the national movement, "We'll never turn back" is to the Mississippi workers. It is a slow song, measured out in grief and determination. The final verse goes,

We have hung our head and cried,
Cried out for those like Lee
who died
Died for you and died for me,
Died for the cause of equality,
  But we will never turn back
  Until we've all been free
  And we have equality, and we have equality.

Love,
Jim

Cesar Chavez to E. L. Barr Jr., President of the California Grape and Tree Fruit League

Inspired by the legacy of Dr. Martin Luther King Jr., Cesar Chavez was a migrant farmworker determined to bring an end to unfair labor practices, substandard wages, and unhealthy working conditions (such as the spraying of pesticides over fields as farmworkers picked produce) through nonviolent means. Chavez organized marches, fasts, and strikes, as well as the United Farmworkers Union (UFW), the first union of its kind. Through Chavez and the UFW, the farmworkers led a successful nationwide boycott against grapes and other handpicked fruits. In the following letter, written to one of the farmworkers' greatest antagonists, the California Grape and Tree Fruit League, Chavez articulates what he hopes to achieve.

Good Friday 1969
E.L. Barr, Jr. President
California Grape and Tree Fruit League
717 Market St.
San Francisco, California

Dear Mr. Barr,

I am sad to hear about your accusations in the press that our union movement and table grape boycott have been successful because we have used violence and terror tactics. If what you say is true, I have been a failure and should withdraw from the struggle; but you are left with the awesome moral responsibility, before God and Man, to come forward with whatever information you have so that corrective action can begin at once. If for any reason you fail to come forth to substantiate your charges, then you must be held responsible for committing violence against us, albeit of the tongue. I am convinced that you as a human being did not mean what you said but rather acted hastily under pressure from the public relations firm that has been hired to try to counteract the tremendous moral force of our movement. How many times we ourselves have felt the need to lash out in anger and bitterness.

Today on Good Friday, 1969, we remember the life and the sacrifice of Martin Luther King, Jr., who gave himself totally to the nonviolent struggle for peace and justice. In his *Letter From a Birmingham Jail* Dr. King describes better than I could our hopes for the strike and boycott: "Injustice must be exposed, with all the tensions its exposure creates, to the light of human conscience and the air of national opinion before it can be cured." For our part I admit that we have seized upon every tactic and strategy consistent with the morality of our cause to expose that injustice and thus to heighten the sensitivity of the American conscience so that farmworkers will have, without bloodshed, their own union and the dignity of bargaining with their agribusiness employers. By lying about the nature of our movement, Mr. Barr, you are working against nonviolent social change. Unwittingly perhaps, you may unleash the other force which our union by discipline and deed, censure and education has sought to avoid, that panacean shortcut: that senseless violence which honors no color, class, or neighborhood.

You must understand—I must make you understand—that our membership and the hopes and aspirations of the hundreds and thousands of the poor and dispossessed that have been raised on our account are, above all, human beings, no better and no worse than any other cross-section of human society; we are not saints because we are poor, but by the same measure neither are we immoral. We are men and women who have suffered and endured much, and not only because of our abject poverty but because we have been kept poor. The colors of our skins, the languages of our cultural and native origins, the lack of our formal education, the exclusion from the democratic process, the numbers of our men slain in recent wars—through all these burdens generation after generation have sought to demoralize us, to break our human spirit. But God knows that we are not beasts of burden, agricultural implements or rented slaves; we are men. And mark this well Mr. Barr, we are men locked in a death struggle against man's inhumanity to man in the industry that you represent. And this struggle itself gives meaning to our life and ennobles our dying.

As your industry has experienced, our strikers here in Delano and those who represent us throughout the world are well trained for this struggle. They have been under the gun, they have been kicked and beaten and herded by dogs, they have been cursed and ridiculed, they have been stripped and chained and jailed, they have been sprayed with the poisons used in the vineyards; but they have been taught not to lie down and die nor flee in shame, but to resist with every ounce of human endurance and spirit. To resist not with retaliation in kind but to overcome with love and compassion, with ingenuity and creativity, with hard work and longer hours, with stamina and patient tenacity, with truth and public appeal, with friends and allies, with mobility and discipline, with politics and law, and with prayer and fasting. They were not trained in a month or even a year; after all, this new harvest season will mark our fourth full year of strike and even now we continue to plan and prepare for the years to come. Time accomplishes for the poor what money does for the rich.

This is not to pretend that we have everywhere been successful enough or that we have not made mistakes. And while we do not belittle or underestimate our adversaries—for they are the rich and the powerful and they possess the land—we are not afraid nor do we cringe from the confrontation. We welcome it! We have planned for it. We know that our cause is just, that history is a story of social revolution, and that the poor shall inherit the land.

Once again, I appeal to you as the representative of your industry and as a man. I ask you to recognize and bargain with our union before the economic pressure of the boycott and strike takes an irrevocable toil; but if not, I ask you to at least sit down with us to discuss the safeguards necessary to keep our historic struggle free of violence. I make this appeal because as one of the leaders of our nonviolent movement, I know and accept my responsibility for preventing, if possible, the destruction of human life and property. For these reasons, and knowing Gandhi's admonition that fasting is the last resort in place of the sword, during a most critical time in our movement last February 1968 I undertook a 25-day fast. I repeat to you the principle enunciated to the membership at the start of the fast: if to build our union required the deliberate taking of life, either the life of a grower or his child, or the life of a farmworker or his child, then I choose not to see the union built.

Mr. Barr, let me be painfully honest with you. You must understand these things. We advocate militant nonviolence as our means for social revolution and to achieve justice for our people, but we are not blind or deaf to the desperate and moody winds of human frustration, impatience and rage that blow among us. Gandhi himself admitted that if his only choice were cowardice or violence, he would choose violence. Men are not angels, and time and tide wait for no man. Precisely because of these powerful human emotions, we have tried to involve masses of people in their own struggle. Participation and self-determination remain the best experience of freedom, and free men instinctively prefer democratic change and even protect the rights guaranteed to seek it. Only the enslaved in despair have need of violent overthrow.

This letter does not express all that is in my heart, Mr. Barr. But if it says nothing else it says that we do not hate you or rejoice to see your industry destroyed; we hate the agribusiness system that seeks to keep us enslaved and we shall overcome and change it not by retaliation or bloodshed but by a determined nonviolent struggle carried on by those masses of farm workers who intend to be free and human.

Sincerely yours,
Cesar E. Chavez
United Farm Workers Organizing Committee
A.F.L.-C.I.O. *Delano, California*

E. L. Barr Jr. did not respond.

Margie Brauer to William Yaeger

In early May 1986, almost two months before Margie Brauer and her husband, Ernie, were officially declared bankrupt, Mrs. Brauer handwrote the following letter to William Yaeger, the court-appointed trustee in the bankruptcy proceedings. The Brauers, who owned a farm in rural North Carolina, were hit hard by the grain embargo imposed by President Jimmy Carter. (Although the intention was to punish the Soviet Union for its 1979 invasion of Afghanistan, many American farmers, unable to sell their grain to Russia, suffered tremendous losses.) Unfamiliar with the procedures of declaring bankruptcy, Mrs. Brauer asked Yaeger what she and her family should expect and what, if anything, could be salvaged.

Mr. William L. Yaeger
Durham, N.C.
Re: Case No. B-86-00887C-7

Dear Mr. Yaeger,

I suppose that bankruptcy is intended to be a "cut and dried" business decision, and in the final analysis perhaps that is the end result. However, with first hand knowledge, I do know there is a far greater involvement, especially the emotional traumas of seeing the upheaval and disposal of a lifetime of very hard work.

My husband and I are from farm families of many generations. Except for brief periods of our lives, we have always farmed and know little of any other way of life. Ernie, at 69 years of age, was off the farm during the years of 1939–1945 while he was in service during World War II with 30 months overseas. When he returned in 1945 we were promptly married, having known each other for many years. In early 1946 we bargained for a very run-down piece of land on which we spent $800 to build a two-room cottage without the amenities of plumbing or electricity on a rural unpaved road. Conditions eventually improved—the road was paved and we did get electricity and running water, but no bath facility for 16 years.

Our two daughters were born while we lived in that little house—one was nine years old and the other three when we moved into our modest FHA-financed home. The intervening years were good because we loved the work of clearing those rolling hills and turning red clay into beautiful green pastures and fields—grabbing up roots and stumps and hauling off endless rocks. It should have mattered that we never had any money at the end of the year, but we always felt the promise and the hope of a better year next year. I worked off the farm at a local bank, an insurance company, a truck line (some of the time at two jobs) along with canning and freezing fruits and vegetables to make ends meet. I sewed for the children and if I needed new curtains or a bedspread, I made them. So much of what we made from the farm went back into the farm, but we didn't require a lot for family living and we simply plowed everything back to the farm.

Out of it all, we raised two very special girls—not extremely beautiful or extremely intellectual, but attractive and smart—pretty stable and altogether satisfactory. Through work-study programs, loans, and scholarships, they both acquired a fairly good basic education. One teaches, the other is a health educator with our local health department. Both have apparently solid and satisfactory marriages. The older one has two little girls, the younger has a new little daughter.

I am not sure why I am writing you this except that perhaps I need to reaffirm to myself that our dilemma is not the result of high and riotous living—that we are and have always been a plain, hard-working farm family. We've had a few health problems, none of which were very expensive, three or four really bad drought years that really set us back, perhaps some bad business decisions and maybe some management weakness. Actually we were not in bad shape until the years with the terrible interest rates and the grain embargo—it seems in retrospect that was the real beginning of a long, painful decline to this sorry state of affairs.

I think I want to tell you that, faced with the certainty of Federal land bank and Farmers Home foreclosure, we came to the conclusion that Chapter 7, with its inherent finality, seemed the preferred route out of the morass of worry and debt. We are trying to maintain our self-respect and a degree of dignity (all honor & pride have gone by the way), trying to get through this most difficult of times with our sanity intact and see what we can do to maintain a livelihood so that we need not resort to public assistance or dependence on our children. At Ernie's age, it will be difficult to find work; his knees are worn out, too; but his Social Security of $296 monthly will help. I was able to get work at a nearby hospital at $4.10 hourly as a ward clerk—completely out of my past experience of book-keeping and accounting but it will pay routine bills, if we are very, very frugal.

Mr. Yaeger, we are very ignorant about bankruptcy, never having had anyone in either of our families or any of our associates involved in bankruptcy. We believe that when this is over, we will be relieved of all our holdings and of all our debts in their entirety and we will be left with our household goods and clothing. I would like to know if it would be possible for me to get a new pair of glasses (mine have not been changed in four or five years and the bifocal is no longer right for my vision). This would probably cost one half of a cow or about $130. I also have two teeth badly in need of repair—one needs a cap in order to save it and the other is in pretty bad shape also—will probably cost two cows or about $500. Also electric bills are continuing for the poultry house and will need to be paid soon. How will the auctioneer be paid? How will you be paid? Is there any way we can come out of this with even a few hundred dollars? We have nothing. We have acquired and accumulated nothing—with the 40 productive years of our life down the drain. How long can we remain in our house?

Our oldest daughter and her husband own a mobile home into which we will move. This has to be relocated since it now is located on a part of the bankruptcy property. Would it be possible or reasonable to request that we be allowed to live in our house perhaps as long as 60 days from probable discharge or until late September or October?

If you do not have the time to dictate a letter answering these questions, perhaps you can call me. Thank you for your time in reading this rather long letter. Perhaps it will establish that we are real flesh and blood people with very real problems and not merely a case number. I pray that the agonizing we have done in order to accept the inevitability of this decision has been the worst part of it and we will greatly appreciate anything you can do to ease the finalizing technicalities and to enable us to pick up the fragments of our lives.

Sincerely,
Margie M. Brauer

After reading her letter, Bill Yaeger replied to Mrs. Brauer that he had "never received such an eloquent description of the financial and economic plight which you, and so many of your neighbors, are presently enduring." He concluded: "I hope that we can work together to reduce the pain of the bankruptcy." Although the Brauers did, ultimately, lose their farm, they were able to stay in their house.

PART II

Letters of Humor & Personal Contempt

Dear Sir:

The enclosed letter arrived on my desk a few days ago. I am sending it to you in the belief that as a responsible citizen you should know that some idiot is sending out letters over your signature.

Variously ascribed

The Indians of the Six Nations to William & Mary College

Hoping to "rehabilitate" Indians from their, as he saw it, strange and sometimes wicked ways, General James A. Carleton of the United States Army recommended in a letter to a colleague what should be done with them: "Gather them together little by little onto a Reservation [and] teach their children how to read and write: teach them the art of peace; teach them the truths of Christianity. [. . .] Little by little they will become a happy and contented people." Many Native Americans, however, saw things a bit differently. In June 1744, in an offer not unlike General Carleton's, the College of William & Mary in Virginia invited the Indians of the Six Nations to send twelve young men to their college to be "properly" educated. Soon after, William & Mary received the following reply.

Sirs,

We know that you highly esteem the kind of learning taught in Colleges, and that the Maintenance of our young Men, while with you, would be very expensive to you. We are convinc'd, therefore, that you mean to do us Good by your Proposal; and we thank you heartily. But you, who are wise, must know that different Nations have different Conceptions of things; and you will therefore not take it amiss, if our Ideas of this kind of Education happen not to be the same with yours. We have had some Experience of it. Several of our Young People were formerly brought up at the Colleges of the Northern Provinces; they were instructed in all your Sciences; but, when they came back to us, they were bad Runners, ignorant of every means of living in the Woods, unable to bear either Cold or Hunger, knew neither how to build a Cabin, take a Deer, or kill an Enemy, spoke our Language imperfectly, were therefore neither fit for Hunters, Warriors, nor Counsellors; they were totally good for nothing. We are, however, not the less oblig'd by your kind Offer, tho' we decline accepting it; and, to show our grateful Sense of it, if the Gentlemen of Virginia will send us a Dozen of their Sons, we will take care of their Education; instruct them in all we know, and make Men of them.

Abraham Lincoln to Mrs. Orville H. Browning

A twenty-nine-year-old lawyer finds himself in a dilemma. Having committed himself to marrying a certain young lady, he finally meets her for the second time, three years after his first encounter, only to find that her appearance is not at all what he remembered. The young man relates his predicament—and its surprising conclusion—in the following letter to Mrs. Orville H. Browning, the wife of a close friend.

Springfield, April 1. 1838.

Dear Madam:

Without appologising for being egotistical, I shall make the history of so much of my own life, as has elapsed since I saw you, the subject of this letter. And by the way, I now discover, that, in order to give a full and inteligible account of the things I have done and suffered *since* I saw you, I shall necessarily have to relate some that happened *before*.

It was, then, in the autumn of 1836, that a married lady of my acquaintance, and who was a great friend of mine, being about to pay a visit to her father and other relatives residing in Kentucky, proposed to me, that on her return she would bring a sister of hers with her, upon condition that I would engage to become her brother-in-law with all convenient dispach. I, of course, accepted the proposal; for you know I could not have done otherwise, had I really been averse to it; but privately between you and me, I was most confoundedly well pleased with the project. I had seen the said sister some three years before, thought her inteligent and agreeable, and saw no good objection to plodding life through hand in hand with her. Time passed on, the lady took her journey and in due time returned, sister in company sure enough. This stomached me a little; for it appeared to me, that her coming so readily showed that she was a trifle too willing; but on reflection it occured to me, that she might have been prevailed upon by her married sister to come, without any thing concerning me ever having been mentioned to her; and so I concluded that if no other objection presented itself, I would consent to wave this. All this occured to me upon my *hearing* of her arrival in the neighborhood; for, be it remembered, I had not yet *seen* her, except about three years previous, as above mentioned.

In a few days we had an interview, and, although I had seen her before, she did not look as my immagination had pictured her. I knew she was over-size, but she now appeared a fair match for Falstaff; I knew she was called an "old maid," and I felt no doubt of the truth of at least half of the appelation, but now, when I beheld her, I could not for my life avoid thinking of my mother; and this, not from withered features, for her skin was too full of fat to permit of its contracting into wrinkles; but from her want of teeth, weather-beaten appearance in general, and from a kind of notion that ran in my head, that *nothing* could have commenced at the size of infancy, and reached her present bulk in less than thirty-five or forty years; and, in short, I was not at all pleased with her. But what could I do? I had told her sister that I would take her for better or for worse; and I made a point of honor and conscience in all things to stick to my word, especially if others had been induced to act on it, which in this case, I doubted not they had, for I was now fairly convinced, that no other man on earth would have her, and hence the conclusion that they were bent on holding me to my bargain. Well, thought I, I have said it, and, be the consequences what they may, it shall not be my fault if I fail to do it. At once I determined to consider her my wife; and this done, all my powers of discovery were put to the rack, in search of perfections in her, which might be fairly set-off against her defects. I tried to imagine she was handsome, which, but for her unfortunate corpulency, was actually true. Exclusive of this, no woman that I have seen has a finer face. I also tried to convince myself, that the mind was much more to be valued than the person; and in this, she was not inferior, as I could discover, to any with whom I had been acquainted.

Shortly after this, without attempting to come to any positive understanding with her, I set out for Vandalia, where and when you first saw me. During my stay there, I had letters from her which did not change my opinion of either her intelect or intention, but, on the contrary, confirmed it in both.

All this while, although I was fixed "firm as the surge repelling rock" in my resolution, I found I was continually repenting the rashness, which had led me to make it. Through life I have been in no bondage, either real or immaginary, from the thraldom of which I so much desired to be free.

After my return home, I saw nothing to change my opinion of her in any particular. She was the same and so was I. I now spent my time planning how I might get along through life after my contemplated change in circumstances should have taken place; and how I might procrastinate the evil day for a time, which I really dreaded as much—perhaps more, than an irishman does the halter.

After all my sufferings upon this deeply interesting subject, here I am, wholly unexpectedly, completely out of the "scrape," and I now want to know if you can guess how I got out of it. Out clear, in every sense of the term; no violation of word, honor or conscience. I dont believe you can guess, and so I may as well tell you at once. As the lawyer says, it was done in the manner following, to wit: After I had delayed the matter as long as I thought I could in honor do, which by the way had brought me round into the last fall, I concluded I might as well bring it to a consumation without further delay; and so I mustered my resolution, and made the proposal to her direct; but, shocking to relate, she answered, No. At first I supposed she did it through an affectation of modesty, which I thought but ill-become her, under the particular circumstances of her case; but on my renewal of the charge, I found she repeled it with greater firmness than before. I tried it again and again, but with the same success, or rather with the same want of success.

I finally was forced to give it up, at which I verry unexpectedly found myself mortified almost beyond endurance. I was mortified, it seemed to me, in a hundred different ways. My vanity was deeply wounded by the reflection, that I had so long been too stupid to discover her intentions, and at the same time never doubting that I understood them perfectly; and also, that she whom I had taught myself to believe nobody else would have, had actually rejected me with all my fancied greatness; and, to cap the whole, I then, for the first time, began to suspect that I was really a little in love with her. But let it all go. I'll try and outlive it. Others have been made fools of by the girls; but this can never be with truth said of me. I most emphatically, in this instance, made a fool of myself. I have now come to the conclusion never again to think of marrying; and for this reason; I can never be satisfied with any one who would be block-head enough to have me.

When you receive this, write me a long yarn about something to amuse me. Give my respects to Mr. Browning.

Your sincere friend,
A. Lincoln

Despite his aversion to marriage, four years later Abraham Lincoln married Mary Todd, from Kentucky, who became his wife of over twenty-two years.

Mark Twain to the Gas Company

"When angry," Mark Twain (Samuel Clemens) advised, "count four; when very angry, swear." Twain, who could express himself with great tenderness in letters to relatives and close friends, was not shy to spit out a mouthful of curses at those who infuriated him. Twain reportedly sent a scathing letter to The New York Times *demanding to know why, considering that seats on the "goddam railroad" all cost the same amount, seats at the opera were all a different "goddam price." He then forwarded a copy of the letter to his friend (and well-known man of letters) William Dean Howells, with a note explaining that he had signed Howells's name to the letter to give it "more weight." When the local gas company shut off Twain's service in the middle of winter without notifying him first, Twain was apoplectic and responded with the following.*

Hartford, February 12, 1891

Dear Sirs:

Some day you will move me almost to the verge of irritation by your chuckle-headed Goddamned fashion of shutting your Goddamned gas off without giving any notice to your Goddamned parishioners. Several times you have come within an ace of smothering half of this household in their beds and blowing up the other half by this idiotic, not to say criminal, custom of yours. And it has happened again to-day. Haven't you a telephone?

Ys
S L Clemens

Erle Stanley Gardner to *Black Mask* Magazine

Erle Stanley Gardner, a lawyer by trade who later become known for his Perry Mason novels, submitted short stories to mystery and detective magazines as a young writer in the 1920s. The popular Black Mask *magazine occasionally ran Gardner's stories but rejected many as well—and often with brutal candor; "Dear Mr. Gardner:" one editor wrote, "This is terrible. Sincerely, H. C. North, Associate Editor." Frustrated by such responses and constant editorial changes to the stories they did accept, Gardner sent the following brief letter to* Black Mask, *along with a manuscript he hoped to see published.*

"Three O'Clock in the Morning" is a damned good story. If you have any comments on it, write 'em on the back of a check.

Erle Stanley Gardner

Black Mask *published "Three O'Clock in the Morning" and featured Gardner's message in the magazine's introduction.*

Ernest Hemingway to F. Scott Fitzgerald

They had both achieved fame at a young age—F. Scott Fitzgerald for The Great Gatsby *and* This Side of Paradise, *which he wrote before he was thirty; Ernest Hemingway for many of his best short stories and* A Farewell to Arms, *also written before he turned thirty. And they were both prolific letter writers who often looked to one other for advice, criticism, praise, and gossip. In the following letter to Fitzgerald, Hemingway articulates, in a friendly fashion, their distinctly contrasting views of the world. (Hadley is Hemingway's wife; Zelda is Fitzgerald's.)*

Burguete, Spain, 1 July 1925

Dear Scott:

We are going in to Pamplona tomorrow. Been trout fishing here. How are you? And how is Zelda?

I am feeling better than I've ever felt—havent drunk anything but wine since I left Paris. God it has been wonderful country. But you hate country. All right omit description of country. I wonder what your idea of heaven would be—A beautiful vacuum filled with wealthy monogamists, all powerful and members of the best families all drinking themselves to death. And hell would probably [be] an ugly vacuum full of poor polygamists unable to obtain booze or with chronic stomach disorders that they called secret sorrows.

To me heaven would be a big bull ring with me holding two barrera seats and a trout stream outside that no one else was allowed to fish in and two lovely houses in the town; one where I would have my wife and children and be monogamous and love them truly and well and the other where I would have my nine beautiful mistresses on 9 different floors and one house would be fitted up with special copies of the Dial printed on soft tissue and kept in the toilets on every floor and in the other house we would use the American Mercury and the New Republic. Then there would be a fine church like in Pamplona where I could go and be confessed on the way from one house to the other and I would get on my horse and ride out with my son to my bull ranch named Hacienda Hadley and toss coins to all my illegitimate children that lived [along] the road. I would write out at the Hacienda and send my son in to lock the chastity belts onto my mistresses because someone had just galloped up with the news that a notorious monogamist named Fitzgerald had been seen riding toward the town at the head of a company of strolling drinkers.

Well anyway we're going into town tomorrow early in the morning. Write me at the / Hotel Quintana

Pamplona
Spain

Or dont you like to write letters. I do because it's such a swell way to keep from working and yet feel you've done something.

So long and love to Zelda from us both,

Yours,
Ernest

Edna St. Vincent Millay to the League of American Penwomen

In March 1927 Elinor Wylie was invited, along with her friend and fellow poet Edna St. Vincent Millay, to be a guest of honor at a breakfast hosted by the League of American Penwomen. One week later, and much to Wylie's surprise, she was disinvited at the insistence of league members who disapproved of Wylie's divorce from her first husband, followed by her elopement with another man. Wylie was crestfallen by the retraction. Millay was so enraged by the league's treatment of her friend that she fired off the following letter.

April 18, '27

Ladies:

I have received from you recently several communications, inviting me to be your Guest of Honour at a function to take place in Washington some time this month. I replied, not only that I was unable to attend, but that I regretted this inability; I said that I was sensible to the honour you did me, and that I hoped you would invite me again.

Your recent gross and shocking insolence to one of the most distinguished writers of our time has changed all that.

It is not in the power of an organization which has insulted Elinor Wylie, to honour me.

And indeed I should feel it unbecoming on my part, to sit as Guest of Honour in a gathering of writers, where honour is tendered not so much for the excellence of one's literary accomplishment as for the circumspection of one's personal life.

Believe me, if the eminent object of your pusillanimous attack has not directed her movements in conformity with your timid philosophies, no more have I mine. I too am eligible for your disesteem. Strike me too from your lists, and permit me, I beg you, to share with Elinor Wylie a brilliant exile from your fusty province.

Very truly yours,
Edna St. Vincent Millay

Dorothy Thompson to an Admirer of Her Husband Sinclair Lewis

In 1930 Sinclair Lewis became the first American to win the Nobel Prize for Literature, and soon after he began receiving considerable fan mail. One letter was from a young woman who wanted to be his secretary; "Dear Mr. Lewis," she wrote, "I'll do everything for you—and when I say everything I mean everything." Dorothy Thompson, Sinclair Lewis's wife, saw the letter and responded with the following.

My dear Miss—:

My husband already has a stenographer who handles his work for him. And, as for "everything" I take care of that myself—and when I say everything I mean everything.

Dorothy Thompson
(Mrs. Sinclair Lewis to you.)

Fred Allen to Everett Rattray

Starting out in vaudeville in the early 1920s, Fred Allen became one of the stars of radio comedy in the 1930s and 1940s. Despite the fact that his radio program—which he wrote, revised, edited, and performed—left him very little free time, Allen sent out numerous letters each day to friends, relatives, fans, and show business associates. Typing in his distinctive lowercase style, he sent the following letter to Everett Rattray, the son of a family friend to whom Allen and his wife, Portland, had recently given a book as a gift.

february
7th
1944

dear everett . . .

portland and i received your letter this morning. you didn't have to bother thanking us for the book. portland picked it out. she noticed a little space between two books on your father's bookshelves and she really bought the book to plug up that crevice. if you want to read the book before you used it for that purpose i am sure portland wouldn't mind. if you enjoy the book, too, i know she will be happy when i tell her.

i guess you are too busy poking around the barn, and trying to fly your kite in that high wind you get at east hampton, to bother much with your mail. you had better be careful with those old shells. you can't drive a nail very far into a shell and expect to be in the barn for long. if you have closed the barn door you may rise unexpectedly, hammer in hand, through the roof.

at the end of your letter you say "i guess i will stop writing. i am coming to the bottom of the page." it is always best to stop a letter when you arrive at the bottom of the page. i know a boy who never stopped his letters in time. he would keep on writing past the bottom of the page and write down one leg of the table until he finished. then when he mailed his letter he had to saw a piece out of the table and cut off the leg of the table, too, and send it along in a large paper bag instead of an envelope. another time, this boy was writing on a desk he didn't stop again but wrote down the front of the desk along the floor for nearly two feet. when he mailed that letter he had to tear off the front of the desk and pry up two feet of the floor. this left a big hole in the floor. his father and mother both fell through the hole and since the boy lived on a houseboat and his father and mother couldn't swim the boy became an orphan. this is why it is always better to finish a letter when you come to the bottom of the page.

give dave and your mother and father our best wishes. we will see you when you come to the city. meantime, best wishes . . .

fred allen

Groucho Marx to Warner Bros.

While preparing to film a movie entitled A Night in Casablanca, *the Marx Brothers received a letter from Warner Bros. threatening legal action if they did not change the film's title. Warner Bros. deemed the film's title too similar to their own* Casablanca, *released almost five years earlier in 1942, with Humphrey Bogart and Ingrid Bergman. In response Groucho Marx dispatched the following letter to the studio's legal department.*

Dear Warner Brothers,

Apparently there is more than one way of conquering a city and holding it as your own. For example, up to the time that we contemplated making this picture, I had no idea that the city of Casablanca belonged exclusively to Warner Brothers. However, it was only a few days after our announcement appeared that we received your long, ominous legal document warning us not to use the name Casablanca.

It seems that in 1471, Ferdinand Balboa Warner, your great-great-grandfather, while looking for a shortcut to the city of Burbank, had stumbled on the shores of Africa and, raising his alpenstock (which he later turned in for a hundred shares of the common), named it Casablanca.

I just don't understand your attitude. Even if you plan on re-releasing your picture, I am sure that the average movie fan could learn in time to distinguish between Ingrid Bergman and Harpo. I don't know whether I could, but I certainly would like to try.

You claim you own Casablanca and that no one else can use that name without your permission. What about "Warner Brothers"? Do you own that, too? You probably have the right to use the name Warner, but what about the name Brothers? Professionally, we were brothers long before you were. We were touring the sticks as the The Marx Brothers when Vitaphone was still a gleam in the inventor's eye, and even before us there had been other brothers—the Smith Brothers; the Brothers Karamazov; Dan Brothers, an outfielder with Detroit; and "Brother, Can You Spare a Dime?" (This was orginally "Brothers, Can You Spare a Dime?" but this was spreading a dime pretty thin, so they threw out one brother, gave all the money to the other one and whittled it down to, "Brother, Can You Spare a Dime?")

Now Jack, how about you? Do you maintain that yours is an original name? Well, it's not. It was used long before you were born. Offhand, I can think of two Jacks—there was Jack of "Jack and the Beanstalk," and Jack the Ripper, who cut quite a figure in his day.

As for you, Harry, you probably sign your checks, sure in the belief that you are the first Harry of all time and that all other Harrys are impostors. I can think of two Harrys that preceded you. There was Lighthouse Harry of Revolutionary fame and a Harry Appelbaum who lived on the corner of 93rd Street and Lexington Avenue. Unfortunately, Appelbaum wasn't too well- known. The last I heard of him, he was selling neckties at Weber and Heilbroner.

Now about the Burbank studio. I believe this is what you brothers call your place. Old man Burbank is gone. Perhaps you remember him. He was a great man in a garden. His wife often said Luther had ten green thumbs. What a witty woman she must have been! Burbank was the wizard who crossed all those fruits and vegetables until he had the poor plants in such a confused and jittery condition that they could never decide whether to enter the dining room on the meat platter or the dessert dish.

This is pure conjecture, of course, but who knows—perhaps Burbank's survivors aren't too happy with the fact that a plant that grinds out pictures on a quota settled in their town, appropriated Burbank's name and uses it as a front for their films. It is even possible that the Burbank family is prouder of the potato produced by the old man than they are of the fact that from your studio emerged "Casablanca" or even "Gold Diggers of 1931."

This all seems to add up to a pretty bitter tirade, but I assure you it's not meant to. I love Warners. Some of my best friends are Warner Brothers. It is even possible that I am doing you an injustice and that you, yourselves, know nothing at all about this dog-in-the-Wanger attitude. It wouldn't surprise me at all to discover that the heads of your legal department are unaware of this absurd dispute, for I am acquainted with many of them and they are fine fellows with curly back hair, double-breasted suits and a love of their fellow man that out-Saroyans Saroyan.

I have a hunch that this attempt to prevent us from using the title is the brainchild of some ferret-faced shyster, serving a brief apprenticeship in your legal department. I know the type well—hot out of law school, hungry for success and too ambitious to follow the natural laws of promotion. This bar sinister probably needled your attorneys, most of whom are fine fellows with curly black hair, double-breasted suits, etc., into attempting to enjoin us. Well, he won't get away with it! We'll fight him to the highest court! No pasty-faced legal adventurer is going to cause bad blood between the Warners and the Marxes. We are all brothers under the skin and we'll remain friends till the last reel of "A Night in Casablanca" goes tumbling over the spool.

Sincerely,
Groucho Marx

Unamused, Warner Bros. requested that the Marx Brothers at least outline the premise of their film. Groucho responded with an utterly ridiculous storyline, and, sure enough, received another stern letter requesting clarification. He obliged and went on to describe a plot more preposterous than the first, claiming that he, Groucho, would be playing "Bordello, the sweetheart of Humphrey Bogart." No doubt exasperated, Warner Bros. did not respond. A Night in Casablanca *was released in 1946.*

President Harry S. Truman to Music Critic Paul Hume & A Father Who Lost a Son in the Korean War to President Truman

When President Harry Truman picked up the Washington Post *early on December 6, 1950, to read a review of his daughter Margaret Truman's singing performance, he was livid. Though conceding that Miss Truman was "extremely attractive," Paul Hume, the* Post*'s *music critic, stated bluntly that "Miss Truman cannot sing very well" and "has not improved" over the years. The president wrote the following letter to the thirty-four-year-old Hume, whom he compared to the columnist Westbrook Pegler ("a rat," in Truman's view).*

THE WHITE HOUSE
WASHINGTON

Mr. Hume:

I've just read your lousy review of Margaret's concert. I've come to the conclusion that you are an "eight ulcer man on four ulcer pay."

It seems to me that you are a frustrated old man who wishes he could have been successful. When you write such poppy-cock as was in the back section of the paper you work for it shows conclusively that you're off the beam and at least four of your ulcers are at work.

Some day I hope to meet you. When that happens you'll need a new nose, a lot of beefsteak for black eyes, and perhaps a supporter below!

Pegler, a gutter snipe, is a gentleman alongside you. I hope you'll accept that statement as a worse insult than a reflection on your ancestry.

H. S. T.

Neither Hume, possibly sympathetic to the president's feelings as a father, nor his editor wanted to run the letter. Nevertheless, it leaked out and ultimately appeared on the front page of a tabloid, the now-defunct Washington News, *earning Truman the ire of countless Americans who were incensed by his "filthy" language. Parents of American soldiers fighting in Korea flooded the White House with letters and telegrams expressing their outrage that the president seemed more concerned with his daughter's singing than their children's lives. One parent, Mr. William Banning of New Canaan, Connecticut, sent Truman the following letter and enclosed a Purple Heart, one of the highest awards a soldier can receive.*

Mr. Truman:

As you have been directly responsible for the loss of our son's life in Korea, you might just as well keep this emblem on display in your trophy room, as a memory of one of your historic deeds.

Our major regret at this time is that your daughter was not there to receive the same treatment as our son received in Korea.

William Banning

According to Truman biographer David McCullough, the president kept Mr. Banning's letter in his desk for several years.

E. B. White to the ASPCA

It was not, apparently, a good mail day for novelist and essayist E. B. White. "I am being accused in New York State of dodging my dog tax," White wrote to the Internal Revenue Service (IRS), explaining an unpaid notice, "and accused in Maine of being behind in my federal tax, and I believe I'm going to have to rearrange my life somehow or other so that everything can be brought together, all in one state, maybe Delaware." The IRS, White's letter claimed, had issued a warrant for the "seizure and sale of [his] house in Maine," and he wanted them to know certain peculiarities about the house, such as how to handle the goose in the barn: "I hope you can manage everything so as not to disturb her until she has brought off her goslings. I'll give you one, if you want. Or would they belong to the federal government anyway, even though the eggs were laid before the [warrant] was mailed?" The payment was resolved, but there was still the matter of "dodging" that dog tax, which White tried to rectify in the following letter to the ASPCA.

12 April 1951
The American Society for the Prevention of Cruelty to Animals
York Avenue and East 92nd Street
New York, 28, NY

Dear Sirs:

I have your letter, undated, saying that I am harboring an unlicensed dog in violation of the law. If by "harboring" you mean getting up two or three times every night to pull Minnie's blanket up over her, I am harboring a dog all right. The blanket keeps slipping off. I suppose you are wondering by now why I don't get her a sweater instead. That's a joke on you. She has a knitted sweater, but she doesn't like to wear it for sleeping; her legs are so short they work out of a sweater and her toenails get caught in the mesh, and this disturbs her rest. If Minnie doesn't get her rest, she feels it right away. I do myself, and of course with this night duty of mine, the way the blanket slips and all, I haven't had any real rest in years. Minnie is twelve.

In spite of what your inspector reported, she has a license. She is licensed in the state of Maine as an unspayed bitch, or what is more commonly called an "unspaded" bitch. She wears her metal license tag but I must say I don't particularly care for it, as it is in the shape of a hydrant, which seems to me a feeble gag, besides being pointless in the case of a female. It is hard to believe that any state in the Union would circulate a gag like that and make people pay money for it, but Maine is always thinking of something. Maine puts up roadside crosses along the highways to mark the spots where people have lost their lives in motor accidents, so the highways are beginning to take on the appearance of a cemetery, and motoring in Maine has become a solemn experience, when one thinks mostly about death. I was driving along a road near Kittery the other day thinking about death and all of a sudden I heard the spring peepers. That changed me right away and I suddenly thought about life. It was the nicest feeling.

You asked about Minnie's name, sex, breed, and phone number. She doesn't answer the phone. She is a dachshund and can't reach it, but she wouldn't answer it even if she could, as she has no interest in outside calls. I did have a dachshund once, a male, who was interested in the telephone, and who got a great many calls, but Fred was an exceptional dog (his name was Fred) and I can't think of anything offhand that he wasn't interested in. The telephone was only one of a thousand things. He loved life—that is, he loved life if by "life" you mean "trouble," and of course the phone is almost synonymous with trouble. Minnie loves life, too, but her idea of life is a warm bed, preferably with an electric pad, and a friend in bed with her, and plenty of shut-eye, night and days. She's almost twelve. I guess I've already mentioned that. I got her from Dr. Clarence Little in 1939. He was using dachshunds in his cancer-research experiments (that was before Winchell was running the thing) and he had a couple of extra puppies, so I wheedled Minnie out of him. She later had puppies by her own father, at Dr. Little's request. What do you think about that for a scandal? I know what Fred thought about it. He was some put out.

Sincerely yours,
E. B. White

John Steinbeck to Pascal "Pat" Covici

Every morning before working on his epic novel East of Eden, *John Steinbeck composed a letter to his close friend and editor, Pascal "Pat" Covici. Steinbeck used his daily letters to explore plot lines, character development, and other ideas before committing them to the novel. For nine months he labored over the book until finally, on November 1, 1951,* East of Eden *was complete. Then, for the book's dedication page, he wrote a letter to Covici expressing the exhilaration, angst, rewards, and frustrations of being a writer. The following is the first draft of Steinbeck's letter.*

Dear Pat.

I have decided for this, my book, *East of Eden*, to write dedication, prologue, argument, apology, epilogue and perhaps epitaph all in one.

The dedication is to you with all the admiration and affection that have been distilled from our singularly blessed association of many years. This book is inscribed to you because you have been part of its birth and growth.

As you know, a prologue is written last but placed first to explain the book's shortcomings and to ask the reader to be kind. But a prologue is also a note of farewell from the writer to his book. For years the writer and his book have been together—friends or bitter enemies but very close as only love and fighting can accomplish.

Then suddenly the book is done. It is a kind of death. This is the requiem.

Miguel Cervantes invented the modern novel and with his Don Quijote set a mark high and bright. In his prologue, he said best what writers feel—The gladness and The terror.

"Idling reader" Cervantes wrote, "you may believe me when I tell you that I should have liked this book, which is the child of my brain, to be The fairest. The sprightliest and The cleverest that could be imagined, but I have not been able to contravene the law of nature which would have it that like begets like—"

And so it is with me, Pat. Although some times I have felt that I held fire in my hands and spread a page with shining—I have never lost the weight of clumsiness, of ignorance, of aching inability.

A book is like a man—clever and dull, brave and cowardly, beautiful and ugly. For every flowering thought there will be a page like a wet and mangy mongrel, and for every looping flight a tap on the wing and a reminder that wax cannot hold the feathers firm too near the sun.

Well—then the book is done. It has no virtue any more. The writer wants to cry out—"Bring it back! Let me rewrite it or better—Let me burn it. Don't let it out in the unfriendly cold in that condition."

As you know better than most, Pat, the book does not go from writer to reader. It goes first to the lions—editors, publishers, critics, copy readers, sales department. It is kicked and slashed and gouged. And its bloodied father stands attorney.

EDITOR

The book is out of balance. The reader expects one thing and you give him something else. You have written two books and stuck them together. The reader will not understand.

WRITER

No, sir. It goes together. I have written about one family and used stories about another family as well as counterpoint, as rest, as contrast in pace and color.

EDITOR

The reader won't understand. What you call counterpoint only slows the book.

WRITER

It has to be slowed—else how would you know when it goes fast.

EDITOR

You have stopped the book and gone into discussions of God knows what.

WRITER

Yes, I have. I don't know why. Just wanted to. Perhaps I was wrong.

EDITOR

Right in the middle you throw in a story about your mother and an airplane. The reader wants to know where it ties in and, by God, it doesn't tie in at all. That disappoints a reader.

WRITER

Yes, sir. I guess you're right. Shall I cut out the story of my mother and the airplane?

EDITOR

That's entirely up to you.

SALES DEPARTMENT

The book's too long. Costs are up. We'll have to charge five dollars for it. People won't pay five dollars. They won't buy it.

WRITER

My last book was short. You said then that people won't buy a short book.

PROOFREADER

The chronology is full of holes. The grammar has no relation to English. On page so-and-so you have a man look in the World Almanac for steamship rates. They aren't there. I checked. You've got Chinese New Year wrong. The characters aren't consistent. You describe Liza Hamilton one way and then have her act a different way.

EDITOR

You make Cathy too black. The reader won't believe her. You make Sam Hamilton too white. The reader won't believe him. No Irishman ever talked like that.

WRITER

My grandfather did.

EDITOR

Who'll believe it.

SECOND EDITOR

No children ever talked like that.

WRITER

(losing temper as a refuge from despair)

God dam it. This is my book. I'll make the children talk any way I want. My book is about good and evil. Maybe the theme got into the execution. Do you want to publish it or not?

EDITORS

Let's see if we can fix it up. It won't be much work. You want it to be good, don't you? For instance the ending. The reader won't understand it.

WRITER

Do you?

EDITOR

Yes, but the reader won't.

PROOFREADER

My god, how you do dangle a participle. Turn to page so-and-so.

There you are, Pat. You came in with a box of glory and there you stand with an armful of damp garbage.

And from this meeting a new character has emerged. He is called the Reader.

THE READER

He is so stupid you can't trust him with an idea.
He is so clever he will catch you in the least error.
He will not buy short books.
He will not buy long books.
He is part moron, part genius and part ogre.
There is some doubt as to whether he can read.

Well, by God, Pat, he's just like me, no stranger at all. He'll take from my book what he can bring to it. The dull witted will get dullness and the brilliant may find things in my book I didn't know were there.

And just as he is like me, I hope my book is enough like him so that he may find in it interest and recognition and some beauty as one finds in a friend.

Cervantes ends his prologue with a lovely line. I want to use it, Pat, and then I will have done. He says to the reader:

"May God give you health—and may He be not unmindful of me, as well."

JOHN STEINBECK
New York 1952

J. B. Lee Jr. to Congressman Ed Foreman

Approximately seventeen to twenty million letters addressed to members of the U.S. Congress are delivered each year to the United States Capitol building in Washington, D.C. Many constituents write in to suggest ideas for legislation, request favors, make complaints (the most frequent), offer praise (not so frequent), and simply express their views on a wide range of social issues. The following letter, written by a west Texan facetiously hoping to take advantage of the U.S. Government's farm subsidies, was sent to Rep. Ed Foreman.

March 20, 1963

The Honorable Ed Foreman
House of Representatives
Congressional District #16
Washington 25, D.C.

Dear Sir:

My friend over in Terebone Parish received a $1,000 check from the government this year for not raising hogs. So I am going into the not-raising hogs business next year.

What I want to know is, in your opinion, what is the best kind of farm not to raise hogs on and the best kind of hogs not to raise? I would prefer not to raise Razorbacks, but if that is not a good breed not to raise, I will just as gladly not raise any Berkshires or Durocs.

The hardest work in this business is going to be in keeping an inventory of how many hogs I haven't raised.

My friend is very joyful about the future of his business. He has been raising hogs for more than 20 years and the best he ever made was $400, until this year, when he got $1,000 for not raising hogs.

If I can get $1,000 for not raising 50 hogs, then will I get $2,000 for not raising 100 hogs? I plan to operate on a small scale at first, holding myself down to 4,000 hogs which means I will have $80,000 coming from the government.

Now, another thing: these hogs I will not raise will not eat 100,000 bushels of corn. I understand that you also pay farmers for not raising corn. So will you pay me anything for not raising 100,000 bushels of corn not to feed the hogs I am not raising?

I want to get started as soon as possible as this seems to be a good time of the year for not raising hogs.

One thing more, can I raise 10 or 12 hogs on the side while I am in the not-raising-hog-business just enough to get a few sides of bacon to eat?

Very truly yours,
J. B. Lee, Jr.
Potential Hog Raiser

John Cheever to Josephine Herbst
& Cheever to Malcolm Cowley

In 1961 John Cheever and his wife, Mary, were asked to care for a cat owned by their friend and fellow writer Josephine Herbst. Cheever and the cat took an immediate dislike to one another. The animosity was sealed when the cat, whom Cheever named after the poet Delmore Schwartz, began "squirting the walls." In retaliation, Cheever took Delmore to the vet to be "fixed." In the following letter, written in December 1963, Cheever updates Herbst on his ongoing feud with the unforgiving feline.

Cedar Lane
Ossining

Some Friday

Dear Josie,

It's been years since we had anything but the most sketchy communication. [. . .] I've long since owed you an account of the destiny of your cat and here we go.

The cat, after your leaving him, seemed not certain of his character or his place and we changed his name to Delmore which immediately made him more vivid. The first sign of his vividness came when he dumped a load in a Kleenex box while I was suffering from a cold. During a paroxysm of sneezing I grabbed for some kleenex. I shall not overlook my own failures in this tale but when I got the cat shit off my face and the ceiling I took Delmore to the kitchen door and drop-kicked him into the clothesyard. This was an intolerable cruelty and I have not yet been forgiven. He is not a forgiving cat. Indeed he is proud. Spring came on then and as I was about to remove the clear glass storm window from Fred's room, Delmore, thinking the window to be open, hurled himself against the glass. This hurt his nose and his psyche badly. Mary and the children then went to the Mountains and I spent a reasonably happy summer cooking for Delmore. The next eventfulness came on Thanksgiving. When the family had gathered for dinner and I was about to carve the turkey there came a strangling noise from the bathroom. I ran there and found Delmore sitting in the toilet, neck-deep in cold water and very sore. I got him out and dried him with towels but there was no forgiveness. Shortly after Christmas a Hollywood writer and his wife came to lunch. My usual salutation to Delmore is: Up your's, and when the lady heard me say this she scorned me and gathered Delmore to her breasts. Delmore, in a flash, started to unscrew her right eyeball and the lady, trying to separate herself from Delmore lost a big piece of an Italian dress she was wearing which Mary said cost $250.00. This was not held against Delmore and a few days later when we had a skating party I urged Delmore to come to the pond with us. He seemed pleased and frisked along like a family-loving cat but at that moment a little wind came from the north-east and spilled the snow off a hemlock onto Delmore. he gave me a dirty look, went back to the house and dumped another load int the kleenex box. This time he got the cleaning-woman and they remain unfriendly.

This is not meant at all to be a rancorous account and I think Delmore enjoys himself. I have been accused of cruelty and a woman named Ruth Hershberger keeps writing Elizabeth Pollet, telling her to take the cat away from me, but Delmore contributes a dynamic to all our relationships. People who dislike me go directly to his side and he is, thus, a peace-maker. He loves to play with toilet paper. He does not like catnip mice. He does not kill song birds. In the spring the rabbits chase him around the lawn but they leave after the lettuce has been eaten and he has the terrace pretty much to himself. He is very fat these days and his step, Carl Sandburg not withstanding, sounds more like that of a barefoot middle-aged man on his way to the toilet than the settling in of a winter fog but he has his role and we all respect it and here endeth my report on Delmore the cat.

I hope all is well with you. Mary teaches, I write, the children go to various schools and all is well.

Best,
John

In March 1964, Cheever was featured on the cover of Time *magazine. In the following letter Cheever shares another story—related to the* Time *article—with the famous editor and literary critic Malcolm Cowley about a nosy neighbor.*

John Cheever
Cedar Lane
Ossining, New York

Dear Malcolm,

The TIME grilling has been unfunny but there was one funny story. Sally Ziegler, a small-town Georgian who lives in the cottage on the hill, has been preparing herself for the TIME interview for a month. On Friday the doorbell rang and she let the man in. "I don't approve of this kind of sneaky journalism," she said, "but the truth is that I know a lot about him because I can see him from my windows. I mean to say that I know he's a very heavy drinker and I often see him out there at twelve o'clock noon with a martini cocktail in his hand. And he sometimes chases his wife through the orchard in full view of my children. And he almost never wears his bathing-suit when he goes swimming and I've always thought there was something peculiar about men who go swimming without their bathing-suits. But as I say I don't approve of this kind of gossip and if you'll ask me some suitable questions about his habits I'll try to answer them to the best of my ability." Then the man said: "Lady, I'm your Fuller Brush representative."

As ever,
John

Elvis Presley to President Richard M. Nixon

A famous photograph of President Richard Nixon warmly shaking hands with a dazed Elvis Presley was the result of an impromptu meeting after Presley sent the president a letter while visiting Washington, D.C. Written by Presley on five pages of American Airlines notepaper in a barely legible scrawl, the letter expresses deep admiration for the president and a willingness to serve as a "Federal Agent at Large" to help stem America's growing drug problem. Inconceivable as the whole scenario may seem, the letter, reprinted here, is real.

Dear Mr. President,

First, I would like to introduce myself. I am Elvis Presley and admire you and have Great Respect for your office. I talked to Vice President Agnew in Palm Springs three weeks ago and expressed my concern for our country. The drug culture, the hippie elements, the SDS, Black Panthers, etc. do *not* consider me as their enemy or as they call it, The Establishment. I call it America and I love it. Sir, I can and will be of any service that I can to help The Country out. I have no concerns or Motives other than helping the country out. So I wish not to be given a title or an appointed position. I can and will do more good if I were made a Federal Agent at Large and I will help out by doing it my way through my communications with people of all ages. First and foremost, I am an entertainer, but all I need is the Federal credentials. I am on this plane with Senator George Murphy and we have been discussing the problems that our country is faced with.

Sir, I am staying at the Washington Hotel, Room 505-506-507. I have two men who work with me by the name of Jerry Schilling and Sonny West. I am registered under the name of Jon Burrows. I will be here for as long as it takes to get the credentials of a Federal Agent. I have done an in-depth study of drug abuse and Communist brainwashing techniques and I am right in the middle of the whole thing where I can and will do the most good.

I am Glad to help just so long as it is kept very Private. You can have your staff or whomever call me anytime today, tonight, or tomorrow. I was nominated this coming year one of America's Ten Most Outstanding Young Men. That will be in January 18 in my home town of Memphis, Tennessee. I am sending you the short autobiography about myself so you can better understand this approach. I would love to meet you just to say hello if you're not too busy.

Respectfully,
Elvis Presley

P.S. I believe that you, Sir, were one of the Top Ten Outstanding Men of America also.

I have a personal gift for you which I would like to present to you and you can accept it or I will keep it for you until you can take it.

President Nixon invited Presley to the White House, and an aide took notes of the December 21, 1970, meeting; "[Presley] mentioned that he has been studying the drug culture for over ten years. He mentioned that he knew a lot about this and was accepted by the hippies. He said he could go right into a group of young people or hippies and be accepted which he felt could be helpful to him in his drug drive. The President indicated again his concern that Presley retain his credibility. At the conclusion of the meeting,

Presley again told the President how much he supported him, and then, in a surprising, spontaneous gesture, put his left arm around the President and hugged him." President Nixon later sent Presley a note thanking him for the personal gift—a commemorative World War II pistol—and provided Presley with an honorary badge. Presley was not, however, given "Federal Agent credentials."

Lazlo Toth, "Super Patriot," to the Makers of Mr. Bubble

Don Novello, a comedian best known for his role as the chain-smoking priest Father Guido Sarducci on "Saturday Night Live," assumed the name "Lazlo Toth" and wrote to numerous politicians, heads of state, military leaders, and corporations in the 1970s. In what seemed to be the sincerest of prose, Toth praised corrupt politicians (most notably President Richard M. Nixon), asked military dictators for autographed photos, and sent in ridiculous ideas and questions to major companies concerning their products. The Gold Seal Company, the makers of Mr. Bubble, were just one of Toth's many epistolary victims.

164 Palm
San Rafael, Calif.
February 18, 1974

Mr. Bubble
Gold Seal Co.
Bismark, N.D. 58501

Dear Gentlemen:

I want you to know first of all that I enjoy your product. It's always refreshing to spend some time in the tub with some bubbles.

However, I must confess I am puzzled by some of the instructions on the box. It says: "KEEP DRY". How can you use it if you keep it dry?

Thought you'd be interested to know someone like me caught the mistake.

I thought you'd like to know.

Sincerely,

Lazlo Toth

One week later Toth received a courteous reply from the Gold Seal Company thanking him for his letter and patiently explaining that the instructions "KEEP DRY" refer only to keeping the product "protected against dampness, such as moisture in the bathroom if the box is not put away." The letter concludes by pitching "SNOWY" BLEACH, another Gold Seal product, and saying "We are enclosing [along with some coupons] an educational bulletin based on our 'SNOWY' BLEACH, which we would appreciate your giving to your mother." Toth immediately responded.

164 Palm
San Rafael,
California
March 1, 1974

M. Hershey
Consumer Relations Dir.
Gold Seal Company
10303 Northwest Freeway
Houston, Texas 77018-ZIP

Dear M. Hershey,

I was being nice to tell you about the error you have on your box and you send me coupons and tell me to give an educational bulletin about stains to my Mother.

To begin with, I wouldn't give your lousy educational bulletin #22 to nobody! Everybody I know knows more about stains and that stuff than your fancy company will ever know! Why you don't even know how to thank someone when they offer you an intelligent suggestion! And then you have the nerve to try to give me some pitch about your BLEACH!

I was writing about MR. BUBBLE, I don't care about BLEACH! What does BLEACH have to do with it? Come on!

And how come the only words in capitals are your SNOWY BLEACH and MR. BUBBLE while my Mother doesn't even get a capital for her *M*!

This is a warning that I'm thinking of moving on to another bubble bath.

Stand by our President!

With a right to be angry,
Lazlo Toth

Encl.
Bulletin #22
SNOWY and MR. BUBBLE
Coupons

The Gold Seal Company sent another letter, expressing regret that Toth's first letter was not answered satisfactorily. They insisted that they truly appreciated his suggestion to eliminate the words "KEEP DRY" on the box but, nevertheless, could not do so for the reasons they stated before. The letter also explained why they sent the coupons and bleach-related materials and assured Toth they were sorry the materials offended him. They were, the company emphasized, meant only as "a friendly gesture." The letter concluded by saying that they hoped Toth "would continue to use and enjoy 'MR BUBBLE.'" There was no mention of Toth's mother.

A Fed-Up Wife to *Ms.* Magazine

From public displays of animosity to private expressions of stony indifference, personal contempt can, of course, manifest itself in different ways. One woman relates, in the following December 1976 letter to Ms. *magazine, the creative (if not a bit devious) manner she has found to express her pent-up anger at her husband's chauvinistic habits.*

Dear Ms.

After working full time and attending ten hours of evening classes each week, I can't begin to describe the rage I feel when performing 100 percent of the household duties—not to mention being zoo-keeper for an overly energetic Great Dane and a cat—while my husband leisurely reads.

Because numerous discussions on this matter have not changed the situation, I am continually searching for new tactics to help him see the folly of his ways.

In the meantime, I have found that the occasional lacing of his dinner with the cat's food has done wonders for my spirit. *Bon appetit!*

Name withheld

Letters of Love & Friendship

*B*everly, there is something happening between us that is way out of the ordinary. Ours is one for the books, for the poets to draw new inspiration from, one to silence the cynics, and one to humble us by reminding us of how little we know about human beings, about ourselves. I did not know that I had all these feelings inside me. They have never been aroused before. Now they cascade down upon my head and threaten to beat me down to the ground, into the dust. But because of the strength of the magnetic pull I feel toward you, I am not fazed and I know that I can stand against the tide.

Eldridge Cleaver, in prison, to his lawyer (and, soon after, his lover) Beverly Axelrod; September 15, 1965

Benjamin Franklin to a Young Friend

"There are three faithful friends," wrote Benjamin Franklin in Poor Richard's Almanac, *"an old wife, an old dog, and ready money." Franklin elaborates his views on taking "an old wife" in the following letter to a young acquaintance who had asked for advice on love and women.*

June 25, 1745

My Dear Friend;—

I know of no Medicine fit to diminish the violent natural Inclinations you mention; and if I did, I think I should not communicate it to you. Marriage is the proper Remedy. It is the most natural State of Man, and therefore the State in which you are most likely to find solid Happiness. Your Reasons against entering into it at present, appear to me not well-founded. The circumstantial Advantages you have in View by Postponing it, are not only uncertain, but they are small in comparison with that of the Thing itself, the being *married and settled*. It is the Man and Woman united that make the compleat human Being. Separate, she wants his Force of Body and Strength of Reason; he, her Softness, Sensibility, and acute Discernment. Together they are more likely to succeed in the World. A single Man has not nearly the Value he would have in that State of Union. He is an incomplete Animal. He resembles the odd Half of a Pair of Scissors. If you get a prudent, healthy Wife, your Industry in your Profession, with her good Economy, will be a Fortune sufficient.

But if you will not take this Counsel, and persist in thinking a Commerce with the Sex inevitable, then I repeat my former Advice, that in all your Amours you should *prefer old Women to young ones*. You call this a Paradox, and demand my Reasons.

They are these:

1—Because they have more Knowledge of the World, and their Minds are better stor'd with Observations, their Conversation is more improving, and more lastingly agreeable.

2—Because when Women cease to be handsome, they study to be good. To maintain their Influence over Men, they supply the Diminution of Beauty by an Augmentation of Utility. They learn to do a 1000 Services, small and great, and are the most tender and useful of all Friends when you are sick. Thus they continue amiable. And hence there is hardly such a thing to be found as an old Woman who is not a good Woman.

3—Because there is no hazard of Children, which irregularly produc'd may be attended with much Inconvenience.

4—Because thro' more Experience they are more prudent and discreet in conducting an Intrigue to prevent Suspicion. The Commerce with them is therefore safer with regard to your Reputation. And with regard to theirs, if the Affair should happen to be known, considerate People might be rather inclin'd to excuse an old Woman, who would kindly take care of a young Man, form his Manners by her good Counsels, and prevent his ruining Health and Fortune among mercenary Prostitutes.

5—Because in every Animal that walks upright, the Deficiency of the Fluids that fill the Muscles appears first in the highest Part: The Face first grows lank and wrinkled; then the Neck; then the Breast and Arms; the lower Parts continuing to the last as plump as ever; So that covering all above with a Basket, and regarding only what is below the Girdle, it is impossible of two Women to know an old from a young one. And as in the Dark all Cats are grey, the Pleasure of corporal Enjoyment with an old Woman is at least equal, and frequently superior; every Knack being by Practice capable of Improvement.

6—Because the Sin is less. The debauching of a Virgin may be her Ruin, and make her Life unhappy.

7—Because the Compunction is less. The having made a young Girl *miserable* may give you frequent bitter Reflections; none of which can attend the making an old Woman *happy*.

8th & lastly.—They are *so grateful*!!

Thus much for my Paradox. But still I advise you to marry directly; being sincerely

Your affectionate Friend,
Benj. Franklin

It is not known if the young man took Franklin's advice. But while Franklin himself was living in France in 1780, he proposed to his neighbor, Madame Helvétius—a reportedly charming and cultivated widow—who happened to be eleven years younger than he. She rejected his proposal. (But they did remain friends.)

Nathaniel Hawthorne to His Fiancée Sophia Peabody & Peabody to Hawthorne

When Nathaniel Hawthorne arrived at the Peabody home in Salem, Massachusetts, for a friendly visit in November 1837, Elizabeth Peabody was said to have exclaimed to her sister, "Oh Sophia, you must come down. The Hawthornes are here and you never saw anything so splendid—he is handsomer than Lord Byron." Sophia, 28, was a semi-invalid who painted and rarely ventured out of her room. Her sister's enticing description of the young writer failed to bring her downstairs. During a later visit, Hawthorne, who was extremely shy himself, eventually did meet Sophia, and the two became close friends. Hawthorne soon discovered he was in love with her, and in April 1839 he proposed to her. During their engagement they exchanged numerous love letters, and though they did not marry until 1842 (Hawthorne wanted to be more financially secure before starting a family), he felt they were already "married" in spirit.

Boston, July 24th, 1839—8 o'clock p.m.

Mine Own,

I am tired this evening, as usual, with my long day's toil; and my head wants its pillow—and my soul yearns for the friend whom God has given it—whose soul He has married to my soul. Oh, my dearest, how that thought thrills me! We *are* married! I felt it long ago; and sometimes, when I was seeking for some fondest word, it has been on my lips to call you—"Wife"! I hardly know what restrained me from speaking it—unless a dread (for *that* would have been an infinite pang to me) of feeling you shrink back from my bosom, and thereby discovering that there was yet a deep place in your soul which did not know me.

Mine own Dove, need I fear it now? Are we not married? God knows we are. Often, while holding you in my arms, I have silently given myself to you, and received you for my portion of human love and happiness, and have prayed Him to consecrate and bless the union. And any one of our innocent embraces—even when our lips did but touch for a moment, and then were withdrawn—dearest, was it not the symbol of a bond between our Souls, infinitely stronger than any external rite could twine around us?

Yes—we are married; and as God Himself has joined us, we may trust never to be separated, neither in Heaven nor on Earth. We will wait patiently and quietly, and He will lead us onward hand in hand (as He has done all along) like little children, and will guide us to our perfect happiness—and will teach us when our union is to be revealed to the world. My beloved, why should we be silent to one another—why should our lips be silent—any longer on this subject? The world might, as yet, misjudge us; and therefore we will not speak to the world; but when I hold you in my arms, why should we not commune together about all our hopes of earthly and external, as well as our faith of inward and eternal union?

Farewell for to-night, my dearest—my soul's bride! Oh, my heart is thirsty for your kisses; they are the dew which should restore its freshness every night, when the hot sunshiny day has parched it. Kiss me in your dreams; and perhaps my heart will feel it.

Hawthorne, who authored The Scarlet Letter *(1850) and* The House of the Seven Gables *(1851), discouraged his wife from pursuing a literary career. Sophia was an accomplished writer, however, and published a book of her own—*Notes in England and Italy*—after his death. And while they were engaged, she, too, wrote heartfelt, poetic letters to her fiancé.*

31 December, 1839

Best Beloved,—

I send you some allumettes wherewith to kindle the taper. There are very few but my second finger could no longer perform extra duty. These will serve till the wounded one be healed, however. How beautiful it is to provide even this slightest convenience for you, dearest! I cannot tell you how much I love you, in this back-handed style. My love is not in this attitude,—it rather bends forwards to meet you.

What a year this has been to us! My definition of Beauty is, that it is love, and therefore includes both truth and good. But those only who love as we do can feel the significance and force of this.

My ideas will not flow in these crooked strokes. God be with you. I am very well, and have walked far in Danvers this cold morning. I am full of the glory of the day. God bless you this night of the old year. It has proved the year of our nativity. Has not the old earth passed away from us?—are not all things new?

Your Sophie

Edgar Allan Poe to Annie L. Richmond

The life of Edgar Allan Poe unfolded not unlike one of his stories. Haunted by persistent poverty and alcoholism, Poe frequently slipped into bouts of despair. In 1835, at age twenty-six, he married his beautiful, thirteen-year-old cousin Virginia, who died in 1847 of tuberculosis. Soon after Virginia's death, Poe fell madly in love with two women, Sarah Helen Whitman—a widow—and Annie Richmond, a married woman. On November 14, 1848, Poe wrote to Whitman: "beloved of my heart of my imagination of my intellect—life of my life—soul of my soul . . . dear dearest *Helen be true to me . . ." He sent the following letter to Annie Richmond just two days later, expressing his eternal love for her and describing a bizarre suicide attempt on his part to get her to visit him. (Poe refers to Richmond several times as his "sister," which she was not.)*

Fordham Nov. 16th 1848—

Ah, Annie Annie! *my* Annie! what cruel thoughts about your Eddy must have been torturing your heart during the last terrible fortnight, in which you have heard *nothing* from me—not even one little word to say that I still lived & loved you. But Annie I know that you *felt* too deeply the nature of my love for you, to doubt *that*, even for one moment, & this thought has comforted me in my bitter sorrow—I could bear that you should imagine *every other evil except that one*—that my soul had been untrue to yours. Why am I not *with* you now *darling* that I might sit by your side, press your dear hand in mine, & look deep down into the clear Heaven of your eyes—so that the words which I now can only *write*, might sink into your heart, and make you comprehend what it is that I would say—And yet Annie, *all* that I wish to say—all that my soul pines to express at this instant, is included in the one word, *love*—To be with you now—so that I might whisper in your ear the divine emotion[s], which agitate me—I would willingly—oh *joyfully* abandon this world with all my hopes of another:—but you *believe* this, Annie—you do believe it, & will always believe it—So long as I think that you *know* I love you, as no man ever loved woman—so long as I think you comprehend in some measure, the fervor with which I adore you, *so* long, no worldly trouble can ever render me absolutely wretched. But oh, *my darling, my* Annie, my own sweet *sister* Annie, my *pure* beautiful angel—*wife* of my soul—to be mine hereafter & *forever in the Heavens*—how shall I explain to you the *bitter, bitter* anguish which has tortured me since I left you? You saw, you *felt* the agony of grief with which I bade you farewell—You remember my expressions of gloom—of a dreadful horrible foreboding of ill—Indeed—*indeed* it seemed to me that death approached me even then, & that I was involved in the shadow which went before him—As I clasped you to my heart, I said to myself—"it is for the last time, until we meet in Heaven"—I remember nothing distinctly, from that moment until I found myself in Providence—I went to bed & wept through a long, long, hideous night of despair—When the day broke, I arose, &

endeavored to quiet my mind by a rapid walk in the cold, keen air—but all *would* not do—the demon tormented me still. Finally I procured two ounces of laud[a]num & without returning to my Hotel, took the cars back to Boston. When I arrived, I wrote you a letter, in which I opened my whole heart to you—to *you*—my Annie, whom I so madly, so distractedly love—I told you how my struggles were more than I could bear—how my soul revolted from saying the words which were to be said—and that not even for your dear sake, could I bring myself to say them. I then reminded you of that holy promise, which was the last I exacted from you in parting—the promise that, under all circumstances, you would come to me on my bed of death—I implored you to come *then*—mentioning the place where I should be found in Boston—Having written this letter, I swallowed about half the laud[a]num & hurried to the Post-Office—intending not to take the rest until I saw you—for, I did not doubt for one moment, that *my own* Annie would keep her sacred promise—But I had not calculated on the strength of the laudanum, for, before I reached the Post Office my reason was entirely gone, & the letter was never put in. Let me pass over, my darling *sister*, the awful horrors which succeeded—A friend was at hand, who aided & (if it can be called saving) saved me—but it is only within the last three days that I have been able to remember what occurred in that dreary interval—It appears that, after the laudanum was rejected from the stomach, I became calm, & to a casual observer, sane—so that I was suffered to go back to Providence—Here I saw *her*, & spoke, for *your* sake, the words which you urged me to speak—Ah Annie Annie! *my* Annie—*is* your heart *so* strong?—is there *no* hope!—is there *none*?—I feel that I *must* die if I persist, & yet, how can I now retract with honor?—Ah *beloved*, think—think for *me* & for yourself—do I not *love* you Annie? do you not *love me*? Is not this *all*? Beyond this blissful thought, what other consideration *can* there be in this dreary world! It is not *much* that I ask, *sweet sister Annie*—my mother & myself would take a small cottage at Westford—oh *so* small—so *very* humble—I should be far away from the tumult of the world—from the ambition which I loathe—I would labor day & night, and with industry, I could accomplish *so* much—Annie! it would be a Paradise beyond my wildest hopes—I could see some of your beloved family *every* day, & you often—oh VERY often—I would hear from you continually—regularly & *our* dear mother would be with us & love us both—ah *darling*—do not these pictures touch your inmost heart? Think—oh *think* for me—before the words—the vows are spoken, which put yet another terrible *bar* between us—before the time goes by, beyond which there must be *no* thinking—I call upon you in the name of God—in the name of the holy love I bear you, to be *sincere* with me—*Can* you, *my* Annie, *bear* to think I am another's? *It would give me supreme—infinite bliss* to hear you say that you could *not* bear it—I am at home now with my dear muddie who is endeavoring to comfort me—but the sole words which soothe me, are those in which she speaks of "*my Annie*"—she tells me that she has written you, begging you to come on to Fordham—ah beloved Annie, IS IT NOT POSSIBLE? I am so *ill*—so terribly, hopelessly ILL in body and mind, that I feel I CANNOT live, unless I can feel your sweet, gentle, loving hand pressed upon my forehead—oh my *pure, virtuous, generous, beautiful, beautiful sister* Annie!—is it not POSSIBLE for you to come—if only for one little week?—until I subdue this fearful agitation, which if continued, will either destroy my life, drive me hopelessly mad—Farewell—here & hereafter—

forever your own
Eddy—

Poe later became involved with yet a third woman, a Mrs. Shelton, whom he was to marry. But the wedding was not to be. The forty-year-old writer, who penned such classics as "The Raven," "The Pit and the Pendulum," and "The Tell-Tale Heart," was found outside a Baltimore saloon in an alcoholic stupor on October 3, 1849, and died four days later.

Herman Melville to Nathaniel Hawthorne

As Herman Melville labored tirelessly on his "Whale," the book that eventually became Moby-Dick, *he found a soulmate and favorable audience in Nathaniel Hawthorne, who lived in a neighboring town. Though Melville was fifteen years younger, he was already a celebrated writer of two popular works,* Typee *and* Omoo. *Melville wrote lengthy, almost stream-of-conscious and immodest letters, but he was aware of his indiscretions; "I talk all about myself, and this is selfishness and egotism. Granted. But how help it? I am writing to you; I know little about you, but something about myself. So I write about myself." But within his sometimes rambling paragraphs there are flashes of profound thoughtfulness and humanity. In the following letter, Melville writes about himself and his thoughts on* Moby-Dick, *but also about how meaningful his friendship and correspondence with Hawthorne are to him.*

[November 1851]
Pittsfield, Monday afternoon.

My Dear Hawthorne,—

People think that if a man has undergone any hardship, he should have a reward; but for my part, if I have done the hardest possible day's work, and then come to sit down in a corner and eat my supper comfortably—why, then I don't think I deserve any reward for my hard day's work—for am I not now at peace? Is not my supper good? My peace and my supper are my reward, my dear Hawthorne. So your joy-giving and exultation-breeding letter is not my reward for my ditcher's work with that book, but is the good goddess's bonus over and above what was stipulated for—for not one man in five cycles, who is wise, will expect appreciative recognition from his fellows, or any one of them. Appreciation! Recognition! Is love appreciated? Why, ever since Adam, who has got to the meaning of this great allegory—the world? Then we pygmies must be content to have our paper allegories but ill comprehended. I say your appreciation is my glorious gratuity. In my proud, humble way,—a shepherd-king,—I was lord of a little vale in the solitary Crimea; but you have now given me the crown of India. But on trying it on my head, I found it fell down on my ears, notwithstanding their asinine length—for it's only such ears that sustain such crowns.

Your letter was handed me last night on the road going to Mr. Morewood's, and I read it there. Had I been at home, I would have sat down at once and answered it. In me divine magnanimities are spontaneous and instantaneous—catch them while you can. The world goes round, and the other side comes up. So now I can't write what I felt. But I felt pantheistic then—your heart beat in my ribs and mine in yours, and both in God's. A sense of unspeakable security is in me this moment, on account of your having understood the book. I have written a wicked book, and feel spotless as the lamb. Ineffable socialities are in me. I would sit down and dine with you and all the gods in old Rome's Pantheon. It is a strange feeling—no hopefulness is in it, no despair. Content—that is it; and irresponsibility; but without licentious inclination. I speak now of my profoundest sense of being, not of an incidental feeling.

Whence come you, Hawthorne? By what right do you drink from my flagon of life? And when I put it to my lips—lo, they are yours and not mine. I feel that the Godhead is broken up like the bread at the Supper, and that we are the pieces. Hence this infinite fraternity of feeling. Now, sympathizing with the paper, my angel turns over another page. You did not care a penny for the book. But, now and then as you read, you understood the pervading thought that impelled the book—and that you praised. Was it not so? You were archangel enough to despise the imperfect body, and embrace the soul. Once you hugged the ugly Socrates because you saw the flame in the mouth, and heard the rushing of the demon,—the familiar,—and recognized the sound; for you have heard it in your own solitudes.

My dear Hawthorne, the atmospheric skepticisms steal into me now, and make me doubtful of my sanity in writing you thus. But, believe me, I am not mad, most noble Festus! But truth is ever incoherent, and when the big hearts strike together, the concussion is a little stunning. Farewell. Don't write a word about the book. That would be robbing me of my miserly delight. I am heartily sorry I ever wrote anything about you—it was paltry. Lord, when shall we be done growing? As long as we have anything more to do, we have done nothing. So, now, let us add Moby Dick to our blessing, and step from that. Leviathan is not the biggest fish;—I have heard of Krakens.

This is a long letter, but you are not at all bound to answer it. Possibly, if you do answer it, and direct it to Herman Melville, you will missend it—for the very fingers that now guide this pen are not precisely the same that just took it up and put it on this paper. Lord, when shall we be done changing? Ah! it's a long stage, and no inn in sight, and night coming, and the body cold. But with you for a passenger, I am content and can be happy. I shall leave the world, I feel, with more satisfaction for having come to know you. Knowing you persuades me more than the Bible of our immortality.

What a pity, that, for your plain, bluff letter, you should get such gibberish! Mention me to Mrs. Hawthorne and to the children, and so, good-by to you, with my blessing.

Herman

P.S. I can't stop yet. If the world was entirely made up of Magians, I'll tell you what I should do. I should have a papermill established at one end of the house, and so have an endless riband of foolscap rolling in upon my desk; and upon that endless riband I should write a thousand—a million—billion thoughts, all under the form of a letter to you. The divine magnet is on you, and my magnet responds. Which is the biggest? A foolish question—they are *One*.

H.

P.P.S. Don't think that by writing me a letter, you shall always be bored with an immediate reply to it—and so keep both of us delving over a writing-desk eternally. No such thing! I sh'n't always answer your letters, and you may do just as you please.

Emily Dickinson to Susan Gilbert

"If it is finished," the poet Emily Dickinson wrote to Susan Gilbert of their friendship, "tell me, and I will raise the lid to my box of Phantoms, and lay one more love in; but if it lives *and* beats *still, still lives and beats for* me, *then say me so." There has been considerable speculation as to the relationship between Dickinson and Gilbert, who later married Dickinson's brother, Austin. Dickinson's letters are unquestionably effusive in their declarations of love, but whether they are the writings of an actual lover or simply those of a dear friend expressing herself in a manner more familiar to the 1800s is uncertain. Either way, Dickinson's letters to Gilbert (not unlike her letters to other friends and family members) are remarkably whimsical, warm, and tender, and, when she believes Gilbert to be too long in responding, expressive of genuine heartache—as demonstrated in the following letter, written in early February of 1852, when Dickinson was twenty-one. ("Vinnie" is Dickinson's younger sister, Lavinia.)*

Will you let me come dear Susie—looking just as I do, my dress soiled and worn, my grand old apron, and my hair—Oh Susie, time would fail me to enumerate my appearance, yet I love you just as dearly as if I was e'er so fine, so you wont care, will you? I am so glad dear Susie—that our hearts are always clean, and always neat and lovely, so not to be ashamed. I have been hard at work this morning, and I ought to be working now—but I cannot deny myself the luxury of a minute or two with you.

The dishes may wait dear Susie—and the uncleared table stand, *them* I have always with me, but you, I have "not always"—*why* Susie, Christ hath saints *manie*—and I have *few*, but thee—the angels shant have Susie—no—no—no!

Vinnie is sewing away like a *fictitious* seamstress, and I half expect some knight will arrive at the door, confess himself a *nothing* in presence of her loveliness, and present his heart and hand as the only vestige of him worthy to be refused.

Vinnie and I have been talking about growing old, today. Vinnie thinks *twenty* must be a fearful position for one to occupy—I tell her I dont care if I am young or not, had as lief be thirty, and you, as most anything else. Vinnie expresses her sympathy at my "sere and yellow leaf" and resumes her work, dear Susie, tell me how *you* feel—ar'nt there days in one's life when to be old dont seem a thing so sad—

I do feel gray and grim, this morning, and I feel it would be a comfort to have a piping voice, and broken back, and scare little children. Dont *you* run, Susie dear, for I wont do any harm, and I do love you dearly tho' I do feel so frightful.

Oh my darling one, how long you wander from me, how weary I grow of waiting and looking, and calling for you; sometimes I shut my eyes, and shut my heart towards you, and try hard to forget you because you grieve me so, but you'll never go away, Oh you never will—say, Susie, promise me again, and I will smile faintly—and take up my little cross again of sad—*sad* separation. How vain it seems to *write*, when one knows how to feel—how much more near and dear to sit beside you, talk with you, hear the tones of your voice; so hard to "deny thyself, and take up thy cross, and follow me"—give me strength, Susie, write me of hope and love, and of hearts that *endured*, and great was their reward of "Our Father who art in Heaven." I dont know how I shall bear it, when the gentle spring comes; if she should come and see me and talk to me of you, Oh it would surely kill me! While the frost clings to the windows, and the World is stern and drear; this absence is easier; the *Earth* mourns too, for all her little birds; but when they all come back again, and she sings and is so merry—pray, what will become of me? Susie, forgive me, forget all I say, get some sweet little scholar to read a gentle hymn, about Bethle[h]em and Mary, and you will sleep on sweetly and have as peaceful dreams, as if I had never written you all these ugly things. Never mind the letter Susie, I wont be angry with you if you dont give me any at all—for I know how busy you are, and how little of that dear strength remains when it is evening, with which to think and write. Only *want* to write me, only sometimes sigh that you are far from me, and that will do, Susie! Dont you think we are good and patient, to let you go so long; and dont we think you're a darling, a real beautiful hero, to toil for people, and teach them, and leave your own dear home? Because we pine and repine, dont think we forget the precious patriot at war in other lands! Never be mournful, Susie—be happy and have cheer, for how many of the long days have gone away since I wrote you—and it is almost noon, and soon the night will come, and then there is one less day of the long pilgrimage. Mattie is very smart, talks of you *much*, my darling; I must leave you now—"one little hour of Heaven," thank who did give it me, and will he also grant me one longer and *more* when it shall please his love—bring Susie home, ie! Love always, and ever, and true!

Emily—

Polygamist Rudger Clawson to His Second Plural Wife Lydia

On October 25, 1884, Rudger Clawson earned his place in history by being the first Mormon to be convicted and imprisoned for violating the 1882 Edmunds Act, legislation passed to outlaw polygamy. Fined eight hundred dollars and sentenced to four years in a Salt Lake City prison, Clawson watched as murderers and thieves were released in less time than he. Throughout his imprisonment he wrote frequently to Lydia Spencer, his second plural wife (his first wife, Florence, was less enthusiastic about the arrangement), expressing his passionate love for her and his intense scorn for those who do not adhere to the early Mormon belief in polygamy. The following letter was written in late March 1885, just a few weeks after Lydia bore their first child, Remus.

My dearest Lydia:

Another chance has offered itself, so I write you a few lines. How very much disappointed I was in not seeing you on Thursday, I do not care to say. It is certainly a very great hardship for a man's family to be denied the privilege of visiting him, but when the wicked rule the people mourn. Possess thy soul in patience, however, my dearest sweetheart, for this cannot last forever. We have no reason to be sorrowful and unhappy, but should rejoice continually, for it must not be forgotten that we are struggling to introduce and maintain, in opposition to the world, one of the most glorious principles ever revealed from heaven.

Two or three years imprisonment is nothing compared to the wretchedness that would result from dishonoring God in the least degree. Happy are we whether in prison or out of prison, whether in life or in death, so long as we are true and faithful to the Great Jehovah, and magnify His Holy Name in every act of our lives. Under existing circumstances two or three years appear to be a very long time, but when we remember that there is an eternity before us, they dwindle down to insignificance. Fret not thy soul, therefore, but lift up thy head and rejoice in the thought that up to this time we have been faithful to the great principle which will exalt us in the presence of God.

Those who denied you the privilege of coming to see me will receive a just reward. The measure they have measured to you will be measured to them again, pressed down and running over. When they are thrust into Hell and see their wives and children given to men more worthy than they, how then think you they will feel. Will not their torment be almost more than they can bear? I think so. This is undoubtedly their fate, lest they speedily repent and make restitution for the great wrongs they have done.

The present brief separation will knit our hearts firmly together in the bonds of affection and will cause us to look forward in anticipation to the joy and pleasure of our reunion. My love is *thine*, and thine is mine, and the thought comforts me. How very much I long to clasp thee in my arms and press thee to my heart. Can greater happiness be derived from any source than from the fond embraces of pure love? Not the love of the world, but love that springs from a pure heart.

And when our thoughts turn to little Remus, so pure, so innocent, so lovely, who has been sent from heaven to bless and cement our union, what reason have we to grieve and worry over a short separation? Hug and kiss him a thousand times for me, and may heaven watch over and bless you both.

Whenever you feel disposed to give way to sorrowful thoughts and feelings of unhappiness, read this and my other letter and know that I love you.

Clawson was pardoned by President Grover Cleveland after serving over three years of his four-year sentence. The Mormon church officially banned polygamy in 1890, but it continued secretly for many years afterward. Clawson is believed to have married a third plural wife, Pearl Udall, in 1904.

Paul Laurence Dunbar to Alice Ruth Moore

"You will pardon my boldness in addressing you, I hope," a twenty-two-year-old Paul Laurence Dunbar wrote to Alice Ruth Moore in 1895, "and let my interest in your work be my excuse." Dunbar was genuinely interested in Moore's work—she was an accomplished African American poet and journalist, and Dunbar, who was also gaining acclaim as an African American writer, asked if the two could "exchange opinions and work." Moore accepted the invitation, and the pair corresponded for two years. They finally met in 1897 and fell in love soon after. In the spring of that same year, Dunbar, traveling in England, sent Moore the following letter.

16 Imperial Mansions,
Oxford Street
London, W.C.
7th March '97

Alice:—My Darling, Someday, when I can hold you in my arms and punctuate every sentence with a kiss and an embrace I may be able to tell you how happy your letter has made me. Happy and yet unhappy from the very strength of my longing to be with you, a longing not to be satisfied it seems to so distant a day.

You love me, Alice, you say; ah yes but could you know the

intensity with which I worship you, you would realize that your strongest feelings are weak beside. You gave me no time to think or to resist had I willed to do so! You took my heart captive at once. I yielded bravely, weak coward that I am, without a struggle. And how glad I am of my full surrender. I would rather be your captive than another woman's king. You have made life a new thing to me—a precious and sacred trust.

Will I love you tenderly and faithfully? Darling, darling, can you ask! You who are my heart, my all, my life. I will love you as no man has ever loved before. Already I am living for you and working for you and through the gray days and the long nights I am longing and yearning for you;—for the sound of your voice, the touch of your hand, the magic of your presence, the thrill of your kiss.

You did wrong to kiss me? Oh sweet heart of mine, does the flower that turns its golden face up to the amorous kisses of the sun do wrong? Does the crystal wave that wrinkles at the touch of the moving wind do wrong? Does the cloud that clasps the mountain close to its dewy breast do wrong? Do any of the eternal forces of nature do wrong? If so then you have done a wrong. But darling you could not have helped it. This love of ours was predestined. I had thought that I loved you before, and I had. I loved Alice Ruth Moore the writer of "Violets," but now I love Alice Ruth Moore, the woman,—and my queen. "All the current of my being runs to thee."

I am writing wildly my dear I know, but I am not stopping to think. My head has retired and it is my heart and my pen for it.

For your sake I will be true and pure. You will help me to be this for you are always in my thoughts. Last night as I started out upon a rather new undertaking or rather phase of action, I took your letter with me and read it as I drove down town. "It will give me heart," I said. It did and I have never had before such a brilliant success. It was at a dinner of the Savage Club, artists, literateurs, scientists and actors, where every man could do some thing. I was an honored guest and held a unique position as the representative of a whole race. I took my turn with the rest, and,—dear is this egotism?—was received with wonderful enthusiasm.

You were with me all the time! You do not leave my thoughts. Alice, Alice, how I love you! Tell me over and over again that you love me. It will hearten me for the larger task that I have set myself here. I am so afraid that you may grow to care less for me. May God forbid! But if you do, let me know at once. I love you so that I am mindful only of your happiness. This is why I shall not complain about your being in New York although I do not like it. It is a *dangerous* place. But I know, darling that you will do me no injustice, and yourself no dishonor, so I am content. Go often to Miss Brown's but do not entirely usurp my place in the heart of that queen of women. Love me, dear, and tell me so. Write to me often and believe me ever

Your Devoted Lover, *Paul*
Low's Exchange
3 Northumberland Ave
Trafalgar Square

Albert Einstein to Mileva Maric

Like many young lovers, Albert Einstein and Mileva Maric were confronted with a vexing obstacle to their relationship—disapproving parents. Einstein's parents, worried that their twenty-one-year-old son was not financially secure enough to marry, discouraged him from seeing Maric. Referring to his mother and father, Einstein writes to Maric in one letter: "They think of a wife as a man's luxury, which he can afford only when he is making a comfortable living. I have a low opinion of this view [. . .] because it makes the wife and the prostitute distinguishable only insofar as the former is able to secure a lifelong contract." In the following letter, written in the fall of 1900, the young Einstein further expresses the extent to which his parents are grating on his nerves.

My dear kitten,

Today I received your registered letter, from which I could tell you were afraid it might fall into someone else's hands. No, darling, I received all of your dear little letters on time, even the money you sent me in Melchtal a while ago. Feel free to write what's on your mind, because it would be as unwise as it would be useless for my parents to keep one of your letters from me. You shouldn't worry about such things because I don't think my parents are capable of behaving like that. I've already put Mama to the test. My parents are very worried about my love for you. Mama often cries bitterly and I don't have a single moment of peace here. My parents weep for me almost as if I had died. Again and again they complain that I have brought misfortune upon myself by my devotion to you, they think you aren't healthy . . . Oh Dollie, it's enough to drive one mad! You wouldn't believe how I suffer when I see how much they both love me, and yet are so inconsolable you would think I had committed the greatest crime, and had gone against what my heart and conscience told me was indisputably true. If only they knew you! But it's as if they're under a spell, thinking all the while that I am. On Saturday I'm going on the business trip with Papa, and then to Venice. I was so distraught that I didn't want to go with him; but this alarmed them so much that I became quite frightened.

I'll only be able to recover from this vacation gradually, by being in your arms—there are worse things in life than exams. Now I know. This is worse than any external problem.

My only diversion is studying, which I am pursuing with redoubled effort, and my only hope is you, my dear, faithful soul. Without the thought of you I would no longer want to live among this sorry herd of humans. But having you makes me proud, and your love makes me happy. I will be doubly happy when I can press you close to my heart once again and see those loving eyes which shine for me alone, and kiss your sweet mouth which trembles blissfully for me alone.

Thank God that August has slipped away. Four more weeks and

we'll be together again and can live to bring each other joy. But then I won't let you go away again so soon!

I've been spending many evenings at Michele's. I like him a great deal because of his sharp mind and his simplicity. I also like Anna, and especially their little kid. His house is simple and cozy, though some of the details lack taste.

Kissing you from the bottom of my heart, your

Sweetheart

Einstein and Maric eloped in 1903; one year later Maric gave birth to a girl who was put up for adoption and whose fate is still unknown. They had two more children, but by 1914 the marriage was in shambles and they separated. Maric and Einstein officially divorced in February 1919. Later that year, Einstein married Elsa Einstein Lowenthal, his cousin.

Edith Wharton to W. Morton Fullerton

Caught up in a marriage that began disastrously and grew worse with time, the novelist Edith Wharton discovered true passion in the arms of W. Morton Fullerton, an American she met in Paris in 1907 who wrote for the London Times. *Fullerton, several years Wharton's junior, was in Wharton's eyes a sophisticated, brilliant, charming, and handsome gentleman who also happened to be closely acquainted with many of Wharton's dearest friends, the writer Henry James being the most notable. But Wharton's affair with Fullerton was also marked by profound despair, as he would inexplicably become remote and then ignore her repeated pleas for some word of love or assurance. After one prolonged silence, Wharton finally addressed him icily in a letter as "Dear Mr. Fullerton" and requested that he return all her letters. But soon after, as he had done before and would do again, he made amends, and the affair continued. The following letter, written by Wharton during one of Fullerton's "distant" periods in August 1908, demonstrates the degree to which his indifference was wounding her.*

August 26

Dear, won't you tell me soon the meaning of this silence?

At first I thought it might mean that your sentimental mood had cooled, & that you feared to let me see the change; & I wrote, nearly a month ago, to tell you how natural I should think such a change on your part, & how I hoped that our friendship—so dear to me!—might survive it.—It would have been easy, after that letter, to send a friendly: "Yes, chère amie—"surely, having known me so well all those months, you could have trusted to my understanding it?

But the silence continues! It was not *that* you wanted? For a time I fancied you were too busy & happy to think of writing—perhaps even to glance at my letters when they came. But even so—there are degrees in the lapse from such intimacy as ours into complete silence & oblivion; & if the inclination to write had died out, must not you, who are so sensitive & imaginative, have asked yourself to what conjectures you were leaving me, & how I should suffer at being so abruptly & inexplicably cut off from all news of you?

I re-read your letters the other day, & I will not believe that the man who wrote them did not feel them, & did not know enough of the woman to whom they were written to trust to her love & courage, rather than to leave her to this aching uncertainty.

What has brought about such a change? Oh, no matter what it is—*only tell me!* I could take my life up again courageously if I only understood; for whatever those months were to you, to me they were a great gift, a wonderful enrichment; & still I rejoice & give thanks for them! You woke me from a long lethargy, a dull acquiescence in conventional restrictions, a needless self-effacement. If I was awkward & inarticulate it was because, literally, all one side of me was asleep.

I remember, that night we went to the "Figlia di Iorio," that in the scene in the cave, where the Figlia sends him back to his mother (I forget all their names), & as he goes he turns & kisses her, & *then she can't let him go*—I remember you turned to me & said laughing: "That's something you don't know anything about."

Well! I *did* know, soon afterward; & if I still remained inexpressive, unwilling, "always drawing away," as you said, it was because I discovered in myself such possibilities of feeling on that side that I feared, if I let you love me too much, I might lose courage when the time came to go away!—Surely you saw this, & understood how I dreaded to be to you, *even for an instant*, the "donna non più giovane" who clings & encumbers—how, situated as I was, I thought I could best show my love by refraining—& abstaining? You saw it was all because I loved you?

And when you spoke of your uncertain future, your longing to break away & do the work you really like, didn't you see how my heart *broke* with the thought that, if I had been younger & prettier, everything might have been different—that we might have had together, at least for a short time, a life of exquisite collaborations—a life in which your gifts would have had full scope, & you would have been able to do the distinguished & beautiful things that you ought to do?—Now, I hope, your future has after all arranged itself happily, just as you despaired,—but remember that *those were my thoughts* when you were calling me "conventional" . . .

I never expected to tell you this; but under the weight of this silence I don't know what to say or leave unsaid. After nearly a month my frank tender of friendship remains unanswered. If that was not what you wished, what *is* then your feeling for me? My reason rejects the idea that a man like you, who has felt a warm sympathy for a woman like me, can suddenly, from one day to another, without any act or word on her part, lose even a friendly regard for her, & discard the mere outward signs of consideration by which friendship speaks. And so I am almost driven to conclude that your silence has another meaning, which I have not guessed. If any feeling subsists under it, may these words reach it, & tell you what I felt in silence when we were together!

Yes, dear, I loved you then, & I love you now, as you then wished me to; only I have learned that one must put all happiness one can into each moment, & I will never again love you "sadly," since that displeases you.

You see I am once more assuming that you *do* care what I feel, in spite of this mystery! How can it be that the sympathy between two people like ourselves, so many-sided, so steeped in imagination, should end from one day to another like a mere "passade"—end by my passing, within a few weeks, utterly out of your memory? By all that I know you are, by all I am myself conscious of being, I declare that I am unable to believe it!

You told me once I should write better for this experience of loving. I felt it to be so, & I came home so fired by the desire that my work should please you! But this incomprehensible silence, the sense of your utter indifference to everything that concerns me, has stunned me. It has come so suddenly . . .

This is the last time I will write you, dear, unless the strange spell is broken. And my last word is one of tenderness for the friend I love—for the lover I worshipped.

Goodbye, dear.

Oh, I don't want my letters back, dearest! I said that in my other letter only to make it easier for you if you were seeking a transition—

Do you suppose I care what becomes of them if you don't care?

Is it really to my dear friend—*to Henry's friend*—to "dearest Morton"—that I have written this?

Fullerton eventually responded, and his affair with Wharton lasted until 1911, when the two decided simply to maintain a platonic friendship. Near the end of their affair, Wharton wrote to Fullerton, lamenting: "When one is a lonely-hearted & remembering creature, as I am, it is a misfortune to love too late, & as completely as I have loved you. Everything else grows so ghostly afterward."

Georgia O'Keeffe to Anita Pollitzer

Having first met as graduate students at Columbia Unversity, Anita Pollitzer and Georgia "Pat" O'Keeffe shared an intense love for art that led to a friendship that would last, off and on, for almost thirty-five years. "Your letters are certainly like drinks of fine cold spring water on a hot day," O'Keeffe wrote to Pollitzer in August 1915. "They have a spark of the kind of fire in them that makes life worthwhile—That nervous energy that makes people like you and I want and go after everything in the world." But O'Keeffe, who was more introspective and reserved (and seven years older) than her more outgoing friend, found Pollitzer's energy and enthusiasm overwhelming at times. In the following letter from Columbia, South Carolina, in October 1915, O'Keeffe gently chastises Pollitzer for an emotional letter she had just written—a letter that has not survived—and shares her own perspective on life and living. (The love interest O'Keeffe mentions is Arthur Macmahon, a fellow teacher, and "Dorothy" is Dorothy True, a mutual friend.)

Anita:
My dear little girl:

You mustn't get so excited. Remember how I made you cry at lunch one day last winter telling you that. You wear out the most precious things you have by letting your emotions and feelings run riot at such a rate

I understand how you feel—and I think I understand too—that you havent decided yet exactly what things are most worth while to you in the world and in life—All I ask—no Ill not ask it—Ill not even advise it—Ill merely ask it as a question dont you think we need to conserve our energies—emotions and feelings for what we are going to make the big things in our lives instead of letting so much run away on the little things everyday

Self control is a wonderful thing—I think we must even keep ourselves from feeling too much—often—if we are going to keep sane and see with a clear unprejudiced vision—

I do not want to preach to you—I like you like you are—but I would like to think you had a string on yourself and that you were not wearing yourself all out of feeling and living now—save a little so you can *live* always—

It always seems to me that so few people *live*—they just seem to exist and I don't see any reason why we shouldn't *live always*—til we die physically—why do it in our teens and twenties

I have to keep my head for purely physical reasons—it wears me out too much not to

You shouldn't have been so excited on my behalf over the letter I sent you—I sent it because people dont often express so much of themselves in words and it was honest and interesting—

I dont love him—I don't pretend to—sometimes when Im very tired I used to want him because he is restful—I probably will again—though—I doubt it.

He is to nice to let go—and to nice to keep—so I will do both—because he doesn't want to—go—We will always be friends

I almost want to say—don't mention loving anyone to me.

It is a curious thing—don't let it get you Anita if you value your peace of mind—it will eat you up and swallow you whole—

Enough for today—I am afraid you will not like this—It seems almost like a scolding

Another thing—Dorothy knows me in a different way than you do—different people always call out different things in us—I could not possibly seem the same to you both—you call for such different responses—but Anita—you mustn't expect too much of me for your bubble is bound to burst if you do—

Pat.

Pollitzer assured O'Keeffe that she did not expect too much of her, but she was not sorry for her first letter; "P'raps your little sermons about not letting my emotions run riot are true, but it is more of a physical strain Pat to keep them quiet when they want to come out—I'd lots rather live hard than long!"

Agnes von Kurowsky to Ernest Hemingway

Serving as an ambulance driver in Italy during World War I, an eighteen-year-old Ernest Hemingway was taken to a Milan hospital after an explosion badly injured his leg. In that hospital he met one of the great loves of his life—Agnes Hannah von Kurowsky, a twenty-six-year-old American nurse who cared for Hemingway as he recuperated. Hemingway was infatuated with von Kurowsky from the start, and for a time she seemed to have feelings for him as well, though von Kurowsky later said she merely "liked" him and that their relationship was nothing more than a "flirtation." Hemingway wanted them to get married, but von Kurowsky—because of the age difference, her belief that Hemingway was immature and aimless, and her interest in other men—rejected the idea. In January 1919 Hemingway left the hospital but continued to write to her. Von Kurowsky decided she finally had to convince him it was over, and on March 7, 1919, she wrote Hemingway the following letter.

Ernie, dear boy,

I am writing this late at night after a long think by myself, & I am afraid it is going to hurt you, but, I'm sure it won't harm you permanently.

For quite awhile before you left, I was trying to convince myself it was a real love-affair, because, we always seemed to disagree, & then arguments always wore me out so that I finally gave in to keep you from doing something desperate.

Now, after a couple of months away from you, I know that I am still very fond of you, but, it is more as a mother than as a sweetheart. It's alright to say I'm a Kid, but, I'm not, & I'm getting less & less so every day.

So, Kid (still Kid to me, & always will be) can you forgive me some day for unwittingly deceiving you? You know I'm not really bad, & don't mean to do wrong, & now I realize it was my fault in the beginning that you cared for me, & regret it from the bottom of my heart. But, I am now & always will be too old, & that's the truth, & I can't get away from the fact that you're just a boy—a kid.

I somehow feel that some day I'll have reason to be proud of you, but, dear boy, I can't wait for that day, & it was wrong to hurry a career.

I tried hard to make you understand a bit of what I was thinking on that trip from Padua to Milan, but, you acted like a spoiled child, & I couldn't keep on hurting you. Now, I only have the courage because I'm far away.

Then—& believe me when I say this is sudden for me, too—I expect to be married soon. And I hope & pray that after you have thought things out, you'll be able to forgive me & start a wonderful career & show what a man you really are.

Ever admiringly & fondly
Your friend,
Aggie

Hemingway's response to this letter is not known because one of von Kurowsky's boyfriends burned all of his letters. But in a June 1919 letter to his friend Howell Jenkins, Hemingway wrote: "I loved her once and then she gypped me. And I don't blame her. But I set out to cauterize out her memory and I burnt it out with a course of booze and other women and now it's gone." But not gone entirely—Agnes von Kurowsky became the basis for Catherine Barkley, the beautiful young American nurse who treats and falls in love with an American soldier in an Italian hospital in Hemingway's 1929 classic A Farewell to Arms.

Zelda Sayre to F. Scott Fitzgerald

The relationship between the great American writer F. Scott Fitzgerald and Zelda Sayre was plagued by arguments and accusations from the start and did not improve with marriage. Fitzgerald died in 1940, at the age of forty-four, in the home of his lover, Sheilah Graham. Zelda, who had been institutionalized after a series of nervous breakdowns, died eight years later in a fire at the hospital. The intensity of their initial love for each another, as well as the seeds of their destruction, are evident in the following letter written by Zelda in the spring of 1919, a year before they married.

Sweetheart,

Please, please don't be so depressed—We'll be married soon, and then these lonesome nights will be over forever—and until we are, I am loving, loving every tiny minute of the day and night—Maybe you won't understand this, but sometimes when I miss you most, it's hardest to write—and you always know when I make myself—Just the ache of it all—and I *can't* tell you. If we were together, you'd feel how strong it is—you're so sweet when you're melancholy. I love your sad tenderness—when I've hurt you—That's one of the reasons I could never be sorry for our quarrels—and they bothered you so—Those dear, dear little fusses, when I always tried so hard to make you kiss and forget—

Scott—there's nothing in all the world I want but you—and your precious love—All the material things are nothing. I'd just hate to live a sordid, colorless existence—because you'd soon love me less—and less—and I'd do anything—anything—to keep your heart for my own—I don't want to live—I want to love first, and live incidentally—Why don't you feel that I'm waiting—I'll come to you, Lover, when you're ready—Don't—don't ever think of the things you can't give me—You've trusted me with the dearest heart of all—and it's so damn much more than anybody else in all the world has ever had—

How can you think deliberately of life without me—If you should die—O Darling—darling Scott—It'd be like going blind. I know I would, too,—I'd have no purpose in life—just a pretty—decoration. Don't you think I was made for you? I feel like you had me ordered—and I was delivered to you—to be worn—I want you to wear me, like a watch—charm or a button hole bouquet—to the world. And then, when we're alone, I want to help—to know that you can't do *anything* without me.

I'm glad you wrote Mamma. It was such a nice sincere letter—

and mine to St Paul was very evasive and rambling. I've never, in all my life, been able to say anything to people older than me—Somehow I just instinctively avoid personal things with them—even my family. Kids are so much nicer.

Ogden Nash to Frances Leonard

Dragged by his sister to a formal dinner dance in Baltimore, a twenty-six-year-old Ogden Nash was soon thinking of ways he could duck out of the event without insulting his host. And then Frances Leonard entered the room. Nash was thunderstruck by her beauty and, after learning her name, secretly switched the place cards so that he would be seated next to her at dinner. "My aim was then, as it is now," Nash later recalled, "to persuade her to stay beside me for the rest of my life." She did. The two dated for several years, married in 1931, and eventually had two children together. Nash became a celebrated writer and lyricist especially known for his amusing and witty poems. The following letter, which displays his warm and whimsical style, was written less than a year after his fateful evening with Frances Leonard.

Sunday night
August 25, 1929

Frances darling,

Have you heard that I love you? I'm not sure that I made it clear to you, and I don't want to have any misunderstandings. It's such a young love yet—just nine and a half months old, born November 13th 1928 at about nine o'clock in the evening. But it's big for its age, and seems much older. I do hope you're going to like it, I'm sending you some now for you to try; but if it's not satisfactory, don't ever let me know.

This is a peculiarly gifted and intelligent pen. Look what it's writing now: I love you. That's a phrase I can't get out of my head—but I don't want to. I've wanted to try it out for a long time; I like the look of it and the sound of it and the meaning of it.

It's past one now and I've got to have some sleep before I face Nelson Doubleday tomorrow. But tell me something before I leave. I was told tonight on what seemed to me the best authority that you are fond of me. Can you confirm this rumor?

Then there's another problem. As long as I'm thinking about you I can't go to sleep; and I'd rather think about you than go to sleep; how am I to sleep?

Oh Frances, do tell me that everything really happened, that it wasn't just something that I wanted so much that it crystallized in my imagination.

Good night. I've just sent St. Joseph off to watch you on the train; he has promised that he will do his duty like an honest saint.

I do love you.

Ogden

Aline Bernstein to Thomas Wolfe

Written over an eleven-year period, the letters between Aline Bernstein and Thomas Wolfe chronicle a tempestuous love affair. When they first met he was twenty-five and she was forty-four. Wolfe was a struggling writer, and Bernstein was a successful stage and costume designer who provided him with financial support to complete what would become one of the great novels of the twentieth cenutury, Look Homeward, Angel. *With Bernstein working in theaters in New York and Wolfe writing in Europe, the two were often separated for long periods at a time. The distance was not conducive to a strong relationship, and in March 1931 Wolfe tried to end it completely. Bernstein nevertheless continued to write him, and Wolfe, who admitted he would love her forever, often wrote back. But in 1932 he ignored almost all her letters and cables, and by 1933 she realized it was clearly over. In the following letter, Bernstein comes to terms with the separation and expresses, one last time, all that Wolfe has meant to her.*

Armonk, N.Y./September 28, 1933

Dear Tom.—

I have lost track of how many years ago we met, and lunched together on your last birthday, but I have not forgotten, and I will carry with me to my death the mark you left upon me, and my deep love for you. It will never lessen, I will never change. I do not know whether you have the slightest interest in me, but this time since we finally parted has been a terrible and wonderful time. I have conquered myself, my outer self, and still preserved the treasure of my love. I am not in constant pain, and I know now that I must never see you again, that my future companionship with you must be in my mind and heart. In spite of all the black and dreadful years I have spent, I realize the beautiful thing that happened to me, that you and the way I loved you has released such wonder in my whole being, I have seen through you, through your touch upon me, a world that was dormant before. Have you seen a boy release homing pigeons from a cage? One day coming to see you in Brooklyn I watched that on a roof, and thought then how like it was to my own state with you. I wish for your happiness and success. I wish that I understood better what came between to destroy whatever good I held for you. I think you can look down to the very centre of yourself, and find beneath the hate for me, just one drop left of pure love.—God bless you, God help you to use your genius. I thought once that I could. I have the utmost faith in your greatness, and I send you, on this birthday, my whole heart of love.

Aline

I have no idea where you are, I hope this will reach you the right day.

Gertrude Stein to Carl Van Vechten

From 1913 until her death in 1946 the writer Gertrude Stein maintained an extensive correspondence with the novelist and music/drama critic Carl Van Vechten. Their letters are personal and loving, almost familial, and the two even addressed one another, somewhat inexplicably, as "Papa Woojums" (Van Vechten) and "Baby Woojumses" (Stein and her companion, Alice Toklas). Raised for the most part in California, Stein eventually moved to Paris, where she lived for the rest of her life. She returned to the United States in 1934 for a lecture tour and, writing from her hotel on December 20th, 1934, recounts her travels to Van Vechten in her own unique style.

The Commodore Perry
Toledo, Ohio

My dearest Carl,

What do you mean by saying that I don't tell you about your letters why we are being most dreadfully spoiled the most spoiled Woojumses in history but the thing that spoils us the most and the sweetest is the finding a letter from Carl whenever we get here if we did not have that we will be lost in this large sized America but we do have that we always do and that makes us all not lost, we passed Marion Ohio, yesterday and were so xcited the home of Harding and the home of the mother of Harding's child and the home of Mrs. Harding and the home of the sister of Harding who was the school-teacher the high school teacher of the mother of Harding's child, could anything be more historical and then we were right near Dayton Ohio, where Wilbur Wright was and now we are in Toledo where poor dear Max Ewing was, Europe nothing in Europe was ever anything to this,

We have just been taken out to drive up the river where Tecumseh fought and bled, and on the way in a magnificent house I heard lived the man and his wife who gave the Champion spark plugs to the world, and to us, to our little Fords we drove so long, so I said I must see them so the procession stopped and we were taken in to see them and they were so nice and they are sending me glass souvenir champion spark plugs, it's a wonderful world, lots of nice stories, and we are remembering them, in the back parts of Columbus two perfectly nice citizens stopped me and said solemnly we just wanted to say that if there was anything that we needed to be done that was not being done for us they would be most glad to do it, anything connected with the police or anything as they were old Columbus families and here were their names, and a reporter girl, told me and she swears she did not make it up here in Toledo that she went to the station to meet us on a train we did not come on and she asked the gate man if we had come through and he looked blank and a shabby citizen leaning on the wall said no she did not come through and the ticket man said who and the shabby man said sure I know her I never saw her but she would not get by here without my knowing her and then he said to the porter, you know her the one who said a rose is a rose is a rose is a rose you know her.

Do you believe that can be true.

Now we go to Cleveland and then all aboard the airplane to Baltimore, and when and where and how do we see you, we are in Washington the 29–30–31, I wish we would be seeing you somewhere your dear envelopes and letters are a comfort but your darling large sizedness would be more even more of a comfort because the Woojums love you with all their hearts and they always tell you so every way

Always
Gertrude

Ansel Adams to Cedric Wright

Ansel Adams, whose black-and-white photographs of nature are renowned for their stunning clarity, started taking pictures at the age of fourteen in Yosemite National Park. "The complexities of the modern world," Adams wrote to his friend Cedric Wright in 1928, "[are] supremely foolish in the face of the eternal openness and beauty of these mountains."

Nine years later, when Adams was thirty-five, a visit to Yosemite inspired the following letter to Wright.

June 10, 1937

Dear Cedric,

A strange thing happened to me today. I saw a big thundercloud move down over Half Dome, and it was so big and clear and brilliant that it made me see many things that were drifting around inside of me; things that related to those who are loved and those who are real friends.

For the first time I *know* what love is; what friends are; and what art should be.

Love is a seeking for a way of life; the way that cannot be followed alone; the resonance of all spiritual and physical things. Children are not only of flesh and blood—children may be ideas, thoughts, emotions. The person of the one who is loved is a form composed of a myriad mirrors reflecting and illuminating the powers and the thoughts and the emotions that are within you, and flashing another kind of light from within. No words or deeds may encompass it.

Friendship is another form of love—more passive perhaps, but full of the transmitting and acceptance of things like thunderclouds and grass and the clean reality of granite.

Art is both love and friendship, and understanding; the desire to give. It is not charity, which is the giving of Things, it is more than kindness which is the giving of self. It is both the taking and giving of beauty, the turning out to the light the inner folds of the awareness of the spirit. It is the recreation on another plane of the realities of the world; the tragic and wonderful realities of earth and men, and of all the inter-relations of these.

I wish the thundercloud had moved up over Tahoe and let loose on you; I could wish you nothing finer.

Ansel

Dr. Charles Drew to Lenore Robbins

"For years I have done little but work, plan and dream of making myself a good doctor, an able surgeon and in my wildest moments perhaps also playing some part in establishing a real school of thought among Negro physicians," wrote Dr. Charles R. Drew to his fiancée, Lenore Robbins. "Then I met you and for the first time mistress medicine met her match and went down almost without a fight." Dr. Drew eventually became not only a "good" doctor but one of the nation's most respected. He was promoted to the position of chief surgeon of Freedman Hospital in Washington, D.C., and, most notably, he helped revolutionize blood preservation so that blood could be saved and then used in emergencies. In 1940 he was working at Columbia University's College of Physicians and Surgeons, and, while struggling to keep his mind on medicine, dashed off the following letter to his new wife describing a peculiar malady that had overcome him.

Sunday Afternoon

Darn it all Lenore,

I'm supposed to be here working, but work is the farthest thing from my mind. I'm simply no good at it. It's terribly disturbing, disorganizing, inefficient, demoralizing, upsetting, frustrating, understandable—delightful. The sap has gone crazy, grins at himself, preens, struts, blushes, smiles, laughs, whistles, sings and then just sits in a daze. Got heartburn, palpitation, indigestion, anorexia, psychasthenia, euphoria and delusions of grandeur. Hallucinations by day and insomnia by night. Got misery and ecstasy. Dear Dr. Robbins what is my trouble? Only you can tell me. Please answer soon. I'm in bad shape.

Charlie

Jack Kerouac to Sebastian Sampas

Born in 1922 to French-Canadian immigrants, Jean ("Jack") Louis Lebris de Kerouac grew up in Lowell, Massachusetts, and then spent brief stints at Columbia University and in the U.S. Navy before focusing almost entirely on writing. Throughout his childhood and early twenties Kerouac was best friends with Sebastian Sampas, whom he described as "a great kid, knightlike, i.e., noble, a poet, goodlooking, crazy, sweet, sad, everything a man should want as a friend." Kerouac's letters to Sampas are written in the same free-spirited, "spontaneous prose" (as Kerouac called it) as his Beat classic On the Road, *published in 1957. In March 1943 Kerouac sent Sampas the following letter suggesting what they should do with their lives. (In his letters Kerouac often alternated between English and Québécois, the language he spoke at home with his parents.)*

Drunken letter

Sebastian!

You magnificent bastard! I was just thinking about you, and all of a sudden, I feel
very Sebastianish,
very Bohemian!
very Baroque!
very GAY! (TURN!)
I was thinking, in a flash of glory, about all things we've done!!!—and all the others we're going to do!

AFTER THE WAR, WE MUST GO TO FRANCE AND SEE THAT THE REVOLUTION GOES WELL! AND GERMANY TOO! AND ITALY TOO! AND *RUSSIA!*

For 1. Vodka
2. Love
3. Glory.

We must find Pat Reel and get drunk with him; we must get tanked up with Phillipe: like Paxton Hibben, we must lay a wreath on Jack Reed's grave in Moscow—

Harvard boy—died in MOSCOW!

Sebastian you son of a beetch!
HOW ARE YOU?
I AM DRUNK!
Do you hear me? Do not die, *live!* We must go to Paris and see that the revolution goes well! And the counter-revolutions in GERMANY, SPAIN, ITALY, YUGOSLAVIA, POLAND ETC.ETC.ETC.
We must go to Bataan and pick a flower. . . .
SEBASTIAN!
SYMPATHY!
To hell with
La Bourgeoisie!
No, *La Bourgueosie!*
To hell with
Hearst
To hell with
Everything
That does not
add up
TO
Brothers living together and laughing their labours to fruition!
DECK THYSELF *NOW* WITH MAJESTY AND EXCELLENCY:
CAST DOWN THE WICKED IN THEIR PLACE. . . .
Au diable
AVEC
les cochons capitalistes,
y los cabrones
cientificos!
STRUMBOUTSOMOUGAVALA
with the Salops Riches!
SYMPATHIE!
C'est le bon mot . . .
C'est le seul mot . . .
La Sympathie et l'humeur—
J'AIME MES FRÈRES:

ILS SONT TRAGIQUES,

BEAUX, BONS, Beaucoup de noblesse—

A l'avant!

Sebastian:—

Red Wine, I have just written to Norma, my Gretchen, my Humanist—Socialist—Psychologist—Amorous love!

This isn't folly, this is me! I am mad with ardor for all things AND Sebastian!

THE LEAF UNTURNED

In a month or so, if I don't hear from the Navy, I shall ship out, I shall go to Camp Lee, and see you, I shall infuse you with new hope.

You're not cheated! You're magnificent!

JEAN Louis le Brise de Kerouac, Baron de Bretagne, retired. AU REVOIR.

Almost a year later, Kerouac learned that Sampas died in North Africa after being wounded on the Anzio beachhead. He wrote a letter of farewell to his friend, concluding with the lines: "Sebastian, really, your death has never ceased making of me a damned sentimentalist like yourself. [. . .] You bastard, you, I shan't ever forgive you!"

Anne Morrow Lindbergh to Charles Lindbergh

On May 21, 1927, Charles A. Lindbergh flew solo across the Atlantic Ocean in a single-engine plane—a feat never before accomplished—and earned himself a place in the record books. The kidnapping and murder of Lindbergh's baby in 1932 further catapulted him and his wife, Anne Morrow Lindbergh, into international repute. Often when he was away Mrs. Lindbergh wrote her husband love letters that greeted him upon his arrival. The following letter, which concludes with a passage by the poet John Jay Chapman, was written on July 2, 1944, on a train heading from Chicago to San Francisco.

Dear Charles,

I am on my way West. I hope to meet you. I feel madly extravagant and altogether quite mad, speeding over the country with not much certainty of when or where I'll meet you.

But I feel happy tonight. I have sat and watched the cornfields of Iowa darken, seen the homesteads pass by—a white house, a red barn and a brave cluster of green trees in the midst of oceans of flat fields—like an oasis in a desert. The glossy flanks of horses and the glossy leaves of corn. And I have been overcome by the beauty and richness of this country I have flown over so many times with you. And overcome with the beauty and richness of our life together, those early mornings setting out, those evenings gleaming with rivers and lakes below us, still holding the last light. Those fields of daisies we landed on—and dusty fields and desert stretches. Memories of many skies and many earths beneath us—many days, many nights of stars. "How are the waters of the world sweet—if we should die, we have drunk them. If we should sin—or separate—if we should fail or secede—we have tasted of happiness—we must be written in the book of the blessed. We have had what life could give, we have eaten of the tree of knowledge, we have known—we have been the mystery of the universe."

Good night—

Ayn Rand to Joanne Rondeau

"Altruism (living for others)," Ayn Rand wrote to a friend, "is actually the most vicious principle ever stated, the source of all evil, the principle of slavery, dependence and degradation." It was just this perspective on life, coupled with her belief that "the proper moral ideal is independence—*spiritual independence—which means absolute egosim," that made Rand a best-selling novelist/philosopher in the 1940s, 1950s, and 1960s with such books as* Atlas Shrugged *and* The Fountainhead. *In 1948, a fan named Joanne Rondeau wrote to Rand asking her to elaborate on the phrase "I*

love you" as it appears in one of her works. Rand responded with the following.

May 22, 1948

Dear Ms. Rondeau:

You asked me to explain the meaning of my sentence in *The Fountainhead*: "To say 'I love you' one must know first how to say the 'I.'"

The meaning of that sentence is contained in the whole of *The Fountainhead*. And it is stated right in the speech on page 400 from which you took that sentence. The meaning of the "I" is an independent, self-sufficient entity that *does not* exist for the sake of any other person.

A person who exists only for the sake of his loved one is not an independent entity, but a spiritual parasite. The love of a parasite is worth nothing.

The usual (and very vicious) nonsense preached on the subject of love claims that love is self-sacrifice. A man's *self* is his spirit. If one sacrifices his spirit, who or what is left to feel the love? True love is profoundly *selfish*, in the noblest meaning of the word—it is an expression of one's *self*, of one's highest values. When a person is in love, he seeks his own happiness—and *not* his sacrifice to the loved one. And the loved one would be a monster if she wanted or expected sacrifice.

Any person who wants to live *for* others—for one sweetheart or for the whole of mankind—is a selfless nonentity. An independent "I" is a person who exists for his own sake. Such a person does not make any vicious pretense of self-sacrifice and does not demand it from the person he loves. Which is the only way to be in love and the only form of a self-respecting relationship between two people.

John Steinbeck to His Son Thom

John Steinbeck, the best-selling author and Nobel laureate, enjoyed the duties of fatherhood and dispensed advice to his two sons when it was requested—and sometimes when it was not. When Steinbeck's son Thom was fourteen he attended boarding school in Connecticut and met a young girl named Susan with whom he thought he might be in love. His father, then living in New York with his second wife, Elaine, offered his views on the matter.

November 10, 1958

Dear Thom:

We had your letter this morning. I will answer it from my point of view and of course Elaine will from hers.

First—if you are in love—that's a good thing—that's about the best thing that can happen to anyone. Don't let anyone make it small or light to you.

Second—There are several kinds of love. One is a selfish, mean, grasping, egotistical thing which uses love for self-importance. This is the ugly and crippling kind. The other is an outpouring of everything good in you—of kindness, and consideration and respect—not only the social respect of manners but the greater respect which is recognition of another person as unique and valuable. The first kind can make you sick and small and weak but the second can release in you strength, and courage and goodness and even wisdom you didn't know you had.

You say this is not puppy love. If you feel so deeply—of course it isn't puppy love.

But I don't think you were asking me what you feel. You know that better than anyone. What you wanted me to help you with is what to do about it—and that I can tell you.

Glory in it for one thing and be very glad and grateful for it.

The object of love is the best and most beautiful. Try to live up to it.

If you love someone—there is no possible harm in saying so—

only you must remember that some people are very shy and sometimes the saying must take that shyness into consideration.

Girls have a way of knowing or feeling what you feel, but they usually like to hear it also.

It sometimes happens that what you feel is not returned for one reason or another—but that does not make your feeling less valuable and good.

Lastly, I know your feeling because I have it and I am glad you have it.

We will be glad to meet Susan. She will be very welcome. But Elaine will make all such arrangements because that is her province and she will be very glad to. She knows about love too and maybe she can give you more help than I can.

And don't worry about losing. If it is right, it happens—The main thing is not to hurry. Nothing good gets away.

Love

Fa

Thomas Merton to Henry Miller & Miller to Brenda Venus

Thomas Merton was a Trappist monk dedicated to a life of prayer and celibacy. Henry Miller was a notorious drinker and womanizer whose books were banned in the United States until 1960 due to their sexual content. Despite these differences, the two men clearly enjoyed each other's epistolary company. Enclosed with one letter, Merton sent Miller a picture of himself with a young poet named Miguel Grinberg. Miller observed that they (i.e., Miller and Merton) looked alike and, further, that they both resembled the French writer and social outcast Jean Genet. "You too have a look of an ex-convict," Miller wrote to Merton in a July fourth letter, "of one who has been through hell and I think bear the traces of it." Far from offended, Merton seemed pleased by the remark and replied with the following.

August 16, 1964

I am glad you liked the photos. By now you must have seen Grinberg himself in person. He is a promising young guy and the thing I like best about him is that he is free of the bitterness and frustration and self-pity that is eating up so many of the good young poets. He has really decided that things are good and that he is going to try to make them better. His is the kind that will not blow the world up. Maybe some of his elders will get to it before he has a chance. But if his gang make it, perhaps there is hope.

Yes, I have often thought of the resemblance between our faces. I had not associated Genet with it, not knowing what he looks like. I suppose the person I most resemble, usually, is Picasso. That's what everybody says. Still I think it is a distinction to look like Picasso, Henry Miller, and Genet all at once. Pretty comprehensive. It seems to imply some kind of responsibility.

As to the ex-con slant: I am very glad you mention it. It seems to me that the only justification for a man's existence in this present world is for him to either be a convict, or a victim of plague, or a leper, or at least to look like one of these things. In a world of furnaces and DP's it would be hideously immoral for someone, especially a priest, to be well, totally sane, perfectly content with everything, knowing which end is always up and keeping it that way too, knowing who thinks right all the time and staying with him only and beating the others over the head etc. etc. Yes, I have got some good hellburns all over me. We all exist. Thank God.

The boys at N[ew] D[irections, a publishing house] have not sent me your new book yet. I will get after them. They sent a couple of good books of poetry recently. I am doing a book of selections from Gandhi which I think you will like. Long introduction.

I know how it is about finding time to write, and about being deluged with letters. People going down for the third time think a letter will keep them afloat. But often what they are going down in is itself an illusion, and the letter itself will be to them an illusion. Sometimes I answer sometimes I can't and I mean not to worry about it. There is a destiny involved there too. But there is no question that we spent our lives battling with mountains of crap, and this is no mean exercise. I do not know if it helps one to improve his faculties. Perhaps that does not matter either. We are all in the plague. Have you read Camus's book on that? I just finished it and it is very true and sobering. The plague is unquestionable, irrefutable. It need not silence a stoical joy. What is real is the emptiness which is always on the side of Being, not of non-being. I will get Powys's autobiography and perhaps a novel or two from one of the college libraries around here.

Very best wishes always. By all means call me by my name which is

TOM

Miller loved, married, and had affairs with countless women throughout his life. His last great love affair, however, was an essentially platonic one. In 1976 an actress by the name of Brenda Venus wrote to Miller to say how much she admired his books and that she would love to meet him. The beautiful young woman enclosed a photograph. Miller, 84, responded immediately. What ensued was a four-year correspondence of over four thousand pages of letters. Venus playfully endured, and sometimes even encouraged, Miller's lusty propositions, but there was also a tenderness to his letters which she recognized and appreciated. In one of his last letters to her before he died in June 1980, the elderly writer articulates how meaningful their relationship has been to him.

And now, a man of 87, madly in love with a young woman who writes me the most extraordinary letters, who loves me to death, who keeps me alive and in love (a perfect love for the first time), who writes me such profound and touching thoughts that I am joyous and confused as only a teenager could be. But more than that—grateful, thankful, lucky. Do I really deserve all the beautiful praises you heap on me? You cause me to wonder exactly who I am, do I really know who and what I am? You leave me swimming in mystery. For that I love you all the more. I get down on my knees, I pray for you, I bless you with what little sainthood is in me. May you fare well, dearest Brenda, and never regret this romance in the midst of your young life. We have been both blessed. We are not of this world. We are of the stars and the universe beyond.

Long live Brenda Venus!

God give her joy and fulfillment and love eternal!

Henry

Ben Washam to Chuck Jones

"We were grotesquely underpaid," recalls Chuck Jones, "but we were being paid to do what we enjoyed doing. We were being paid to associate every day with people we loved and respected, people who were eager, excited, and joyfully willing to try almost anything." Jones and his colleagues were part of the team of writers and animators who brought to the world Bugs Bunny, Daffy Duck, Elmer Fudd, Wile E. Coyote ("Genius"), and a host of other Warner Brothers cartoon characters. Ben Washam, a Warner Bros. animator, expresses his affection for Jones in the following letter written on the occasion of Jones's sixty-ninth birthday.

September 14, 1981

Dear Chuck—

On my tenth birthday my father gave me a mule. It was truly love at first sight. I named him Spencer after a rifle I saw advertised in a Sears, Roebuck catalog.

The spring and summer that followed were the most wonderful in my memory. We rode over and through every hill and swamp in northeast Arkansas.

In the fall after the crops were in, everybody went to the county fair, especially Spencer and me.

Aside from judging cows, pigs, chickens, cakes, pies and the like, stump pulling was a community favorite.

The stumps were dynamited out of the ground (a few days

before the fair started), then a mule was hitched to the stump. The mule that pulled the greatest distance won—Spencer and me won.

First prize was a Rhode Island Red Rooster and a blue ribbon with Robert E. Lee's face painted on it with gold paint. I was so proud I kissed Spencer. Everybody laughed and my mother made me wash my face.

At this time I learned about evil. I learned evil lurks in unsuspected places and, like a spider, attacks without warning.

An aunt, who later turned out to be unsavory, invited me to have a soda pop with her.

Leaving Spencer eating hay and my rooster tied to a wagon wheel, we went off to the refreshment tent.

Everything was fine. I even got a piece of cake. The soda pop was great—I saved half of it for Spencer.

When I returned to the wagon, Spencer was gone. I grabbed a pitchfork and went looking for the thief. After looking all over the fairgrounds they finally told me that some Yankee from Chicago gave my father fifty dollars for Spencer.

My devastation was complete that evening—my mother cooked my rooster for supper.

I spent the next day planning revenge. The thought of putting a water moccasin in my father's bed was pleasant. Then it occurred to me that anybody that mean wouldn't be troubled by a water moccasin. By the end of the day I had concluded that I couldn't fight them, but I could make sure that I never became one of them—so I made a vow never to become an adult, or care for an adult.

To make sure that I would never break the vow, I ate a green persimmon—eating a green persimmon was a sure way to test a person's sincerity. Anyone who would eat a green persimmon to back up their word had to be honest. That was especially true in courtships—however, I don't remember ever hearing of any girl eating a green persimmon.

From that time I walked into the hills and valleys of life, secure in the knowledge that I was free from adults, Yankees and unsavory aunts in particular. (It was my aunt who lured me away from

Spencer with the promise of a soda pop. Deep in my heart I know that old harridan dwells in the north side of hell with all the Yankees.)

I have mellowed over the years. My vow has not been broken, only bent a little. So it is that I can tell you that you are one of the few adults I have come to love and respect.

My reason for telling you this is because I want to wish you a happy birthday and impress upon you that such a wish coming from me is no small effort.

Ben

LETTERS OF FAMILY

Miss McMillan said to me that I had been a help to her in her work, that it was my education which inspired her with the idea of training those poor children in a new way. She thought: if my senses could be developed to such a high degree, what might she not do in developing the five senses of her many little pupils! [. . .] And you too, mother, you have a share in this beautiful work. For you helped me all you could in my first years, you kept me healthy and active, you strove to stimulate my mind, so that it would not be quenched in darkness and silence. How precious your motherhood is as I think what a blessing you have helped to bring to mothers all over the world.

Helen Keller to Kate Heller; October 11, 1912

Benjamin and Julia Rush to Their Son John

Dr. Benjamin Rush was not only the most prominent physician of his time, he was one of America's founding fathers—contributing to both the Declaration of Independence and the Constitution. His advice was frequently sought by Thomas Jefferson, James Madison, John Adams, and other esteemed men on issues relating to health, politics, international affairs, business, and travel (he advised Lewis and Clark before their famous expedition). Before his own son, John, left for a trip to India, Dr. Rush and his wife penned the following letter to guide their son morally, physically and financially on his journey.

Directions and advice to Jno. Rush from his father and mother composed the evening before he sailed for Calcutta, May 18th, 1796.

We shall divide these directions into four heads, as they relate to *morals*, *knowledge*, *health* and *business*.

I. MORALS

1. Be punctual in committing your soul and body to the protection of your Creator every morning and evening. Implore at the same time his mercy in the name of his Son, our Lord and Saviour Jesus Christ.

2. Read in your Bible frequently, more especially on Sundays.

3. Avoid swearing and even an irreverent use of your Creator's name. *Flee* youthful lusts.

4. Be courteous and gentle in your behavior to your fellow passengers, and respectful and obedient to the captain of the vessel.

5. Attend public worship regularly every Sunday when you arrive at Calcutta.

II. KNOWLEDGE

1. Begin by studying Guthrie's *Geography*.

2. Read your other books *through* carefully, and converse daily upon the subjects of your reading.

3. Keep a diary of every day's studies, conversations, and transactions at sea and on shore. Let it be composed in a fair, legible hand. Insert in it an account of the population, manners, climate, diseases, &c., of the places you visit.

4. Preserve an account of every person's name and disease whom you attend.

III. HEALTH

1. Be temperate in eating, more especially of animal food. Never *taste* distilled spirits of any kind, and drink fermented liquors very sparingly.

2. Avoid the night air in sickly situations. Let your dress be rather warmer than the weather would seem to require. Carefully avoid fatigue from all causes both of body and mind.

IV. BUSINESS

1. Take no step in laying out your money without the advice and consent of the captain or supercargo.

2. Keep an exact account of all your expenditures. Preserve as vouchers of them all your bills.

3. Take care of all your instruments, books, clothes, &c.

Be sober and vigilant. Remember at all times that while you are seeing the world, the world will see you. Recollect further that you are always under the eye of the Supreme Being. One more consideration shall close this parting testimony of our affection. Whenever you are tempted to do an improper thing, fancy that you see your father and mother kneeling before you and imploring you with tears in their eyes to refrain yielding to the temptation, and assuring you at the same time that your yielding to it will be the means of hurrying them to a premature grave.

Bnjn Rush
Julia Rush

Mary Moody Emerson to Her Nephew Charles Chauncy Emerson

Ralph Waldo Emerson, the eminent nineteenth-century writer and lecturer, claimed that no other individual had a greater influence on his education than his aunt Mary Moody Emerson. A tiny, eccentric woman (she had her bed made into the shape of a coffin), she was well read and sent out a seemingly endless stream of profoundly theological and philosophical letters, particularly to young relatives and acquaintances whom she hoped to cultivate morally and spiritually. (Emerson called his aunt's letters works of "Genius, always new, frolicsome, musical, unpredictable.") She was especially close to the children of her brother, William, who died in 1811 and left behind a young widow with two girls and six boys, all under the age of fourteen. Emerson sent the following letter to her nephew Charles, who was nine at the time, on avoiding eternal damnation.

Elm Vale Jan. 1, 1818

A happy year to my dear Charles, if it be one of virtue. How important is every day of this new year! Tho the earth runs her wonted Journey without complaining of the idleness of her inhabitants, which she constantly carries down the stream of time, yet you know there is an account made of all the days she travels. She will continue to begin and end her journies with the same velocity, when you and all the present generation are intombed within her bosom, as now you are playing and bustling on her surface.

But where will be the immortal souls of this vast multitude then? *Where will you be*, and how occupied? You, my dear boy, who have been my joy and companion for so many years, where will you be some long years hence? Who will associate with you? *The spirits of the just made happy?* Shall you so govern your temper, so cultivate generous amiable dispositions as to be admitted into a state of honor and employed in delightfull pursuits—in acts of love and charity?

But how dreadfull is sin! One wrong act only in the affairs of this life has been known to throw the whole of a man's fortunes into the dark and gloomy paths of abject poverty disgrace and uselessness. But after all this, the same unfortunate man has become religious—has died happily—and in the language of scripture *forgotten his miseries as waters which pass away*. But the splendid and famous in this worlds goods have often *died without hope*. One wrong action persisted in—how inexpressible its' consequences! Who can tell that has entered the invisible world, and been denied the blessing and protection of God and the Redeemer.

I tremble while I write. God of mercy spare my dearest child from the misery which awaits the ungodly, the Proud and deceitfull.

Your Aunt
MM Emerson

James Russell Lowell to His Nephew Charlie

In a letter written to a close friend during a visit to the country, the diplomat and poet James Russell Lowell exclaimed, "How I do love this unemphatic landscape, which suggests but never defines, in which so much license is left to conjecture and divination, as when one looks into the mysterious beyond." Lowell hoped to instill this same love of the natural world, with its ability to inspire mind and soul, in his young nephew Charlie R. Lowell. When Charlie was fourteen, Lowell sent him the following letter.

Elmwood, June 11, 1849

My dear Charlie,—

I have so much to do in the way of writing during the past week that I have not had time sooner to answer your letter, which came to me in due course of mail, and for which I am much obliged to you.

I am very glad to hear that you are enjoying yourself so much, and also that the poor musquash dug faster than you did. I was not so long ago a boy as not to remember what sincere satisfaction there is in a good ducking, and how the spirit of maritime adventure is ministered to by a raft which will not float. I congratulate you on both experiences.

And now let me assume the privilege of my uncleship to give you a little advice. Let me counsel you to make use of all your visits to the country as opportunities for an education which is of great importance, which town-bred boys are commonly lacking in, and which can never be so cheaply acquired as in boyhood. Remember that a man is valuable in our day for what he *knows*, and that his company will always be desired by others in exact proportion to the amount of intelligence and instruction he brings with him. I assure you that one of the earliest pieces of definite knowledge we acquire after we become men is this—that our company will be desired no longer than we honestly pay our proper share in the general reckoning of mutual entertainment. A man who knows more than another knows *incalculably* more, be sure of that, and a person with eyes in his head cannot look even into a pigsty without learning something that will be useful to him at one time or another. Not that we should educate ourselves for the mere selfish sake of that advantage of superiority which it will give us. But knowledge is power in this noblest sense, that it enables us to *benefit* others and to pay our way honorably in life by being of *use*.

Now, when you are at school in Boston you are furnishing your brain with what can be obtained from books. You are training and enriching your intellect. While you are in the country you should remember that you are in the great school of the senses. Train your eyes and ears. Learn to know all the trees by their bark and leaves, by their general shape and manner of growth. Sometimes you can be able to say positively what a tree is *not* by simply examining the lichens on the bark, for you will find that particular varieties of lichen love particular trees. Learn also to know all birds by sight, by their notes, by their manner of flying; all the animals by their general appearance and gait or the localities they frequent.

You would be ashamed not to know the name and use of every piece of furniture in the house, and we ought to be as familiar with every object in the world—which is only a larger kind of house.

You recollect the pretty story of Pizarro and the Peruvian Inca: how the Inca asked one of his Spaniards to write the word *Dio* (God) upon his thumb-nail, and then, showing it to the rest, found only Pizarro unable to read it! Well, you will find as you grow older that this same name of God is written all over the world in little phenomena that occur under our eyes every moment, and I confess that I feel very much inclined to hang my head with Pizarro when I cannot translate these hieroglyphics into my own vernacular.

Now, I write all this to you, my dear Charlie, not in the least because it is considered proper for uncles to bore their nephews with musty moralities and advice; but I should be quite willing that you should think me a bore, if I could only be the means of impressing upon you the importance of *observing*, and the great fact that we cannot properly observe till we have learned *how*. Education, practice, and especially a determination not to be satisfied with remarking that side of an object which happens to catch our eye at first when we first see it—these gradually make an observer. The faculty, once acquired, becomes at length another sense which works mechanically.

I think I have sometimes noticed in you an *impatience* of mind which you should guard against carefully. Pin this maxim up in your memory—that Nature abhors the credit system, and that we never get anything in life till we have paid for it. Anything good, I mean; evil things we always pay for afterwards, and always when we find it hardest to do. By paying for them, of course, I mean *laboring* for them. Tell me how much good solid *work* a young man has in him, and I will erect a horoscope for him as accurate as Guy Mannering's for young Bertram. Talents are absolutely nothing to a man except he have the faculty of work along with them. They, in fact, turn upon him and worry him, as Actaeon's dogs did—you remember the story? Patience and perservance—these are the sails and the rudder even of genius, without which it is only a wretched hulk upon the waters.

It is not fair to look a gift horse in the mouth, unless, indeed, it be a wooden horse, like that which carried the Greeks into Troy; but my lecture on patience and *finish* was apropos of your letters, which was more careless in its chirography and (here and there) in its composition than I liked. Always make a thing as good as you can. Otherwise it was an excellent letter, because it told what you had seen and what you were doing—certainly better as a *letter* than this of mine, which is rather a sermon. But read it, my dear Charlie, as the advice of one who takes a sincere interest in you. I hope to hear from you again, and my answer to your next shall be more entertaining.

I remain your loving uncle,
J. R. Lowell

William James to His Father Henry James Sr.

William James, the distinguished American psychologist and philosopher, was traveling in Europe when he learned through his sister, Alice, that their father, living in New York, was on the verge of death. James, doubtful he could return to the States in time, wrote a letter of farewell to his father on December 14. But the letter did not make it in time—it arrived eleven days after Henry Sr., a prominent theologian, died, on December 19. On December 31, William's brother, the famed novelist Henry ("Harry") James, read the letter aloud before their father's grave.

Bolton St., London, Dec. 14, 1882

Darling old Father,

Two letters, one from Alice last night, and one from Aunt Kate to Harry just now, have somewhat dispelled the mystery in which the telegrams left your condition; and although their news is several days earlier than the telegrams, I am free to suppose that the latter report only an aggravation of the symptoms the letters describe. It is far more agreeable to think of this than of some dreadful unknown and sudden malady.

We have been so long accustomed to the hypothesis of your being taken away from us, especially during the past ten months, that the thought that this may be your last illness conveys no very sudden shock. You are old enough, you've given your message to the world in many ways and will not be forgotten; you are here left alone, and on the other side, let us hope and pray, dear, dear old Mother is waiting for you to join her. If you go, it will not be an inharmonious thing. Only, if you are still in possession of your normal consciousness, I should like to see you once again before we part. I stayed here only in obedience to the last telegram, and am waiting now for Harry—who knows the exact state of my mind, and who will know yours—to telegraph again what I shall do. Meanwhile, my blessed old Father, I scribble this line (which may reach you though I should come too late), just to tell you how full of the tenderest memories and feelings about you my heart has for the last few days been filled. In that mysterious gulf of the past into which the present soon will fall and go back and back, yours is still for me the central figure. All my intellectual life I derive from you; and though we have often seemed at odds in the expression thereof, I'm sure there's a harmony somewhere, and that our strivings will combine. What my debt to you is goes beyond all my power of estimating,—so early, so penetrating and so constant has been the influence. You need be in no anxiety about your literary remains. I will see them well taken care of, and that your words shall not suffer for being concealed. At Paris I heard that Milsand, whose name you may remember in the "Revue des Deux Mondes" and elsewhere, was an admirer of the "Secret of Swedenborg," and Hodgson told me your last book had deeply impressed him. So will it be; especially, I think, if a collection of *extracts* from your various writings were published, after the manner of the extracts from Carlyle, Ruskin, & Co. I have long thought such a volume would be the best monument to you.—As for us; we shall live on each in his way,—feeling somewhat unprotected, old as we are, for the absence of the parental bosoms as a refuge, but holding fast together in that common sacred memory. We will stand by each other and by Alice, try to transmit the torch in our offspring as you did in us, and when the time comes for being gathered in, I pray we may all, if not all, some at least, be as ripe as you. As for myself, I know what trouble I've given you at various times through my peculiarities;

and as my own boys grow up, I shall learn more and more of the kind of trial you had to overcome in superintending the development of a creature different from yourself, for whom you felt responsible. I say this merely to show how my *sympathy* with you is likely to grow much livelier, rather than to fade—and not for the sake of regrets.—As for the other side, and Mother, and our all possibly meeting, I *can't* say anything. More than ever at this moment do I feel that if that *were* true, all would be solved and justified. And it comes strangely over me in bidding you good-bye how a life is but a day and expresses mainly but a single note. It is so much like the act of bidding an ordinary good-night. Good-night, my sacred old Father! If I don't see you again—Farewell! a blessed farewell!

Your
William

Jack London to His Daughter Joan

By the time he was twenty-one, Jack London had freeloaded rides on freight trains throughout the United States, worked as a sailor, been arrested and jailed for vagrancy, went to college after teaching himself enough to be admitted, and then dropped out to seek (unsuccessfully) a quick fortune in the Klondike gold rush of 1897. He was a bold, adventurous spirit who later gained acclaim as the author of such works as White Fang *and* The Call of the Wild. *"Right here at the start," London warned his publisher, "please know you are dealing with a man who is always hopelessly frank." The same applied to his family; he did not mince words in his letters to his first wife, Bessie, or to his daughters, Joan and Bess. In the following letter, London gives a fourteen-year-old Joan some rather direct advice about developing her mind and body.*

Glen Ellen, California,
September 16, 1915.

Dear Joan:

First of all, I had Aunt Eliza send you the check for $7.00 so that you might buy the two pairs of boots for yourself and Bess.

Second of all, I promised to reply to your letter.

Third of all, and very important, please remember that your Daddy is a very busy man. When you write to society people, or to young people, who have plenty of time, write on your fine stationery and write on both sides of the paper. But, please, when you write to Daddy, take any kind of paper, the cheapest paper for that matter, and write on one side only. This makes it ever so much easier for Daddy to read. A two-sheet letter, such as yours that I am now looking at, written on both sides, is like a Chinese puzzle to a busy man. I take more time trying to find my way from one of the four portions into which your two-sided sheet is divided than I do in reading the letter itself.

Some day I should like to see your French heeled slippers. Joan, you are on the right track. Never hesitate at making yourself a dainty, delightful girl and woman. There is a girl's pride and a woman's pride in this, and it is indeed a fine pride. On the one hand, of course, never over-dress. On the other hand, never be a frump. No matter how wonderful are the thoughts that burn in your brain, always, physically, and in dress, make yourself a delight to all eyes that behold you.

I have met a number of philosophers. They were real philosophers. Their minds were wonderful minds. But they did not take baths, and they did not change their socks and it almost turned one's stomach to sit at table with them.

Our bodies are as glorious as our minds, and, just as one cannot maintain a high mind in a filthy body, by the same token one cannot keep a high mind and high pride when said body is not dressed beautifully, delightfully, charmingly. Nothing would your Daddy ask better of you in this world than that you have a high mind, a high pride, a fine body, and, just as all the rest, a beautifully dressed body.

I do not think you will lose your head. I think, as I read this last letter of yours, that I understand that you have balance, and a woman's balance at that. Never forget the noble things of the spirit, on the other hand, never let your body be ignoble, never let the garmenture of your body be ignoble. As regards the garmenture of your body, learn to do much with little, never to over-do, and to keep such a balance between your garmenture and your mind that both garmenture and mind are beautiful.

I shall not say anything to you about your method of saving, about Bess's method of saving, but there is much I should like to say to you, and, in the meantime I think a lot about it. You are on the right track. Go ahead. Develop your mind to its utmost beauty; and keep your body in pace with your mind.

Daddy

Maxwell Perkins to His Daughter Jane

Maxwell Perkins, the legendary book editor who nurtured such writers as F. Scott Fitzgerald and Thomas Wolfe, was the father of five daughters. Although the Perkins family lived in New Jersey, Perkins sent his daughters to Vermont in the summer—away from the city's sweltering heat and grime—to enjoy the beauty of the outdoors. His frequent letters from his office in New York were playful and loving, and he often drew illustrations on them and on the envelopes. The following, which Perkins wrote in verse, was addressed to his five-year-old daughter, Jane, for Valentine's Day and included sketches of goats and of Cupid pulling his bow.

To Janey

There was a maiden loved me—
Oh that was long ago!
We tramped the hills together—
O, that we still did so.
And of a Sunday morning, howe'er
the day might be,

We'd search the shaggy mountain sides
The sprightly goats to see.

She rode my shoulders then—
Ah, but she rides no more!
For she learned to skip, and hop,
and bound about the floor.
The sprightly goats she's quite forgot,
To me she pays no heed,
For of my mighty shoulder now
She has no further need.

Alone I stride the mountains
in sunlight and in rain:
Alone I climb the rocky trails
I used to climb with Jane!
The goats now gaze upon me
With eyes of sad reproof:
They shake their horns in sorrow,
They point a scornful hoof.

So little cupid hear me:—
This day this prayer I make,
Not only for my lonely self, but
for a poor goat's sake—
Shoot at the heart of Janey
An arrow keen and fine
So that she may at last consent
To be my Valentine.

Sherwood Anderson to His Son John

Born in 1876 in Camden, Ohio, Sherwood Anderson held a variety of industrial and unskilled labor jobs until he began to write short stories in his spare time. Influenced by the works of Gertrude Stein and Ernest Hemingway, Anderson's prose style was based on everyday speech and dialogue. At the age of forty he published Windy McPherson's Son, *the first of many novels, including his best-seller* Dark Laughter. *His son John, who wanted to be a painter, wrote to his father often about art and literature. The following was written by Anderson to his son in the spring of 1927, while John was traveling in France. (Anderson did not include a salutation with the letter, and he had a habit of neglecting the "s" at the end of plural words.)*

Something I should have said in my letter yesterday.

In relation to painting.

Don't be carried off your feet by anything because it is modern, the latest thing.

Got to the Louvre often and spend a good deal of time before the Rembrandts, the Delacroix's.

Learn to draw. Try to make your hand so unconsciously adept that it will put down what you feel without your having to think of your hands.

Then you can think of the thing before you.

Draw things that have some meaning to you. An apple, what does it mean?

The object drawn doesn't matter so much. It's what you feel about it, what it means to you.

A masterpiece could be made of a dish of turnips.

Draw, draw, hundreds of drawing.

Try to remain humble. Smartness kills everything.

The object of art is not to make salable pictures. It is to save yourself.

Any cleanness I have in my own life is due to my feeling for words.

The fools who write articles about me think that one morning I suddenly decided to write and began to produce masterpieces.

There is no special trick about writing or painting either. I wrote constantly for 15 years before I produced anything with any solidity to it.

For days, weeks, and months now I can't do it.

You saw me in Paris this winter. I was in a dead, blank time. You have to live through such times all your life.

The thing, of course, is to make yourself alive. Most people remain all of their lives in a stupor.

The point of being an artist is that you may live.

Such things as you suggested in your letter the other day. I said, "Don't do what you would be ashamed to tell me about."

I was wrong.

You can't depend on me. Don't do what you would be ashamed of before a sheet of white paper or a canvas.

The materials have to take the place of God.

About color. Be careful. Go to nature all you can. Instead of paintshops, other men's palettes, look at the sides of buildings in every light. Learn to observe little thing, a red apple lying on a grey cloth.

Trees, trees against hill, everything. I know little enough. It seems to me that if I wanted to learn about color, I would try always to make a separation. There is a plowed field here before me, below it a meadow, half-decayed cornstalk in the meadow making yellow lines, stumps, sometimes like looking into an ink bottle, sometimes almost blue.

The same in nature is a composition.

You look at it, thinking, "What made up that color?" I have walked over a piece of ground, after seeing it from a distance, trying to see what made the color I saw.

Light makes so much difference.

You won't arrive. It is an endless search.

I write as though you were a man. Well, you must know my heart is set on you.

It isn't your success I want. There is a possibility of your having a decent attitude toward people and work. That alone may make a man of you

Tell Church that David Prall finally got the Cézanne prints.

Also tell the man at the shop where you go for the Picasso book, or if you have been there, drop him a note—the shop, I mean.

Charles Adams to His Son Ansel

Charles Adams's relation to his son Ansel was a close and loving one. When Ansel went off to Yosemite National Park as a young man, the two corresponded frequently. When Ansel became a father himself, Charles wrote to him and his wife, Virginia: "This boy of yours will reach down into the depths of your hearts and touch the strings there, to sound such rich chords [. . . that] will fill your being with a joy unknown before and a happiness, which we cannot define, through many, many years." In the following letter, sent five years earlier when Ansel was twenty-six and about to be married, Charles writes of his devotion to his own wife, Ollie, and to her sister Mary, his faith and hopes in the face of financial ruin, and his love for the natural world that Ansel Adams would go on to display so brilliantly as a photographer.

San Francisco
January 30, 1928

My Dear Ansel:

This letter is for you and Virginia and not for another soul. Your mother will know of it. In other words it is just for us!

Do not think, in reading this, that I am ill, or that I am going to die, or even that I am depressed and blue and unhappy. Far from it, for I am happier than I have been in many a year. Happy because you have Virginia and because *we* have her too, for through you, we have taken into our home and our hearts one of the finest girls in the whole world. So, how can I be unhappy? As I told you a few evenings ago, when you two were home with us I was almost afraid and could not understand why so much happiness had come to me. Everything in my life during the past twenty-five years has brought nothing to cheer, nothing to hope for, and much responsibility. A future which is at times as black as a ton of coal. You know how fond I am of our dear Ollie; you know her life is mine; that her happiness, her sorrows and her cares are mine, and so, when one disappointment after another came to me; when one mistake after another brought to me the conclusion that my life had been a failure, my journey had been a rather up-hill one. However, I am not one to lie down, to give up, to grovel. I have fought a fair, honest fight and am not ashamed. Further, I am still fighting and working and hoping and aiming at success ahead and will win out yet, so that I may leave dear old Ollie provided for and free from cares and worries, and that I might leave you and Virginia so that you may have your lives full of the joys of living. I don't care to make enough to leave you *rich*, even if that were possible, for that would only weaken your chances for happiness. I want you to have enough so that your high ideals may be realized; so that you, of whom I am so proud, shall fulfill a destiny as great as I dream of. I want Virginia to share with you a full, happy life, for God knows she deserves all there is in this world that is good and kind and true.

Now, before going any farther with this I want to tell you one very important thing. Don't think I have worried and suffered alone. Your mother has gone through it all with me. She has suffered far more than I, for I have been on the "firing line;" fighting and having all the excitement, the rough and tumble of a man's life. It was only when I stopped and rested that worry and care strode in. On the other hand, your mother has sat at home, alone in her thoughts, hoping for my success and finding naught but failure and disappointment. She could not get the stimulus of the fight, but must wait alone and bear the burden in silence and stand by my side to cheer me up, when her own heart was torn. She has never faltered, never was she impatient with me; always giving me her heart and her hand to lift me up and strengthen me! Ansel, always be gentle with her. Be gentle with Mary, for she too loves you and hopes for you, and while it may seem hard at times to overlook "things," you will do it for me, I know.

Here endeth a rambling prelude, but it had to come out before I could go ahead with the rest of letter.

In the first place, the human being is a very peculiar little atom in this interesting universe of ours. He rushes about, through the years, often blindly, striving for something and always striving in his own way. For some reason or another, he never profits by the experience of those who have gone before him. Individuals and races are alike in this. They come into being, live a life which is perhaps successful, perhaps not, but generally a life of their own making, and then comes the end. Whatever they do, they do *not* take advantage of the experience of others. Experiences which have brought failure or brought success. If they would only stop once in a while and think of what certain things brought to certain people or peoples, perhaps much trouble could be avoided and much happiness assured.

As you read along, you will better understand what I ask of you and why.

Twenty-six years old! Just beginning your life. What an opportunity lies ahead of you, Ansel, if you but truly shape your course. You have strength and energy and high ideals, and aims that are worth working for and worth realizing. Life to you now is like a wonderful sunrise in your beloved Mountains. I am so glad for you.

Later in life, there will come a time when things will change. High noon will have passed and the afternoon shadows will come and will fall upon you and Virginia with a softness and kindness that will bring a lustre of gold to your hearts and minds and you will want to set aside the heavy cares of life and to sit down for a while and look back through the years that have passed and into the time which is yet to come. When comes this autumn of life, a little peace, a little quiet and rest is so good, so good. I want your lives to be so planned that you may together have these happy years, free from the burdens of worry and care.

With your youth, strength and power to work and with your wonderful gifts, you have a capital which is invaluable. I believe your ideals and your character to be so high that none of the human weaknesses will turn you aside in your career. I say these things, Ansel, because I know them to be true, and I know too that you will so live that my estimation of you will not be shaken.

Great is your responsibility! When you were alone it was very important that you maintain these high standards, but now that another very dear life is in your hands, it is obligatory. What a wonderful thing is life! And what a terrible thing that in our hands is given the power of making a life a heaven on earth or of bringing unhappiness and misery, though ever so unwittingly to one whom we love.

I can see in the years to come, when you will have worked hard and faithfully, there will come a day when you will wish to rest, when you will wish to give to her whom you love and whom you will love the more as the years pass, your own time, your own self, that you two may go hand in hand into the winter, unafraid and unburdened by cares and sorrows.

The twenty years to come are your best working years. Try and plan so that at the end of each month something may be set aside to provide for this later time. Let Virginia be your guide in this. She can see that the idea is carried out better than you and your time will be free to work.

This I ask, Ansel, that you may have no regrets, and that this wonderful girl who is yours will not have to worry later in life. That she and you may have those golden years as I would wish.

I love you so much that I cannot help but write this letter and tell you. I love you *both* so much that I can look ahead through the time to come and offer a suggestion and ask that you follow it, that the setting sun of your lives may be as glorious as is now the dawn.

Dad

Mrs. Colbert to Her Daughter Jane

In her best-selling book, My Mother/My Self: The Daughter's Search for Identity, *Nancy Friday explores the underlying tensions that affect many parent/child relationships, including her own with her mother, Jane Colbert. Friday's mother was fourteen years old when, in 1930,* her *mother left her husband—an emotionally cold, argumentative, and distant man—and four of their five children (she took the youngest with her) to live on her own. Knowing that Jane would be especially devastated by her absence, Colbert left behind a letter to remind her daughter how much she loved and would miss her. Jane Colbert held onto the letter and finally showed it to Nancy when Nancy became an adult. "Unable to speak to me herself," Friday writes in her book, "but resonating in her depths to my sense that I too had somehow been deserted when I was little just as she had been, my mother used her mother's own words to tell me she recognized my anger, to say that she had always loved me even if imperfectly, and to ask me to forgive her" (which Friday did). The following letter is the one Mrs. Colbert wrote to her daughter before leaving.*

My darling Jane:

When you read this I want you to do it with an open heart. Forget the things that have been said—the thoughts you may have had, and try to remember only the better, more beautiful phase of life. When I am not there with you, it is going to be your task to try to help the little ones to see things. Try to guide them in the right away. This is your work and your duty.

To me motherhood has been the most beautiful thing in my life. The wonder of it never ceases for me—to see you all developing from tiny helpless babies into big strong girls and boys, to see your minds changing with your years and to remember that some day you will be grown men and women. It is overwhelming.

All my life as a child I looked forward to the time when I would have children of my own—and in spite of my so-called talents or urges toward other things, underneath was that spark which had to burst into flame sometime. And when I held you, Jane—my first baby—in my arms, I had the greatest thrill I have ever experienced. I felt almost saintly, as if I had really entered heaven, and now I know that every time a mother receives a new baby she really does enter heaven. There is nothing else in life like it. And anyone who receives such a blessing should be eternally grateful.

I am telling you this, Jane, just so you will understand my love and feeling for you. Always remember this and as you grow older, think of me sometime and try to understand what I am trying to convey to you.

My heart is full, but I could not write the things I feel in a thousand years. Love each other and be good to daddy and he will take care of you. This is the hardest, bitterest moment of my life, leaving you, but I cannot do anything else. I cannot see through my tears. God bless you all,

Mama

Mrs. Colbert did, in fact, return to her family, but she died two years later of "sleeping sickness," an illness that affects the central nervous system.

F. Scott Fitzgerald to His Daughter "Pie"

"Please, *turn back and read this letter over!" F. Scott Fitzgerald instructed his daughter, Scottie, "It is too packed with considered thought to digest the first time." Fitzgerald frequently implored his daughter to listen carefully to his advice, which was at times supportive and loving, other times bitter and scornful. At the conclusion of one letter, written thirteen years after novels like* This Side of Paradise *and* The Great Gatsby *brought Fitzgerald international fame, he even reminded his daughter that "at the* Saturday Evening Post *rate this letter is worth $4000 [. . . so] won't you read it twice?" Fitzgerald's tendency both to encourage and criticize his teenage daughter are evident in the following letter, in which he tells Scottie, nicknamed "Pie," what her priorities in life should be.*

La Paix, Rodger's Forge
Towson, Maryland

August 8, 1933

Dear Pie:

I feel very strongly about you doing [your] duty. Would you give me a little more documentation about your reading in French? I am glad you are happy—but I never believe much in happiness. I never believe in misery either. Those are things you see on the stage or the screen or the printed page, they never really happen to you in life.

All I believe in in life is the rewards for virtue (according to your talents) and the *punishments* for not fulfilling your duties, which are doubly costly. If there is such a volume in the camp library, will you ask Mrs. Tyson to let you look up a sonnet of Shakespeare's in which the line occurs *"Lilies that fester smell worse than weeds."*

Have had no thoughts today, life seems composed of getting up a *Saturday Evening Post* story. I think of you, and always pleasantly; but if you call me "Pappy" again I am going to take the White Cat out and beat his bottom *hard, six times for every time you are impertinent*. Do you react to that?

I will arrange the camp bill.

Halfwit, I will conclude.

Things to worry about:

Worry about courage

Worry about cleanliness

Worry about efficiency

Worry about horsemanship

Worry about . . .

Things not to worry about:

Don't worry about popular opinion

Don't worry about dolls

Don't worry about the past

Don't worry about the future

Don't worry about growing up

Don't worry about anybody getting ahead of you

Don't worry about triumph

Don't worry about failure unless it comes through your own fault

Don't worry about mosquitos

Don't worry about flies

Don't worry about insects in general

Don't worry about parents

Don't worry about boys

Don't worry about disappointments

Don't worry about pleasures

Don't worry about satisfactions
Things to think about:
What am I really aiming at?
How good am I really in comparison to my contemporaries in regard to:
(a) Scholarship
(b) Do I really understand about people and am I able to get along with them?
(c) Am I trying to make my body a useful instrument or am I neglecting it?

With dearest love,
Daddy

P. S. My come-back to your calling me Pappy is christening you by the word Egg, which implies that you belong to a very rudimentary state of life and that I could break you up and crack you open at my will and I think it would be a word that would hang on if I ever told it to your contemporaries. "Egg Fitzgerald." How would you like that to go through life with—"Eggie Fitzgerald" or "Bad Egg Fitzgerald" or any form that might occur to fertile minds? Try it once more and I swear to God I will hang it on you and it will be up to you to shake it off. Why borrow trouble?

Love anyhow.

Sylvia Plath to Her Mother Aurelia

When Sylvia Plath took her life at the age of thirty she left behind an enormous collection of poems, journals, short stories, and letters. Throughout her years in college, her trips away from home, and, ultimately, her move to England in 1955, Plath corresponded frequently with her brother, Warren, and her mother, Aurelia. The letters between the two women, in particular, chronicle Sylvia's frequent bouts of despair, including her nervous breakdown in 1953. In the following letter Sylvia's mother is the one in need of encouragement, having recently undergone an operation, and Sylvia emphasizes the fun they will have together when her mother comes to visit. (Aurelia Plath edited her daughter's letters substantially before making them public—cutting out almost everything that reflected negatively on her—and although obvious in some cases, it is not always clear which ellipses represent deletions and which are in the original.)

April 23, 1956

Dearest Mother,

Well, finally the blundering American Express sent me your letter from Rome . . . our minds certainly work on the same track!

. . . I have already planned to stay in London three nights and have written to reserve a room for us; we'll just eat and talk the day you come, but for the next two I'll get some theater tickets and we'll plan jaunts to flowering parks, Piccadilly, Trafalgar Square . . . walking, strolling, feeding pigeons and sunning ourselves like happy clams. Then, to Cambridge, where I have already reserved a room for you two nights . . . I have made a contract with one of my husky men to teach me how to manage a punt before you come, so you shall step one afternoon from your room at the beautiful Garden House Hotel right onto the Cam and be boated up to Granchester through weeping willows for tea in an orchard! Worry about nothing. Just let me know your predilections and it shall be accomplished. . . .

You, alone, of all, have had crosses that would cause many a stronger woman to break under the never-ceasing load. You have borne daddy's long, hard death and taken on a man's portion in your work; you have fought your own ulcer attacks, kept us children sheltered, happy, rich with art and music lessons, camp and play; you have seen me through that black night when the only word I knew was No and when I thought I could never write or think again; and, you have been brave through your own operation. Now, just as you begin to breathe, this terrible slow, dragging pain comes upon you, almost as if it would be too easy to free you so soon from the deepest, most exhausting care and giving of love.

. . . know with a certain knowing that *you* deserve, too, to be with the loved ones who can give you strength in your trouble:

Warren and myself. Think of your trip here as a trip to the heart of strength in your daughter who loves you more dearly than words can say. I am waiting for you, and your trip shall be for your own soul's health and growing. You need . . . a context where all burdens are not on your shoulders, where some loving person comes to heft the hardest, to walk beside you. Know this, and know that it is right you should come. You need to imbibe power and health and serenity to return to your job . . .

I feel with all my joy and life that these are qualities I can give you, from the fulness and brimming of my heart. So come, and slowly we will walk through green gardens and marvel at this strange and sweet world.

Your own loving sivvy

James Baldwin to His Nephew James

Born in 1924 and raised in Harlem, James Baldwin went on to become one of America's most influential writers, publishing plays, essays, and novels of great emotional intensity. Encountering persistent racism wherever he went in the States, he left for France in 1948—for good, he thought—but then came back for months and years at a time as work and other commitments demanded. His searing look at race relations in the United States, The Fire Next Time, *was published in 1963 and became an immediate sensation. The work begins with the following letter Baldwin wrote, on the hundreth anniversary of the Emancipation Proclamation, to his young nephew James.*

Dear James:

I have begun this letter five times and torn it up five times. I keep seeing your face, which is also the face of your father and my brother. Like him, you are tough, dark, vulnerable, moody—with a very definite tendency to sound truculent because you want no one to think you are soft. You may be like your grandfather in this, I don't know, but certainly both you and your father resemble him very much physically. Well, he is dead, he never saw you, and he had a terrible life; he was defeated long before he died because, at the bottom of his heart, he really believed what white people said about him. This is one of the reasons that he became so holy. I am sure that your father has told you something about all that. Neither you nor your father exhibit any tendency towards holiness: you really *are* of another era, part of what happened when the Negro left the land and came into what the late E. Franklin Frazier called "the cities of destruction." You can only be destroyed by believing that you really are what the white world calls a *nigger*. I tell you this because I love you, and please don't you ever forget it.

I have known both of you all your lives, have carried your Daddy in my arms and on my shoulders, kissed and spanked him and watched him learn to walk. I don't know if you've ever known anybody from that far back; if you've loved anybody that long, first as an infant, then as a child, then as a man, you gain a strange perspective on time and human pain and effort. Other people cannot see what I see whenever I look into your father's face, for behind your father's face as it is today are all those other faces which were his. Let him laugh and I see a cellar your father does not remember and a house he does not remember and I hear in his present laughter his laughter as a child. Let him curse and I remember him falling down the cellar steps, and howling, and I remember, with pain, his tears, which my hand or your grandmother's so easily wiped away. But no one's hand can wipe away those tears he sheds invisibly today, which one hears in his laughter and in his speech and in his songs. I know what the world has done to my brother and how narrowly he has survived it. And I know, which is much worse, and this is the crime of which I accuse my country and my countrymen, and for which neither I nor time nor history will ever forgive them, that they have destroyed and are destroying hundreds of thousands of lives and do not know it and do not want to know it. One can be, indeed one must strive to become, tough and philosophical concerning destruction and death, for this is what most of mankind has been best at since we have heard of man. (But remember: *most* of mankind is not *all* of mankind.) But it is not permissible that the authors of devastation should also be innocent. It is the innocence which constitutes the crime.

Now, my dear namesake, these innocent and well-meaning people, your countrymen, have caused you to be born under conditions not very far removed from those described for us by Charles Dickens in the London of more than a hundred years ago. (I hear the chorus of the innocents screaming, "No! This is not true! How *bitter* you are!"—but I am writing this letter to *you*, to try to tell you something about how to handle *them*, for most of them do not yet really know that you exist. I *know* the conditions under which you were born, for I was there. Your countrymen were *not* there, and haven't made it yet. Your grandmother was also there, and no one has ever accused her of being bitter. I suggest that the innocents check with her. She isn't hard to find. Your countrymen don't know that *she* exists, either, though she has been working for them all their lives.)

Well, you were born, here you came, something like fourteen years ago; and though your father and mother and grandmother, looking about the streets through which they were carrying you, staring at the walls into which they brought you, had every reason to be heavyhearted, yet they were not. For here you were, Big James, named for me—you were a big baby, I was not—here you were: to be loved. To be loved, baby, hard, at once, and forever, to strengthen you against the loveless world. Remember that: I know how black it looks today, for you. It looked bad that day, too, yes, we were trembling. We have not stopped trembling yet, but if we had not loved each other none of us would have survived. And now you must survive because we love you, and for the sake of your children and your children's children.

This innocent country set you down in a ghetto in which, in fact, it intended that you should perish. Let me spell out precisely what I mean by that, for the heart of the matter is here, and the root of my dispute with my country. You were born where you were born and faced the future that you faced because you were black and *for no other reason*. The limits of your ambition were, thus, expected to be set forever. You were born into a society which spelled out with brutal clarity, and in as many ways as possible, that you were a worthless human being. You were not expected to aspire to excellence: you were expected to make peace with mediocrity. Wherever you have turned, James, in your short time on this earth, you have been told where you could go and what you could do (and *how* you could do it) and where you could live and whom you could marry. I know your countrymen do not agree with me about this, and I hear them saying, "You exaggerate." They do not know Harlem, and I do. So do you. Take no one's word for anything, including mine—but trust your experience. Know whence you came. If you know whence you came, there is really no limit to where you can go. The details and symbols of your life have been deliberately constructed to make you believe what white poeple say about you. Please try to remember what they believe, as well as what they do and cause you to endure, does not testify to your inferiority but to their humanity and fear. Please try to be clear, dear James, through the storm which rages about your youthful head today, about the reality which lies behind the words *acceptance* and *integration*. There is no reason for you to try to become like white people and there is no basis whatever for their impertinent assumption that *they* must accept *you*. The really terrible thing, old buddy, is that *you* must accept *them*. And I mean that very seriously. You must accept them and accept them with love. For these innocent people have no other hope. They are, in effect, still trapped in a history which they do not understand; and until they understand it, they cannot be released from it. They have had to believe for many years, and for innumerable reasons, that black men are inferior to white men. Many of them, indeed, know better, but, as you will discover, people find it very difficult to act on what they know. To act is to be committed, and to be committed is to be in danger. In this case, the danger, in the minds of most white Americans, is the loss of their identity. Try to imagine how you would feel if you woke up one morning to find the sun shining and all the stars aflame. You would be frightened because it is out of the order of nature. Any upheaval in the universe is terrifying because it so profoundly attacks one's sense of one's own reality. Well, the black man has functioned in the white man's world as a fixed star, as an immovable pillar: and as he moves out of his place, heaven and earth are shaken to their foundations. You, don't be afraid. I said that it was intended that you should perish in the ghetto, perish by never being allowed to go behind the white man's definitions, by never being allowed to spell your proper name. You have, and many of us have, defeated this intention; and, by a terrible law, a terrible paradox, those innocents who believed that your imprisonment made them safe are losing their grasp of reality. But these young men are your brothers—your lost, younger brothers. And if the word *integration* means anything, this is what it means: that we, with love, shall force our brothers to see themselves as they are, to cease fleeing from reality and begin to change it. For this is your home, my friend, do not be driven from it; great men have done great things here, and will again, and we can make America what America must become. It will be hard, James, but you come from sturdy, peasant stock, men who picked cotton and dammed rivers and built railroads, and, in the teeth of the most terrifying odds, achieved an unassailable and monumental dignity. You come from a long line of great poets, some of the greatest poets since Homer. One of them said, *The very time I thought I was lost, My dungeon shook and my chains fell off.*

You know, and I know, that the country is celebrating one hundred years of freedom one hundred years too soon. We cannot be free until they are free. God bless you, James, and Godspeed.

Your uncle,
James

David Rothenberg to His Mother

In 1974, at the age of forty, David Rothenberg decided it was time to share a secret about his life that he had been keeping from his mother. Rothenberg was serving as the executive director of the Fortune Society, a New York–based nonprofit organization that helped ex-convicts find employment and rebuild their lives. He was encouraging former inmates to be open and honest about their past, and he realized he had not been forthcoming about his own life with his family. After sharing the news with his sister over the phone, Rothenberg sent the following letter to his mother, who was then living in Florida.

Dear Mother:

For weeks I have been flirting with the notion of sharing some truths about myself with you—and have arrived at the juncture where honesty and love can meet.

For the first time in my life, I am beginning to get a sense of contentment and of self-acceptance. This is important to our relationship, son-to-mother, mother-to-son. I have held back with you, filled my being with moody silences that I now realize were underlined with fears of rejection. It is my deepest hope that as I have learned to accept myself, it will fill in some of the blank spaces of our friendship and love.

This is all by way of saying to you that I have, at last, accepted a truth about myself—and in doing so, it makes my life bearable. An enormous weight has been lifted. It is that I am, and always have been, homosexual.

Growing up in New Jersey—unknowing and affected by small town mores, I felt cursed. I saw myself on the outside looking in. Now I have learned that I am a total human being with much to be proud of, with much to offer, and my sexual orientation is a problem only if I permit it to be, and if I am obsessed with the rejection of an unknowing outside world. I can no longer live in fear, with suspicions of what some unknown third party will think.

I have talked with parents of other homosexuals about talking or sharing this with you. They have urged me to do so. I do so now in the hope that you will accept me as I have accepted myself—and, in turn, am a happier person. Parents, I have heard, often lament, "Where have I failed?", but since my life has been filled with purpose and meaning, your question *should* be, rather, "How have I contributed to this success?"

This letter is written to you with an enormity that I hope you can understand, with tears running down my face because at last I am asking you, whom I love with every ounce of my breath, to accept me as I am, not in pretense.

I am your son, with a growing sense of freedom, who loves you.

David

Rothenberg's mother responded positively; "She cried when she read it," he later remarked, "because of all the years that I felt I could not share with her. I went down and spent some days with her—and it was the first time in thirty years that we were able to have a totally honest conversation."

Anne Sexton to Her Daughter Linda

Although written over five years before she took her own life on October 4, 1974, the following letter by Anne Sexton was in many ways her "final" letter to her fifteen-year-old daughter, Linda. Sexton, a Pulitzer Prize–winning poet, had attempted suicide before and was frequently hospitalized for depression. Sexton knew her death would be painful for her two daughters, and she wanted Linda, the elder, especially to understand how much she loved her, and that they could continue to converse with one another through her works. Anne Sexton was forty years old when she wrote the letter in April 1969.

Wed — 2:45 p.m.

Dear Linda,

I am in the middle of a flight to St. Louis to give a reading. I was reading a *New Yorker* story that made me think of my mother and all alone in the seat I whispered to her "I know, Mother, I know." (Found a pen!) And I thought of you—someday flying somewhere all alone and me dead perhaps and you wishing to speak to me.

And I want to speak back. (Linda, maybe it won't be flying, maybe it will be at your *own* kitchen table drinking tea some afternoon when you are 40. *Anytime*.)—I want to say back.

1st I love you.

2. You *never* let me down.

3. I know. I was there once. I *too*, was 40 and with a dead mother who I needed still.

This is my message to the 40-year-old Linda. No matter what happens you were always my bobolink, my special Linda Gray. Life is not easy. It is awfully lonely. *I* know that. Now you too know it—wherever you are, Linda, talking to me. But I've had a good life—I wrote unhappy—but I lived to the hilt. You too, Linda—Live to the HILT! To the top. I love you, 40-year-old Linda, and I love what you do, what you find, what you are!—Be your own woman. Belong to those you love. Talk to my poems, and talk to your heart—I'm in both: if you need me. I lied, Linda. I did love my mother and she loved me. She never held me but I miss her, so that I have to deny I ever loved her—or she me! Silly Anne! So there!

XOXOXO
Mom

Ita Ford to Her Niece Jennifer Sullivan

In July 1980 a young woman named Ita Ford traveled as a Maryknoll volunteer to El Salvador to serve the poor of the region. A relentless cam-

paign of violence was being waged against students, peasants, community organizers, and Catholic priests by the government, and Ford worked with other sisters and lay volunteers to help deliver food and supplies to needy families, transport refugees, and accompany grief-stricken families in search of loved ones who had disappeared. The life was a dangerous one, but, as Ford expressed in a letter to her sister, she felt the risks were necessary; "You say you don't want anything to happen to me. I'd prefer it that way myself—but [. . .] if you choose to enter into other people's suffering, to love others, you at least have to consent in some way to the possible consequences." Tragically, the worst "possible consequences" became a reality when Ita Ford and three other American churchwomen—Jean Donovan, Dorothy Kazel, and Maura Clarke—were found murdered near the remote village of Santiago Nonualco. Three months before her death, Ford wrote the following letter to her niece, Jennifer, living in Brooklyn.

August 18, 1980

Dear Jennifer,

The odds that this note will arrive for your birthday are poor, but know that I'm with you in spirit as you celebrate 16 big ones. I hope it's a special day for you.

I want to say something to you and I wish I were there to talk to you because sometimes letters don't get across all the meaning and feeling. But, I'll give it a try anyway.

First of all, I love you and care about you and how you are. I'm sure you know that. That holds if you're an angel or a goof-off, a genius or a jerk. A lot of that is up to you, and what you decide to do with your life. What I want to say . . . some of it isn't too jolly birthday talk, but it's real . . . Yesterday I stood looking down at a 16-year-old who had been killed a few hours earlier. I know a lot of kids even younger who are dead. This is a terrible time in El Salvador for youth. A lot of idealism and commitment is getting snuffed out here now. The reasons why so many people are being killed are quite complicated, yet there are some clear, simple strands. One is that many people have found a meaning to life, to sacrifice, struggle, and even to death. And whether their life span is 16 years, 60 or 90, for them, their life has had a purpose. In many ways, they are fortunate people.

Brooklyn is not passing through the drama of El Salvador, but some things hold true wherever one is, and at whatever age. What I'm saying is, I hope you come to find that which gives life a deep meaning for you . . . something worth living for, maybe even worth dying for . . . something that energizes you, enthuses you, enables you to keep moving ahead. I can't tell you what it might be—that's for you to find, to choose, to love. I can just encourage you to start looking, and support you in the search.

I hope this doesn't sound like some kind of a sermon because I don't mean it that way. Rather, it's something that you learn here, and I want to share it with you. In fact, it's my birthday present to you. If it doesn't make sense right at this moment, keep this and read it sometime from now. Maybe it will be clearer. Or ask me about it, OK?

A very happy birthday to you and much, much love,

Ita

Allison West to His Daughter Tracey

Allison West, now in semiretirement after having worked as a businessman and as the owner of a small manufacturing company in eastern New York, often writes letters to his two grown children, Darrell and Tracey, on special occasions. On Darrell's thirty-first birthday, West wrote: "To release the love that was stored up in me required [your] birth. Like most fathers when their sons are born, it's their rebirth." Not long after writing this letter, West's daughter delivered a baby boy named Nicholas. In the following letter, West expresses what Tracey's childhood and Nicholas's birth have meant to him.

December 23, 1994

Dear Tracey,

I haven't had an opportunity to talk to you since this lovable despot came into the family. His whimpers are our commands. All I can do is watch you care for him and listen to you lecture your mother and me on baby-sitting for our grandchild. I won't test your love and tell you what we say about you after you are out of ear reach.

The more I see your child, the more I see my daughter, and a kaleidoscope of colorful memories, unique and precious, crystallizes inside me. At his age, you decided my shoulder was more appetizing and soothing than your teething ring. You gummed me, then bit me, and if I would have allowed you, I'm certain you would've nibbled away my shoulder. You taught me how painless your needs were.

The years were greedy with us. They gobbled up my little girl and left a young lady who tried to conceal the child I visioned. On numerous occasions you informed me you were a woman. Even when you became a lawyer, your voicing it was unacceptable evidence. When we marched down the aisle at your wedding, I didn't feel I was giving you away, just adding to our life. And all that has happened since has proven me correct. It was not until I saw you with your child did I see you anew. The happiness in your face when you looked at him. The way you talked and played with him, burying your face in his stomach, entangling your hair in his grasping hands. Both laughing as if laughter were the song of love.

What I saw I never imagined. All the other phases of your life I peeped into your future and glimpsed them before they arrived. Why was it that I never saw you with child? Did I knowingly blind that vision because of its irrefutability: my child would be gone and replaced by a woman? What do I see now when I look at you holding your child? You were never lovelier. You were never more loving. You were never more lovable. You were never more.

I don't know if it is possible for me to love you more. But I do know there is so much for me to love and to know about my love.

Love,

Dad

Michele Song to Her Birth Mother

Ever since she was a young girl Michele Song, who was adopted as an infant, wanted to know who her birth parents were. Song's adoption records, however, were sealed by law. It was not until she was thirty-one years old that, after thirteen years of petitioning, she got the courts to allow a social worker to examine their contents. (As with virtually all adoptions, under no circumstances would Song ever be allowed to see the file.) Pam Hirsch was the intermediary assigned by the agency that oversaw the adoption, Catholic Charities, and she told Song she would do everything she could to locate an address or phone number for her birth mother (the birth father, it was learned, had died two years after Song was born). And though neither Hirsch nor Song knew where the mother was—or if she were still alive—Hirsch encouraged Song to write a letter to her just in case an opportunity presented itself to establish contact. On August 15, 1996, Michele Song wrote the following letter to her birth mother, not knowing if it would ever be received. (Unsure of how to address her birth mother, Song did not include a salutation.)

I don't know quite how to begin this letter. I have waited a very long time to get to this point. I have wanted to find you since I was 8 years old, and I am finally at a point in my life that I could take the risk of finding you. Will you want to meet me? Do you want to see me? Get to know me? Would it be OK to contact you? Or do you want to forget me? That last question has kept me from moving on in this quest.

I would always watch those TV shows that reunited long lost parents with their children they gave up for adoption and I would cry every time. I dreamed of how that could be us. That you would want to meet me. At least once.

I have good parents, wonderful brothers and sister, and a great extended family. I have lived a middle class life. I had all the essentials and worked hard for the extras. I have been given wonderful opportunities and tried to take advantage of them. Yet through all of this there has been a hole in my heart that nothing has filled. Not the beautiful man that is my husband who has supported me in this endeavor nor my incredible daughter who makes me realize how hard of a decision you faced in giving me up. That hole is where you and my biological father are.

Becoming pregnant with Shannon is what finally gave me strength to try to find you. I chose to go through Catholic Charities since I wanted to make sure that I did not disrupt your life unduly, so that you could make a choice that was good for you. I don't know the circumstances of your life and didn't want to put you in a bad position or intrude in case others in your life don't know about me. Don't get me wrong, I'm praying with all my heart that you want to at least talk with me and maybe even meet with me. After giving birth to Shannon, I realized how hard it must have been to give me away. You and I were as one for 9 months and then suddenly we were apart. I cannot imagine being apart from Shannon. This made me think that maybe you would be open to hearing from me.

Several years ago, I wrote to Catholic Charities to get any non-identifying information I could get. It took a year to get but it was well worth the wait because I got information about you, your family, my biological father and his family. For the first time I felt like I was human. Before that I felt that I had been dropped here from Mars. Shortly after Shannon's birth, Jay (my husband) and I filed a petition with the DC family court to break the seal of my adoption through Catholic Charities in order to obtain medical information and the opportunity to meet you. This was granted July 1. I met with Pam Hirsch just a couple of days ago. She went through the file and gave me even more information, like what time I was born, how big I was, etc. But the real prize (and surprise) came the next night with the letter you had written your social worker just a few weeks after giving birth to me. Pam read the letter to me and my husband (edited of course to protect your identity). In that letter you said if you could have done things differently, you would have kept me. I had always believed that you didn't want me. What a joy it was to hear that I was wrong!! Another surprise to me was that my biological father knew of my existence and asked you about me. It seems I was wrong about that, too.

I really hope that things are well in your world. I also hope that before too much longer you and I might meet. I understand it's been a long time and that your life has gone on. I don't want much. Just to see if I look like you, get a chance to ask some questions, and if you allow it, a chance to get to know you.

Thank you for loving me enough to give me up so that I might have a better life. It must have been a hard decision. Getting to know you in what ever way is best for you will complete things for me. God bless!!

Michele Song

Several weeks later Hirsch located Song's birth mother, Judie Randall, who was alive and well. Hirsch asked Randall's permission to pass on her phone number to Song, and Randall agreed. Hours later Song spoke to her mother for the first time, and the two have since met and kept in close contact. "It's as if I was always part of the family and she kept a place for me," Song remarked. "It's far better than anything I expected."

Letters on Death & Dying

Good-night! I can't stay any longer in a world of death. Austin is ill of fever. I buried my garden last week—our man, Dick, lost a little girl through the scarlet fever. I thought perhaps that you were dead, and not knowing the sexton's address, interrogate the daisies. Ah! dainty—dainty Death! Ah! democratic Death! Grasping the proudest zinnia from my purple garden,—then deep to his bosom calling the serf's child! Say, is he everywhere? Where shall I hide my things?

Emily Dickinson to Mr. and Mrs. Hollands; November 6, 1858

Benjamin Franklin to Elizabeth Hubbart

The letters of Benjamin Franklin cover a seemingly limitless range of issues, from his views on virtue, happiness, religion, racial equality, marriage, and war to his opinions on the teachings of Confucius, scientific discoveries, and even the health benefits of working in a cold room "without any clothes [on]." On a more serious note, Franklin offered a reflection on death in a letter of condolence to his brother John Franklin's stepdaughter, Elizabeth Hubbart, who was deeply shaken by her stepfather's passing.

Philadelphia, February 22, 1756

Dear Child,

I condole with you, we have lost a most dear and valuable relation, but it is the will of God and Nature that these mortal bodies be laid aside, when the soul is to enter into real life; 'tis rather an embrio state, a preparation for living; a man is not completely born until he be dead: Why then should we grieve that a new child is born among the immortals? A new member added to their happy society? We are spirits. That bodies should be lent us, while they can afford us pleasure, assist us in acquiring knowledge, or doing good to our fellow creatures, is a kind and benevolent act of God—when they become unfit for these purposes and afford us pain instead of pleasure—instead of an aid, become an incumbrance and answer none of the intentions for which they were given, it is equally kind and benevolent that a way is provided by which we may get rid of them. Death is that way. We ourselves prudently choose a partial death. In some cases a mangled painful limb, which cannot be restored, we willingly cut off—He who plucks out a tooth, parts with it freely since the pain goes with it, and he that quits the whole body, parts at once with all pains and possibilities of pains and diseases it was liable to, or capable of making him suffer.

Our friend and we are invited abroad on a party of pleasure—that is to last forever—His chair was first ready and he is gone before us—we could not all conveniently start together, and why should you and I be grieved at this, since we are soon to follow, and we know where to find him.

Adieu,
B. Franklin

Alexander Hamilton to His Wife Eliza

It is not known exactly what Alexander Hamilton said about Aaron Burr in the summer of 1804, but it was apparently offensive enough to prompt Burr to challenge Hamilton to a duel. The two men had traded insults before, and on July 11 of that year, Hamilton, an author of the United States Constitution and former secretary of the treasury, and Burr, a former vice president of the United States, met face to face to settle their animosity once and for all. One week before the confrontation, Hamilton wrote the following letter to his wife to be read in the event of his death.

My dear Eliza—

This letter, my very dear Eliza, will not be delivered to you, unless I shall first have terminated my earthly career; to begin, as I humbly hope from redeeming grace and divine mercy, a happy immortality.

If it had been possible for me to have avoided the interview, my love for you and my precious children would have been alone a decisive motive. But it was not possible, without sacrifices which would have rendered me unworthy of your esteem. I need not tell you of the pangs I feel, from the idea of quitting you and exposing you to the anguish which I know you would feel. Nor could I dwell on the topic, lest it should unman me.

The consolations of Religion, my beloved, can alone support you; and these you have a right to enjoy. Fly to the bosom of your God and be comforted. With my last idea; I shall cherish the sweet hope of meeting you in a better world.

Adieu, best of wives and best of Women. Embrace all my darling Children for me.

Ever Yours

AH

Eyewitness accounts of the event reported that Hamilton, who was opposed to the duel, fired straight up in the air. Burr shot directly at his opponent, mortally wounding him. Hamilton died the next day.

Thomas Jefferson to John Adams

"There is a ripeness of time for death," a seventy-three-year-old Thomas Jefferson wrote to John Adams in August 1816. "It is reasonable we should drop off, and make room for another growth. When we have lived our generation out, we should not wish to encroach on another." Though Jefferson often discussed death in objective terms, he was not unfamiliar with the devastating impact it had on those who have lost loved ones—he was a widower at the age of thirty-nine, and five of his six children died in his lifetime. When Jefferson learned that Abigail Adams, John's wife of fifty-four years, had passed away in November 1818, he sent his friend the following letter.

Monticello November 13, 1818

The public papers, my dear friend, announce the fatal event of which your letter of October 20th had given me ominous forebodings. Tried myself in the school of affliction, by the loss of every form of connection which can rive the human heart, I know well and feel what you have lost, what you have suffered, are suffering, and have yet to endure. The same trials have taught me that for ills so immeasurable, time and silence are the only medicines. I will not, therefore, by useless condolences, open afresh the sluices of your grief, nor, altho' mingling sincerely my tears with yours, will I say a word more where words are vain, but that it is of some comfort to us both that the time is not very distant at which we are to deposit in the same cerement our sorrows and suffering bodies, and to ascend in essence to an ecstatic meeting with the friends we have loved and lost, and whom we shall still love and never lose again. God bless you and support you under your heavy affliction.

Th. Jefferson

Remarkably, Jefferson and Adams, who had written the Declaration of Independence together, died of natural causes on the same day in 1826—July 4.

Henry David Thoreau to Ralph Waldo Emerson

In 1845, at the age of twenty-seven, Henry David Thoreau built a small cottage by the shores of Walden Pond on land owned by Ralph Waldo Emerson, whose religious beliefs had been a great influence on his life. For two years Thoreau recorded his experiences living an austere life close to nature in a journal, selections of which were published in 1854 as Walden. *In January 1842 Thoreau's brother John died suddenly. Two weeks later Emerson's little boy Waldo, whom Thoreau adored, came down with scarlet fever and died soon after. Thoreau was so traumatized by the deaths that for almost two months he wrote nothing. Then, on March 11, he sent Emerson the following letter.*

Concord

Dear Friend,

I see so many "carvels ticht, fast tending throw the sea" to your El Dorado, that I am in haste to plant my flag in season on that distant beach, in the name of God and King Henry. There seems to be no occasion why I who have so little to say to you here at home should take pains to send you any of my silence in a letter—Yet since no correspondence can hope to rise above the level of those homely speechless hours, as no spring ever bursts above the level of the still mountain tarn whence it issued—I will not delay to send a venture. As if I were to send you a piece of the house-sill—or a loose casement rather. Do not neighbors sometimes halloo with good will across a field, who yet never chat over a fence?

The sun has just burst through the fog, and I hear blue-birds, song-sparrows, larks, and robins, down in the meadow. The other day I walked in the woods, but found myself rather denaturalized by late habits. Yet it is the same nature that Burns and Wordsworth loved—the same life that Shakespeare and Milton lived. The wind still roars in the wood, as if nothing had happened out of the course of nature. The sound of the waterfall is not interrupted more than if a feather had fallen.

Nature is not ruffled by the rudest blast—The hurricane only snaps a few twigs in some nook of the forest. The snow attains its average depth each winter, and the chic-adee lisps the same notes. The old laws prevail in spite of pestilence and famine. No genius or virtue so rare & revolutionary appears in town or village, that the pine ceases to exude resin in the wood, or beast or bird lays aside its habits.

How plain that death is only the phenomenon of the individual or class. Nature does not recognize it, she finds her own again under new forms without loss. Yet death is beautiful when seen to be a law, and not an accident—It is as common as life. Men die in Tartary—in Ethiopia—in England—in Wisconsin. And after all what portion of this so serene and living nature can be said to be alive? Do this year's grasses and foliage outnumber all the past?

Every blade in the field—every leaf in the forest—lays down its life in its season as beautifully as it was taken up. It is the pastime of a full quarter of the year. Dead trees—sere leaves—dried grass and herbs—are not these a good part of our life? And what is that pride of our autumnal scenery but the hectic flush—the sallow and cadaverous countenance of vegetation—its painted throes—with the November air for canvas—

When we look over the fields we are not saddened because these particular flowers or grasses will wither—for the law of their death is the law of new life. Will not the land be in good heart *because* the crops die down from year to year? The herbage cheerfully consents to bloom, and wither, and give place to a new.

So it is with the human plant. We are partial and selfish when we lament the death of the individual, unless our plaint be a paean to the departed soul, and a sigh as the wind sighs over the fields, which no shrub interprets into its private grief.

One might as well go into mourning for every sere leaf—but the more innocent and wiser soul will snuff a fragrance in the gales of autumn, and congratulate Nature upon her health.

After I have imagined thus much will not the Gods feel under obligation to make me realize something as good?

I have just read some good verse by the old Scotch poet John Bellenden—

"The fynest gold or silver that we se,
May nocht be wrocht to our utilitie,
Bot flammis kein & bitter violence;
The more distress, the more intelligence.
Quhay sailis lang in hie prosperitie,
Ar sone ourest be stormis without defence."

From your friend,
Henry D. Thoreau

Harriet Beecher Stowe to Her Husband Calvin

Legend has it that upon meeting Harriet Beecher Stowe for the first time, Abraham Lincoln remarked, "So this is the little lady who started the big war." The story is believed to be apocryphal, but Stowe's Uncle Tom's Cabin *unquestionably had an enormous impact on the American public in the ten years preceding the Civil War. In an 1853 letter to an acquaintance, Stowe remarked that it was the death of her baby boy Charley to cholera that inspired much of* Uncle Tom's Cabin*; "It was at his dying bed and at his grave," Stowe wrote, "that I learned what a poor slave mother may feel when her child is torn away from her. [. . . I]t was my only prayer to God that such anguish might not be suffered in vain." Stowe wrote the follow-*

ing letter to her husband, Calvin Ellis Stowe, on July 26, 1849, soon after Charley died.

My Dear Husband,—At last it is over, and our dear little one is gone from us. He is among the blessed. My Charley—my beautiful, loving, gladsome baby, so loving, so sweet, so full of life and hope and strength now lies shrouded, pale and cold, in the room below. Never was he anything to me but a comfort. He has been my pride and joy. Many a heartache has he cured for me. Many an anxious night have I held him to my bosom and felt the sorrow and loneliness pass out of me with the touch of his little warm hands. Yet I have just seen him in his death agony, looked on his imploring face when I could not help nor soothe nor do one thing, not one, to mitigate his cruel suffering, do nothing but pray in my anguish that he might die soon. I write as though there were no sorrow like my sorrow, yet there has been in this city, as in the land of Egypt, scarce a house without its dead. This heart-break, this anguish, has been everywhere, and when it will end God alone knows.

John A. Copeland to His Family

John A. Copeland, a fugitive slave, was one of five black men who joined John Brown on his fateful raid on Harpers Ferry, Virginia, in October 1859. Ten of the eighteen members of Brown's makeshift army were killed in the attempt, and the rest were captured and tried for treason. Copeland, like Brown, was sentenced to death, and his execution was scheduled for December 16. Hours before he was hanged, Copeland sent the following letter to his family.

Dear Father, Mother, Brothers Henry, William and Freddy and Sisters Sarah and Mary:

The last Sabbath with me on earth has passed away. The last Monday, Tuesday, Wednesday and Thursday that I shall ever see on this earth, have now passed by. God's glorious sun, which he has placed in the heavens to illuminate this earth—whose warm rays make man's home on earth pleasant—whose refulgent beams are watched for by the poor invalid, to enter and make as it were a heaven of the room in which he is confined—I have seen declining behind the western mountains for the last time. Last night, for the last time, I beheld the soft bright moon as it rose, casting its mellow light into my felon's cell, dissipating the darkness, and filling it with that soft pleasant light which causes such thrills of joy to all those in like circumstances with myself. This morning, for the last time, I beheld the glorious sun of yesterday rising in the far-off East, away off in the country where our Lord Jesus Christ first proclaimed salvation to man; and now, as he rises higher and his bright light takes the place of the pale, soft moonlight, I will take my pen, for the last time, to write you who are bound to me by those strong ties, (yea, the strongest that God ever instituted,) the ties of blood and relationship. *I am well, both in body and in mind.* And now, dear ones, if it were not that I knew your hearts will be filled with sorrow at my fate, I could pass from this earth without a regret. Why should you sorrow? Why should your hearts be wracked with grief? Have I not everything to gain, and nothing to lose by the change? I fully believe that not only myself, but also all three of my poor comrades who are to ascend the same scaffold—(a scaffold already made sacred to the cause of freedom by the death of that great champion of human freedom—Captain John Brown) are *prepared* to meet our God.

I am only leaving a world filled with sorrow and woe, to enter one in which there is but one lasting day of happiness and bliss. I feel that God, in his mercy, has spoken peace to my soul, and that all my numerous sins are forgiven.

Dear parents, brothers and sisters, it is true that I am now in a few hours to start on a journey from which no traveler returns. Yes, long before this reaches you, I shall, as I sincerely hope, have met our brother and sister who have for years been worshipping God around his throne—singing praises to him and thanking him that he gave his Son to die that they might have eternal life. I pray daily and hourly that I may be fitted to have my home with them, and that you, one and all, may prepare your souls to meet your God, that so, in the end, though we meet no more on earth, we shall meet in heaven, where we shall not be parted by the demands of the cruel and unjust monster Slavery.

But think not that I am complaining, for I feel reconciled to meet my fate. *I pray God that his will be done, not mine.*

Let me tell you that it is not the mere fact of having to meet death, which I should regret, (if I should express regret I mean,) but that such an unjust institution should exist as the one which demands my life, and not my life only, but the lives of those to whom my life bears but the relative value of zero to the infinite. I beg of you, one and all, that you will not grieve about me; but that you will thank God that he spared me to make my peace with him.

And now, dear ones, attach no blame to any one for my coming here, for not any person but myself is to blame.

I have no antipathy against any one. I have freed my mind of all hard feelings against every living being, and I ask all who have any thing against me to do the same.

And now, dear Parents, Brothers and Sisters, I must bid you to serve your God, and meet me in heaven.

I must with a very few words close my correspondence with those who are the most near and dear to me: but I hope, in the end, we may again commune never more to cease.

Dear ones, he who writes this will, in a few hours, be in this world no longer. Yes, these fingers which hold the pen with which this is written will, before today's sun has reached his meridian, have laid it aside forever, and this poor soul have taken its flight to meet its God.

And now, dear ones, I must bid you that last, long, sad farewell. Good by, Father, Mother, Henry, William and Freddy, Sarah and Mary! Serve your God and meet me in heaven.

Your Son and Brother to eternity,

John A. Copeland

President Abraham Lincoln to Fanny McCullough

One of the most memorable letters attributed to Abraham Lincoln is a short message he sent Mrs. Lydia Bixby, who, the president had been told, lost five sons in the Civil War. The letter read: "I pray that our Heavenly Father may assuage the anguish of your bereavement, and leave you only the cherished memory of the loved and lost, and the solemn pride that must be yours to have laid so costly a sacrifice upon the altar of freedom." It is now believed that the information was erroneous—one of Bixby's sons had come home safely and two others were deserters—and there is some doubt that Lincoln even composed the letter. There is no question, however, that Lincoln sent the following letter of condolence to Miss Fanny McCullough, a young girl whose father, Lt. Col. William McCullough, whom Lincon had known personally, was killed in the war.

Executive Mansion
Washington, December 23, 1862

Dear Fanny:

It is with deep grief that I learn of the death of your kind and brave Father; and, especially that it is affecting your young heart beyond what is common in such cases. In this sad world of ours, sorrow comes to all; and, to the young, it comes with bitterest agony, because it takes them unawares. The older have learned ever to expect it. I am anxious to afford some alleviation of your present distress. Perfect relief is not possible, except with time. You can not now realize that you will ever feel better. Is not this so? And yet it is a mistake. You are sure to be happy again. To know this, which is certainly true, will make you some less miserable now. I have had experience enough to know what I say; and you need only to believe it, to feel better at once. The memory of your dear Father, instead of an agony, will yet be a sad, sweet feeling in your heart, of a purer and holier sort than you have known before.

Please present my kind regards to your afflicted mother.

Your sincere friend, A Lincoln

Earlier that same year, Lincoln's son Willie died unexpectedly. He would have been twelve years old on December 21, 1862, just two days before Lincoln sent his letter to McCullough.

Samuel Clemens (Mark Twain) to Joe Twichell

On August 18, 1896, Samuel L. Clemens, better known as Mark Twain, suffered the most devastating loss of his life—his beloved twenty-four-year-old daughter, Susy, died from meningitis. Clemens was traveling abroad at the time and was not with his daughter when she passed away in their home in Hartford, Connecticut. In a letter to his friend Joe Twichell written several months after Susy's death, Clemens expresses the degree to which the loss is affecting him and Livy, his wife.

London, Jan. 19, '97

Dear Joe,

Do I want you to write to me? Indeed I do. I do not want most people to write but I do want you to do it. The others break my heart but you will not. You have something divine in you that is not in other men. You have the touch that heals, not lacerates. And you know the secret places of our hearts. You know our life—the outside of it—as the others do—and the inside of it—which they do not. You have seen our whole voyage. You have seen us go to sea, a cloud of sail, and the flag at the peak. And you see us now, chartless, adrift—derelicts, battered, water-logged, our sails a ruck of rags, our pride gone. For it is gone. And there is nothing in its place. The vanity of life was all we had, and there is no more vanity left in us. We are even ashamed of that we had, ashamed that we trusted the promises of life and builded high—to come to this!

I did know that Susy was part of us. I did *not* know that she could go away. I did not know that she could go away and take our lives with her, yet leave our dull bodies behind. And I did not know what she was. To me she was but treasure in the bank, the amount known, the need to look at it daily, handle it, weigh it, count it, *realize* it, not necessary. And now that I would do it, it is too late. They tell me it is not there, has vanished away in a night, the bank is broken, my fortune is gone, I am a pauper. How am I to comprehend this? How am I to *have* it? Why am I robbed, and who is benefited?

Ah well, Susy died at *home*. She had that privilege. Her dying eyes rested upon nothing that was strange to them, but only things which they had known and loved always and which had made her young years glad. And she had you and Sue and Katy and John and Ellen. This was happy fortune. I am thankful that it was vouchsafed to her. If she had died in another house—well, I think I could not have borne that. To us, our house was not unsentient matter. It had a heart and a soul and eyes to see us with approvals and solicitudes and deep sympathies. It was of us and we were in its confidence and lived in its grace and in the peace of its benediction. We never came home from an absence that its face did not light up and speak out its eloquent welcome. And we could not enter it unmoved. And could we now, oh how, in spirit we should enter it unshod.

I am trying to add to the "assets" which you estimate so generously. No, I am not. The thought is not in my mind. My purpose is other. I am working but it is for the sake of the work—the "surcease of sorrow" that is found there. I work all the days, and trouble vanishes away when I use that magic. This book will not long stand between it and me now. But that is no matter, I have many unwritten books to fly to for my preservation. The interval between the finishing of this one and the beginning of the next will not be more than an hour, at most. *Continuances*, I mean, for two of them are already well along. In fact have reached exactly the same stage in their journey: 19,000 words each. The present one will contain 180,000 words—130,000 are done. I am well protected.

But Livy! She has nothing in the world to turn to, nothing but housekeeping and doing things for the children and me. She does not see people and cannot. Books have lost their interest for her. She sits solitary, and all the day and all the days wonders how it all happened and why. We others were always busy with our affairs but Susy was her comrade—had to be driven from her loving persecutions—sometimes at 1 in the morning. To Livy the persecutions were welcome. It was heaven to her to be plagued like that. But it is ended now. Livy stands so in need of help, and none among us all could help her like you.

Some day you and I will walk again, Joe, and talk. I hope so. We could have *such* talks! We are grateful to you and Harmony—*how* grateful it is not given to us to say in words. We pay as we can, in love, and in this coin practicing no economy. Goodbye, dear old Joe!

Mark

Ambrose Bierce to His Niece Lora

"Death is not the end," wrote Ambrose Bierce, "there remains litigation over the estate." "Bitter Bierce," as he was often called, was an unapologetic misanthrope who loathed humanity and took pleasure in deflating every inspiring myth or optimistic sentiment with a sharp comment. After serving in the Civil War—and seeing up close the depths to which man could sink—he became a journalist in San Francisco infamous for cutting one-liners and putdowns. In October 1913, at the age of seventy-one, Bierce decided to quit the United States and observe the Pancho Villa revolution in Mexico. Before leaving, he wrote the following letter to his niece Lora. ("Carlt" is her husband, Carlton.)

Dear Lora,

I go away tomorrow for a long time, so this is only to say good-bye. I think there is nothing else worth saying; *therefore* you will naturally expect a long letter. What an intolerable world this would be if we said nothing but what is worth saying! And did nothing foolish—like going into Mexico and South America.

I'm hoping that you will go to the mine soon. You must hunger and thirst for the mountains—Carlt likewise. So do I. Civilization be dinged!—It is the mountains and the desert for me.

Good-bye—if you hear of my being stood up against a Mexican

stone wall and shot to rags please know that I think that a pretty good way to depart this life. It beats old age, disease, or falling down the cellar stairs. To be a Gringo in Mexico—ah, that is euthanasia!

With love to Carlt, affectionately yours,

Ambrose

Lora received another short letter from Bierce on November 6 of that same year, reporting that he was in Laredo, Texas. The letter concluded: "I shall not be here long enough to hear from you, and don't know where I shall be next. Guess it doesn't matter much. Adios, Ambrose." She never heard from him again, and his death remains a mystery.

Eugene O'Neill to His Wife Agnes

James O'Neill Sr., a popular actor and the father of playwright Eugene O'Neill, was diagnosed with intestinal cancer in the spring of 1920 and was given only a short time to live. At the end of July, when his death seemed imminent, Eugene was called down to New London, Connecticut, from Massachusetts to be with his father. O'Neill stayed at his father's bedside and wrote often painfully candid letters to his wife, Agnes Boulton O'Neill, describing his father's condition and the effect his dying was having on them both. The following letter was written approximately a week and a half before James O'Neill finally passed away, on August 10.

Own Sweetheart: Am writing this at the hospital. Papa is lying in bed watching me, his strange eyes staring at me with a queer, uncanny wonder as if, in that veiled borderline between Life and Death in which his soul drifts suspended, a real living being of his own flesh and blood were an incongruous and puzzling spectacle. I feel as if my health, the sun tan on my face contrasted with the unearthly pallor of his, were a spiritual intrusion, an impudence. And yet how his eyes lighted up with grateful affection when he first saw me! It made me feel so glad, so happy I had come!

The situation is frightful! Papa is alive when he ought to be dead. The disease has eaten through his bowels. Internal decomposition has set in—while he is still living! There is a horrible, nauseating smell in the room, the sickening, overpowering odor of a dead thing. His face, his whole body is that of a corpse. He is unspeakably thin and wasted. Only his eyes are alive—and the light that glimmers through their gaze is remote and alien. He suffers incredible tortures—in spite of all their dope. Just a few moments ago he groaned in anguish and cried pitifully: "Oh God, why don't You take me! Why don't You take me!" And Mama and I silently echoed his prayer. But God seems to be in His Omnipotent mood just now and not His All Merciful.

One very pitiful, cruelly ironic thing: He cannot talk plainly any more. Except when he cries out in pain it is impossible to understand him. And all through life his greatest pride has been in his splendid voice and clear articulation! His lips flutter, he tries so hard to say something, only a mumble comes forth—and then he looks at you so helplessly, so like a dog that has been punished it knows not why.

Death seems to be rubbing it in—to demand that he drink the chalice of gall and vinegar to the last bitter drop before peace is finally his. And, dear God, why? Surely he is a fine man as men go, and can look back to a long life in which he has kept an honorable faith and labored hard to get from nothing to the best attainment he knew. Surely the finest test of that attainment is the great affection and respect that all bear him who knew him. I don't believe he ever hurt a living thing intentionally. And he has certainly been a husband to marvel at, and a good father, according to his lights. I know those are the conventional virtues that are inscribed on tombstones—but he is the one person in a million who deserves them. Perhaps these virtues are so common in cemeteries because they are so rare in life. At any rate, looking at it dispassionately, he seems to me a *good* man—in the best sense of the word—and about the only one I have ever known.

Then why should he suffer so—when murderers are granted the blessing of electric chairs? Mankind—and myself—seem to me meaningless gestures, to be mocked at with gales of dreary laughter. The last illusion—the soft beauty of Death—"gone glimmering through the dream of things that were"—one result of this present visit.

There is a man on the floor above—an automobile accident case—who is howling monstrously & with every expulsion of breath—ticking of the clock of agony. He is dying, too, it seems. Like a wounded jackal he bays uncomprehendingly at the setting moon of Life. These hollow cries reverberate echoingly through the wide, cool halls where the nurses march from room to room—fat, buxom, red-armed wenches, mostly. They walk quietly on their rubber soles—insistently efficient with a too-fleshy indifference.

I'm afraid you'll find this letter a false note of drama. It isn't. It's sincere as hell! I'm too keyed up to write convincingly. When the Ultimate plucks you by the sleeve and you stand confronted by a vast enigma—brought home—what more can you do than—stutter! But I hope I've conveyed something.

Later—He was asleep when I was writing the above. Then he woke up and called me over. He made a dreadful effort to speak clearly and I understood a part of what he said, "Glad to go, boy—a better sort of life—another sort—somewhere"—and then he mumbled. He appeared to be trying to tell me what sort—and although I tried my damndest I couldn't understand! (How appropriate! Life is at least consistent!) Then he became clear again: "This sort of life—froth!—rotten!—all of it—no good!" There was a bitter expression on his poor, sunken face. And there you have it—the verdict of a *good* man looking back over seventy-six years: "Froth! Rotten!"

But it's finely consoling to know he believes in a "better sort—somewhere." I could see he did—implicitly! He will die with a sigh of relief. What queer things for him to say, eh? They sound like a dying dialogue in a play I might have written. Yet I swear to you I am quoting verbatim! He didn't mention God, I am sure. His "somehere" didn't appear to be a Catholic Heaven. He tried to tell me and I couldn't understand! Isn't it ghastly?

Oh My Own, we mustn't fight and hurt each other any more! We *mustn't!* It's the unforgivable sin—a crime against the spirit of our love! I can see that the great thing my father hugs to his heart as a something vital, not froth or rotten, is my mother's love and his for her. He has thrown everything else overboard but that remains—the real thing of the seventy-six years—the only meaning of them—the justification of his life because he knows that, at least, is fine and that it will go with him wherever he is going—the principal reason he is not afraid to go, I believe!

So let us protect our love against ourselves—that we may always have the inner courage, the faith to go on—with it to fall back on. All my love.

Gene

P.S. Am keeping my promise. So don't worry—and *rest!*

P.S. again. They expect Father to go any moment now. It can't be long postponed—and they can't be any more definite. His pulse is almost out. I'll write all developments.

Am staying at my cousin's with my Mother.

Archibald MacLeish to His Mother

Archibald MacLeish was a lawyer, professor, poet, journalist, and statesman who served as President Franklin D. Roosevelt's assistant secretary of state from 1944 to 1945 after serving as the librarian of Congress from 1939 to 1944. As a young man, MacLeish went to law school for two years, then volunteered to fight in World War I. Although he returned home safely from the war, his younger brother Kenny, a navy flier, was killed one month before the armistice. Two years later, MacLeish reflected on Kenny's death in the following letter to his mother.

12 October 1920 Cambridge

Dearest Mother:

This should come to you on the second anniversary of Kenneth's death. As time goes by I have a strange impression that it is we who are leaving Kenny, rather than Kenny who has left us.

Two years ago only the reported fact he had been killed altered the situation for us. We really had him still as much as though he had been alive. He was no farther removed from us in our last impression of him then than he would have been had he lived and remained in France. But now days & weeks & months have passed & we must, if we would touch the living Kenny, retrace all that length of time and labor to relimn the images time has been so busy effacing. We dont feel, at least I dont, that Kenny has gone farther from us. But I feel as each period of time goes by that the current of time & change is bearing me away from the things he & I knew together, & gradually wearing out my memory of the tone of his voice & the way he had of laughing as though he were really glad & the carriage of his head & smile. I can still feel the grip at my heart when I write of these things because they still have a vitality & existence. But I know that in a few years I shall not be able truly to feel them. And when I have been so far carried away from the Kenny who was my brother that I cannot reconstitute any single quality or characteristic of him with such certainty as to make the nerves respond as though he had been really there—why, what will Kenny be to me then? I think perhaps he will have a truer because a more idealized existence. Men become the symbols of ideas by losing their familiar & personal qualities. And Kenny as the symbol of brave youth content to die for the battle's sake will really exist when the Kenny who so nearly & intimately touches my heart has a little paled & faded into oblivion. For Kenny is the only one of us all whose immortality is provably sure. He belongs now & will belong more & more as time passes to the immortality of great ideas. He is one of the innumerable points of star fire that make up together man's great conception of the capacity for splendid and generous daring of the human heart. Whether he will live in his own proper person with his own lovliness & gentleness & timbre we cannot know. I, for one, cannot believe he, or any of us, will. But he has immortality nevertheless for his death flung him at one stroke into the heaven of man's deepest faith. Kenny cannot die so long as men believe in youth and the beauty of youth and the perfect generosity of youth's sacrifice.

I don't believe I ever gave you a little verse I wrote at Craigie Lea this summer. You will think of the days when there is a strong East Wind & the gulls hang in the sun motionless between heaven & earth, or slide gently against the wind, just over the lip of the bluff. On those windy days the garden is always very still where the trees & the hedges shield it—

Here in this inland garden
  Unrumorous of surf,
Here where the larches warden
  Only the sunny turf,

Here in the windy weather,
  Here where the lake wind lulls,
Slowly on silver feather
  Drift overhead the gulls.

O heart estranged of grieving,
  What is a sea bird's wing?
What beauty past believing
  Are you remembering?

Dearest love to you all
Archie

Will Rogers to Charles Russell

Will Rogers was born into a Cherokee family in 1879 and raised on a farm in Indian territory in Oklahoma. With a modest demeanor and a keen eye for hypocrisy and hubris in politics, Rogers was a folk hero during the Great Depression and became—through his radio program, syndicated column, stage shows, and movies—the most beloved humorist and entertainer of his time. When his close friend, the artist Charles Russell, passed away in 1926, Rogers wrote the following letter to him and sent it to Nancy Russell, "Charley"'s wife, at her request.

Dear Charley,

I bet you hadn't been up there three days until you had out your pencil and was drawin' something funny. And I bet you that a whole bunch of those great old joshers was just a waitin' for you to pop in with all the latest ones.

And I bet they are regular fellows when you meet 'em, ain't they? Most big men are.

Well, you will run into my old Dad up there, Charley, for he was a real cowhand, and I bet he's runnin' a wagon. And you will pop into some well-kept ranchhouse over under some cool shade trees, and you will be asked to dinner, and it will be the best one you ever had in your life. Well, when you are thankin' the women folks you just tell the sweet lookin' little old lady that you knew her boy, back on an outfit you used to rope for, and tell the daughters that you knew their brother, and if you see a cute little rascal runnin' around there with my brand on him, kiss him for me.

Well, can't write any more, Charley, paper's all wet, it must be raining in this old bunkhouse.

From your old friend,
Will

Amelia Earhart to Her Parents

The first woman to fly solo across the Atlantic, Amelia Earhart attempted an around-the-world flight in 1937 that would, once again, put her in the record books. Tragically, her plane disappeared, and Earhart was never found. Earhart had first learned to fly during World War I, and, after she demonstrated considerable skill as a pilot, her family bought her a small yellow biplane for her twenty-fourth birthday. In 1928 she was asked to ride as a passenger—the first woman to do so—on a transatlantic crossing so secret she did not even tell her parents that she was going. Earhart did, however, leave behind "Popping off Letters," to be opened in the event of her death. One of these letters, discovered later by George Putnam, her husband and biographer, was addressed to her father.

May 20, 1928

Dearest Dad:

Hooray for the last grand adventure! I wish I had won, but it was worth while anyway. You know that.

I have no faith we'll meet anywhere again, but I wish we might.

Anyway, good-by and good luck to you.

Affectionately, your doter,

Mill.

There was another letter, addressed to her mother, which read, simply: "Even though I have lost, the adventure was worth while. Our family tends to be too secure. My life has really been very happy, and I don't mind contemplating its end in the midst of it."

Edmund Wilson to William Rose Benét

Edmund "Bunny" Wilson, one of the great editors and writers of his time, was an ardent admirer and close friend of the poet and novelist Elinor Wylie. After hearing she was in a minor accident but recovering well, Wilson wrote to her on November 19, 1928, "I look forward with eagerness, and even with avidity, to seeing you in December. [. . .] Let's inaugurate the New Year by a spirited dinner together sometime as soon as possible." The dinner was not to be. Less than a month later, on December 16, Wylie died unexpectedly from what was believed to have been exhaustion. Wilson was devastated. As soon as he heard the news from his wife, Mary McCarthy, he sent the following letter to William Rose Benét, a close friend and Wylie's husband of five years.

December 21, 1928
Sunset Limited

Dear Bill:

I heard about Elinor just before I left California. Mary telegraphed me and has asked me to write you for her, as well as for me. It is hard for me to write or even to think about it now, and I know that you will not want to hear much—but I wanted you to know of the sympathy and distress I feel for you when I realize what a hole has been made in my own life. My only consolation is remembering that the last letter I received from Elinor—written from England, after her accident—was the happiest I had ever had from her. She told me that she had never enjoyed life more and that she was coming back in December, and I realized out there in California that seeing you and her again was one of the few things which could make me glad to get back to New York. But it's better to be cut off at the height of life with the head and heart full than to die as most people die. In Elinor's case, it leaves the impression undimmed of her almost supernatural brilliance and energy—it is like the sudden extinction of a sun, which has never been seen to cool—and there is something almost supernatural, too, about such a death, because it is not accompanied by any sign of weakness or decay. Please forgive the illegibility of this letter, which is written on a jolting train—and forgive my clumsy expression of my sympathy in a loss of which it will never be easy for me to write and of which it is peculiarly difficult just now, when my mind refuses to accept it and I have several times found myself thinking of her, as if I should see her when I got back. Such reality as this, such reality as Elinor had, is given to few human beings, and death has no power over it, for it endures in her and our minds, continuing to give us life, as few of the living do. You are fortunate in this, that you had more of it than anyone else. I sometimes envied you when Elinor was alive, and in spite of the grief you must now be in and the bleakness you must be feeling, I do so even now.

Yours always,
Bunny Wilson

John Boettiger to His Wife Virginia

"It was the most difficult letter to write," John Boettiger remarked in a letter to Ted Swanson, his business partner in their failing public relations firm, "and I am not happy with it, but it is the best I could do." The letter in question was Boettiger's final message to his wife, Virginia, before he committed suicide on October 31, 1950. Boettiger had been married previously to Anna Roosevelt, daughter of Franklin and Eleanor Roosevelt, and was still close to the family. Eleanor Roosevelt, in fact, was living in New York just a few blocks from the hotel from which Boetigger jumped and was one of the first to learn of his death. The following letter, among others to Anna Roosevelt and his eleven-year-old son, John, were found in his hotel room.

Virginia, my Darling, I have reached the end of the road. I can see no path ahead that offers any promise of a useful life.

I am filled with sadness that the manner of my leavetaking is such as to bring an unwonted grief to you and others who love me. How comforting it would be if one could slip away quietly and unnoticed!

I would hope to leave with you and my other loved ones the sense that here departs an uncomplaining man who has tasted far greater joys of life than are given to most men.

In thinking about others who have taken their own lives, I have always felt that when a man in good reasoning arrives at the supreme decision that his usefulness in life falls short, his self imposed death should not invoke condemnation or dismay.

I do not challenge the thought that the man who dies to escape his responsibilities is less than admirable. But if he weighs the assets and the liabilities of his life, and the scales fall on the debt side, then his decision might be accepted, at least by those who care for his, as right.

It has seemed to me that the fates have held my life to have been lived. My Darling, I have struggled against such a decision, even up to yesterday when I talked with more people in my efforts to find a right way to carry on. But today I have a full sense of finality. I have searched myself most earnestly, and I have concluded that my course has been run.

The crushing irony in this scheme of fate is that in my personal life I am supremely happy. You have given me deep, inward happiness born of your boundless capacity for devotion and loyalty, companionship and love. Your beauty is of the mind as well as of the body. From you and Victoria I have received great gifts of human relationships. Bless you both, and my equally staunch and devoted Johnny, and may the fates deal more gently with you all, the rest of your days.

The insurance which I leave will help you three in your material needs. This, and the memory of our happy days together, are all that I can bequeath.

I am anxious that you and some others know the thoughts which are in my mind and contributed to my decision.

Some men achieve high purposes and accomplishments in life, and later slip gracefully into an acceptance of lesser aims. I could do this, and would do it gladly, so long as I could feel that I could provide a reasonably good life for my family, and so long as I had a feeling that my tasks were useful ones.

I could never take refuge in a life of intellectual asceticism, nor could I submit to a life of mediocrity. It would be frustrating beyond my power to bear to submit my family to a meager life, even though I know that your love and faith would endure. My Darling, you are made for much better things.

I am a newspaper man. Twice in 29 years I left my profession and entered other work. Both times I was privileged to work with able, successful and sympathetic colleagues. But in my present association, as in the other, I have felt ill adjusted and unable to exert what abilities I possess to real advantage. Quite frankly I feel I am more of a hindrance than a help to my present working companions.

You know how earnestly I have tried to find a place in my own profession. I have sought out publishers and editors of newspapers, and newspaper brokers, all over the country, and in every honorable way I have endeavored to discover a suitable newspaper pursuit. I have uncovered situations in which I knew in my heart I could render highly useful services, to those with whom I proposed connections as well as in society itself. But the proposals failed for one reason or another, and in some instances because people, while conceding my fitness, found it difficult to overlook my past associations.

They could not reconcile the strangely conflicting relationships I had with Franklin Roosevelt, Colonel McCormick and William Randolph Hearst. I must confess that were I on the other side of the table, I myself might hesitate to join efforts with an amorphous character such as I might seem to be!

But the people where my writings were observed, in Chicago and Seattle and Phoenix particularly, know that I searched for the truth and was not afraid to print it.

Life for me has never been dull, and for all the interesting and exciting and worthwhile things I have been permitted to do I have high gratitude toward all those who helped me in the doing. It's been a wonderful world filled with wonderful people!

My spirit rises now in happy memory of all the years I have lived, from the days of my earliest recollections, when my mother gave me her full devotion, through the years gay and full with joys and loves and good jobs to be done, down to the present in which I have cherished your glowing devotion.

Good night, Darling

I love you.

John

P. S. Please, Darling, don't come to New York now. I want you and Victoria to think of me in our happy times. I am leaving a note that there's to be no funeral folderol.

Rachel Carson to Dorothy Freeman

"Love is such an expandable thing," the famed conservationist Rachel Carson wrote to her closest friend, Dorothy Freeman, in December 1954, "and every day since I have known you it has been growing so much it hurts. And what a lovely hurt!" Carson and Freeman maintained an extraordinarily loving and supportive correspondence for eleven years that ended only when Carson finally succumbed to cancer on April 14, 1964. Just over a year before she passed away, Carson wrote the following letter to Freeman, which was found among Carson's belongings and given to Freeman posthumously. (Roger is Carson's adopted son, and Jeffie is her cat.)

January 24, 1963

Darling,

I have been coming to the realization that suddenly there might be no chance to speak to you again and it seems I must leave a word of goodbye. Perhaps you will never read this, for in time—if there is time—I may destroy it. But last night the pains were bad and came so often that I was frightened. No, that isn't quite the word, but I realized there might not come a time when I wouldn't rouse from sleep in time to reach for the pills. And it seemed it might be a little easier for you if there were some message.

Perhaps I shall write this letter a little at a time, as I can and I shall leave it in an envelope addressed to you.

When I think back to the many farewells that have marked the decade (almost) of our friendship, I realize they have almost been inarticulate. I remember chiefly the great welling up of thoughts that somewhow didn't get put into words—the silences heavy with things unsaid. But then, we knew or hoped, there was always to be another chance—and always the letters to fill the gaps.

I have felt, darling, that it is better for you that in this past year, the tempo of our correspondence has slowed down so greatly—to the point where I'm sure you no longer watch for the mailman. When there can be no more letters the wrench won't be quite so great.

What do I most want to say? I think that you must have no regrets in my behalf. I have had a rich life, full of rewards and satisfactions that come to few, and if it must end now, I can feel that I have achieved most of what I wished to do. That wouldn't have been true two years ago, when I first realized my time was short, and I am so grateful to have had this extra time.

My regrets, darling, are for your sadness, for leaving Roger, when I so wanted to see him through to manhood, for dear Jeffie whose life is linked to mine.

Perhaps there is more time than I think. But for the past year I have been able to feel much less optimism. And now this new development! But as to the angina, in a way it is almost like a secret weapon against the grimmer foe—so if it should take me quickly, darling, remember this is the easier way for me.

But enough of that. What I want to write of is the joy and fun and gladness we have shared—for these are the things I want you to remember—I want to live on in your memories of happiness. I shall write more of those things. But tonight I'm weary and must put out the light. Meanwhile, there is this word—and my love that will always live.

Rachel

Elizabeth Bishop to U. T. and Joseph Summers

"When you write my epitaph," Elizabeth Bishop told fellow poet Robert Lowell in 1948, "you must say I was the loneliest person who ever lived." Loss had been a constant for Bishop; at the age of eight months her father died suddenly, and her mother was so traumatized by the event she had to be institutionalized. At the age of five Bishop was taken to live with her grandparents, and she never saw her mother again. After years of heartbreak and dejection, she finally found love and stability in her relationship with a Brazilian woman named Lota Macedo Soares. Bishop and Lota were together for fifteen years until Lota died on September 25, 1967—the aftermath of an intentional, early-morning overdose of sedatives on September 17. Three days after Lota's death, Bishop wrote the following letter to her close friends, U. T. and Joseph Summers.

September 28, 1967

Lota died Monday morning without having regained consciousness. That's about all I have to tell you now—Tuesday was taken up with all the arrangements necessary for sending a "body" (oh god) home to a foreign country—very complicated—and now I have just talked, forever, it seems to the Brazilian Consul here (very nice, although I don't know him—he seems to have known Lota)—about what to say for the newspapers, etc. This is all a great waste of time because I gather it was in them already and god knows what they said. However, we did our best and it may help some . . .

She was a wonderful, remarkable woman and I'm sorry you didn't know her better. I had the 12 or 13 happiest years of my life with her, before she got sick—and I suppose that is a great deal in this unmerciful world.

I just want to repeat (maybe) I was with her for only a few hours, actually, and there was no quarrel or discussion of any sort. I know of N.Y. gossip already so am dreading all this kind of interpretation. In fact her letters had been full of plans for our future together—although knowing her so well, I could see she was still very sick and trying to force herself to sound that way. Oh WHY WHY WHY didn't she wait a few days? Why did I sleep so soundly—why why why—I can't help thinking I might have saved her somehow—go over and over that Sunday afternoon but honestly can't think of anything I did especially wrong—except that I have done many wrong things all my life. Please try to keep on loving me in spite of them, won't you? I am clinging to my friends desperately.

I wanted to go down with her but the doctor persuaded me not to—the Macedo Soares clan is very big and very famous—and I'd just be in the way. I shall have to go as soon as I feel a little better, of course—but I'll keep in touch with you . . .

Norma Shumpert and Chris B. to the NAMES Project Foundation

In an effort to demonstrate the overwhelming human loss behind the AIDS epidemic, the San Francisco–based NAMES Project Foundation began the AIDS Memorial Quilt in 1987. The quilt, which is displayed throughout the country, is made up of individual panels contributed by family members, friends, lovers, and others dedicated to remembering those who have died from the disease. Often, those who send in quilts also include letters expressing grief for their loss, as well as their thanks to The NAMES Project for enabling them to memorialize loved ones in a lasting way.

The following was written by Norma Shumpert on September 14, 1987.

Billy Denver Donald was my brother. He was born in Dorsey, Michigan on June 18, 1936—he died April 23, 1987.

Physically, he was tall with black hair, blue eyes and olive complexion—exceptionally handsome. He was a father to a 19-year old son, a brother to three sisters, a son to a widowed mother, a special nephew to many aunts and uncles, a cousin to about 60, a friend, a highly respected manager to his fellow workers, and so much more.

I was sitting in the hospital waiting room after just being told Bill had AIDS. I mentally became very small—lifted off the sofa—went out the window and landed on the grass. The wind blew a leaf over me and I hid from the world for a few seconds.

With God's help and Bill's courage, we dealt with his illness with all the love within us. And life goes on without him. We will miss him forever.

Norma Shumpert

This letter was written by Chris B. (no last name given) on July 19, 1989.

Dear Brothers and Sisters in the NAMES Project,

It is very hard to describe the life of a good friend within a very few lines. It is harder to describe the feeling of loss at his passing. I believe that these will be more eloquently represented in the panel I made than I could ever cover in words.

When he died last year, I never grieved. I tried for a long time to forget—because it was too painful to remember. But when I saw your logo "Remember My Name," I realized that I must remember—for his sake.

Land never told his parents that he was gay, or that he had AIDS. They still do not know. So I did not include his last name, in respect for his wishes.

Land was a great friend. The best. His concern for others, when he had little himself, his sympathy for others and their suffering, in the face of his own suffering, epitomizes his personality and his character.

He was gentle and kind. He was a black man who knew no color. He was Land . . .

When Land entered the hospital for what he thought was a routine checkup, we spoke on the phone almost every day. Within a week, he was in intensive care. I was barred from seeing him. Three months later, he was dead. I promised I would visit him, but could not. His death came as a shock I could not deal with, so I never went to his funeral.

My panel, I hope, will be the goodbye I never had time to say. A woman friend, whose son I taught a number of years ago, sewed this panel together. She spent many hours working on a memorial to a man she never met. I thank her for that.

The silhouette on this panel is almost an exact likeness of him. It has allowed me to see him at last—and to mourn. I love him. I'll miss him.

Chris B.

Letters of Faith & Hope

As long as there is one upright man, as long as there is one compassionate woman, the contagion may spread and the scene is not desolate. Hope is the thing that is left to us, in a bad time. I shall get up Sunday morning and wind the clock, as a contribution to order and steadfastness.

Sailors have an expression about the weather: they say, the weather is a great bluffer. I guess the same is true of our human society—things can look dark, then a break shows in the clouds, and all is changed, sometimes rather suddenly. It is quite obvious that the human race has made a queer mess of life on this planet. But as a people we probably harbor seeds of goodness that have lain for a long time, waiting to sprout when the conditions are right. Man's curiosity, his relentlessness, his inventiveness, his ingenuity have led him into deep trouble. We can only hope that these same traits will enable him to claw his way out.

Hang on to your hat. Hang on to your hope. And wind the clock, for tomorrow is another day.

E. B. White to Mr. Nadeau; March 30, 1973

Benjamin Franklin to Joseph Huey

Although Benjamin Franklin is best known for his roles as a statesman, legislator, inventor, businessman, and writer, he was also a noted philanthropist. He helped establish the first hospital in Philadelphia, as well as the first fire department and public library in the colonies. In the following letter to Joseph Huey, Franklin offers his views on the importance of "good works," especially as they relate to faith and religion.

Philada. June 6. 1753

Sir,

I received your kind Letter of the 2nd Inst. and am glad to hear that you increase in Strength; I hope you will continue mending till you recover your former Health and Firmness. Let me know whether you still use the cold Bath, and what Effect it has.

As to the Kindness you mention, I wish it could have been of more Service to you. But if it had, the only Thanks I should desire is, that you would always be equally ready to serve any other Person that may need your Assistance, and so let good Offices go round, for Mankind are all of a Family.

For my own Part, when I am employed in serving others, I do not look upon myself as conferring Favours, but as paying Debts. In my Travels and since my Settlement I have received much Kindness from Men, to whom I shall never have any Opportunity of making the least direct Return. And numberless Mercies from God, who is infinitely above being benefited by our Services. These Kindnesses from Men I can therefore only return on their Fellow-Men; and I can only show my Gratitude for those Mercies from God, by a Readiness to help his other Children and my Brethren. For I do not think that Thanks, and Compliments, tho' repeated Weekly, can discharge our real Obligations to each other, and much less those to our Creator.

You will see in this my Notion of Good Works, that I am far from expecting (as you suppose) that I shall merit Heaven by them.

By Heaven we understand, a State of Happiness, infinite in Degree, and eternal in Duration: I can do nothing to deserve such Reward: He that for giving a Draught of Water to a thirsty Person should expect to be paid with a good Plantation, would be modest in his Demands, compar'd to those who think they deserve Heaven for the little Good they do on Earth. Even the mix'd imperfect Pleasures we enjoy in this World are rather from God's Goodness than our Merit; how much more such Happiness of Heaven. For my own part, I have not the Vanity to think I deserve it, the Folly to expect it, nor the Ambition to desire it; but content myself in submitting to the Will and Disposal of that God who made me, who has hitherto preserv'd and bless'd me, and in whose fatherly Goodness I may well confide, that he will never make me miserable, and that even the Afflictions I may at any time suffer shall tend to my Benefit.

The Faith you mention has doubtless its use in the World; I do not desire to see it diminished, nor would I endeavor to lessen it in any Man. But I wish it were more productive of Good Works than I have generally seen it: I mean real Good Works, Works of Kindness, Charity, Mercy, and Publick Spirit; not Holiday-keeping, Sermon-Reading or Hearing, performing Church Ceremonies, or making long Prayers, fill'd with Flatteries and Compliments, despis'd even by wise Men, and much less capable of pleasing the Deity. The Worship of God is a Duty, the hearing and reading of Sermons may be useful; but if Men rest in Hearing and Praying, as too many do, it is as if a Tree should value itself on being water'd and putting forth Leaves, tho' it never produc'd any Fruit.

Your great Master tho't much less of these outward Appearances and Professions than many of his modern Disciples. He prefer'd the Doers of the Word to the meer Hearers; the Son that seemingly refus'd to obey his Father and yet perform'd his Commands, to him that profess'd his Readiness but neglected the Works; the heretical but charitable Samaritan, to the uncharitable tho' orthodox Priest and sanctified Levite: and those who gave Food to the hungry, Drink to the Thirsty, Raiment to the Naked, Entertainment to the Stranger, and Relief to the Sick, &c. tho' they never heard of his Name, he declares shall in the last Day be accepted, when those who cry Lord, Lord; who value themselves on their Faith tho' great enough to perform Miracles but have neglected good Works shall be rejected. He profess'd that he came not to call the Righteous but Sinners to Repentance; which imply'd his modest Opinion that there were some in his Time so good that they need not hear even for Improvement; but now a days we have scarce a little Parson, that does not think it the Duty of every Man within his Reach to sit under his petty Ministrations, and that whoever omits them offends God. I wish to such more Humility, and to you Health and Happiness, being Your friend and Servant

B. Franklin

Col. G. W. Clarke to the Editor of the *Arkansas Intelligencer*

Although a million and a half Irish men, women, and children were able to escape the potato famine of the late 1840s and travel to America, countless others could not afford—or were simply too weak—to leave Ireland. Desperate pleas for assistance poured into the United States, and family members and concerned citizens struggled to raise whatever funds they could to send overseas. When a small group of Choctaw Indians learned of the plight of the starving Irish, they contributed a substantial portion of a $170 donation (worth an estimated $25,000 in present-day dollars) ultimately sent by a relief committee in Memphis. The Choctaws were well aware of the suffering caused by starvation and disease—in the early 1830s they had been forcibly removed by the U.S. Government from their native land in Mississippi to the Indian Territory, and over a quarter of their people died en route. Writing from the Indian Territory in March 1847, Col. G. W. Clarke describes to the editor of the Arkansas Intelligencer *his firsthand account of the Choctaws's compassion.*

Dear Sir—

The cries of famishing Ireland have been heard even in this remote corner of the "great west," and nobly and generously have they been responded to.

On the evening of the 23d inst, a meeting was held at the office of the Superintendent, at which were present most of the neighboring people, and some strangers, who were here on business.

On motion, Majr Wm. Armstrong was appointed chairman, and J. B. Luce, Secretary.

After the reading of a letter from the Irish Relief Committee of Memphis, the chairman adverted to the condition of Ireland, briefly and most feelingly. He spoke of "Old Erin," as men of Irish feeling and Irish blood alone can speak; he said "it was not words she wanted, but substantial food." A subscription list was then opened, and in a short time $170 were subscribed and paid. By reference to the list you will perceive the names of many full-blooded Choctaw Indians, who knew nothing more, cared for nothing more, than the fact that across the Big Water, there were thousands of human beings starving to death. Is not this a sublime spectacle? The Red man of the New, bestowing alms upon the people of the Old world! With them, it is literally complying with that golden rule of Christianity, of returning good for evil.

The funds were immediately forwarded to the Committee at Memphis, Tenn. Can your city, famed as it is for its liberality, beat this[?]

Citizens from Arkansas did, in fact, send funds to Ireland, but the total amount is unknown.

Henry James to Grace Norton

Like his brother, the renowned psychologist and philosopher William James, Henry James experienced severe bouts of depression throughout his life. In the summer of 1883 he received a despairing letter from his friend and fellow author Grace Norton, who was nearing an emotional collapse. James, all too familiar with the sense of hopelessness she faced, wrote the following.

131 Mount Vernon St.,
Boston
July 28th

My dear Grace,

Before the sufferings of others I am always utterly powerless, and the letter you gave me reveals such depths of suffering that I hardly know what to say to you. This indeed is not my last word—but it must be my first. You are not isolated, verily, in such states of feeling as this—that is, in the sense that you appear to make all the misery of mankind your own; only I have a terrible sense that you give all and receive nothing—that there is no reciprocity in your sympathy—that you have all the affliction of it and none of the returns. However—I am determined not to speak with you except with the voice of stoicism. I don't know *why* we live—the gift of life comes to us from I don't know what source or for what purpose; but I believe we can go on living for the reason that (always of course up to a certain point) life is the most valuable thing we know anything about and it is therefore presumptively a great mistake to surrender it while there is any yet left in the cup. In other words consciousness is an illimitable power, and though at times it may seem to be all consciousness of misery, yet in the way it propagates itself from wave to wave, so that we never cease to feel, though at moments we appear to, try to, pray to, there is something that holds one in one's place, makes it a standpoint in the universe which it is probably good not to forsake. You are right in your consciousness that we are all echoes and reverberations of the *same*, and you are noble when your interest and pity as to everything that surrounds you, appears to have a sustaining and harmonizing power. Only don't, I beseech you, *generalize* too much in these sympathies and tendernesses—remember that life is a very special problem which is not yours but another's and content yourself with the terrible algebra of your own. Don't melt too much into the universe, but be as solid and dense and fixed as you can. We all live together, and those of us who love and know, live so most. We help each other—even unconsciously, each in our own effort, we lighten the effort of others, we contribute to the sum of success, make it possible for others to live. Sorrow comes in great waves—no one can know that better than you—but it rolls over us, and though it may almost smother us it leaves us on the spot and we know that if it is strong we are stronger, inasmuch as it passes and we remain. It wears us, uses us, but we wear it and use it in return; and it is blind, whereas we after a manner see. My dear Grace, you are passing through a darkness in which I myself in my ignorance see nothing but that you have been made wretchedly ill by it; but it is only a darkness it is not an end, or *the* end. Don't think, don't feel, any more than you can help, don't conclude or decide—don't do anything but *wait*. Everything will pass, and serenity and *accepted* mysteries and disillusionments, and the tenderness of a few good people, and new opportunities and ever so much of life, in a word, will remain. You will do all sorts of things yet, and I will help you. The only thing is not to *melt* in the meanwhile. I insist upon the necessity of a sort of mechanical condensation—so that however fast the horse may run away there will, when he pulls up, be a somewhat agitated but perfectly identical G.N. left in the saddle. Try not to be ill—that is all; for in that there is a future. You are marked out for success, and you must not fail. You have my tenderest affection and all my confidence.

Ever your faithful friend—
Henry James

Mark Twain to Walt Whitman

The humorist Mark Twain was not especially known for having profound hope for humanity. "When I get over to the other side," he once wrote, "I shall use my influence to have the human race drowned again, and this time drowned good, no omissions, no Ark." But in a letter to the great American poet Walt Whitman, who was celebrating his seventieth birthday, Twain wrote the following uncharacteristically optimistic message.

May 24, 1889

To Walt Whitman:

You have lived just the seventy years which are greatest in the world's history and richest in benefit and advancement to its peoples. These seventy years have done more to widen the interval between man and the other animals than was accomplished by any of the five centuries which preceded them.

What great births have you witnessed! The steam press, the steamship, the steelship, the railroad, the perfect cotton gin, the telegraph, the phonograph, photogravure, the electrotype, the gaslight, the electric light, the sewing machine and the amazing infinitely varied and innumerable products of coal tar, those latest and strangest marvels of a marvelous age. And you have seen even greater births than these; for you have seen the application of anesthesia to surgery-practice, whereby the ancient dominion of pain, which began with the first created life, came to an end on this earth forever, you have seen the slave set free, you have seen monarchy banished from France and reduced in England to a machine which makes an imposing show of diligence and attention to business, but isn't connected with the works. Yes you have indeed seen much—but tarry for a while, for the greatest is yet to come. Wait thirty years, and *then* look out over the earth! You shall see marvels upon marvels added to those whose nativity you have witnessed; and conspicuous above them you shall see their formidable Result—man at almost his full stature at last!—and still growing, visibly growing while you look. Wait till you see that great figure appear, and catch the far glint of the sun upon his banner; then you may depart satisfied, as knowing you have seen him for whom the earth was made, and that he will proclaim that human wheat is more than human tares, and proceed to organize human values on that basis.

Mark Twain

Francis P. Church to Virginia O'Hanlon

To this day it remains one of the most famous editorial replies ever featured in a major newspaper. And it all started when a little girl, looking for a direct answer to an age-old question, sent the following letter to the New York Sun.

New York, Sept. 21, 1897.

Dear Editor: I am 8 years old.
Some of my little friends say there is no Santa Claus.
Papa says "If you see it in The Sun, it's so."
Please tell me the truth: is there a Santa Claus?

Virginia O'Hanlon

115 West Ninety-Fifth Street

The paper's editor, Francis Pharcellus Church, had three choices: tell Virginia the truth, lie, or simply not print her letter at all. Ultimately, he printed her query and responded with the following.

Virginia, your little friends are wrong. They have been affected by the skepticism of a skeptical age. They do not believe except they see. They think that nothing can be which is not comprehensible by their little minds. All minds, Virginia, whether they be men's or children's, are little. In this great universe of ours man is a mere insect, an ant, in his intellect, as compared with the boundless world about him, as measured by the intelligence capable of grasping the whole of truth and knowledge.

Yes, Virginia, there is a Santa Claus. He exists as certainly as love and generosity and devotion exist, and you know that they abound and give to your life its highest beauty and joy. Alas! how dreary would be the world if there were no Santa Claus. It would be as dreary as if there were no Virginias. There would be no childlike faith then, no poetry, no romance to make tolerable this existence. We should have no enjoyment, except in sense and sight. The eternal light with which childhood fills this world would be extinguished.

Not believe in Santa Claus! You might as well not believe in fairies! You might get your papa to hire men to watch in all the chimneys on Christmas Eve to catch Santa Claus, but even if they did not see Santa Claus coming down, what would that prove? Nobody sees Santa Claus, but that is no sign that there is no Santa Claus. The most real things in the world are those that neither children nor men can see. Did you ever see fairies dancing on the lawn? Of course not, but that's no proof that they are not there. Nobody can conceive or imagine all the wonders there are unseen and unseeable in the world.

You may tear apart the baby's rattle and see what makes the noise inside, but there is a veil covering the unseen world which not the strongest man, nor even the united strength of all the strongest men that ever lived, could tear apart. Only faith, fancy, poetry, love, romance, can push aside that curtain and view and picture the supernal beauty and glory beyond. Is it all real? Ah, Virginia, in all this world there is nothing else real and abiding.

No Santa Claus! Thank God! he lives, and he lives forever. A thousand years from now, Virginia, nay, ten times ten thousand years from now, he will continue to make glad the heart of childhood.

Rabbi Stephen Wise to His Wife Louise

A passionate spokesman for a wide range of social causes, from women's suffrage to the labor movement to child welfare, Rabbi Stephen Wise believed deeply in equal rights for all and the inherent goodness of humanity. His commitment to abolishing injustice and fostering peace frequently took him throughout the United States and, at times, overseas. When he traveled he kept in constant touch with his wife, Louise, and children, James and Justine, through a steady stream of letters. Writing from Portland, Oregon, in 1902, Rabbi Wise describes to his wife a sermon he had given on faith, justice, and mercy earlier that day.

I know not where to begin nor when I shall end this letter, wishing as I do to tell you everything. But to begin with that which brightened and gladdened the day, what a delight it was to have James' telegram this morning at seven just as I sat down to my desk for an hour's work. To hear those words, "Dear Father". Tears and smiles succeeded each other very quickly. After a hurried breakfast, I returned to my room and there on the desk were your beautiful gifts, each precious because of the love of the giver. The old flood-tablet is mounted superbly, my dear old father's picture is just what I wished to have on my table all the time. The two *Books of the Twelve Prophets* are fine. Think of it; I turned at once to see what George Adam Smith thought of the Creed of Micah and I found his words so striking that, late as it was, I incorporated them into my address. "These beautiful words, the greatest saying of the Old Testament, express an ideal of religion to which no subsequent century has ever been able to add either grandeur or tenderness." Could any gift have been more timely? When I quoted them, it was as though you were speaking through my lips as I always wish you to do.

The day was perfect. I cannot tell you *how* I spoke but I will tell you what I said. I began by saying that as mariners sailing out upon the sea of the unknown future, we should provide ourselves with chart and compass and remember that from time to time we must look up to the stars. Such a chart I thought could be found in a simple setting of the fundamentals of the Jewish religion. The creed of Israel was not the collection of dogma by Maimonides or by Albo, nor yet the "Shema." A Rabbi had said that the 613 laws of the Pentatuch could be reduced to the eleven of the 15th Psalm, and reduced finally after several gradations to Micah's three, "To do justice, to love mercy and to walk humbly with thy God". Briefly I touched upon Micah's contribution to Jewish religious thought in that he had shown a simplicity and catholicity of faith, had laid broad and deep and enduring the ethical foundations of the Jewish Church and finally had supplemented the mighty Don't of the Prophets with the Do of the great constructive reformer and teacher.

Then I passed on to my theme paper. Justice must be done between man and man, nation and nation. Then I spoke of Emile Zola, mightiest of the modern champions of justice and truth, shut out from the company of the Academy's immortals, but immortal indeed by the side of these pigmy mortals. At this part of my address the people were thoroughly roused—I could feel—I spoke from out the fullness of my heart.

I spoke next of Rumanian injustice to the Jews and of the glorious attempt of Hay and Roosevelt to secure justice for these unhappy beings. I pictured the "Jew-drives à la Rabbit-drives" in which the Rumanians indulge, and told of those poor mothers who have thrown themselves into the Danube sooner than to go back to Rumania, when commanded to do so at the frontier. As a final instance of the need of justice, I spoke of the present industrial conflict, demanding justice from master to workman and from workman and master.

"Loving mercy" I explained by showing that justice would not suffice. Justice and righteousness are not enough for the world; these must be supplemented and crowned by mercy and compassion and love. Herein, Micah had anticipated Jesus' "A new commandment I give unto you" etc.

This skeletonized version of my sermon is not so bare but that it will bore you. Finally, "Walk humbly before God" was commanded anew in Kipling's "Lest We Forget". I pointed out the dangers besetting a nation grown suddenly great and rich: "Let us not strive to make ours an imperial nation, but a nation whose citizens are imperial men. A man without a country is not as tragic a spectacle as a country without a man, without men—doers of justice, lovers of mercy and walking humbly before God". This was to be our chart as we fared forth upon the seas of the future.

Eugene V. Debs to Clara Spalding Ellis

Throughout the early 1900s Eugene V. Debs was a presidential candidate who fought for many of the most debated reform movements of the Progressive Era—compensation for unemployed workers, a graduated income tax, civil rights for minorities, pensions for retirees, and similar issues that stressed workers' rights and social equality. Debs ran for president in every election from 1900 to 1920 except one (1916), and although his campaigns faired poorly, they educated millions of Americans about issues often ignored by other politicians. Clara Spalding Ellis, a journalist working on a book entitled What's Next? or, Shall a Man Live Again, *wrote to Debs and asked him if he believed in immortality. Debs replied with the following.*

Terre Haute, Ind. Feb. 6th 1904

Mrs Clara Spalding Ellis
Montclair N.J.
Dear Mrs Ellis:

Your communication was received during my absence from the city. The question you ask is a large and serious one and it is doubtful if in the hurry of the moment I can make myself intelligible to yourself and readers. I am so busy with the affairs of this life, so much concerned with the wrongs that exist here, with the suffering that prevails now, and so profoundly impressed with the sense of duty I owe myself and my fellowman here and now that I have but little time to think of what lies beyond the grave; and but for the earnestness and anxiety so apparent in your letter, I should feel obliged to decline the attempt to answer a question which at best must still remain unanswered.

The most scientific minds have thus far failed to demonstrate the immortality of human life and yet the normal human being, the wide world over, be he learned or ignorant, wise or foolish, good or evil, longs for, yearns for, hungers and hopes for, if he does not actually believe in life everlasting, and this seems to me to present the strongest proof that immortality is a fact in nature.

There are many truths that are not demonstrable to the ordinary sense and yet they are so obvious and self-evident that it were folly to attempt to deny or contradict them.

Coming more directly to your question, as to whether I, my personal, identical, conscious self, shall continue to live after my body goes back to dust, I confess I do not know, nor do I know of any means of knowing; but as I, in that narrow capacity, am infinitesimally insignificant, it is a question which does not greatly concern me.

I believe firmly, however, in the immortal life of humanity as a whole, and as my little life merges in and becomes an elementary part of that infinitely larger life, I may, and in fact do feel secure in the faith and belief in immortality.

Men are small, but *Man* is tall as God Himself.

The universal life is eternal and will enrich and glorify the world with its divinity after all the planets wheel dead in space.

Yours very truly,
Eugene V. Debs

Edgar Farrar Sr. to Governor Luther E. Hall

On November 1, 1911, in New Orleans, Edgar Farrar Jr. was shot dead in broad daylight by a young burglar named Rene Canton. Farrar was from a prominent family, and the news of his murder caused an immediate sensation. Canton pleaded not guilty, but the evidence was overwhelmingly against him, and on April 15, 1912, he was sentenced to die on December 6 of the same year. Eight days before Canton was to be hanged, a surprising appeal was made on his behalf. Edgar Farrar Sr. wrote the following letter to the governor of Louisiana asking that he be merciful to the man who killed his son.

His Excellency, Luther E. Hall,
Governor of Louisiana,
Baton Rouge, LA.

Dear Sir:

On this day of Thanksgiving, the thoughts of all my household were turned to the chair made empty by the crime of the poor wretch, the date of whose execution you have fixed. This matter has been in our minds for some time, and after mature deliberation, all of us, father, mother, sisters, brothers and widow of my son, have concluded to ask you to reprieve Rene Canton, and to send his case before the Board of Pardons for their consideration as to whether his sentence should not be commuted to imprisonment for life. We feel that this young brute is the product of our system of society, for which all of us, particularly persons of our position, are to some extent responsible. His father and mother are honest, hard working people. With them the struggle for existence was too bitter and exacting to permit them to devote the time and personal care necessary to develop the good and repress the evil in their son, who thus grew up amid the malign influences that surround the children of the poor in a large city. We believe that he shot my son as instinctively as a snake would strike one who crossed his path; and while his act was murder in law and in fact, yet it lacked that forethought and deliberation which make a crime of this sort unpardonable. This man is now in no condition to be sent into the next world. We hope and pray that time and reflection will bring repentance and that his soul may be saved.

Your obedient servant,
Edgar Howard Farrar

On December 28, and with approval from the Board of Pardons, Governor Hall commuted Canton's death sentence to life imprisonment.

Albert Einstein to Phyllis Wright

Educated as a young boy in a Christian school (where he was the only Jew), Albert Einstein fled his native Germany in 1933 when the Nazis came to power. Throughout his life Einstein maintained his identity as a Jew, but his views on Judaism—and religion in general—were complex. "If there is any such concept as a God," Einstein said in an interview, "it is a subtle spirit, not an image of a man. In essence, my religion consists of a humble admiration for this illimitable superior spirit that reveals itself in the slight details that we are able to perceive with our frail and feeble minds." Einstein was often asked to articulate his opinions on faith, especially in relation to science, and one such request came from a sixth-grade student named Phyllis Wright, who asked if scientists pray and, if so, what they pray for. Einstein responded with the following letter.

January 24, 1936

Dear Phyllis,

I have tried to respond to your question as simply as I could. Here is my answer.

Scientific research is based on the idea that everything that takes place is determined by laws of nature, and therefore this holds for the actions of people. For this reason, a research scientist will hardly be inclined to believe that events could be influenced by a prayer, i.e. by a wish addressed to a supernatural Being.

However, it must be admitted that our actual knowledge of these laws is only imperfect and fragmentary, so that, actually, the belief in the existence of basic all-embracing laws in Nature also rests on a sort of faith. All the same this faith has been largely justified so far by the success of scientific research.

But, on the other hand, every one who is seriously involved in the pursuit of science becomes convinced that a spirit is manifest in the laws of the Universe—a spirit vastly superior to that of man, and one in the face of which we with our modest powers must feel humble. In this way the pursuit of science leads to a religious feeling of a special sort, which is indeed quite different from the religiosity of someone more naive.

I hope this answers your question.

Best wishes,
Yours
Albert Einstein

Dorothy Day's "Letter to the Unemployed"

Covering the National Hunger March on Washington, D.C., in December 1932, a young journalist named Dorothy Day was dismayed that only Communists seemed to be on the side of workers and the oppressed. Although she had associated herself with Communists, socialists, and anarchists earlier in her life, she renounced these beliefs and converted to Catholicism in 1927. Six years later she published the first issue of The Catholic Worker, *which asked rhetorically, "Is it not possible to be radical and not atheist?" The newspaper not only served as a voice for the poor and oppressed but promoted "Houses of Hospitality" throughout the country that offered meals to the hungry and the homeless. In the following "Letter to the Unemployed," from the December 1937 edition of* The Catholic Worker, *Day implores the poor and unemployed to maintain their sense of hope no matter how desperate their situation becomes.*

For two and a half months I have been traveling through the country, visiting Detroit, Cleveland, Chicago, Los Angeles, San Francisco, New Orleans, and stopping off at country places in between. And everywhere I have been meeting the unemployed—around the steel mills, the employment agencies, the waterfronts, around the "skid rows" and Boweries of this country, out in the rural districts where the sharecroppers and tenant farmers face lean months of hunger.

Now I am back on Mott street, and as I get up at six-thirty there you are, a long line of hungry men extended all the way to Canal Street, waiting for the coffee and apple butter sandwiches we have to offer.

I remember how hard it was last Christmas to face you men. How could one say "Merry Christmas" to you who are gaunt and cold and ragged? Even the radio with its recipes and offerings of clothes on the installment plan, interspersed with music, did little to brighten things.

It is hard to preach the Gospel to men with empty stomachs, Abbé Lugan said. We are not a mission. We turn off the melancholy religious offerings on the radio in the morning. Religion is joy in the Holy Spirit. "Religion is a fire; it is like the coming of the Paraclete, 'a mighty wind rising'; it is a passion, the most powerful passion known to man. For religion is 'mighty to God unto the pulling down of fortifications.' Religion is a battle," writes Father Gillis.

Because it is a battle, and because you are not weaklings, we fight our own inclinations to feed only bodies to the small extent we can and let this editorial go. But it is a battle to hang on to religion when discouragement sets in. It is a battle to remember that we are made in the image and likeness of God when employers, treating you with less consideration than animals, turn you indifferently away. It is a fierce battle to maintain one's pride and dignity, to remember that we are brothers of Christ, who ennobled our human nature by sharing it.

But that very thought should give courage and should bring hope.

Christ, the Son of Man, lived among us for thirty-three years. For many of those years He lived in obscurity. When He was a baby His foster father had to flee with Him into Egypt. Joseph was a carpenter, a common laborer, and probably had no more savings than the majority of workers. When he tramped the long weary road, in the heat and dust of deserts, he, too, and Mary and the Child were doubtless hungry. Do any of those hitchhikers, fleeing from the dust bowl into southern California across mountain and desert, remember, as they suffer, the flight into Egypt?

George Putnam, who has charge of our Los Angeles house, told me of picking up a man in the desert so starved that for the remaining days of the trip he could hold neither food nor water. Occasionally they had to stop the car and let him lie out on the ground to still the convulsive agony of his stomach. While I was in Los Angeles a young couple came to our place carrying a month-old baby and leading another eighteen months old. Some kindly worker had given them a lift on the last lap of their journey and turned his room over to them since he worked nights and could sleep days. That traveler, the father of the two little ones, was also a carpenter. Did anyone see Joseph in this unemployed man? Did they see the Holy Family, epitomized in this little group? Did they see Christ in the worker who helped them?

Christ was a worker and in the three years He roamed through Palestine He had no place to lay His head. But He said, "Take no thought for what ye shall eat and where ye shall sleep, or what ye shall put on. Seek ye first the Kingdom of God and His righteousness and all these things shall be added unto you. . . . For your Heavenly Father knoweth that you have need of these things."

For one year now, our coffee line has been going on. Right now we are making seventy-five gallons of coffee every morning. There are too many of you for us, who wait on the line, to talk to you. We must think of the other fellow waiting out in the cold, as you remember, for you are very prompt in finishing your breakfast and making way for them. It is a grim and desperate struggle to keep the line going in more ways than one.

It is hard, I repeat, to talk to you of religion. But without faith in each other, we cannot go on. Without hope we cannot go on. Without hope we cannot live. To those who are without hope, I remind you of Christ, your brother. Religion, thought in terms of our brotherhood through Christ, is not the opiate of the people. It is a battle "mighty to God unto the pulling down of fortifications." Do not let either capitalist or Communist kill this noble instinct in you.

Lester B. Granger to Sylvan Gotshal

When Lester B. Granger of the National Urban League—an organization "dedicated to securing equal opportunities for African Americans"—became aware of the persecutions against the Jews in Nazi Germany, he organized an informal collection to donate to the United Jewish Appeal. Granger then sent the contribution along with the following letter to the UJA's president, Sylvan Gotshal.

September, 1943

Dear Mr. Gotshal:

With this letter I am presenting to you checks in the total amount of $755.00 as a contribution from a committee of 77 Negro Americans to the United Jewish Appeal. Our committee has no formal title, neither is this contribution the result of any special campaign. Many of those sharing in this effort have contributed before and will contribute again to the cause of suffering Jewry overseas. We wish, however, to make this special expression of the deep sympathy felt by members of our race for a people whose extremity of anguish is unmatched in the history of modern civilization.

Daily we read with growing horror of the ruthless savagery unleashed against helpless Jews in Nazi-occupied Europe. We who have known deprivation and suffering in our native land, America, stand aghast at the maniacal fury and bestial atrocities practiced against the Jewish people by Hitler and his foul associates. Those crimes of Nazi leadership constitute one further reason why Negroes must remain wholeheartedly committed to this war until the last vestige of Nazism is driven from the earth.

Negroes share a tremendous debt which the world owes to the descendants of Israel—for your scholars and soldiers, scientists and judges, teachers and workers have enriched the living of every nation on the globe. But as Negroes we owe a special debt to those Jews of great spirit who have through the years brought such important material and moral support to the cause of Negro advancement and inter-racial understanding.

The contribution which our committee makes to the United Jewish Appeal is not so much an acknowledgment of that debt as it is a reaffirmation of our conviction that we are under one God, one people united in one cause. May this small gift stand as an additional testimonial to the bond of friendship that must grow between two peoples with a glorious history, and a still more glorious future.

Sincerely yours,
Lester B. Granger

Flannery O'Connor to Alfred Corn

After listening to a talk given at the University of Atlanta by Flannery O'Connor, a freshman named Alfred Corn felt impelled to write to the famous author and explain to her that he was experiencing a crisis of faith. O'Connor, a staunch Catholic, sent the young man the following letter. (Robert Bridges and Gerard Manley Hopkins, both mentioned in the letter, were prominent British poets. Hopkins was of particular interest to O'Connor because he was a Jesuit priest who incorporated religious themes in his poetry.)

Milledgeville
30 May 62

Dear Mr. Corn,

I think that this experience you are having of losing your faith, or as you think, of having lost it, is an experience that in the long run belongs to faith; or at least it can belong to faith if faith is still valuable to you, and it must be or you would not have written me about this.

I don't know how the kind of faith required of a Christian living in the 20th century can be at all if it is not grounded on this experience that you are having right now of unbelief. This may be the case always and not just in the 20th century. Peter said, "Lord, I believe. Help my unbelief." It is the most natural and most human and most agonizing prayer in the gospels, and I think it is the foundation prayer of faith.

As a freshman in college you are bombarded with new ideas, or rather pieces of ideas, new frames of reference, an activation of the intellectual life which is only beginning, but which is already running ahead of your lived experience. After a year of this, you think you cannot believe. You are just beginning to realize how difficult it is to have faith and the measure of a commitment to it, but you are too young to decide you don't have faith just because you feel you can't believe. About the only way we know whether we believe or not is by what we do, and I think from your letter that you will not take the path of least resistance in this matter and simply decide that you have lost your faith and that there is nothing you can do about it.

One result of the stimulation of your intellectual life that takes place in college is usually a shrinking of the imaginative life. This sounds like a paradox, but I have often found it to be true. Students get so bound up with difficulties such as reconciling the clashing of so many different faiths such as Buddhism, Mohammedanism, etc., that they cease to look for God in other ways. Bridges once wrote Gerard Manley Hopkins and asked him to tell him how he, Bridges, could believe. Bridges was an agnostic. He must have expected from Hopkins a long philosophical answer. Hopkins wrote back, "Give alms." He was trying to say to Bridges that God is to be experienced in Charity (in the sense of love for the divine image in human beings). Don't get so entangled with intellectual difficulties that you fail to look for God in this way.

The intellectual difficulties have to be met, however, and you will be meeting them for the rest of your life. When you get a reasonable hold on one, another will come to take its place. At one time, the clash of the different world religions was a difficulty for me. Where you have absolute solutions, however, you have no need of faith. Faith is what you have in the absence of knowledge. The reason this clash doesn't bother me any longer is because I have got, over the years, a sense of the immense sweep of creation, of the evolutionary process in everything, of how incomprehensible God must necessarily be to be the God of heaven and earth. You can't fit the Almighty into your intellectual categories. I might suggest that you look into some of the works of Pierre Teilhard de Chardin (*The Phenomenom of Man* et al.). He was a paleontologist—helped to discover Peking man—and also a man of God. I don't suggest you go to him for answers but for different questions, for that stretching of the imagination that you need to make you a sceptic in the face of much that you are learning, much of which is new and shocking but which when boiled down becomes less so and takes its place in the general scheme of things. What kept me a sceptic in college was precisely my Christian faith. It always said: wait, don't bite on this, get a wider picture, continue to read.

If you want your faith, you have to work for it. It is a gift, but for very few is it a gift given without any demand for equal time devoted to its cultivation. For every book you read that is anti-Christian, make it your business to read one that presents the other side of the picture; if one isn't satisfactory read others. Don't think that you have to abandon reason to be a Christian. A book that might help you is *The Unity of Philosophical Experience* by Etienne Gilson. Another is Newman's *The Grammar of Assent*. To find out about faith, you have to go to the people who have it and you have to go to the most intelligent ones if you are going to stand up intellectually to agnostics and the general run of pagans that you are going to find in the majority of people around you. Much of the criticism of belief that you find today comes from people who are judging it from the standpoint of another and narrower discipline. The Biblical criticism of the 19th century, for instance, was the product of historical disciplines. It has been entirely revamped in the 20th century by applying broader criteria to it, and those people who lost their faith in the 19th century because of it, could better have hung on in blind trust.

Even in the life of a Christian, faith rises and falls like the tides of an invisible sea. It's there, even when he can't see it or feel it, if he wants it to be there. You realize, I think, that it is more valuable, more mysterious, altogether more immense than anything you can learn or decide upon in college. Learn what you can, but cultivate

Christian scepticism. It will keep you free—not free to do anything you please, but free to be formed by something larger than your own intellect or the intellects of those around you.

I don't know if this is the kind of answer that can help you, but any time you care to write me, I can try to do better.

Yours,
Flannery O'Connor

Corn did write back and pursued the issue of faith's being incompatible with reason, which he did not want to give up. O'Connor emphasized he did not have to; "Satisfy your demand for reason always," she wrote, "but remember that charity is beyond reason, and that God can be known through charity." Corn, who is now an accomplished poet, eventually did regain his faith.

William Lederer to Admiral David McDonald

The Ugly American, *published in 1958 by William Lederer and Eugene Burdick, is a fictionalized account of the two men's experiences working in Southeast Asia. Although the book focuses primarily on the deficiencies of America's foreign aid program at the time, it is memorable for its accounts of Americans acting in a boorish and insensitive manner toward the citizens of their host country. While traveling in France almost four years later, however, Lederer witnessed an incident involving an American sailor that touched him so deeply he sent the following letter to the chief of naval operations in Washington, D.C.*

Admiral David L. McDonald, USN
Chief of Naval Operations
Washington, D.C.

Dear Admiral McDonald,

Eighteen people asked me to write this letter to you.

Last year at Christmas time, my wife, three boys and I were in

France, on our way from Paris to Nice. For five wretched days everything had gone wrong. Our hotels were "tourist traps," our rented car broke down; we were all restless and irritable in the crowded car. On Christmas Eve, when we checked into our hotel in Nice, there was no Christmas spirit in our hearts.

It was raining and cold when we went out to eat. We found a drab little restaurant shoddily decorated for the holiday. Only five tables were occupied. There were two German couples, two French families, and an American sailor, by himself. In the corner a piano player listlessly played Christmas music.

I was too tired and miserable to leave. I noticed that the other customers were eating in stony silence. The only person who seemed happy was the American sailor. While eating, he was writing a letter, and a half-smile lighted his face.

My wife ordered our meal in French. The waiter brought us the wrong thing. I scolded my wife for being stupid. The boys defended her, and I felt even worse.

Then, at the table with the French family on our left, the father slapped one of his children for some minor infraction, and the boy began to cry.

On our right, the German wife began berating her husband.

All of us were interrupted by an unpleasant blast of cold air. Through the front door came an old flower woman. She wore a dripping, tattered overcoat, and shuffled in on wet, rundown shoes. She went from one table to the other.

"Flowers, *monsieur*? Only one *franc*."

No one bought any.

Wearily she sat down at a table between the sailor and us. To the waiter she said, "A bowl of soup. I haven't sold a flower all afternoon." To the piano player she said hoarsely, "Can you imagine, Joseph, soup on Christmas Eve?"

He pointed to his empty "tipping plate."

The young sailor finished his meal and got up to leave. Putting on his coat, he walked over to the flower woman's table.

"Happy Christmas," he said, smiling and picking out two corsages. "How much are they?"

"Two *francs*, *monsieur*."

Pressing one of the small corsages flat, he put it into the letter he had written, then handed the woman a 20-*franc* note.

"I don't have change, *monsieur*," she said. "I'll get some from the waiter."

"No, ma'am," said the sailor, leaning over and kissing the ancient cheek. "This is my Christmas present to you."

Then he came to our table, holding the other corsage in front of him. "Sir," he said to me, "may I have permission to present these flowers to your beautiful daughter?"

In one quick motion he gave my wife the corsage, wished us a Merry Christmas and departed.

Everyone had stopped eating. Everyone had been watching the sailor. Everyone was silent.

A few seconds later Christmas exploded throughout the restaurant like a bomb.

The old flower woman jumped up, waving the 20-*franc* note, shouted to the piano player, "Joseph, my Christmas present! And you shall have half so you can have a feast too."

The piano player began to belt out *Good King Wencelaus*, beating the keys with magic hands.

My wife waved her corsage in time to the music. She appeared 20 years younger. She began to sing, and our three sons joined her, bellowing with enthusiasm.

"*Gut! Gut!*" shouted the Germans. They began singing in German.

The waiter embraced the flower woman. Waving their arms, they sang in French.

The Frenchman who had slapped the boy beat rhythm with his fork against a bottle. The lad climbed on his lap, singing in a youthful soprano.

A few hours earlier 18 persons had been spending a miserable evening. It ended up being the happiest, the very best Christmas Eve, they had ever experienced.

This, Admiral McDonald, is what I am writing you about. As the top man in the Navy, you should know about the very special gift that the U.S. Navy gave to my family, to me and to the other people in that French restaurant. Because your young sailor had Christmas spirit in his soul, he released the love and joy that had been smothered within us by anger and disappointment. He gave us Christmas.

Thank you, Sir, very much.

Merry Christmas,
Bill Lederer

Thomas Merton to Chris McNair

On September 15, 1963, a bomb exploded in the Sixteenth Street Baptist Church in Birmingham, Alabama, killing four black children attending Sunday school. Thomas Merton, a Trappist monk and renowned poet who wrote passionately about civil rights and other social issues, was profoundly affected by the event. Look *magazine later published photographs of the young victims before the bombing, and Merton clipped out one photograph in particular, placed it in his journal, and captioned it: "Carole Denise McNair, one of the four bomb-murdered Negro children, never learned to hate." Merton then sent the following letter—along with a poem he wrote, "Picture of a Black Child with a White Doll"—to the girl's father, Chris McNair.*

October 12, 1964

This is not exactly an easy letter to write. There is so much to say, and there are no words in which to say it. I will say it as simply as I can, in the hope that you will understand this message from a total stranger. I saw the pictures you took of Carole Denise in *Look* several months ago. One of them meant so much to me that I cut it out, and kept it. It seemed to say so much, principally about goodness, and about the way in which the goodness of the human heart is invincible, and overcomes the evil and wickedness that may sometimes be present in other men.

Being a writer, and a writer of poems, I eventually was moved to write a poem, and now that it has been published I want to send you at least this copy of it. It is a somewhat angry poem, because I think that a little anger is still called for. I hope that love and compassion also come through, for anger is not enough and never will be.

At any rate, I wanted to say what you already know and believe: that the mercy and goodness of the Lord chose Carole Denise to be with Him forever in His love and His light. Nor is she forgotten on the earth. She remains as a witness to innocence and to love, and an inspiration to all of us who remain to face the labor, the difficulty and the heart-break of the struggle for human rights and dignity.

Malcolm X to His Followers

At the age of four Malcolm Little and his family barely escaped a fire—set by two white men—that destroyed his parents' house. Malcolm Little's bitterness toward whites grew, and in 1948 he became convinced that "all whites were devils." Soon after, he learned of the Honorable Elijah Muhammad, leader of the Nation of Islam, and was inspired enough by the leader's antiwhite views to join the Nation in 1951. Malcolm Little eventually became Malcolm X and, in the mid-1950s and early 1960s, used his powerful oratorical skills to spread the Nation of Islam's message and recruit more converts. But in 1963 and 1964 he began to have serious doubts about the Nation of Islam, its leader, and whether all white people were truly evil. Ultimately, a pilgrimage to Mecca, described in the following letter to his followers in Harlem, marked a fundamental turning point in his thoughts on whites and interracial harmony. The letter is printed in its entirety as it appears in The Autobiography of Malcolm X.

Never have I witnessed such sincere hospitality and the overwhelming spirit of true brotherhood as is practiced by people of all colors and races here in this Ancient Holy Land, the home of

Abraham, Muhammad, and all the other prophets of the Holy Scriptures. For the past week, I have been utterly speechless and spellbound by the graciousness I see displayed all around me by people of all colors.

I have been blessed to visit the Holy City of Mecca. I have made my seven circuits around the Ka'ba, led by a young *Mutawaf* named Muhammad. I drank water from the well of Zem Zem. I ran seven times back and forth between the hills of Mt. Al-Safa and Al-Marwah. I have prayed in the ancient city of Mina, and I have prayed on Mt. Arafat.

There were tens of thousands of pilgrims, from all over the world. They were of all colors, from blue-eyed blonds to black-skinned Africans. But we were all participating in the same ritual, displaying a spirit of unity and brotherhood that my experiences in America had led me to believe never could exist between the white and the non-white.

America needs to understand Islam, because this is the one religion that erases from its society the race problem. Throughout my travels in the Muslim world, I have met, talked to, and even eaten with people who in America would have been considered "white"—but the "white" attitude was removed from their minds by the religion of Islam. I have never before seen *sincere* and *true* brotherhood practiced by all colors together, irrespective of their color.

You may be shocked by these words coming from me. But on this pilgrimage, what I have seen, and experienced, has forced me to *re-arrange* much of my thought-patterns previously held, and to *toss aside* some of my previous conclusions. This was not too difficult for me. Despite my firm convictions, I have been always a man who tries to face facts, and to accept the reality of life as new experience and new knowledge unfolds it. I have always kept an open mind, with every form of intelligent search for truth.

During the past eleven days here in the Muslim world, I have eaten from the same plate, drunk from the same glass, and slept in the same bed (or on the same rug)—while praying to the *same God*—with fellow Muslims, whose eyes were the bluest of blue, whose hair was the blondest of blond, and whose skin was the whitest of white. And in the *words* and in the *actions* and in the *deeds* of the "white" Muslims, I felt the same sincerity that I felt among the black African Muslims of Nigeria, Sudan, and Ghana.

We were *truly* all the same (brothers)—because their belief in one God had removed the "white" from their *minds*, the "white" from their *behavior*, and the "white" from their *attitude*.

I could see from this, that perhaps if white Americans could accept the Oneness of God, then perhaps, too, they could accept in *reality* the Oneness of Man—and cease to measure, and hinder, and harm others in terms of their "differences" in color.

With racism plaguing America like an incurable cancer, the so-called "Christian" white American should be more receptive to a proven solution to such a destructive problem. Perhaps it could be in time to save America from imminent disaster—the same destruction brought upon Germany by racism that eventually destroyed the Germans themselves.

Each hour here in the Holy Land enables me to have greater spiritual insights into what is happening in America between black and white. The American Negro never can be blamed for his racial animosities—he is only reacting to four hundred years of conscious racism of the American whites. But as racism leads America up the suicide path, I do believe, from the experiences I have had with them, that the whites of the younger generation, the colleges and universities, will see the handwriting on the wall and many of them will turn to the *spiritual* path of *truth*—the *only* way left to America to ward off the disaster that racism inevitably must lead to.

Never have I been so highly honored. Never have I been made to feel more humble and unworthy. Who would believe the blessings that have been heaped upon an *American Negro*? A few nights ago, a man who would be called in America a "white" man, a United Nations diplomat, ambassador, a companion of kings, gave me *his* hotel suite, *his* bed. By this man, His Excellency Prince Faisal, who rules this Holy Land, was made aware of my presence here in Jedda. The very next morning, Prince Faisal's son, in person, informed me that by the will and decree of his esteemed father, I was to be a State Guest.

The Deputy Chief of Protocol himself took me before the Hajj Court. His Holiness Sheikh Muhammad Harkon himself okayed my visit to Mecca. His Holiness gave me two books on Islam, with his personal seal and autograph, and he told me that he prayed that I would be a successful preacher of Islam in America. A car, a driver, and a guide, have been placed at my disposal, making it possible for me to travel about this Holy Land almost at will. The government provides air-conditioned quarters and servants in each city that I visit. Never would I have even thought of dreaming that I would ever be a recipient of such honors—honors that in America would be bestowed upon a King—not a Negro.

All praise is due to Allah, the Lord of all the Worlds.

Sincerely,
El-Hajj Malik El-Shabazz
(Malcolm X)

Malcolm X's newfound views on whites—along with his public criticisms of the Hon. Elijah Muhammad—cost him his life. On February 21, 1965, while speaking at the Audubon Ballroom in Harlem, he was gunned down by three men believed to be members of the Nation of Islam.

Marion Lee Kempner to His Great-Aunt

Marion Lee ("Sandy") Kempner, a former Peace Corps volunteer from Galveston, Texas, was sent to Vietnam in July 1966 to serve with the marines. Writing to his great-aunt Mrs. Louis "Fannie" Adoue on October 20, 1966, Kempner addresses the subject of immortality after a seemingly trivial incident.

Dear Aunt Fannie,

This morning, my platoon and I were finishing up a three-day patrol. Struggling over steep hills covered with hedgerows, trees, and generally impenetrable jungle, one of my men turned to me and pointed a hand, filled with cuts and scratches, at a rather distinguished-looking plant with soft red flowers waving gaily in the downpour (which had been going on ever since the patrol began) and said, "That is the first plant I have seen today which didn't have thorns on it." I immediately thought of you.

The plant, and the hill upon which it grew, was also representative of Vietnam. It is a country of thorns and cuts, of guns and marauding, of little hope and of great failure. Yet in the midst of it all, a beautiful thought, gesture, and even person can arise among it waving bravely at the death that pours down upon it. Some day this hill will be burned by napalm, and the red flower will crackle up and die among the thorns. So what was the use of it living and being a beauty among the beasts, if it must, in the end, die because of them, and with them? This is a question which is answered by Gertrude Stein's "A rose is a rose is a rose." You are what you are what you are. Whether you believe in God, fate, or the crumbling cookie, elements are so mixed in a being that make him what he is; his salvation from the thorns around him lies in the fact that he existed at all, in his very own personality. There once was a time when the Jewish idea of heaven and hell was the thoughts and opinions people had of you after you died. But what if the plant was on an isolated hill and was never seen by anyone? That is like the question of whether the falling tree makes a sound in the forest primeval when no one is there to hear it. It makes a sound, and the plant was beautiful and the thought was kind, and the person was humane, and distinguished and brave, not merely because other people recognized it as such, but because it is, and it is, and it is.

The flower will always live in the memory of a tired, wet Marine, and thus has achieved a sort of immortality. But even if we had never gone on that hill, it would still be a distinguished, soft, red, thornless flower growing among the cutting, scratching plants, and that in itself is its own reward.

Love,
Sandy

Less than three weeks after writing this letter, Sandy Kempner was disarming a mine near Tien Phu when one of his men accidentally tripped another mine. Kempner, though seriously injured by the explosion, ordered that the other wounded man be treated first. Kempner was finally placed in a medevac to be taken to the hospital, but he died en route. He was twenty-four years old.

Norman Mailer to Salman Rushdie

Two month after the publication of Salman Rushdie's The Satanic Verses *in December 1988, the Ayatollah Khomeini of Iran declared the book an offense to Islam and issued a* fatwa *that Rushdie must be killed. "Anyone who dies in the cause of ridding the world of Rushdie," the ayatollah declared, "will be a martyr and will go directly to heaven." Rushdie, who was born in India but lived in England, was immediately placed under the protection of armed guards by the British government. The threat was genuine; bookstores that sold* The Satanic Verses *were firebombed, riots ensued in areas where it was believed Rushdie was visiting, and two of the book's translators were stabbed—one fatally—by Muslim extremists. In the midst of it all, many prominent writers sent Rushdie letters of support and encouragement, including the following by the Pulitzer Prize–winning author Norman Mailer.*

Dear Salman Rushdie,

I have thought of you often over the last few years. Many of us begin writing with the inner temerity that if we keep searching for the most dangerous of our voices, why then, sooner or later we will outrage something fundamental in the world, and our lives will be in danger. That is what I thought when I started out, and so have many others, but you, however, are the only one of us who gave proof that this intimation was not ungrounded. Now you live in what must be a living prison of contained paranoia, and the toughening of the will is imperative, no matter the cost to the poetry in yourself. It is no happy position for a serious and talented writer to become a living martyr. One does not need that. It is hard enough to write at one's best without bearing a hundred pounds on one's back each day, but such is your condition, and if I were a man who believed that prayer was productive of results, I might wish to send some sort of vigour and encouragement to you, for if you can transcend this situation, more difficult than any of us have known, if you can come up with a major piece of literary work, then you will rejuvenate all of us, and literature, to that degree, will flower.

So, my best to you, old man, wherever you are ensconced, and may the muses embrace you.

Cheers,
Norman Mailer

Luis J. Rodriguez to the Young Men of the Illinois Youth Center

"This is the world we are enmeshed in," Luis J. Rodriguez once wrote to a friend, "but a world we are endeavoring to transform, even at a great sacrifice." Rodriguez, 42, had just learned that three of his son's friends had been shot at in a gang-related attack. Rodriguez was raised in the barrios of Los Angeles and is familiar with the ways of the streets; he had joined a gang as a teenager and spent time in and out of county jails. Now, as an accomplished writer, he teaches poetry and youth enpowerment classes on a volunteer basis in correctional facilities. The following letter was written to a small group of young men he knew who were incarcerated in the Illinois Youth Center.

May 5, 1995

To the Young Men of I.Y.C.–Joliet:

Cinco de Mayo is a special day—a day of triumph for the people of Mexico, and all the Americas, against foreign intervention from Europe. It is a day to be proud, to always remember.

I hope all of you can see your value as inheritors of this battle. But just as Zapoteca Indians fought barefoot with bows and arrows, against Europe's mightiest Army (France)—and won!—you must struggle to be warriors again.

A true warrior does not waste energy or time. A true warrior fights with creativity, heart (corazon), thoughts and words (poets are warriors). A warrior is wise, learns all the time, and is prepared to train and develop new warriors—this is true in the free world as it is behind bars.

In this country, we are often taught to think that warriors use only physical weapons. This is mostly romanticism. I have learned to judge men not by how many people they can hurt by such weapons (which, as you know, requires no courage or strength). I have learned to judge men by how they strategize, by how they maintain their integrity and vision in the face of fire.

I want to convey these thoughts to you as you celebrate this day. You have before you a lifetime of struggle—every step will require all your innate powers as human beings. Prepare yourself with all the tools you will need to prevail—including language, history, organization, and the arts. I believe in all of you. You hold the key to establishing a future of true justice, peace and equity. I believe you all have the capabilities to become the best warriors, elders, fathers and rulers. The first step is to finally, and decisively, become owners of your life.

En la lucha
Luis J. Rodriguez

Permissions

Grateful acknowledgment is made to the publishers, estates, libraries, individuals, and other copyright owners for permission to reprint and quote from the materials listed below:

Letters from Prague 1939–1941 (Chicago: Academy Chicago Publishers, 1991); From *Dorothy Day: Selected Writings, By Little and By Little* edited by Robert Ellsberg (Maryknoll, N.Y.: Orbis Books, 1992). Copyright © 1983, 1992 by Robert Ellsberg and Tamar Hennessey. Reprinted by permission of Orbis Books; Eugene V. Debs letter courtesy of the Debs Collection, Indiana State University Library; Reprinted by permission of the publishers from *The Letters of Emily Dickinson,* edited by Thomas H. Johnson, Cambridge, Mass.: The Belknap Press of Harvard University Press. Copyright © 1958, 1986 by the President and Fellows of Harvard College; Charles Drew letter reprinted with permission of the Moorland-Springarn Research Center, Founder's Library, Howard University; From *Albert Einstein the Human Side: New Glimpses from His Archives,* edited by Helen Dukas and Banesh Hoffman. Copyright © 1979 by Princeton University Press. Reprinted by permission of Princeton University Press; From *Albert Einstein/Mileva Maric (The Love Letters),* edited by Jurgen Renn and Robert Schulman. Copyright © 1992 by Princeton University Press. Reprinted by permission of Princeton University Press; Dwight D. Eisenhower letter courtesy of and copyright by John S. D. Eisenhower, from his book *Letters to Mamie* (Garden City, N.Y.: Doubleday & Company, 1978); Mary Moody Emerson letter reprinted by permission of the Houghton Library, Harvard University (bMS Am 1280.226 (632)); Guri Endresen letter from *Land of Their Choice: The Immigrants Write Home,* edited by Theodore C. Blegen (Minneapolis: University of Minnesota Press, 1955). Reprinted with permission of the publisher, copyright © 1955 by the University Press of Minnesota; Mary Ewald letter courtesy of and copyright by William and Thomas Ewald; From *Essays, Speeches, and Public Letters* by William Faulkner. Copyright © 1965 by Random House, Inc. Reprinted by permission of Random House, Inc.; Reprinted with permission of Scribner, a Division of Simon & Schuster, from *F. Scott Fitzgerald: A Life in Letters*, edited by Matthew J. Bruccoli. Copyright © 1994 by the Trustees u/a dated 7/3/75 created by Frances Scott Fitzgerald Smith; Joseph Fogg letter courtesy of the United States Holocaust Research Institute Archives, Record Group 09, Liberation, 039: "Joseph G. Fogg letter and obituary"; Ita Ford letter courtesy of and copyright by William Ford and Jennifer Sullivan; Letter to Ed Foreman courtesy of and copyright by the Honorable Ed Foreman; Letter from "George" to "Sis," March 19, 1945, from the Miscellaneous American Letters and Papers, Manuscripts, Archives and Rare Books Division, Schomburg Center for Research in Black Culture, The New York Public Library, Astor, Lenox, and Tilden

Foundations; Lester B. Granger letter courtesy of and copyright by the National Urban League, from *Opportunity Journal,* January–March, 1944, XXII, pp. 18–19; From *The Papers of Ulysses S. Grant*, edited by John Y. Simon, © 1967–1985 by The Ulysses S. Grant Association, published by Southern Illinois University Press. Reprinted by permission of the publisher; Material from *The Letters*, 1813–1843, volume XV of the Centenary Edition of the Works of Nathaniel Hawthorne, is reprinted by permission. Copyright © 1984 by the Ohio State University Press. All rights reserved. From *Ernest Hemingway: Selected Letters 1917–1961,* edited by Carlos Baker (New York: Charles Scribner's Sons, 1981), reprinted by permission of the Ernest Hemingway Foundation & Society. © Hemingway Foreign Rights Trust. All rights outside of U.S., Hemingway Foreign Rights Trust, by a deed of trust of Mary Hemingway, 16 March 1962; Reprinted by permission of the publisher from *Henry James: Selected Letters,* edited by Leon Edel, Cambridge, Mass.: Harvard University Press, Copyright © 1974, 1975, 1980, 1984, 1987: Leon Edel, Editorial, Alexander R. James, James copyrighted material; Helen Keller letter reprinted by permission of the American Foundation for the Blind; Sandy Kempner letter courtesy of Bernard Edelman, editor of *Dear America: Letters Home from Vietnam*, © the New York Vietnam Veterans Memorial Commission; Jack Kerouac letter reprinted by permission of Sterling Lord Literistic, Inc., copyright © the Estate of Stella Kerouac, John Sampas, Literary Representative, 1995; Reprinted by arrangement with The Heirs to the Estate of Martin Luther King Jr., c/o Writers House, Inc. as agent for the proprietor. Copyright © 1963 by Martin Luther King Jr., copyright renewed 1991 by Coretta Scott King; Agnes von Kurowsky letter from *Hemingway in Love and War: The Lost Diary of Agnes von Kurowsky, Her Letters, and Correspondence of Ernest Hemingway,* by Henry Serrano Villard and James Nagel. Copyright 1989 by Henry Serrano Villard and James Nagel. Reprinted with the permission of Northeastern University Press; William Lederer letter courtesy of and copyright by William Lederer; From *The Collected Works of Abraham Lincoln*, Roy P. Basler, ed., copyright © 1953 by the Abraham Lincoln Association. Reprinted by permission of Rutgers University Press; Excerpt from *War Within and Without: Diaries and Letters of Anne Morrow Lindbergh*, 1939–1944, copyright © 1980 by Anne Morrow Lindbergh, reprinted by permission of Harcourt Brace & Company; Reprinted from *The Letters of Jack London*, Three Volumes, edited by Earle Labor, Robert C. Letiz III, and I. Milo Shepard, with the permission of the publishers, Stanford University Press, ©

1988 by the Board of Trustees of the Leland Stanford Junior University; From *The Letters of Archibald Macleish* 1907–1982, edited by R. H. Winnick. Copyright © 1983 by The Estate of Archibald MacLeish and by R. H. Winnick. Reprinted by permission of Houghton Mifflin Company. All rights reserved; Norman Mailer letter reprinted from *The Rushdie Letters: Freedom to Speak, Freedom to Write,* edited by Steve MacDonogh, by permission of the University of Nebraska Press. Compilation © Article 19 and Steve MacDonogh 1993; Reprinted with permission of Simon & Schuster from *The Groucho Letters* by Gourcho Marx. Copyright © 1967 by Groucho Marx; Frithjof Meidell letter from *Land of Their Choice: The Immigrants Write Home,* edited by Theodore C. Blegen (Minneapolis: University of Minnesota Press, 1955). Reprinted with permission of the publisher, copyright © 1955 by the University Press of Minnesota; Reprinted by permission of Louisiana State University Press, from *Selected Letters of Cotton Mather,* compiled and with commentary by Kenneth Silverman, copyright © 1971 by Louisiana State University Press; Reprinted by permission of University of Washington Libraries, from the Iwao Matsushita Papers; From *The Letters of Herman Melville,* edited by Merrell R. Davis and William H. Gilman (New Haven: Yale University Press, 1960). Reprinted with permission of the publisher. Copyright © 1960 Yale University Press, Inc.; Reprinted by permission of Farrar, Straus & Giroux, Inc. from *The Courage for Truth: The Letters of Thomas Merton to Writers* by Thomas Merton, selected and edited by Christine M. Bochen. Copyright © 1993 by The Merton Legacy Trust; and from *Road to Joy: The Letters of Thomas Merton to New and Old Friends* by Thomas Merton, selected and edited by Robert E. Daggy. Copyright © 1989 by The Merton Legacy Trust; "To the League of American Penwomen" (April 18, 1927), letter of Edna St. Vincent Millay. From *Letters of Edna St. Vincent Millay*, Harper & Row. Copyright © 1952, 1980 by Norma Millay Ellis. All rights reserved. Reprinted by permission of Elizabeth Barnett, literary executor; Letter by Henry Miller to Brenda Venus from *Dear, Dear Brenda: The Love Letters of Henry Miller to Brenda Venus*, reprinted by permission of the William Morris Agency, Inc., on behalf of the author. Copyright © 1986 by Brenda Venus and Corwin/Sindell Productions; William Murphy letter courtesy of W. Ronald Thompson and the Deputy Keeper, Public Records Office of Northern Ireland; From *Loving Letters from Ogden Nash* by Nash. Copyright © 1990 by Isabel Nash Eberstadt and Linell Nash Smith. By permission of Little, Brown and Company; Reprinted by permission of Farrar, Straus & Giroux, Inc. from *The Habit of Being* by Flannery

O'Connor, edited by Sally Fitzgerald. Copyright © 1979 by Regina O'Connor; Reprinted with the permission of Simon & Schuster from *Lovingly Georgia: The Complete Correspondence of Georgia O'Keeffe & Anita Pollitzer* by Georgia O'Keeffe, edited by Clive Giboire. Copyright © 1990 by the Estate of Georgia O'Keeffe; Eugene O'Neill letter reprinted by permission of The Harvard Theatre Collection; Maxwell Perkins letter courtesy of and copyright by Bertha S. Frothingham and Louise E. King, from their book *Father to Daughter: The Family Letters of Maxwell Perkins* (Kansas City: Andrews and McMeel, 1995), also edited with Ruth King Porter; From *Letters Home by Sylvia Plath: Correspondence 1950–1963,* by Aurelia Schober Plath. Copyright © 1975 by Aurelia Schober Plath. Reprinted by permission of HarperCollins Publishers, Inc.; From *The Letters of Edgar Allan Poe,* edited by John Ward Ostrom, Cambridge, Mass.: Harvard University Press. Copyright © 1948 by the President and Fellows of Harvard College, 1976 by John Ward Ostrom; From *Letters of Katherine Anne Porter,* edited by Isabel Bayley. Copyright © 1990 by Isabel Bayley. Used by permission of Grove/Atlantic; Willson Price letter courtesy of and copyright by Rose Price; "May 22, 1948, 'Dear Miss Rondeau,' " from *Letters of Ayn Rand* by Ayn Rand, Michael Berliner, editor. Copyright © 1995 by the Estate of Ayn Rand. Introduction Copyright © 1995 by Leonard Peikoff. Used by permission of Dutton Signet, a division of Penguin Books USA Inc.; Ronald Reagan letter courtesy of the Ronald Reagan Library; Paul Revere letter courtesy of the Massachusetts Historical Society; Luis J. Rodriguez letter courtesy of and copyright by Luis J. Rodriguez; Eleanor Roosevelt and Franklin D. Roosevelt letters courtesy of the Franklin D. Roosevelt Library; Theodore Roosevelt letter courtesy of and copyright by Dr. John A. Gable, executive director of the Theodore Roosevelt Association; David Rothenberg letter courtesy of and copyright by David Roth-enberg; Benjamin Rush letters owned by the Library Company of Philadelphia; From *The Letters of Sacco and Vanzetti*, by Marion D. Frankfurter and Gardner Jackson. Copyright 1928, renewed © 1955 by The Viking Press, Inc. Used by permission of Viking Penguin, a division of Penguin Books USA Inc.; George Saito letter gift of Mary S. Tominaga, courtesy of the Japanese American National Museum; Excerpt from *Anne Sexton: A Self-Portrait in Letters,* edited by Linda Gray Sexton and Lois Ames. Copyright © 1977 by Linda Gray Sexton and Loring Conant Jr., executors of the will of Anne Sexton. Reprinted by permission of Houghton Mifflin Co. All rights reserved; Michele Song letter courtesy of and copyright by Michele Song; From *The Sound of*

Mountain Water by Wallace Stegner. Copyright © 1969 by Wallace Stegner. Used by permission of Doubleday, a division of Bantam Doubleday Dell Publishing Group, Inc.; Gertrude Stein letter reprinted courtesy of Calman Levin, © The Estate of Gertrude Stein; From *STEINBECK: A Life in Letters,* by Elaine A. Steinbeck and Robert Wallsten. Copyright 1952 by John Steinbeck, © 1969 by The Estate of John Steinbeck, © 1975 by Elaine A. Steinbeck and Robert Wallsten. Used by permission of Viking Penguin, a division of Penguin Books USA Inc; Ben Washam letter reprinted by permission of Chuck Jones, from *Chuck Amuck: The Life and Times of an Animated Cartoonist* (New York: Farrar, Straus & Giroux, 1989); Allison West letter courtesy of and copyright by Allison West; Reprinted with the permission of Scribner, a Division of Simon & Schuster from *The Letters of Edith Wharton*, edited by R.W.B. Lewis and Nancy Lewis. Copyright © 1988 by R.W.B. Lewis, Nancy Lewis, and William R. Tyler; E. B. White to the ASPCA from "Two Letters, Both Open" from *The Second Tree from the Corner* by E. B. White. Copyright © 1951 by E. B. White. Copyright Renewed. Reprinted by permission of HarperCollins Publishers, Inc.; E. B. White to Mr. Nadeau from *Letters of E. B. White*, Collected and Edited, by Dorothy Lobrano Guth. Copyright © 1976 by E. B. White. Reprinted by permission of HarperCollins Publishers, Inc.; Reprinted by permission of Farrar, Straus & Giroux, Inc. from *Letters on Literature and Politics 1912–1972* by Edmund Wilson, edited by Elena Wilson. Copyright © 1977 by Elena Wilson; From *The Personal Letters of Stephen Wise,* edited by Justine Wise Polier and James Waterman Wise, copyright © 1956 by Justine Wise Polier and James Waterman Wise, reprinted by permission of Beacon Press, Boston; Letter of Frank Lloyd Wright copyright © 1997 by The Frank Lloyd Wright Foundation, Scottsdale, Ariz.; From the *Autobiography of Malcolm X* by Malcolm X with Alex Haley. Copyright © 1964 by Alex Haley and Betty Shabazz. Reprinted by permission of Random House, Inc.

The editor has taken all possible care to trace the ownership of letters in copyright reprinted in this book and to acknowledge their use. If any errors have mistakenly occurred, please contact the publisher so that they can be corrected in subsequent editions.

Additional Sources

Charles Francis Adams, ed., *The Works of John Adams, Second President of the United States* (Boston: Little, Brown, and Company, 1854); Virginia M. Adams, ed., *On the Altar of Freedom: A Black Soldier's Civil War Letters from the Front* (New York: Warner Books, 1991); Malaiko Adero, ed., *Up South: Stories, Studies and Letters of African American Migrations* (New York: The New Press, 1993); Mary Street Alinder and Andrea Gray Stillman, eds., *Ansel Adams: Letters and Images 1916–1984* (Boston: Little, Brown, 1988); Stephen Ambrose, *Undaunted Courage: Meriwether Lewis, Thomas Jefferson, and the Openings of the American West* (New York: Simon & Schuster, 1996); *American Mercury*, July 1940; Herbert Aptheker, ed., *A Documentary History of the Negro People in the United States, Vols. I, II & III* (New York: A Citadel Press Book, 1951); Bernard Asbell, ed., *Mother & Daughter: The Letters of Eleanor and Anna Roosevelt* (New York: Coward, McCann & Geoghegan, 1982); Jerry L. Avord, ed., *Up Against the Ivy Wall: A History of the Columbia Crisis* (New York: Atheneum, 1969); Nina Baym et al., eds., *The Norton Anthology of American Literature*, Fourth Edition (New York: W. W. Norton & Company, 1994); Carl Becker, ed., *The Declaration of Independence: A Study in the History of Political Ideals* (New York: Alfred A. Knopf, 1942); William Bennett, ed., *The Moral Compass: Stories for a Life's Journey* (New York: Simon & Schuster, 1995); Ira Berlin et al., eds., *Free At Last: A Documentary History of Slavery, Freedom, and the Civil War* (New York: The New Press, 1992); Ira Berlin et al., eds., *The Black Military Experience* (New York: The New Press, 1982); John W. Blassingame, ed., *Slave Testimony: Two Centuries of Letters, Speeches, Interviews, and Autobiographies* (Baton Rouge: Louisiana State University Press, 1977); Richard Blow, ed., *Abroad in America: Literary Discoverers of the New World from the Past 500 Years* (New York: Continuum, 1990); John Boettiger letter courtesy of his son John Boettiger; Travis Bogard and Jackson R. Bryer, eds., *Selected Letters of Eugene O'Neill* (New Haven: Yale University Press, 1988); Sarah Bradford, *Harriet Tubman: The Moses of Her People* (Gloucester: Corinth Books, 1981); Edward Burns, ed., *The Letters of Gertrude Stein and Carl Van Vechten 1913–1946, Vol. I 1913–1935* (New York: Columbia University Press, 1986); L. H. Butterfield et al., eds., *The Book of Abigail and John: Selected Letters of the Adams Family 1762–1784* (Cambridge: Harvard University Press, 1975); L. H. Butterfield, ed., *Letters of Benjamin Rush* (Princeton: Princeton University Press, 1951); Hiram

Martin Cittenden and Alfred Talbot Richardson, eds., *Life, Letters and Travels of Father Pierre-Jean De Smet, S. J., 1801–1873* (New York: Francis P. Harper, 1905); Eldridge Cleaver, *Soul on Ice* (New York: A Laurel Book, 1968); Henry Steele Commager and Richard B. Morris, eds., *The Spirit of Seventy Six: The Story of the American Revolution as Told By Participants* (New York: De Capo, 1995); J. Robert Constantine, ed., *Gentle Rebel: Letters of Eugene V. Debs* (Urbana: University of Illinois Press, 1995); Kemper F. Cowing and Courtney Ryley Cooper, eds., *Dear Folks at Home: The Glorious Story of the United States Marines in France as Told by Their Letters from the Battlefield* (Cambridge: The Riverside Press, 1919); Henry Plauché Dart, *Edgar Howard Farrar: A Sketch of His Life and Times* (New Orleans: Andrée Printery, Inc., 1922); Cathy N. Davidson, ed., *The Book of Love: Writers and Their Love Letters* (New York: Plume, 1992); Ellen Carol DuBois, ed., *Elizabeth Cady Stanton, Susan B. Anthony: Correspondence, Writings, Speeches* (New York: Schocken Books, 1981); Letter by Paul Laurence Dunbar from the University of Delaware Library, Newark, Delaware; William G. Eliot, ed., *The Story of Archer Alexander: From Slavery to Freedom* (Boston, 1875); Anne Fields, ed., *Life and Letters of Harriet Beecher Stowe* (Boston: Houghton Mifflin Company, 1897); Philip S. Foner, ed., *Mother Jones Speaks: Collected Writings and Speeches* (New York: Monad Press, 1983); Peter Force, ed., *American Archives: Fifth Series, Containing a Documentary History of the United States of America* (Washington, D.C., 1848–53); Antonia Fraser, ed., *Love Letters* (New York: Crescent Books, 1995); Lucy Freeman and Alma Halbert Bond, *America's First Woman Warrior: The Courage of Deborah Sampson* (New York: Paragon House, 1992); Francis L. and Roberta B. Fugate, eds., *Secrets of the World's Best-Selling Writer: The Storytelling Techniques of Erle Stanley Gardner* (New York: William Morrow, 1980); Minnie A. Harden letter courtesy of the Franklin D. Roosevelt Library, Eleanor Roosevelt papers, series 190 miscellaneous, 1937 H; Walter Harding and Carl Bode, eds., *The Correspondence of Henry David Thoreau* (New York: New York University Press, 1974); Ida Husted Harper, ed., *History of Woman Suffrage,* Vol. 5 (New York: Arnos & the *New York Times,* 1969); Richard B. Harwell, ed., *The Civil War Reader* (New York: Konecky & Konecky, 1957); Alan Heimart and Andrew Delbanco, eds., *The Puritans in America: A Narrative Anthology* (Cambridge: Harvard University Press, 1985); William H. Hobbs, *Peary* (New York: The Macmillan Company, 1936); Rhoda Hoff, ed., *America's Immigrants: Adventures in Eyewitness History* (New York: Henry Z. Walck, Inc., 1967); Harold Holzer, ed., *Dear Mr. Lincoln: Letters to the President* (New York:

Addison-Wesley Publishing Company, 1995); Anne Hulton, *Letters of a Loyalist Lady* (Cambridge: Harvard University Press, 1927); Arthur Crew Inman, ed., *Soldier of the South: General Pickett's War Letters to His Wife* (Cambridge: The Riverside Press, 1918); Donald Jackson, ed., *Letters of the Lewis and Clark Expedition* (Urbana: University of Illinois Press, 1962); Henry James, ed., *The Letters of William James* (Boston: Atlantic Monthly Press, 1920); John William Jones, ed., *Life and Letters of Robert Edward Lee* (New York: Neale Publishing Co., 1906); Katharine M. Jones, ed., *Heroines of Dixie: Confederate Women Tell Their Story of the War* (New York: Konecky & Konecky, 1955); Mary Harris Jones, *Autobiography of Mother Jones* (New York: Arno Press, 1969); Frederick R. Karl, *William Faulkner: American Writer* (New York: Ballantine Books, 1989); John F. Kennedy letter courtesy of the John Fitzgerald Kennedy Library; J. A. Leo Lamay, ed., *Benjamin Franklin: Writings* (New York: The Library of America, 1987); H. Jack Lang, ed., *Dear Wit: Letters from the World's Wits* (New York: Prentice Hall Press, 1990); H. Jack Lang, ed., *Letters in American History: Words to Remember 1770 to the Present* (New York: Harmony Books, 1982); Stan Larson, ed., *Prisoner for Polygamy: The Memoirs and Letters of Rudger Clawson at the Utah Territorial Penitentiary, 1884–87* (Urbana: University of Illinois Press, 1993); R. E. Lee, *Recollections and Letters of General Robert E. Lee* (London: Archibald, Constable, & Co., 1904); Judy Barrett Litoff and David C. Smith, eds., *We're in This War, Too: World War II Letters from American Women in Uniform* (New York: Oxford University Press, 1994); Iris Luce, ed., *Letters from the Peace Corps* (New York: Van Rees Press, 1964); Jay Martin and Gossie H. Hudson, eds., *The Paul Laurence Dunbar Reader* (New York: Dodd, Mead & Company, 1975); Julian D. Mason Jr., ed., *The Poems of Phillis Wheatley* (Chapel Hill: University of North Carolina Press, 1966); Joe McCarthy, ed., *Fred Allen's Letters* (Garden City, N.Y.: Doubleday & Company, Inc., 1965); Sally McClain, *Navajo Weapon* (Boulder: Books Beyond Borders, Inc., 1994); David McCullough, *Truman* (New York: Simon & Schuster, 1992); Robert S. McElvaine, ed., *Down & Out in the Great Depression: Letters from the Forgotten Man* (Chapel Hill: University of North Carolina Press, 1983); T. C. McLuhan, ed., *Touch the Earth: A Self-Portrait of Indian Existence* (New York: Simon & Schuster / Touchstone, 1971); Isaac Metzker, ed., *A Bintel Brief: Sixty Years of Letters from the Lower East Side to the* Jewish Daily Forward (Garden City, N.Y.: Doubleday & Company, Inc., 1971); Kerby Miller and Paul Wagner, *Out of Ireland: The Story of Irish Emigration to America* (Washington, D.C.: Elliott & Clark Publishing, 1994); Linda R. Monk, ed., *Ordi-*

nary Americans: U.S. History Through the Eyes of Everyday People (Alexandria: Close Up Publishing, 1994); Wayne Moquin with Charles Van Doren, eds., *A Documentary History of the Mexican Americans* (New York: Praeger Publishers, 1971); Wayne Moquin with Charles Van Doren, eds., *Great Documents in American Indian History* (New York: Praeger Publishers, 1973); Ruth Barnes Moynihan et al., eds., *Second to None: A Documentary History of American Women* (Lincoln: University of Nebraska Press, 1993); Charles Neider, ed., *The Selected Letters of Mark Twain* (New York: Harper & Row, Publishers, 1917); Brian Niiya, ed., *Japanese American History: An A-to-Z Reference from 1868 to the Present* (New York: Facts on File, 1993); Charles Eliot Norton, ed., *Letters of James Russell Lowell* (New York: Harper & Brothers Publishers, 1894); Angie O'Gorman, ed., *The Universe Bends Toward Justice: A Reader on Christian Nonviolence in the U.S.* (Santa Cruz: New Society Publishers, 1990); Laura Palmer, ed., *Shrapnel in the Heart: Letters and Remembrances from the Vietnam Veterans Memorial* (New York: Random House, 1987); Lindsay Patterson, ed., *A Rock Against the Wind: African-American Poems and Letters of Love and Passion* (New York: Perigee, 1996); Karen Payne, ed., *Between Ourselves: Letters Between Mothers & Daughters 1750–1982* (Boston: Houghton Mifflin Company, 1983); Monte M. Poen, ed., *Strictly Confidential: The Letters Harry Truman Never Mailed* (Boston: Little, Brown and Company, 1982); Bertha Clark Pope, ed., *The Letters of Ambrose Bierce* (New York: Gordian Press, 1922); George Palmer Putnam, *Soaring Wings* (New York: Harcourt, Brace & Company, 1939); Ronald Reagan, *An American Life* (New York: Simon & Schuster, 1990); Byron Johnson Rees, ed., *Nineteenth Century Letters* (New York: Charles Scribner's Sons, 1899); Paul Revere letter courtesy of the Massachusetts Historical Society; Wilbert Rideau and Ron Wikberg, eds., *Life Sentences: Rage and Survival Behind Bars* (New York: Times Books, 1992); Morris U. Schappes, ed., *A Documentary History of the Jews in the United States 1654–1875* (New York: Schocken Books, 1991); M. Lincoln Schuster, ed., *A Treasury of the World's Great Letters* (New York: Simon & Schuster, 1940); Margaret Sanger, *An Autobiography* (New York: W. W. Norton & Company, 1938); Stephen W. Sears, ed., *The Civil War: A Treasury of Art and Literature* (New York: Beaux Arts, Hugh Lauter Levin Associates, Inc., 1992); Reid Sherline, ed., *Letters Home: Celebrated Authors Write to Their Mothers* (New York: Timken Publishers, 1993); Reid Sherline, ed., *Love Anyhow: Famous Fathers Write to Their Children* (New York: Timken Publishers, 1994); William Tecumseh Sherman, *Memoirs of General William T. Sherman* (New York: D. Appleton, 1875); Lynn Sherr, ed., *Failure Is Impossible:*

Susan B. Anthony in Her Own Words (New York: Times Books, 1995); Kenneth Silverman, ed., *Selected Letters of Cotton Mather* (Baton Rouge: Louisiana State University Press, 1971); Liz Smith, ed., *The Mother Book: A Compendium of Trivia and Grandeur Concerning Mothers, Motherhood & Maternity* (New York: Crown Publishers, Inc., 1984); Albert Henry Smyth, ed., *The Writings of Benjamin Franklin,* Vols. 1–10 (London: The Macmillan Company, 1905–07); Jared Sparks, ed., *The Works of Benjamin Franklin,* Vols. 1–10 (Boston: Tappan & Whittemore, 1844); Ed Stackler, ed., *Forever Yours: Letters of Love* (New York: St. Martin's Press, 1991); Elizabeth Cady Stanton, *Elizabeth Cady Stanton Revealed in Her Letters* (New York: Harper & Brothers, 1922); Elinore Prewitt Stewart, *Letters of a Woman Homesteader* (Boston: Houghton Mifflin Company, 1913); William Still, ed., *The Underground Rail Road* (Philadelphia: Porters & Coates, 1872); Hudson Strode, ed., *Jefferson Davis: Private Letters 1823–1889* (New York: Harcourt, Brace, & World, 1966); Suzanne Stutman, ed., *My Other Loneliness: Letters of Thomas Wolfe and Aline Bernstein* (Chapel Hill: University of North Carolina Press, 1983); Elizabeth Sutherland, ed., *Letters from Mississippi* (New York: McGraw Hill, 1965); Harold C. Syrett, ed., *The Papers of Alexander Hamilton* (New York: Columbia University Press, 1962); Lola L. Szladits, ed., *Other People's Mail: Letters of Men and Women of Letters* (New York: The New York Public Library & Readex Books, 1973); Mary Tape letter from *Alta*, April 16, 1885; Mary Thom, ed., *Letters to Ms. 1972–1987* (New York: Henry Holt and Company, 1987); Bernard De Voto, ed., *The Portable Mark Twain* (New York: The Viking Press, 1946); Geoffrey C. Ward et al., eds., *The Civil War: An Illustrated History* (New York: Alfred A. Knopf, 1990); Chief Justice Earl Warren, *The Memoirs of Earl Warren* (Garden City, N.Y.: Doubleday & Company, Inc., 1977); H. A. Washington, ed., *The Writings of Thomas Jefferson* (New York: Derby & Jackson, 1859); Peter Washington, ed., *Love Letters* (New York: Alfred A. Knopf, 1996); Sanford Wexler, ed., *Westward Expansion: An Eyewitness History* (New York: Facts on File, 1991); Robert C. Winthrop, ed., *Life and Letters of John Winthrop* (Boston: Ticknor and Fields, 1867); Paula L. Woods and Felix H. Liddell, eds., *I Hear a Symphony: African Americans Celebrate Love* (New York: Anchor Books, 1994); Carter G. Woodson, ed., *The Mind of the Negro as Reflected in Letters Written During the Crisis 1800–1860* (Washington, D.C.: The Association for the Study of Negro Life and History, 1926).

Index

Roman text represents senders; italicized represents recipients.